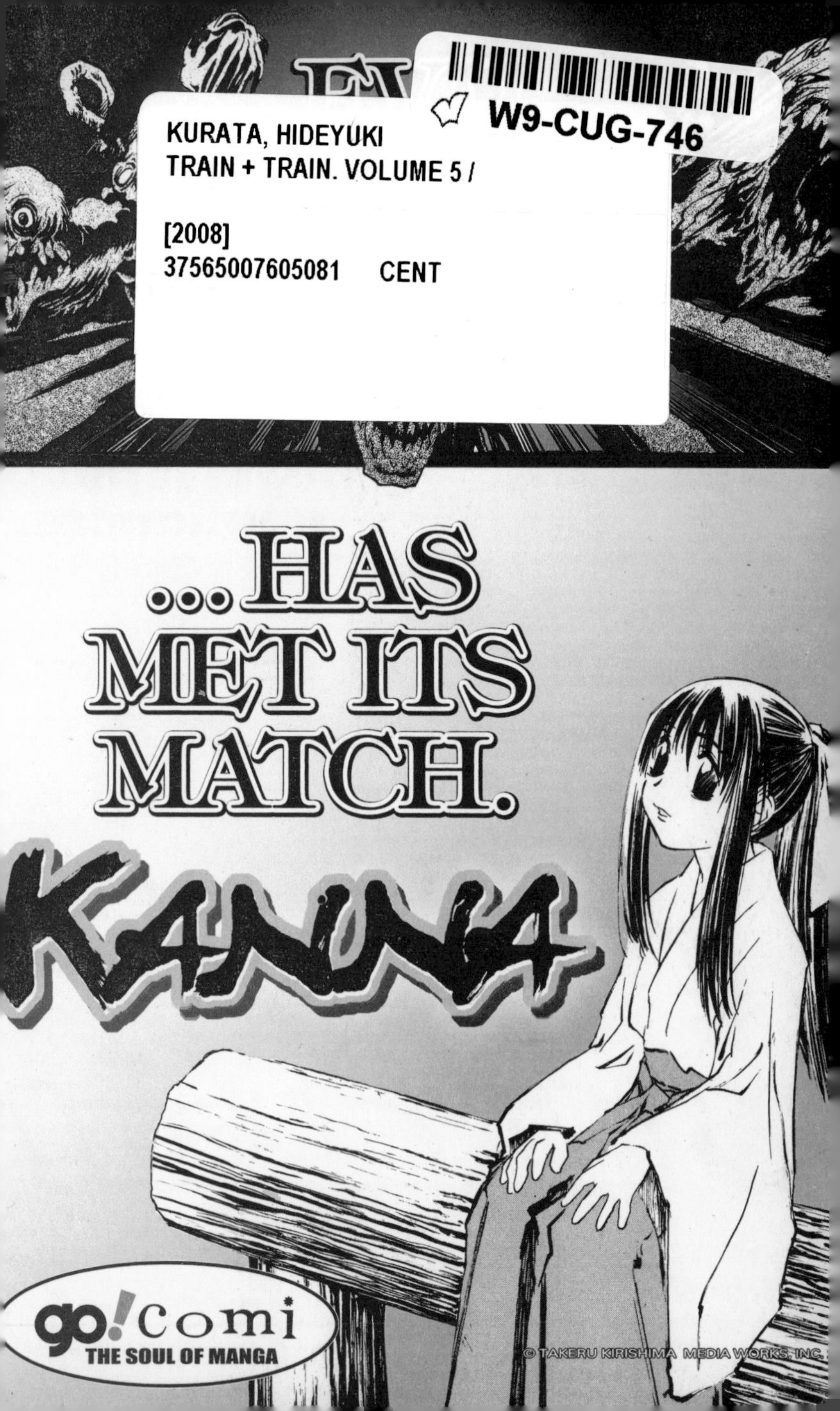
...HAS MET ITS MATCH.
KANNA
go!comi
THE SOUL OF MANGA
© TAKERU KIRISHIMA MEDIA WORKS, INC.

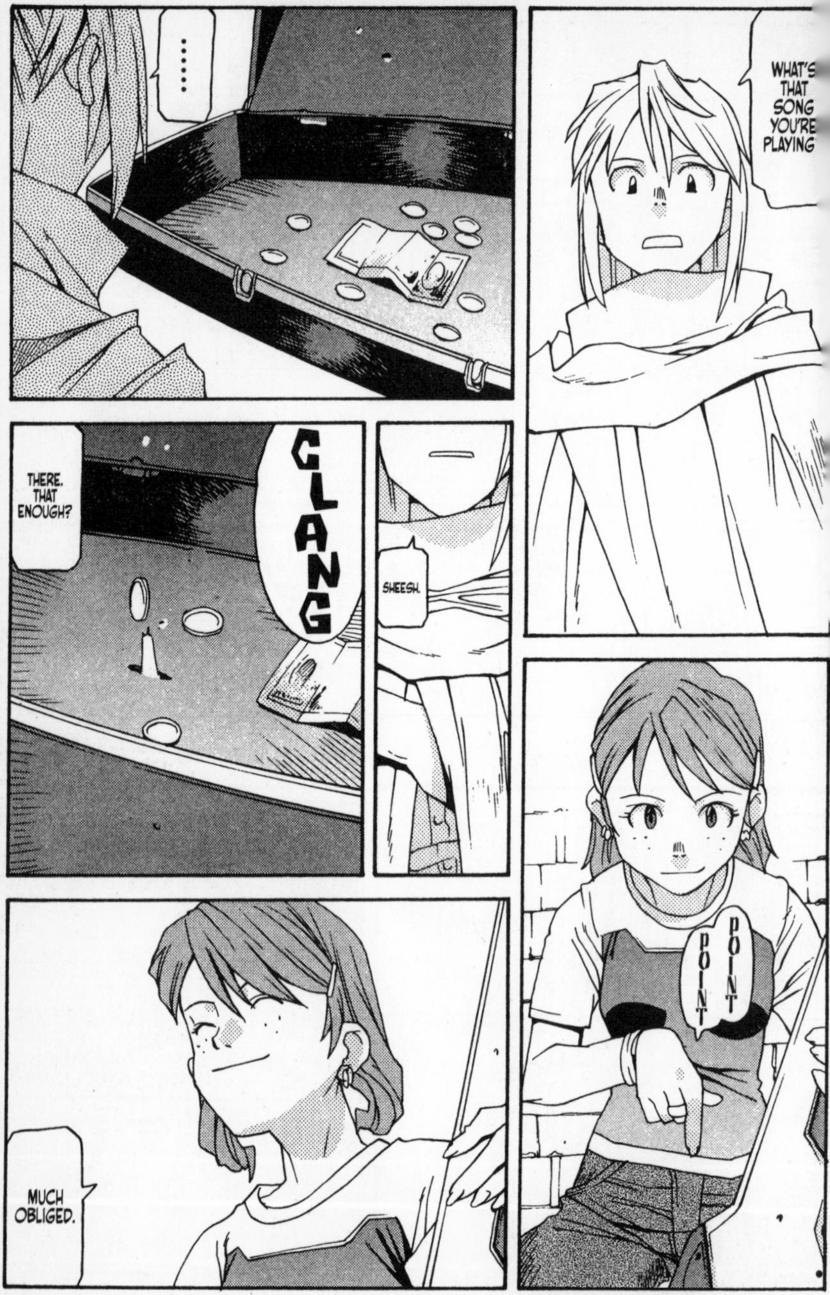
WHAT'S THAT SONG YOU'RE PLAYING
……
SHEESH.
THERE. THAT ENOUGH?
CLANG
POINT POINT
MUCH OBLIGED.

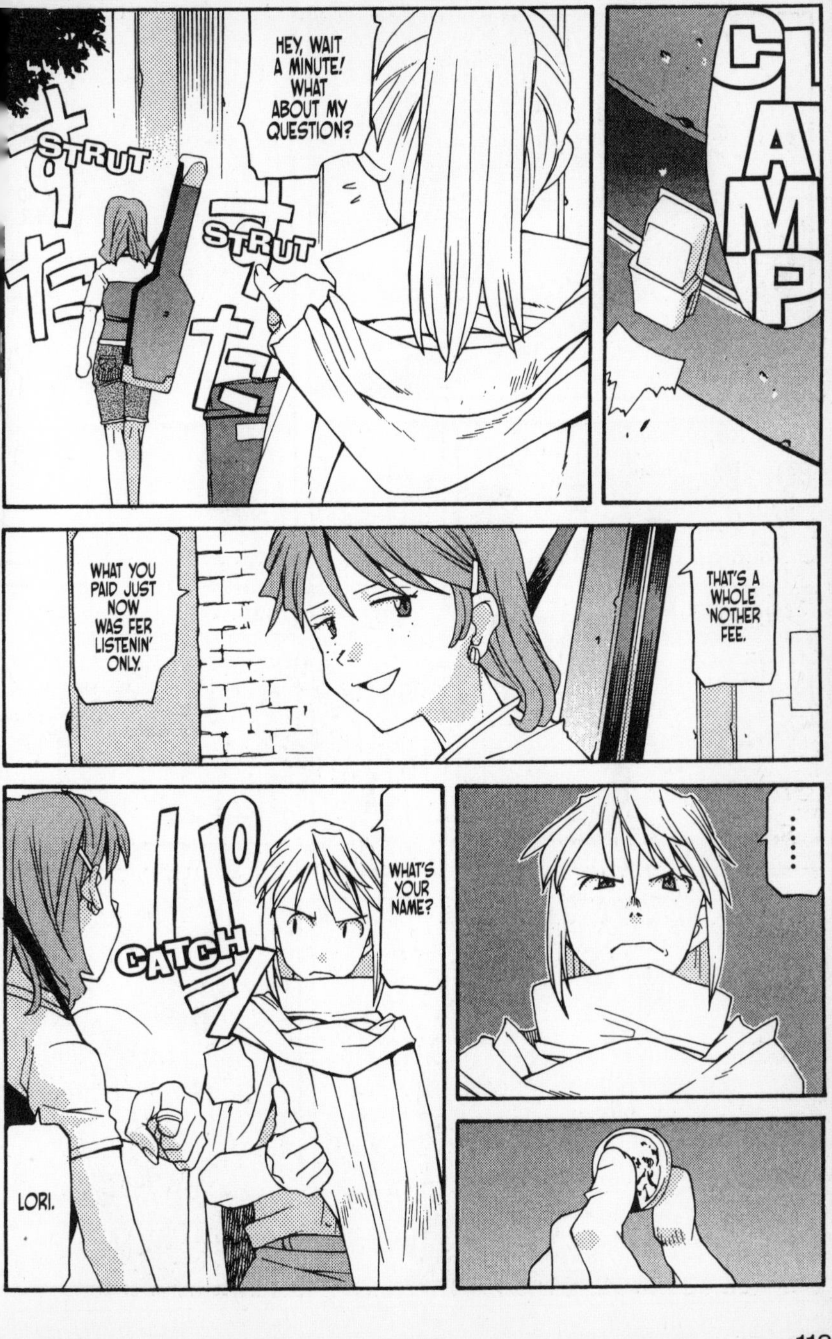
CLAMP
HEY, WAIT A MINUTE! WHAT ABOUT MY QUESTION?
STRUT
STRUT
THAT'S A WHOLE 'NOTHER FEE.
WHAT YOU PAID JUST NOW WAS FER LISTENIN' ONLY.
......
WHAT'S YOUR NAME?
CATCH
LORI.

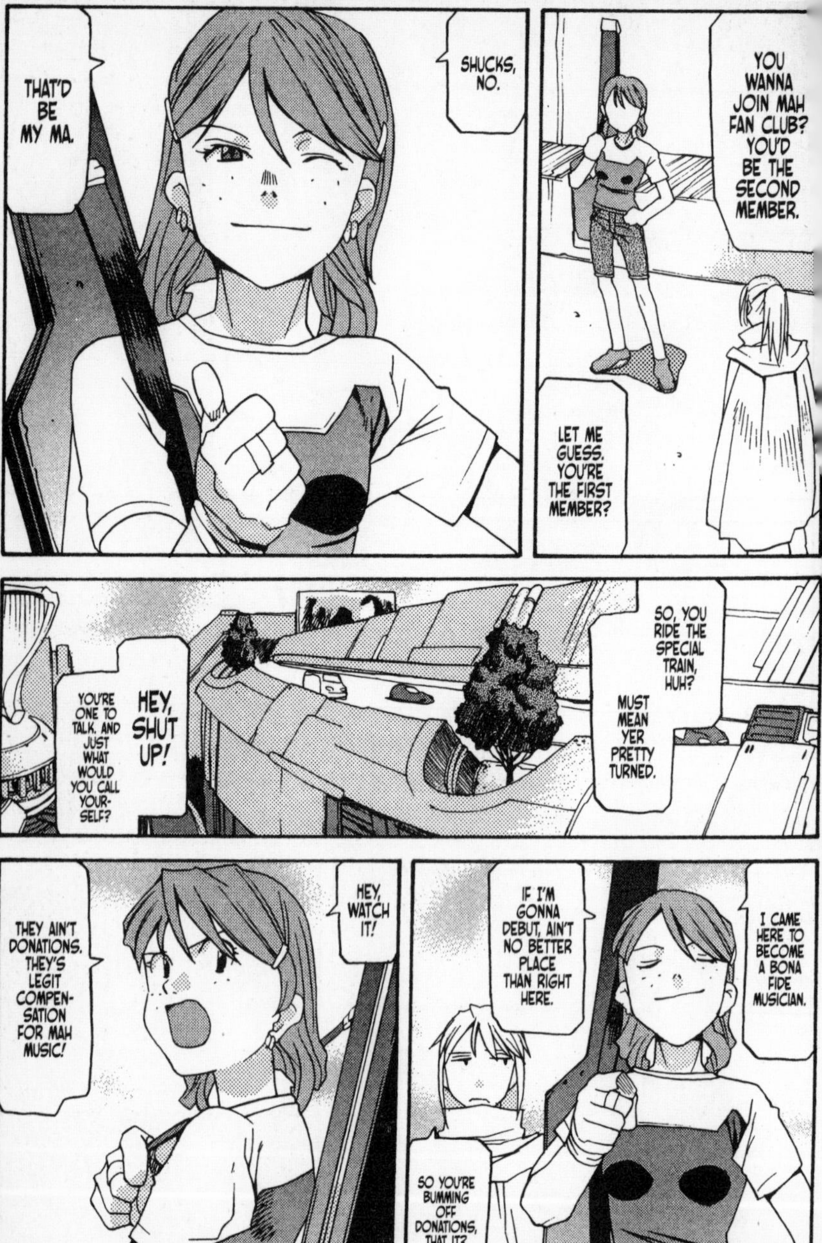
YOU WANNA JOIN MAH FAN CLUB? YOU'D BE THE SECOND MEMBER.
LET ME GUESS. YOU'RE THE FIRST MEMBER?
SHUCKS, NO.
THAT'D BE MY MA.
SO, YOU RIDE THE SPECIAL TRAIN, HUH?
MUST MEAN YER PRETTY TURNED.
HEY, SHUT UP!
YOU'RE ONE TO TALK. AND JUST WHAT WOULD YOU CALL YOUR-SELF?
I CAME HERE TO BECOME A BONA FIDE MUSICIAN.
IF I'M GONNA DEBUT, AIN'T NO BETTER PLACE THAN RIGHT HERE.
SO YOU'RE BUMMING OFF DONATIONS, THAT IT?
HEY, WATCH IT!
THEY AIN'T DONATIONS. THEY'S LEGIT COMPEN-SATION FOR MAH MUSIC!

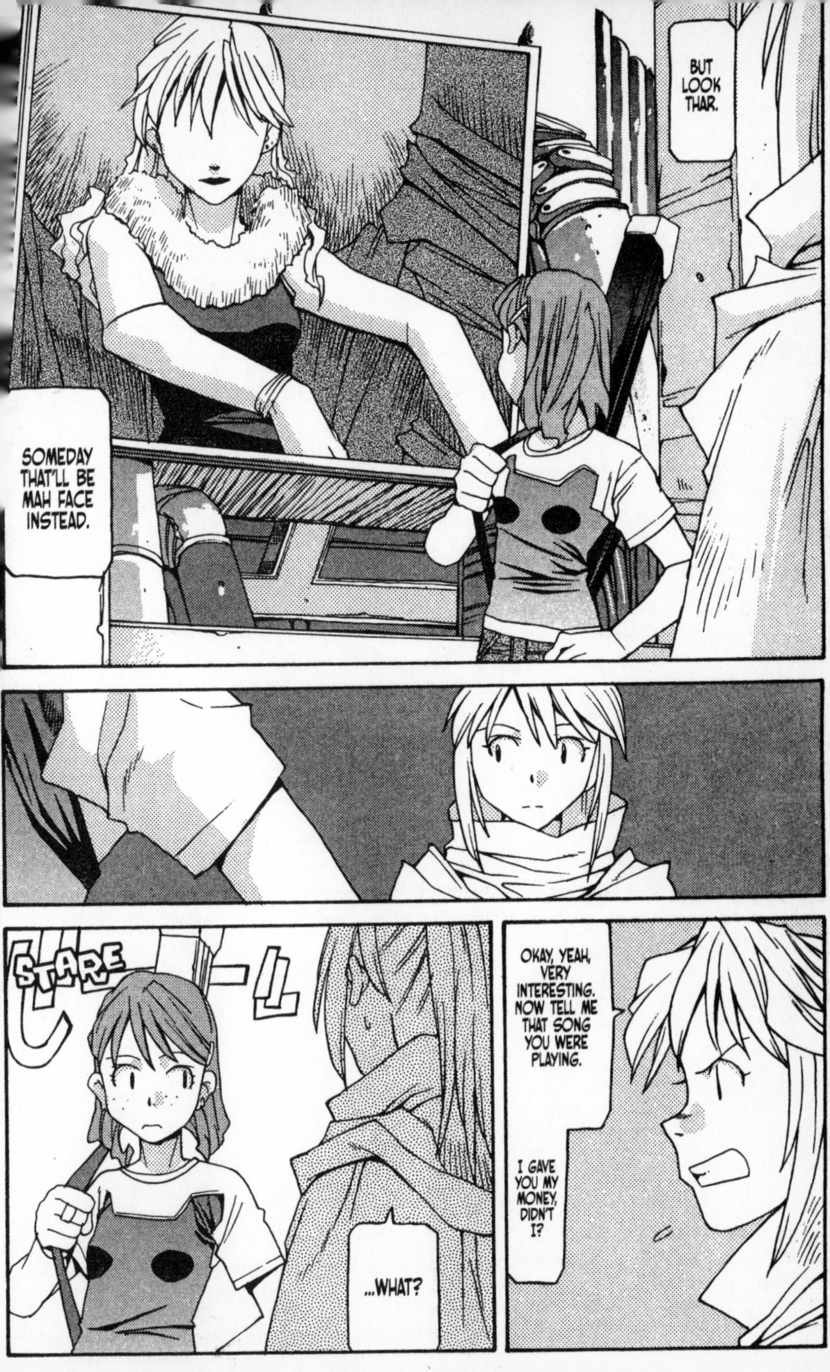
BUT LOOK THAR.
SOMEDAY THAT'LL BE MAH FACE INSTEAD.
OKAY, YEAH, VERY INTERESTING. NOW TELL ME THAT SONG YOU WERE PLAYING.
I GAVE YOU MY MONEY, DIDN'T I?
STARE
...WHAT?

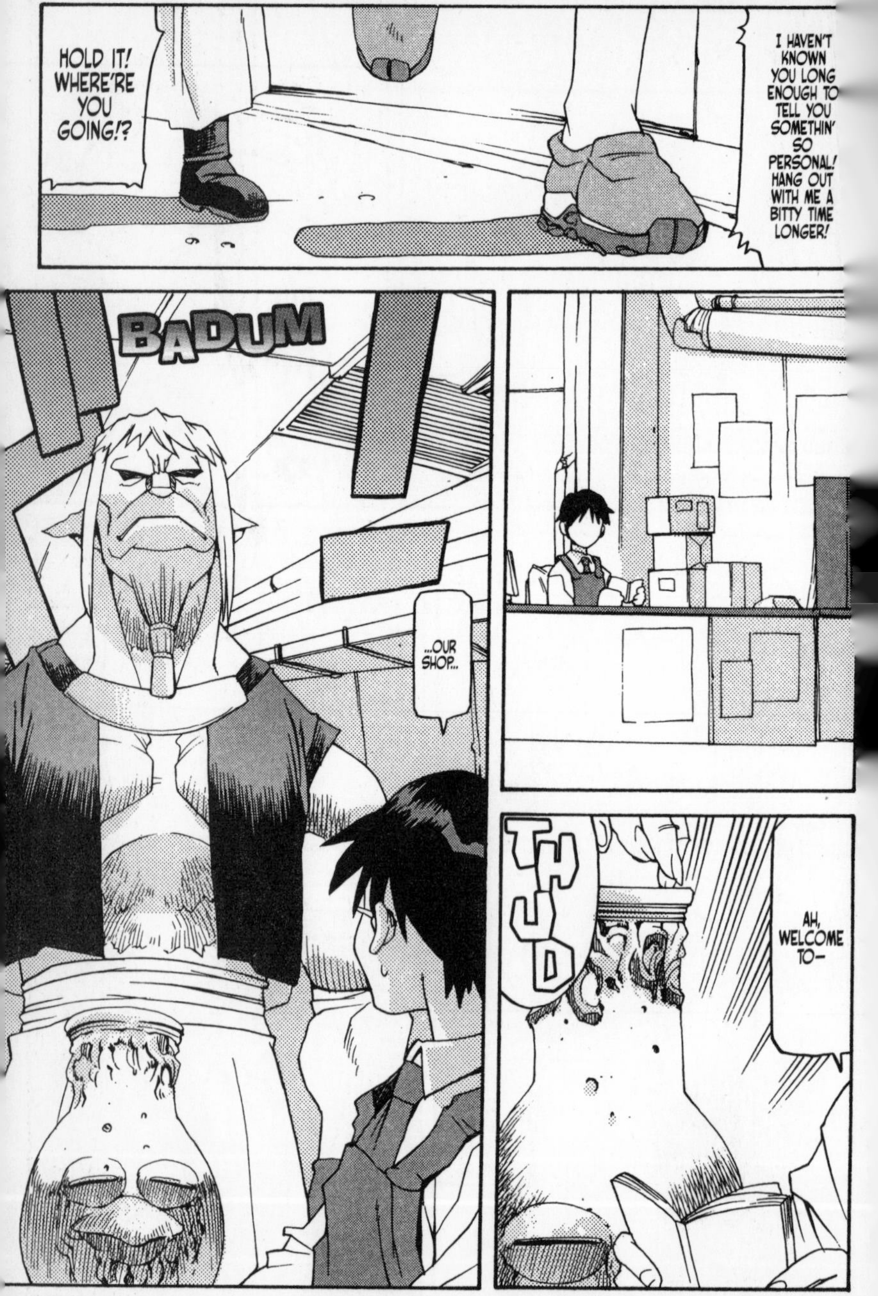
I HAVEN'T KNOWN YOU LONG ENOUGH TO TELL YOU SOMETHIN' SO PERSONAL! HANG OUT WITH ME A BITTY TIME LONGER!
HOLD IT! WHERE'RE YOU GOING!?
THUD
AH, WELCOME TO—
BADUM
...OUR SHOP...

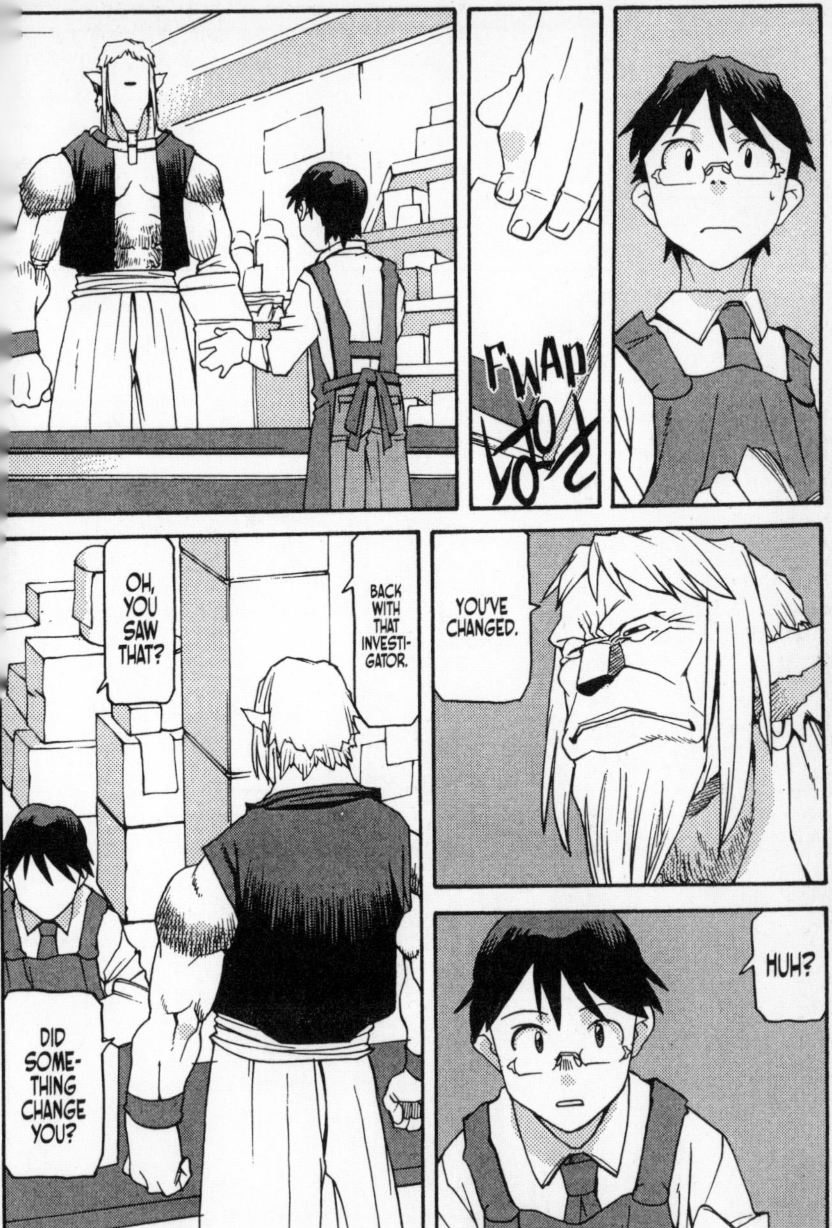
FWAP
YOU'VE CHANGED.
HUH?
BACK WITH THAT INVESTIGATOR.
OH, YOU SAW THAT?
DID SOMETHING CHANGE YOU?

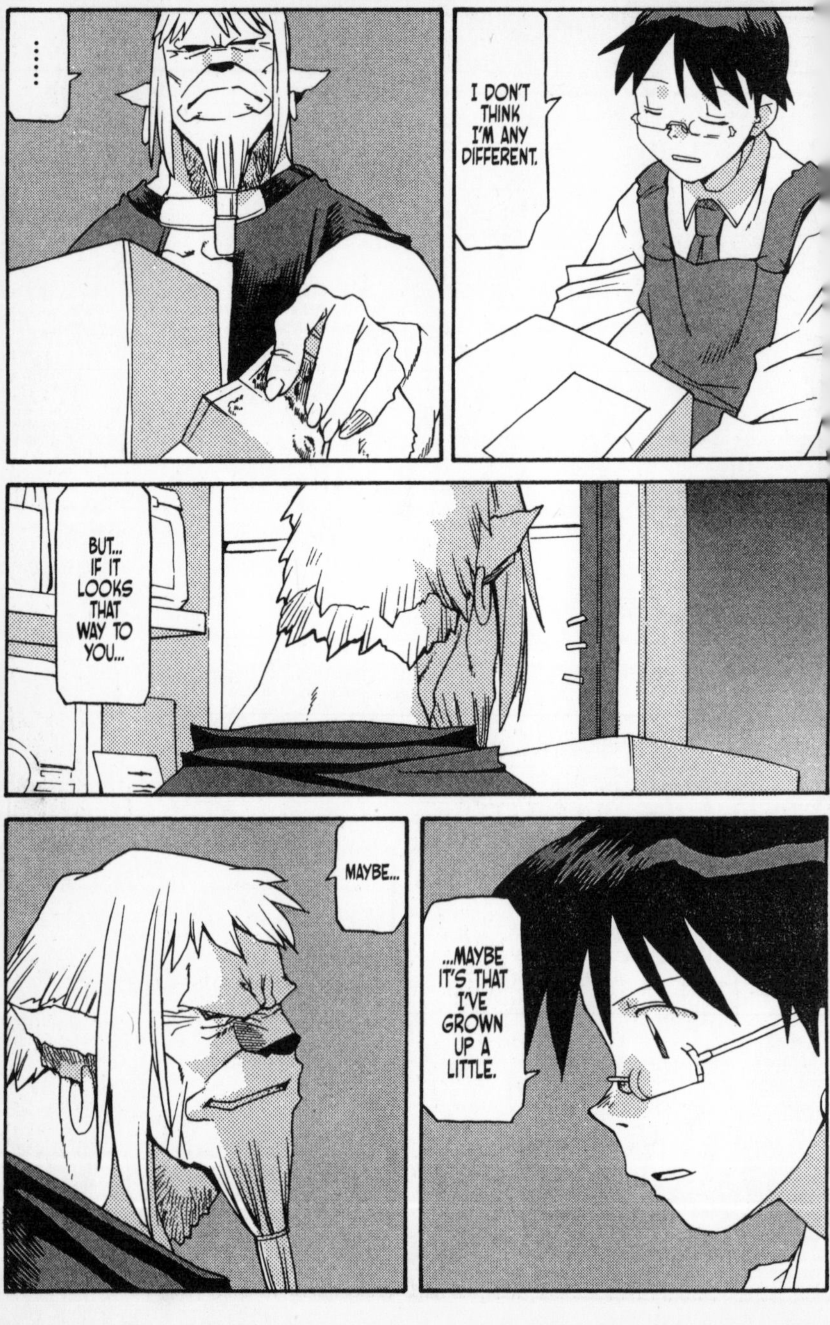
I DON'T THINK I'M ANY DIFFERENT.
......
BUT... IF IT LOOKS THAT WAY TO YOU...
...MAYBE IT'S THAT I'VE GROWN UP A LITTLE.
MAYBE...

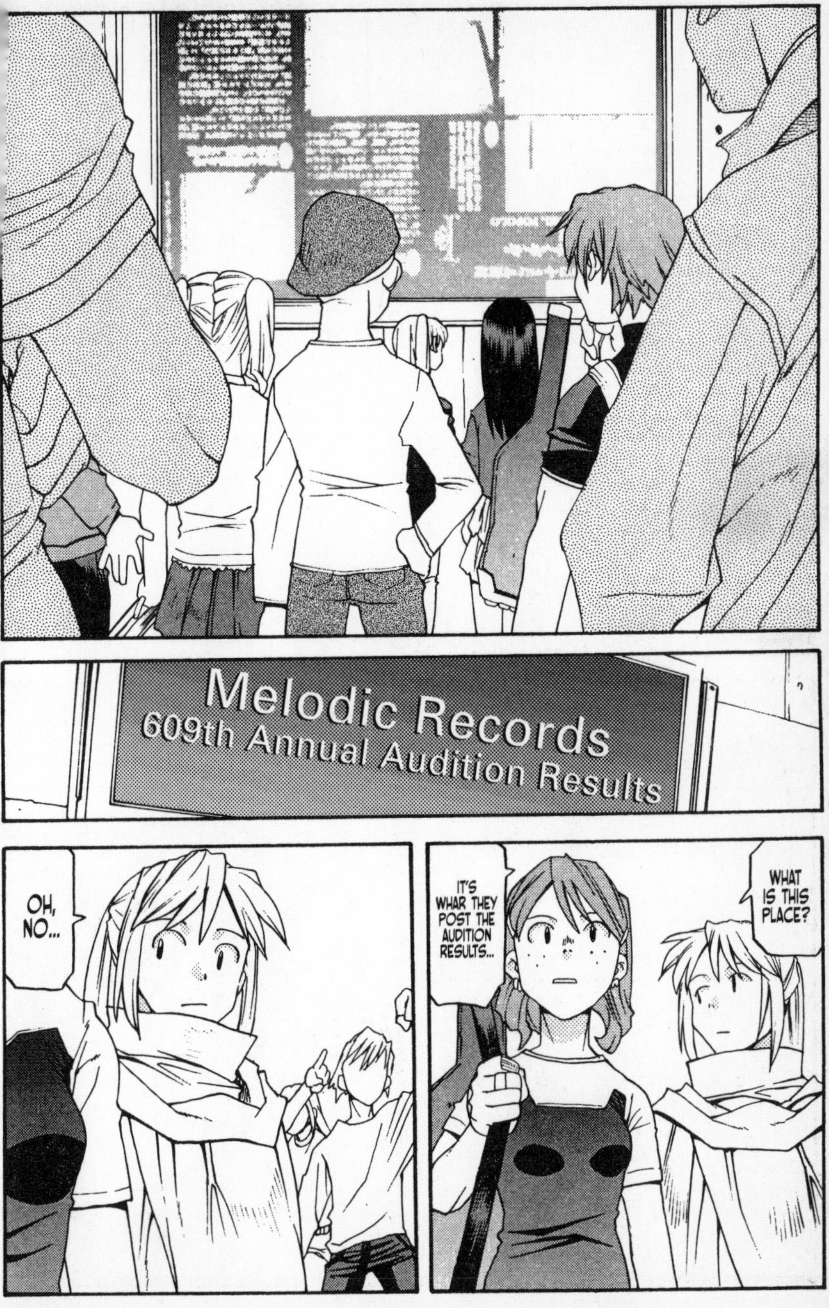
Melodic Records
609th Annual Audition Results
WHAT IS THIS PLACE?
IT'S WHAR THEY POST THE AUDITION RESULTS...
OH, NO...

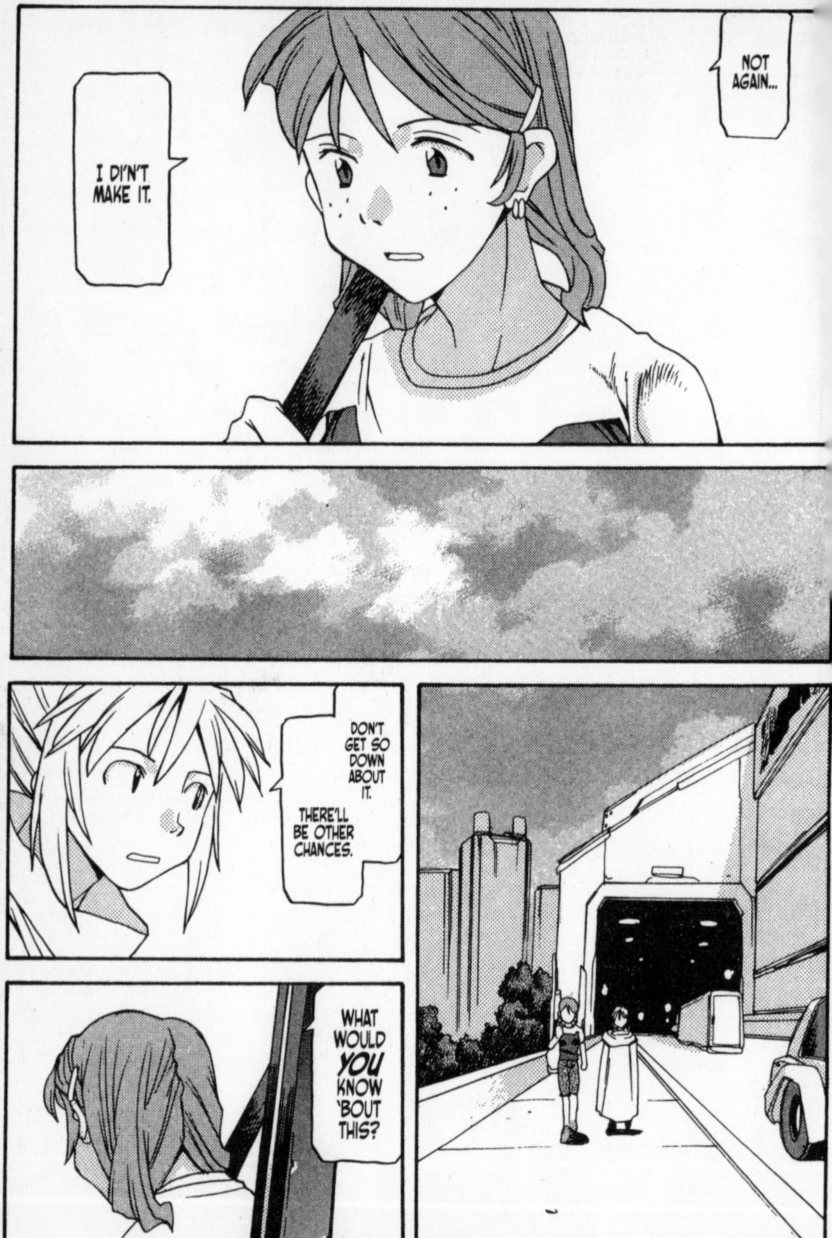
NOT AGAIN...
I DI'N'T MAKE IT.
DON'T GET SO DOWN ABOUT IT.
THERE'LL BE OTHER CHANCES.
WHAT WOULD *YOU* KNOW 'BOUT THIS?

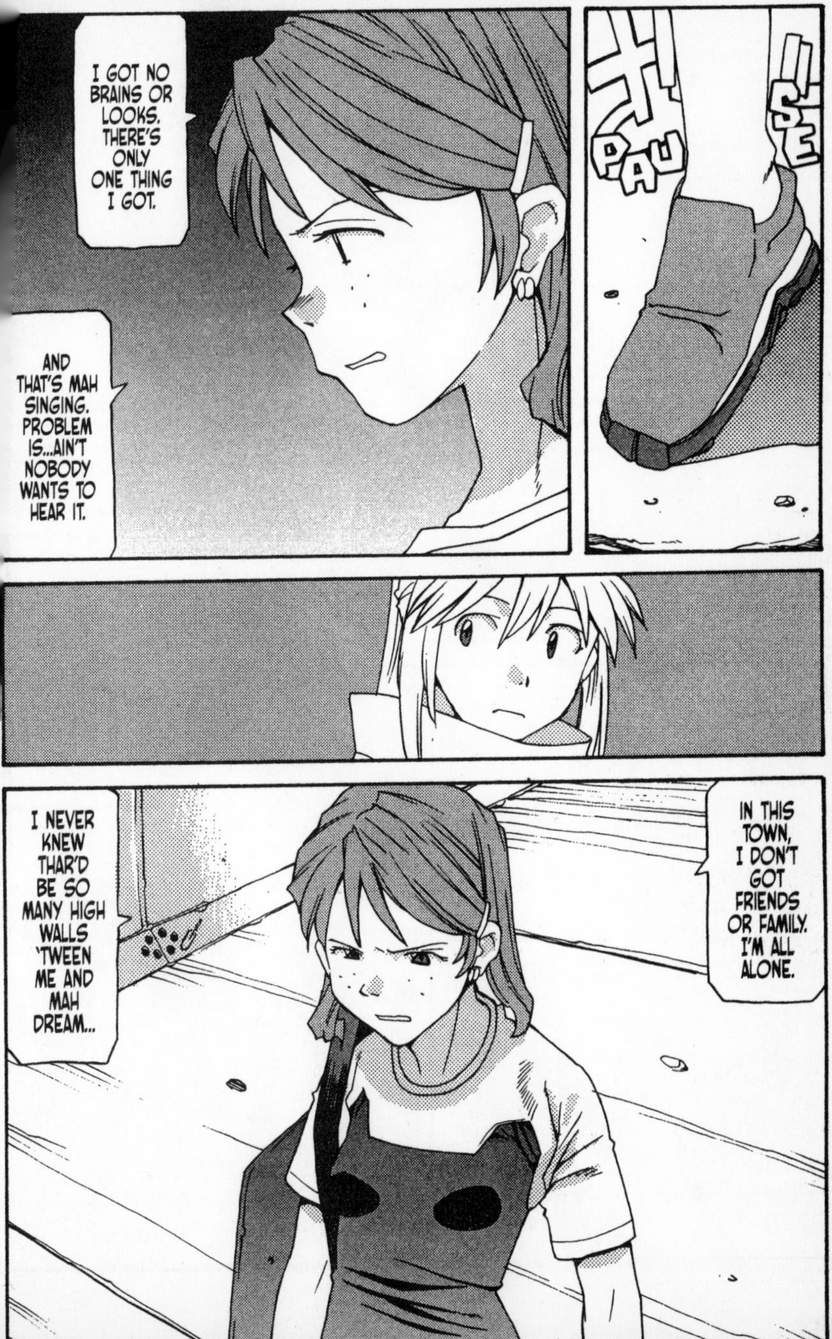
PAUSE
I GOT NO BRAINS OR LOOKS. THERE'S ONLY ONE THING I GOT.
AND THAT'S MAH SINGING. PROBLEM IS...AIN'T NOBODY WANTS TO HEAR IT.
IN THIS TOWN, I DON'T GOT FRIENDS OR FAMILY. I'M ALL ALONE.
I NEVER KNEW THAR'D BE SO MANY HIGH WALLS 'TWEEN ME AND MAH DREAM...

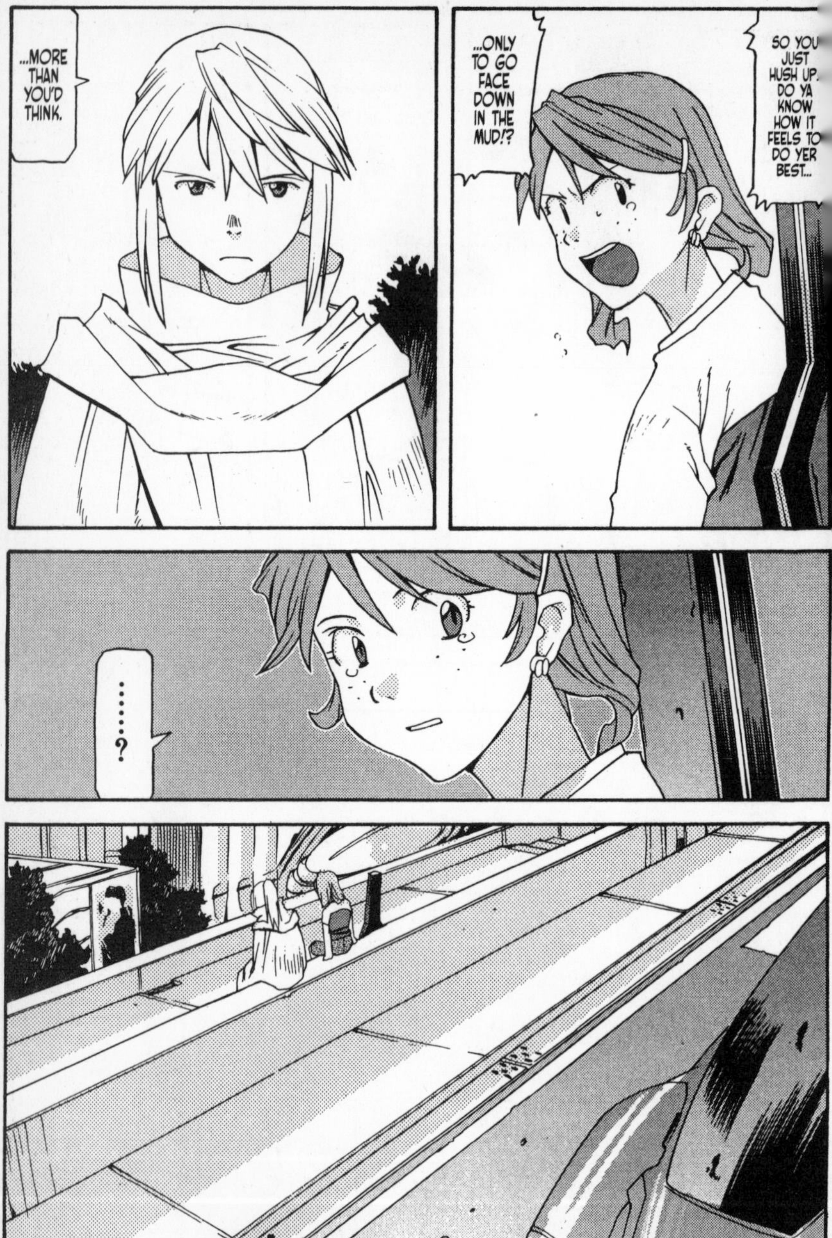
SO YOU JUST HUSH UP. DO YA KNOW HOW IT FEELS TO DO YER BEST...
...ONLY TO GO FACE DOWN IN THE MUD!?
...MORE THAN YOU'D THINK.
......?

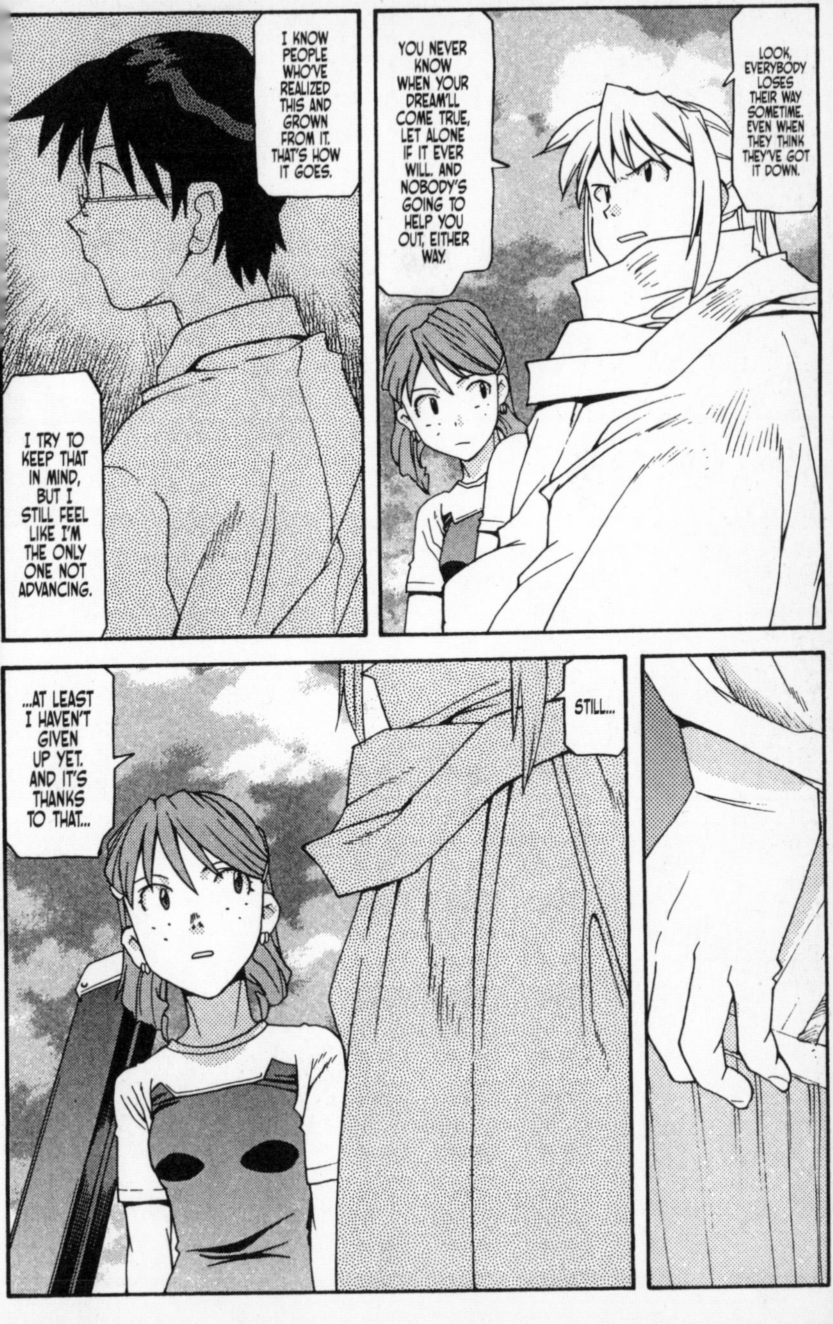
LOOK, EVERYBODY LOSES THEIR WAY SOMETIME. EVEN WHEN THEY THINK THEY'VE GOT IT DOWN.
YOU NEVER KNOW WHEN YOUR DREAM'LL COME TRUE, LET ALONE IF IT EVER WILL. AND NOBODY'S GOING TO HELP YOU OUT, EITHER WAY.
I KNOW PEOPLE WHO'VE REALIZED THIS AND GROWN FROM IT. THAT'S HOW IT GOES.
I TRY TO KEEP THAT IN MIND, BUT I STILL FEEL LIKE I'M THE ONLY ONE NOT ADVANCING.
STILL...
...AT LEAST I HAVEN'T GIVEN UP YET. AND IT'S THANKS TO THAT...

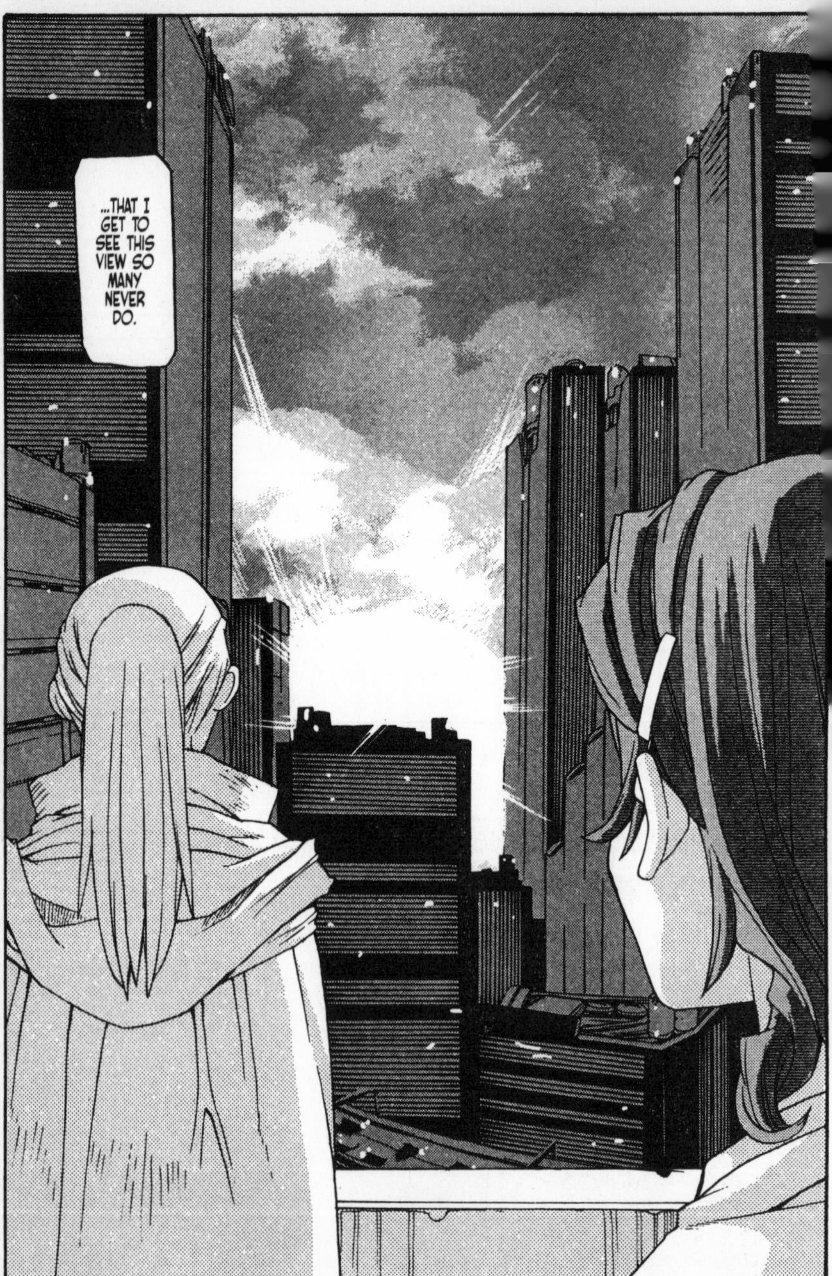
...THAT I GET TO SEE THIS VIEW SO MANY NEVER DO.

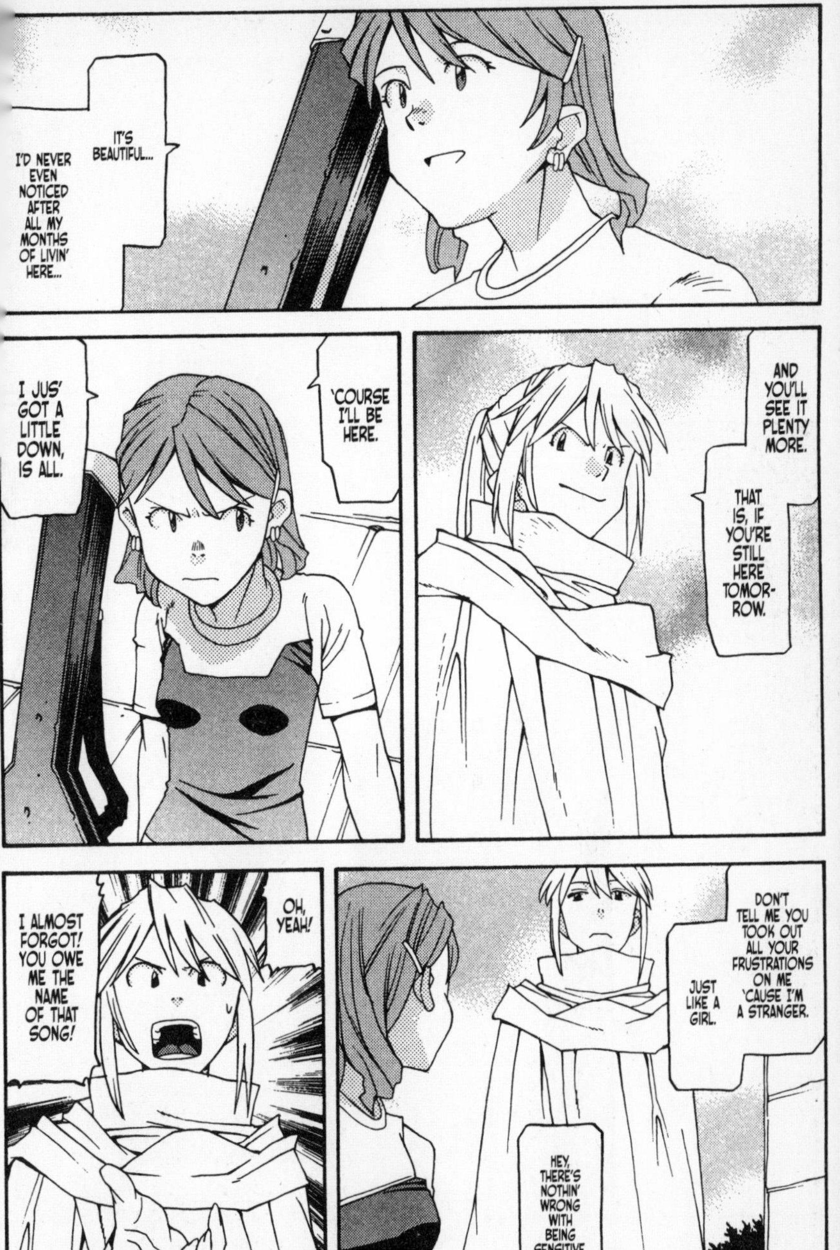
IT'S BEAUTIFUL...
I'D NEVER EVEN NOTICED AFTER ALL MY MONTHS OF LIVIN' HERE...
AND YOU'LL SEE IT PLENTY MORE.
THAT IS, IF YOU'RE STILL HERE TOMORROW.
'COURSE I'LL BE HERE.
I JUS' GOT A LITTLE DOWN, IS ALL.
DON'T TELL ME YOU TOOK OUT ALL YOUR FRUSTRATIONS ON ME 'CAUSE I'M A STRANGER.
JUST LIKE A GIRL.
HEY, THERE'S NOTHIN' WRONG WITH BEING SENSITIVE.
OH, YEAH!
I ALMOST FORGOT! YOU OWE ME THE NAME OF THAT SONG!

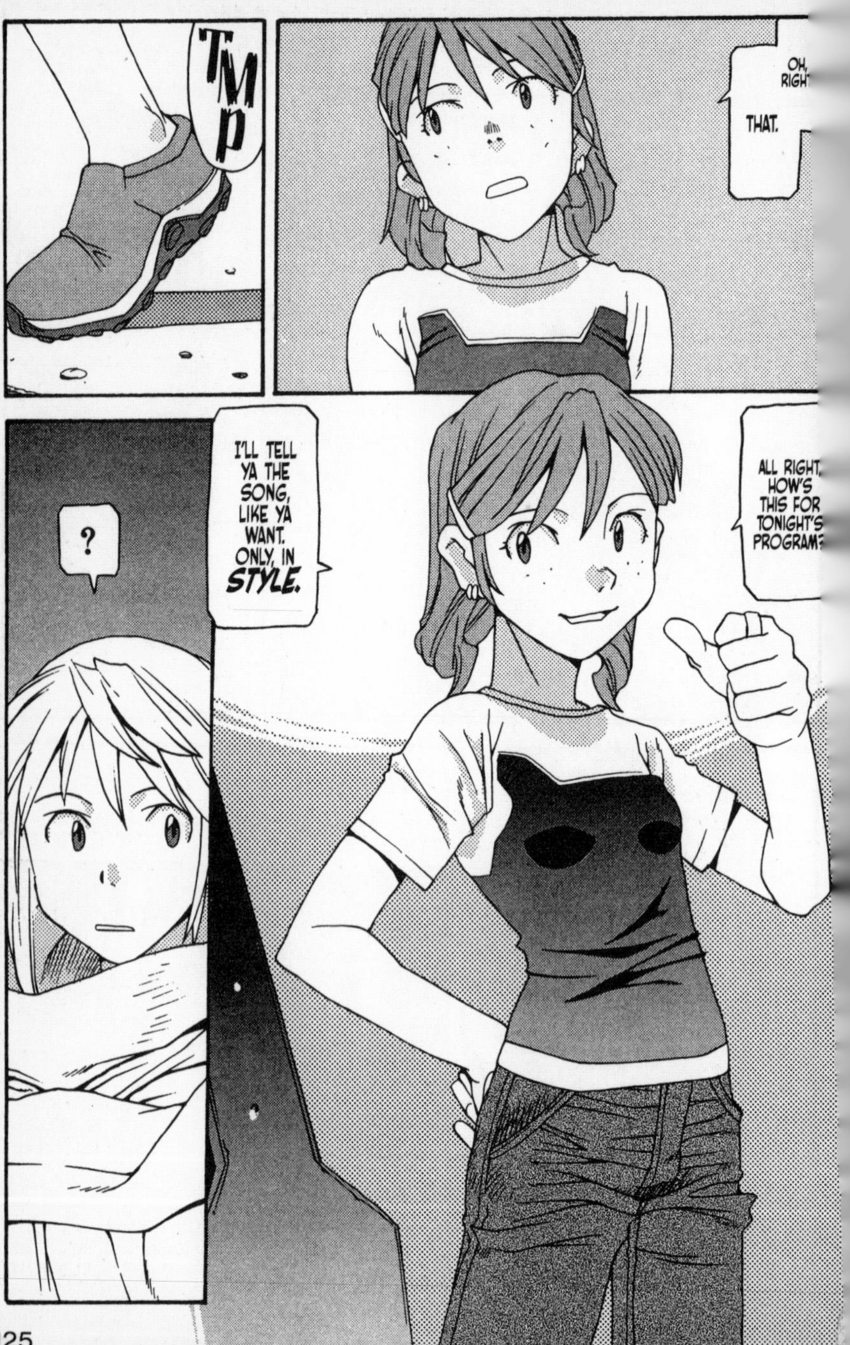

OH, RIGHT THAT.
TMP
ALL RIGHT, HOW'S THIS FOR TONIGHT'S PROGRAM?
I'LL TELL YA THE SONG, LIKE YA WANT. ONLY, IN ***STYLE.***
?

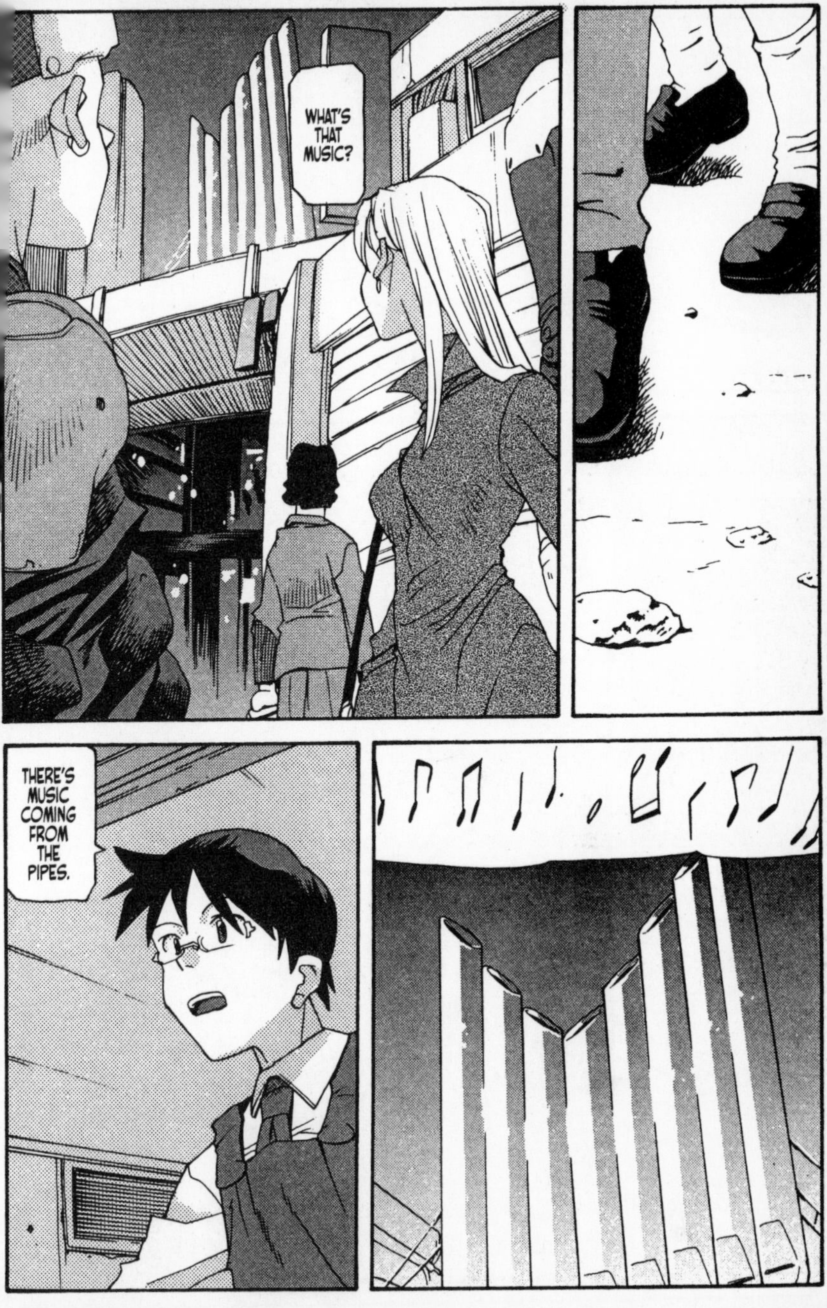
WHAT'S THAT MUSIC?
THERE'S MUSIC COMING FROM THE PIPES.

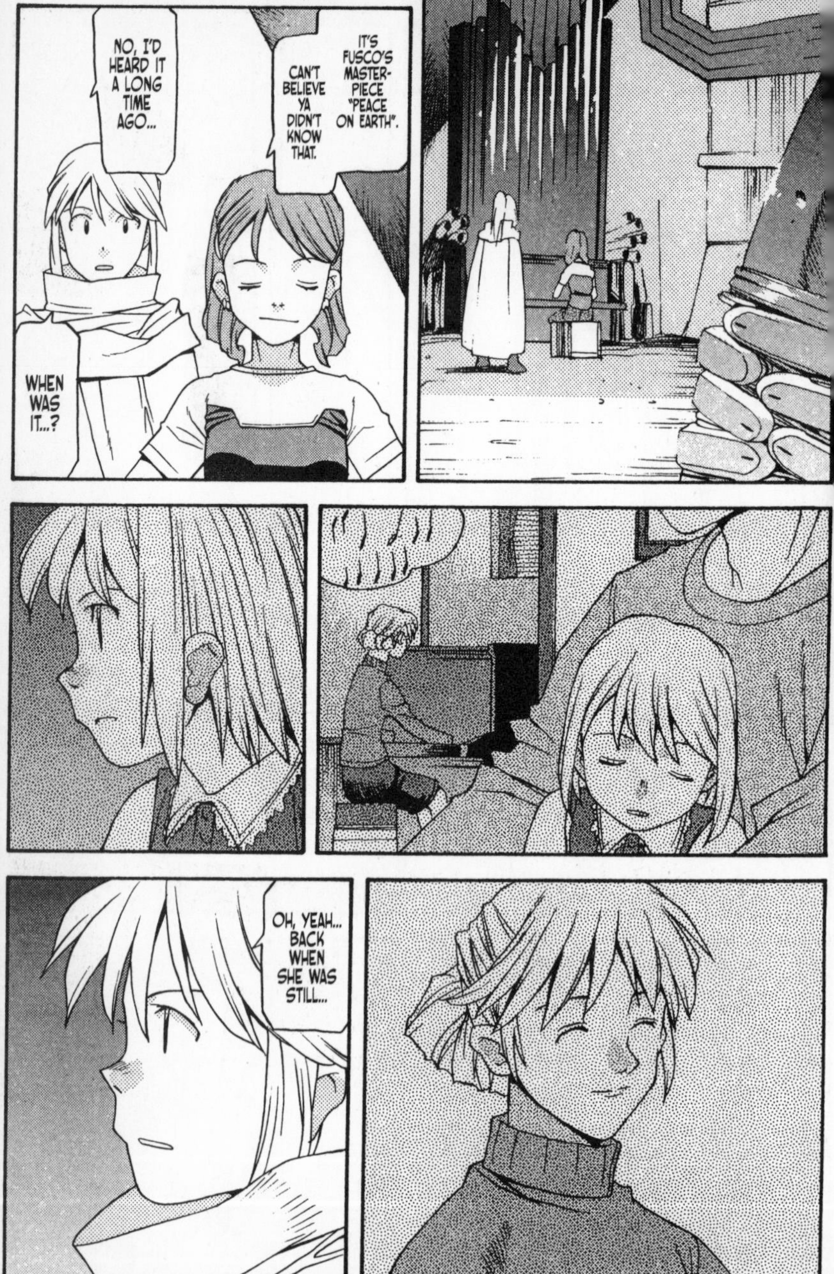
IT'S FUSCO'S MASTERPIECE "PEACE ON EARTH".
CAN'T BELIEVE YA DIDN'T KNOW THAT.
NO, I'D HEARD IT A LONG TIME AGO...
WHEN WAS IT...?
OH, YEAH... BACK WHEN SHE WAS STILL...

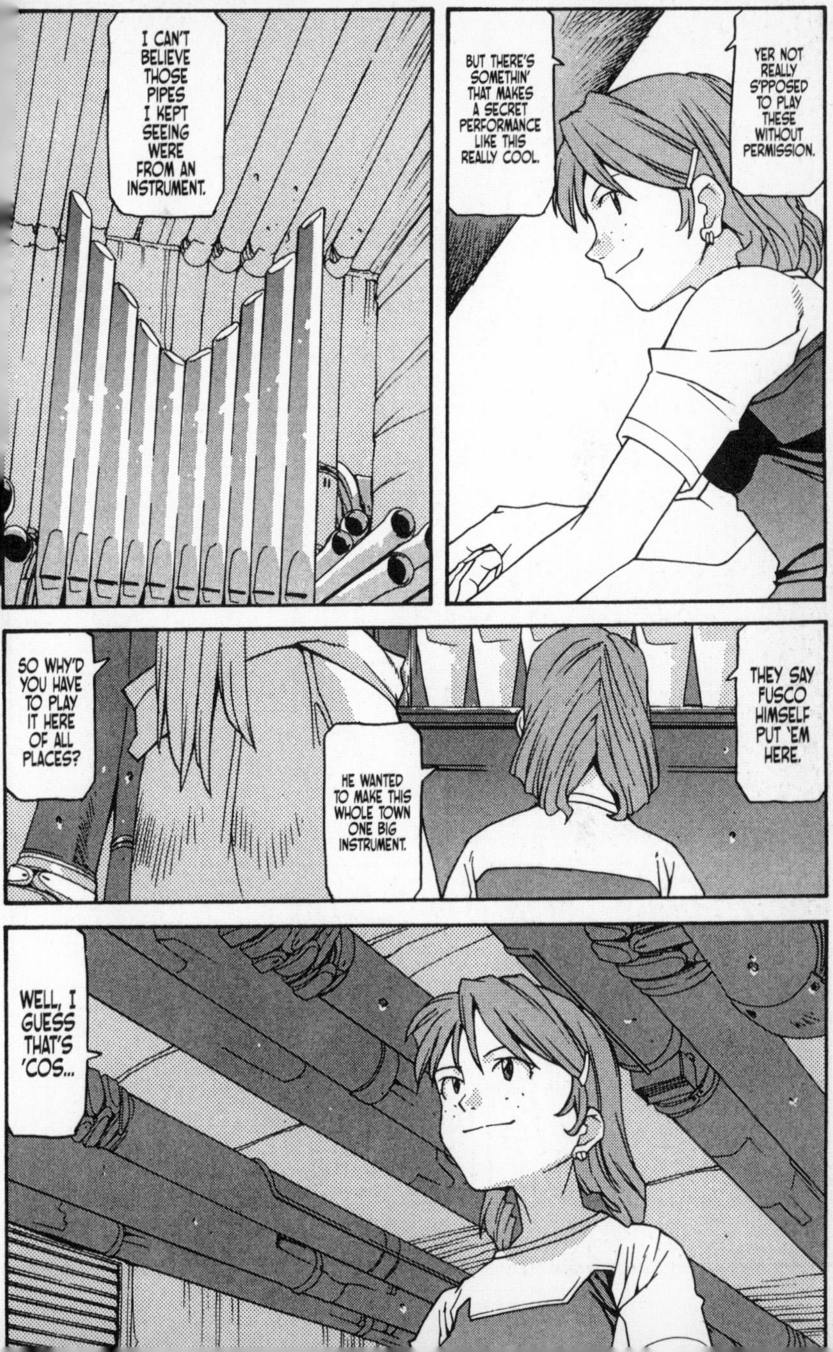
YER NOT REALLY S'PPOSED TO PLAY THESE WITHOUT PERMISSION.
BUT THERE'S SOMETHIN' THAT MAKES A SECRET PERFORMANCE LIKE THIS REALLY COOL.
I CAN'T BELIEVE THOSE PIPES I KEPT SEEING WERE FROM AN INSTRUMENT.
THEY SAY FUSCO HIMSELF PUT 'EM HERE.
HE WANTED TO MAKE THIS WHOLE TOWN ONE BIG INSTRUMENT.
SO WHY'D YOU HAVE TO PLAY IT HERE OF ALL PLACES?
WELL, I GUESS THAT'S 'COS...

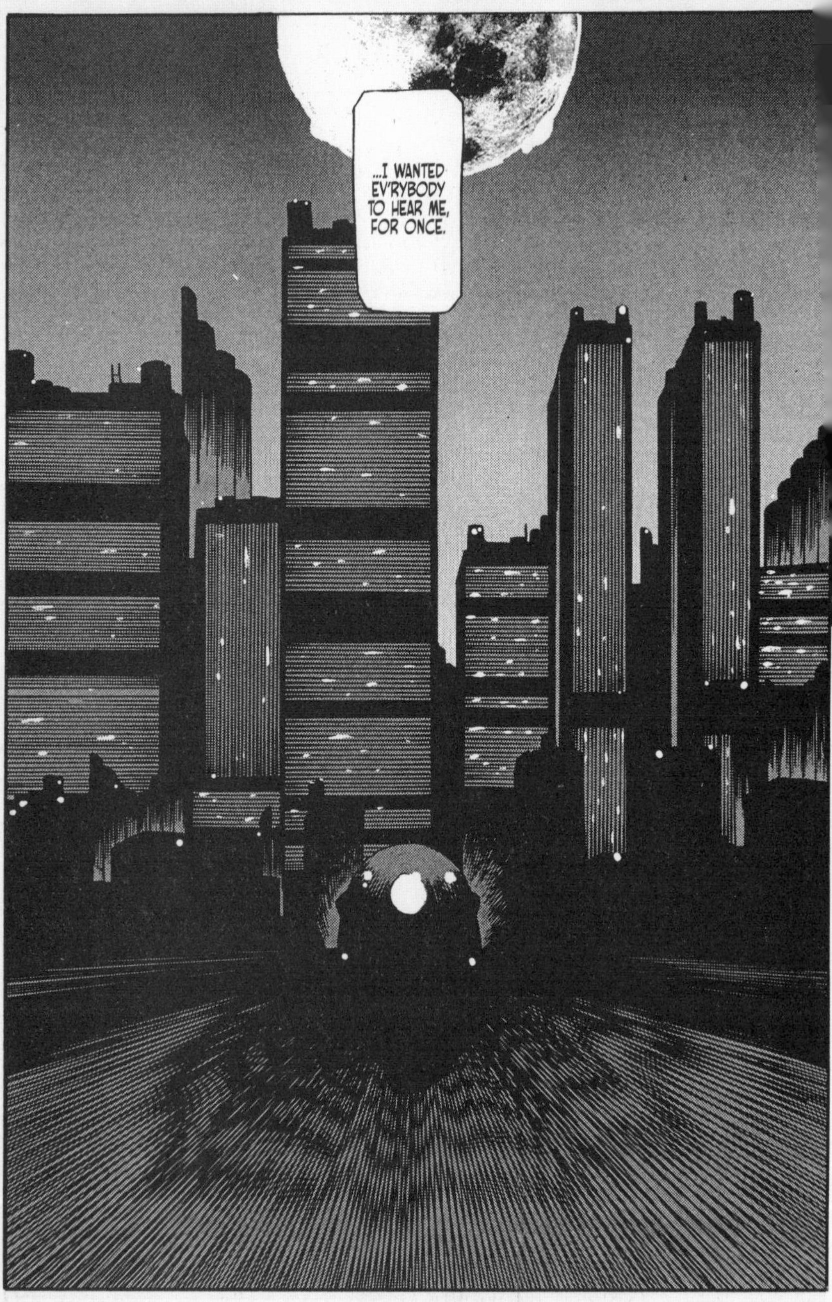
...I WANTED EV'RYBODY TO HEAR ME, FOR ONCE.

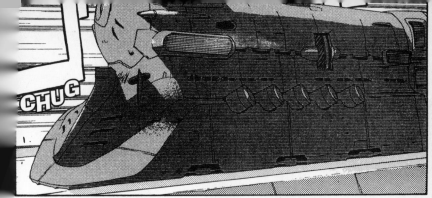

CHUG

TAP

I'LL ADMIT, IT'S A GOOD SONG.

Hang Them High

Lyrics: Arena Pendleton
Composition: Lori Anderson

K-
CUC
K

BUT YOU CAN'T USE PUNK FOR A SCHOOL ANTHEM.

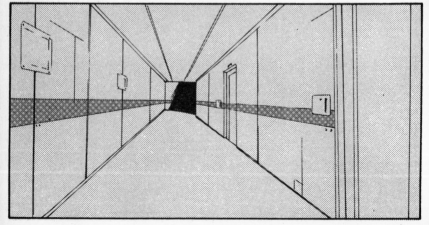

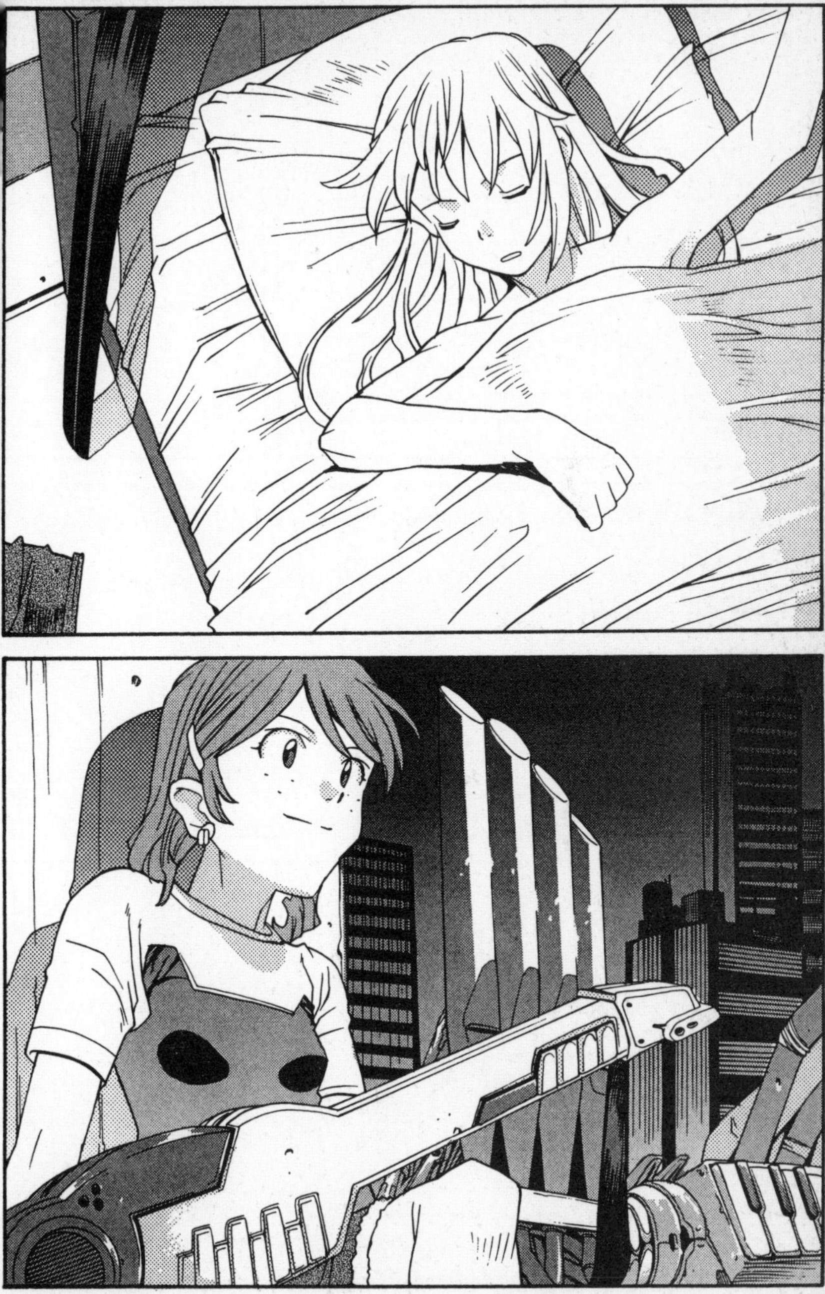

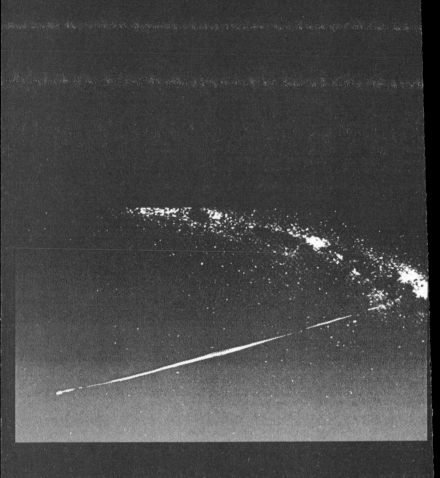

02. 6. 21

TRAIN+TRAIN

Episode.30

Episode 31

INTO THE BLUES

0300

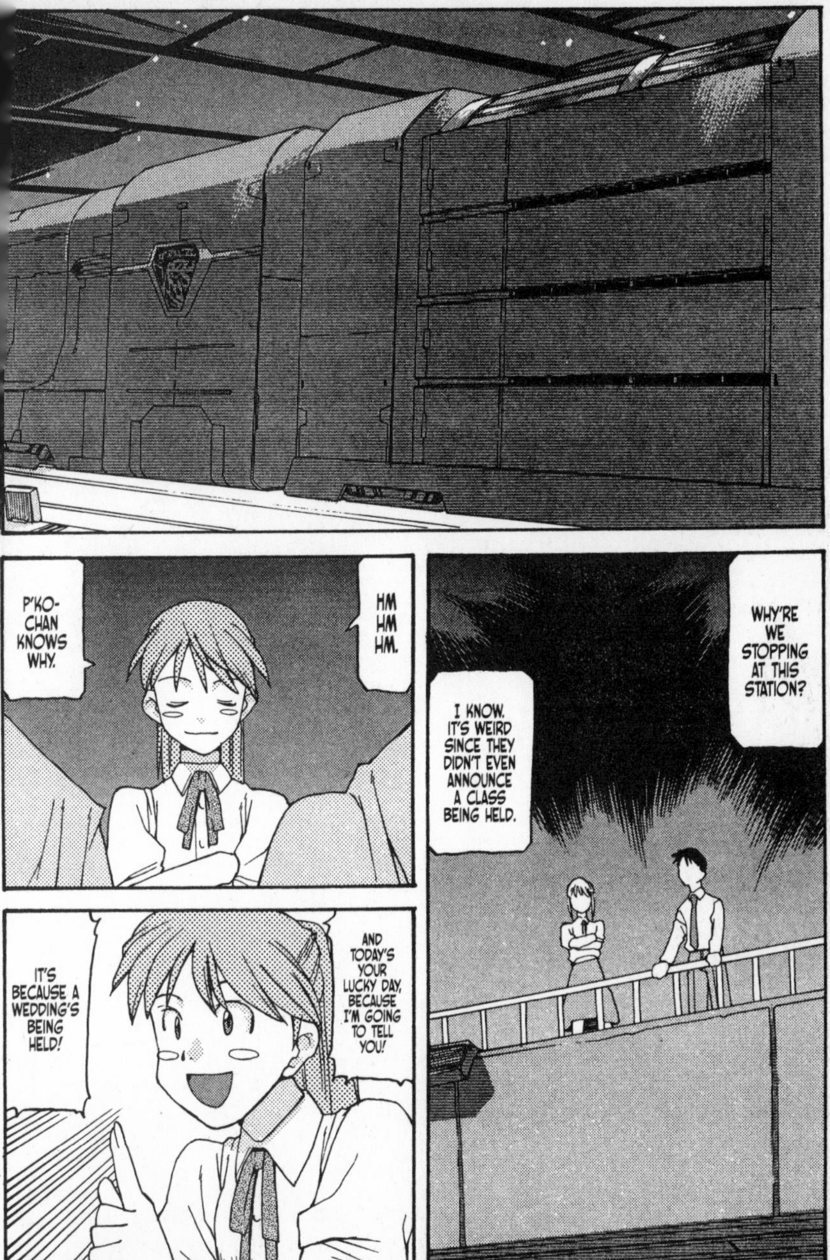
WHY'RE WE STOPPING AT THIS STATION?
I KNOW. IT'S WEIRD SINCE THEY DIDN'T EVEN ANNOUNCE A CLASS BEING HELD.
HM HM HM.
P'KO-CHAN KNOWS WHY.
AND TODAY'S YOUR LUCKY DAY, BECAUSE I'M GOING TO TELL YOU!
IT'S BECAUSE A WEDDING'S BEING HELD!

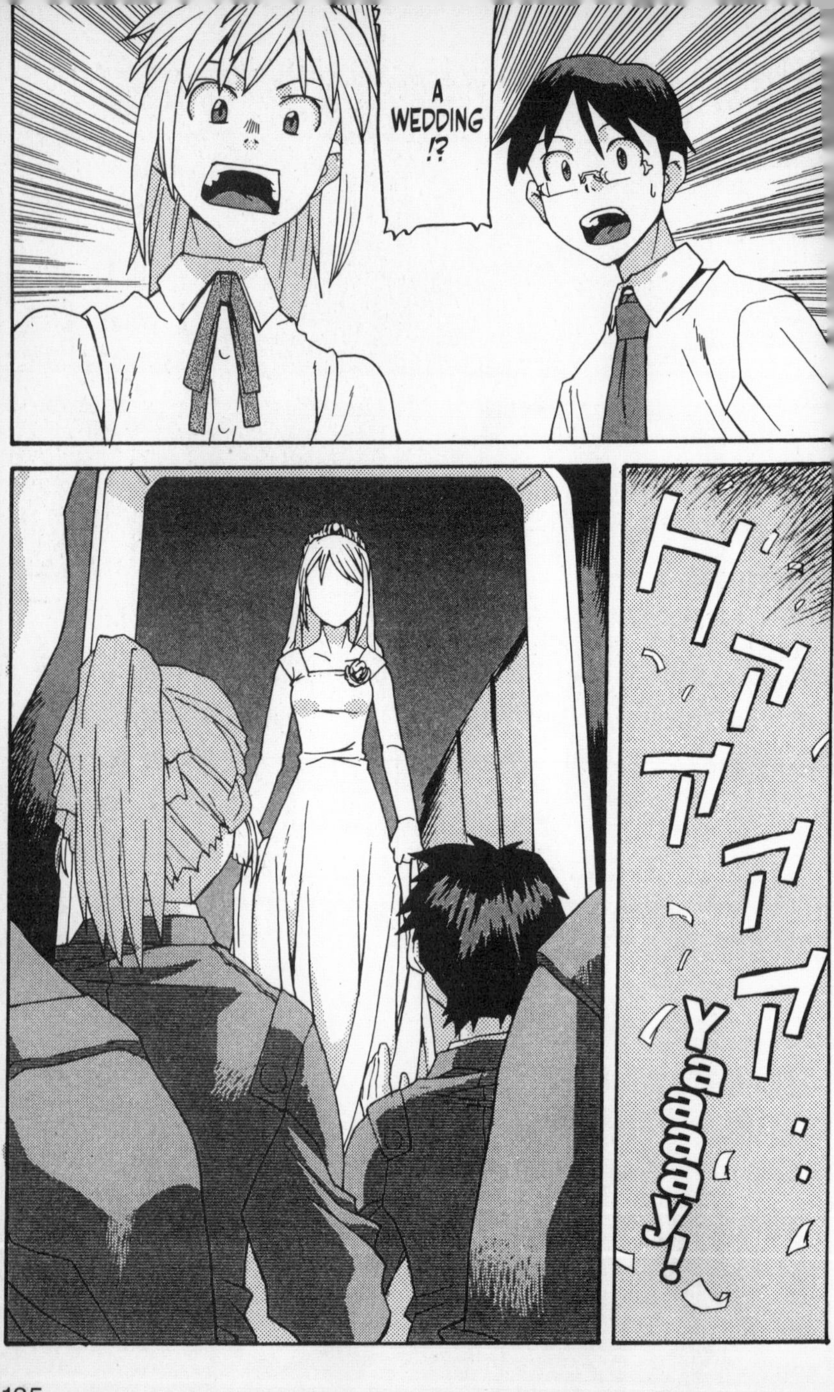
A WEDDING !?
Yaaaay!

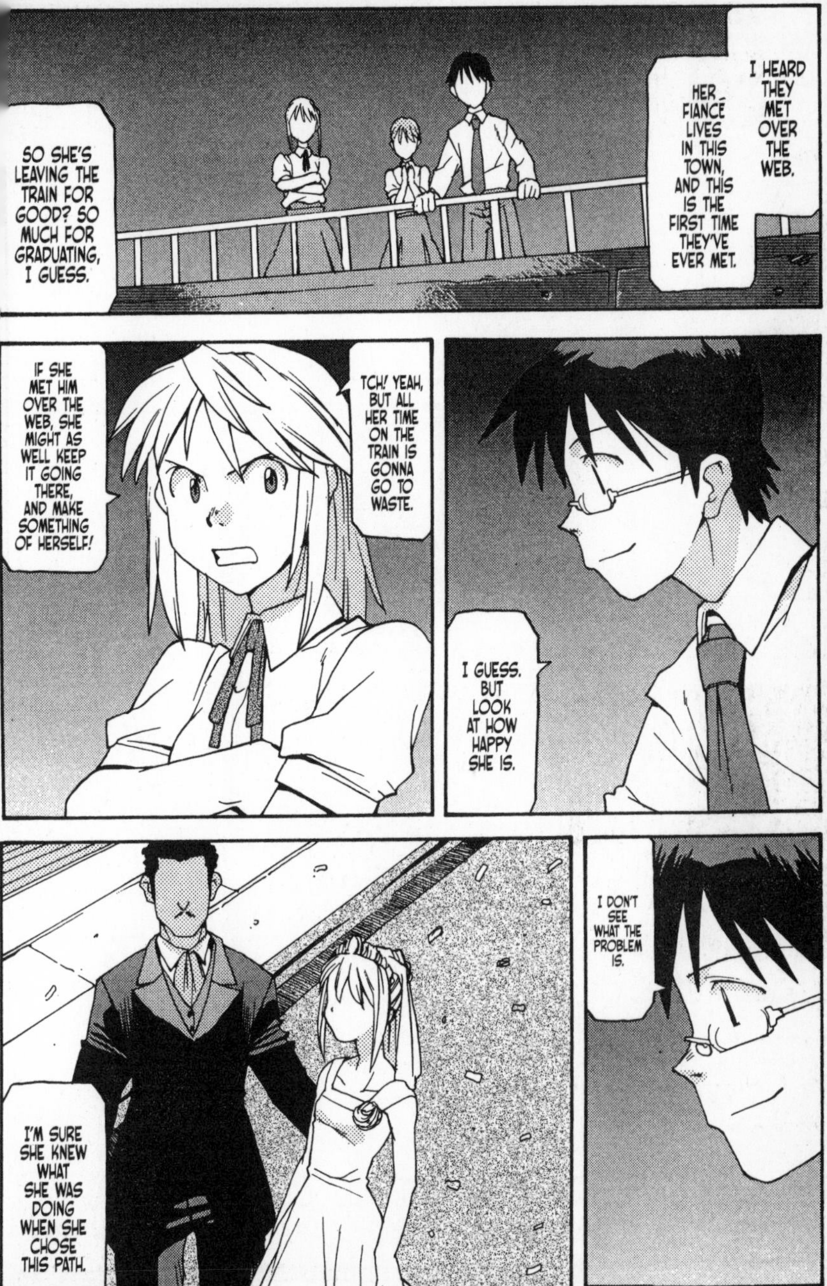
I HEARD THEY MET OVER THE WEB.
HER FIANCÉ LIVES IN THIS TOWN, AND THIS IS THE FIRST TIME THEY'VE EVER MET.
SO SHE'S LEAVING THE TRAIN FOR GOOD? SO MUCH FOR GRADUATING, I GUESS.
I GUESS. BUT LOOK AT HOW HAPPY SHE IS.
TCH! YEAH, BUT ALL HER TIME ON THE TRAIN IS GONNA GO TO WASTE.
IF SHE MET HIM OVER THE WEB, SHE MIGHT AS WELL KEEP IT GOING THERE, AND MAKE SOMETHING OF HERSELF!
I DON'T SEE WHAT THE PROBLEM IS.
I'M SURE SHE KNEW WHAT SHE WAS DOING WHEN SHE CHOSE THIS PATH.

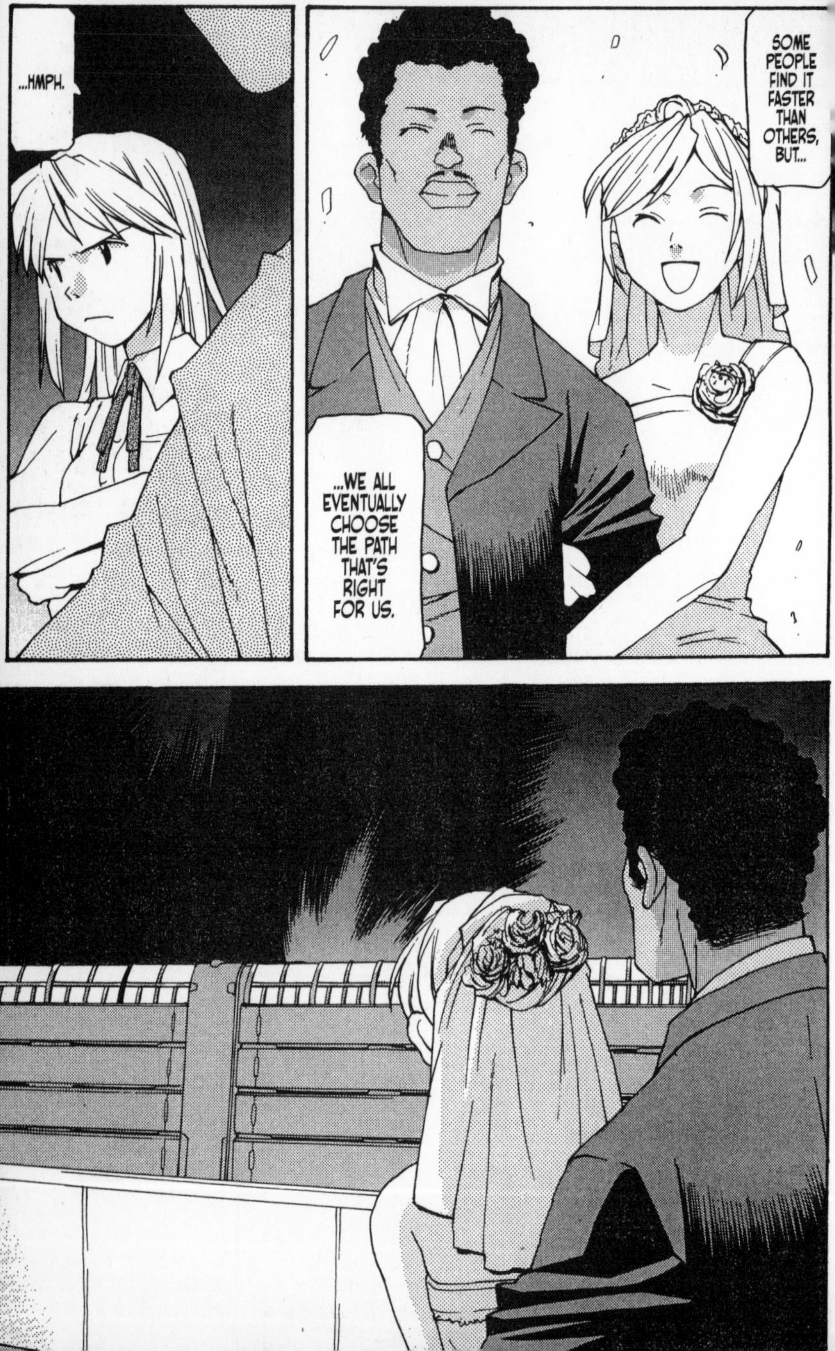
SOME PEOPLE FIND IT FASTER THAN OTHERS, BUT...
...WE ALL EVENTUALLY CHOOSE THE PATH THAT'S RIGHT FOR US.
...HMPH.

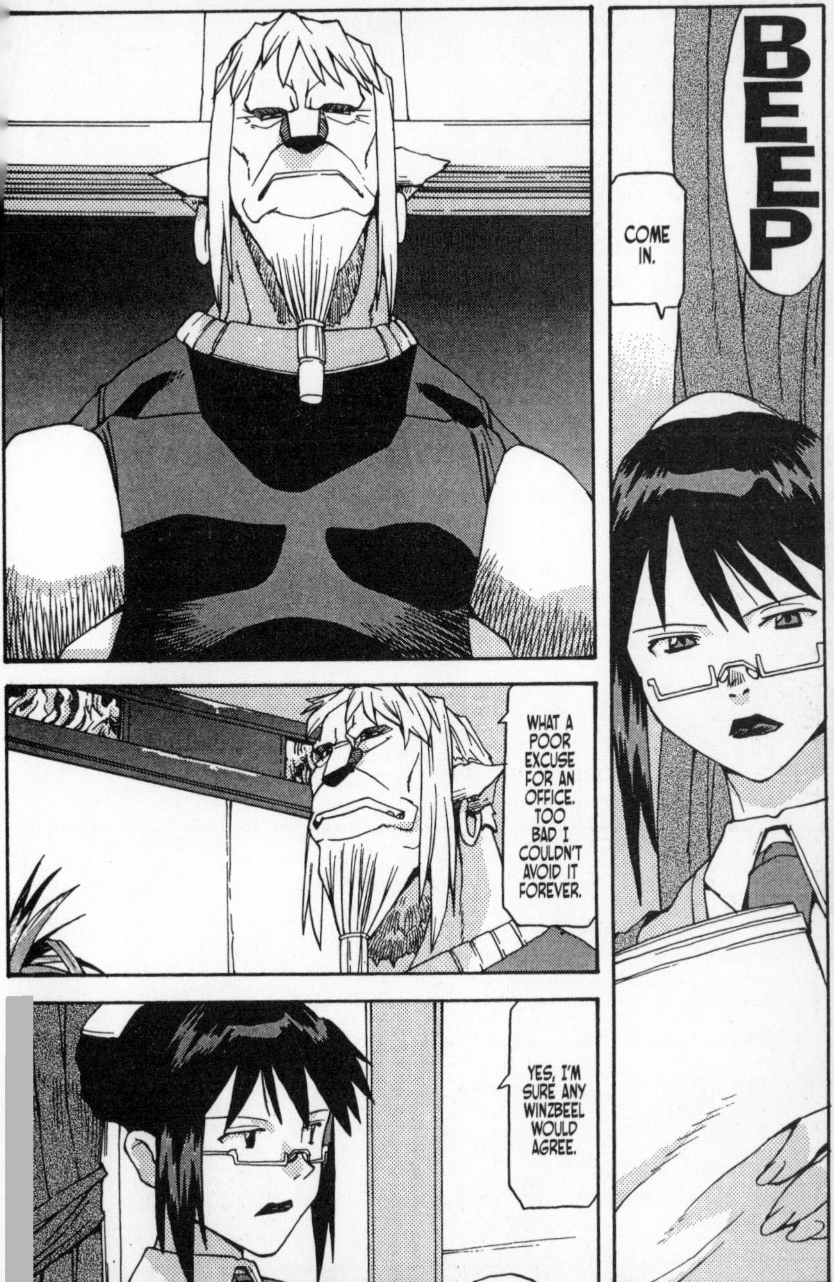
BEEP
COME IN.
WHAT A POOR EXCUSE FOR AN OFFICE. TOO BAD I COULDN'T AVOID IT FOREVER.
YES, I'M SURE ANY WINZBEEL WOULD AGREE.
FWAP

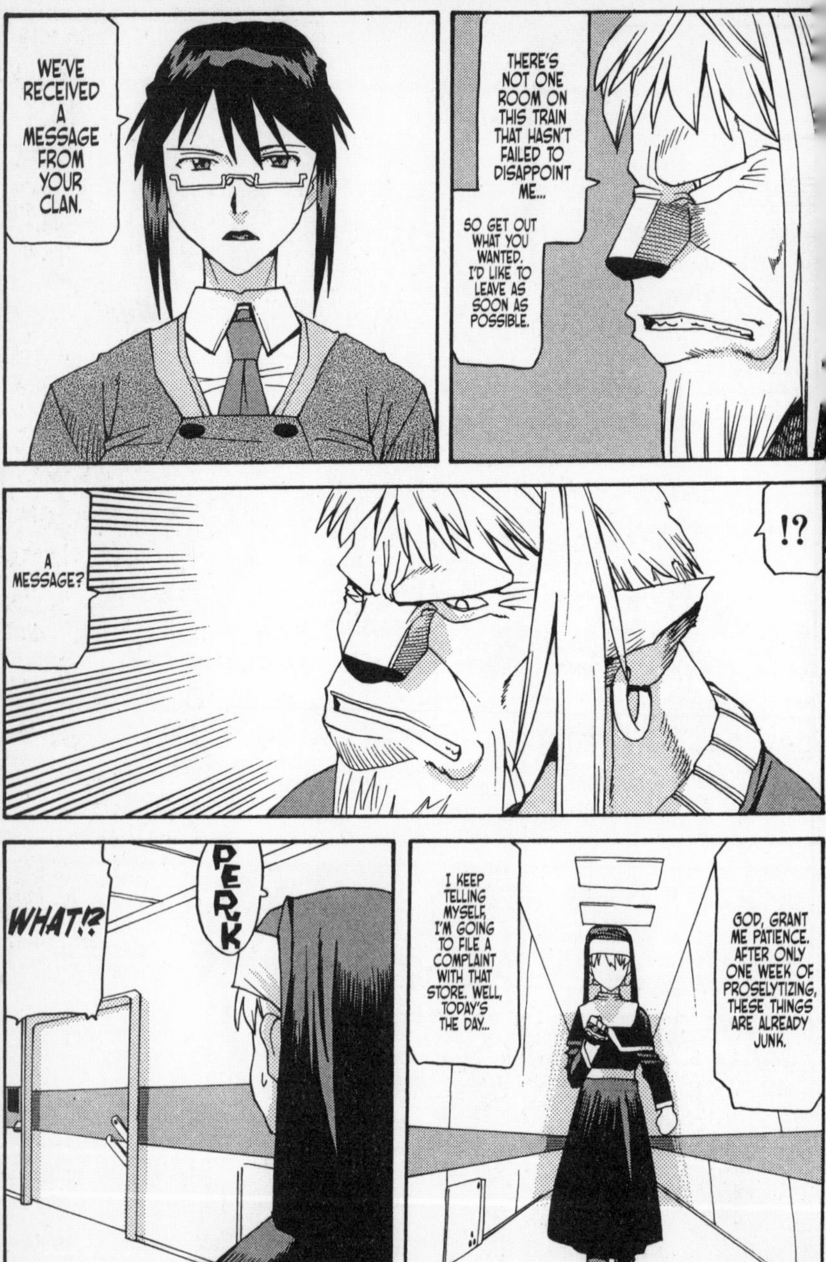
THERE'S NOT ONE ROOM ON THIS TRAIN THAT HASN'T FAILED TO DISAPPOINT ME...
SO GET OUT WHAT YOU WANTED. I'D LIKE TO LEAVE AS SOON AS POSSIBLE.
WE'VE RECEIVED A MESSAGE FROM YOUR CLAN.
!?
A MESSAGE?
GOD, GRANT ME PATIENCE. AFTER ONLY ONE WEEK OF PROSELYTIZING, THESE THINGS ARE ALREADY JUNK.
I KEEP TELLING MYSELF, I'M GOING TO FILE A COMPLAINT WITH THAT STORE. WELL, TODAY'S THE DAY...
PERK
WHAT!?

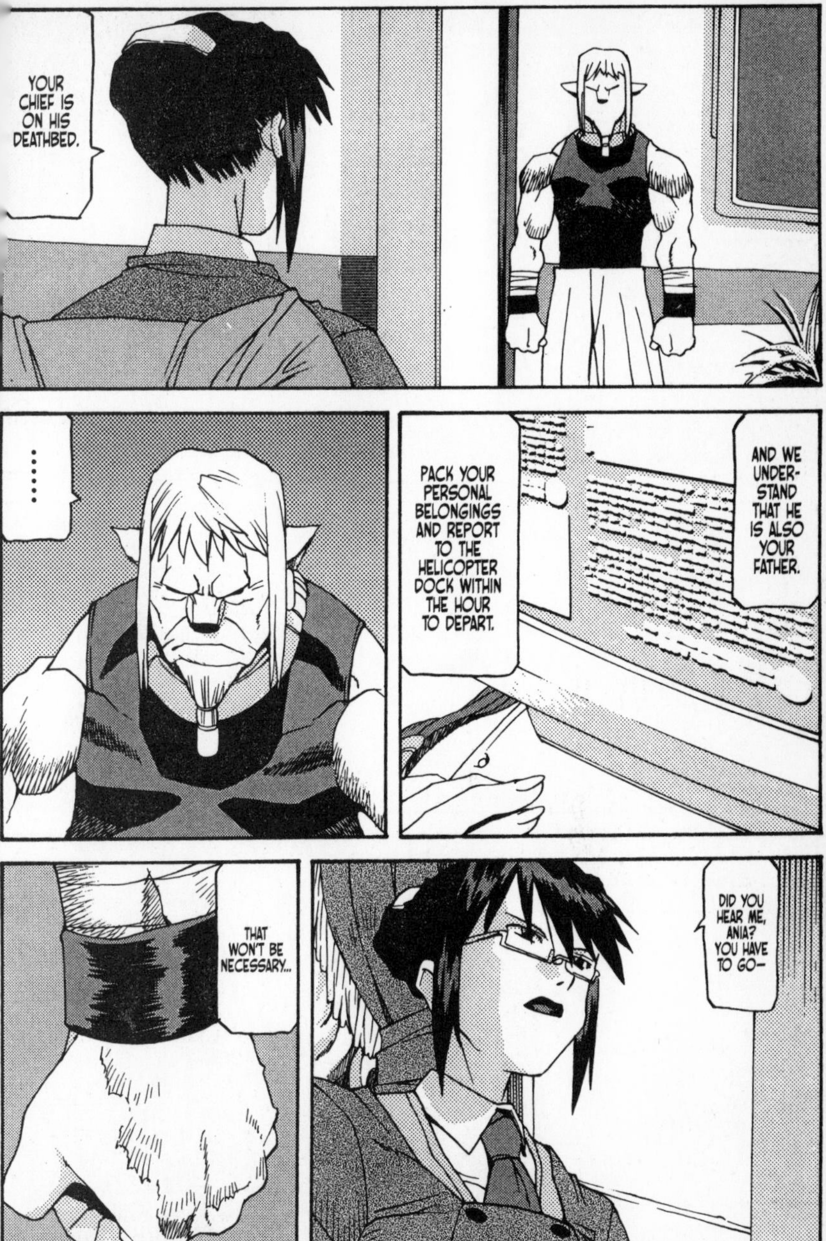
YOUR CHIEF IS ON HIS DEATHBED.
AND WE UNDER-STAND THAT HE IS ALSO YOUR FATHER.
PACK YOUR PERSONAL BELONGINGS AND REPORT TO THE HELICOPTER DOCK WITHIN THE HOUR TO DEPART.
......
DID YOU HEAR ME, ANIA? YOU HAVE TO GO—
THAT WON'T BE NECESSARY...

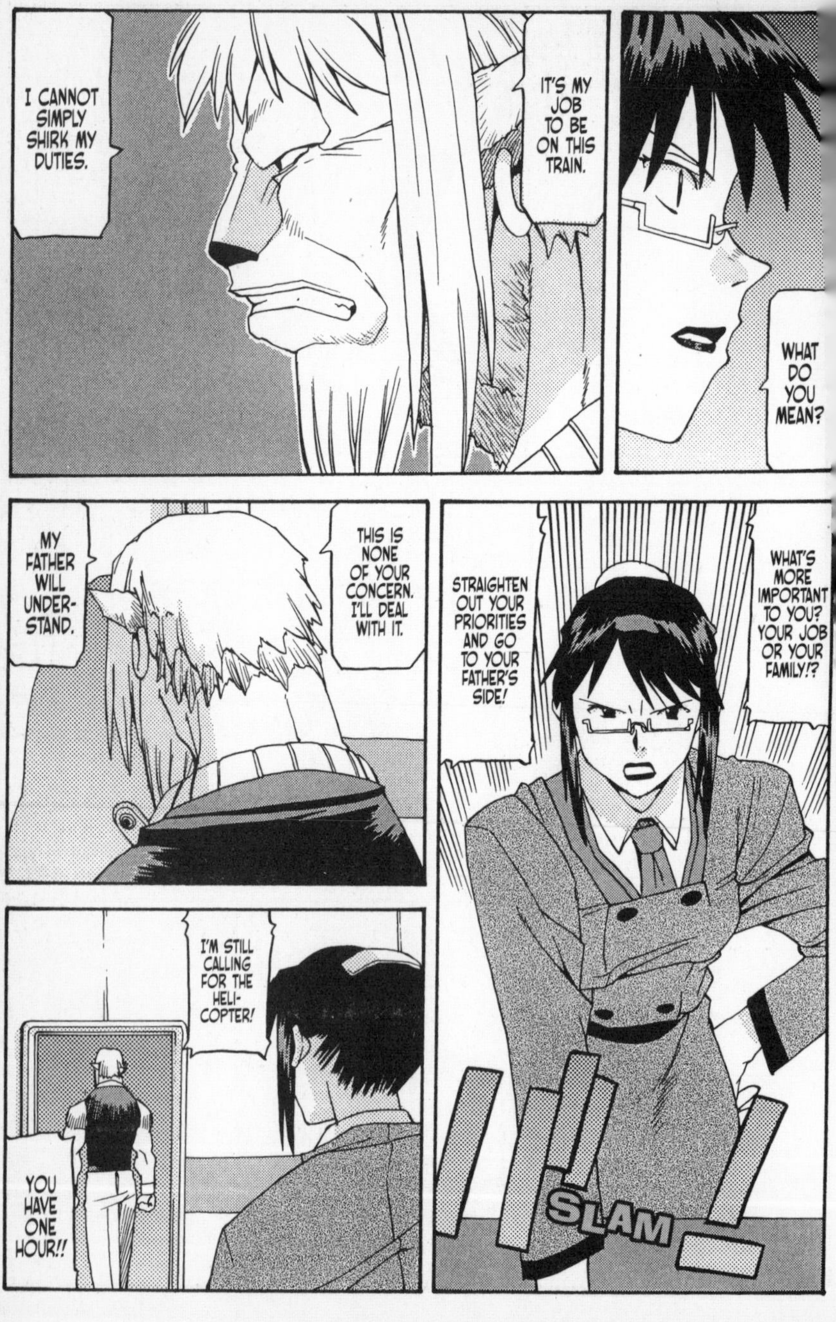
WHAT DO YOU MEAN?
IT'S MY JOB TO BE ON THIS TRAIN.
I CANNOT SIMPLY SHIRK MY DUTIES.
WHAT'S MORE IMPORTANT TO YOU? YOUR JOB OR YOUR FAMILY!?
STRAIGHTEN OUT YOUR PRIORITIES AND GO TO YOUR FATHER'S SIDE!
SLAM
THIS IS NONE OF YOUR CONCERN. I'LL DEAL WITH IT.
MY FATHER WILL UNDER-STAND.
I'M STILL CALLING FOR THE HELI-COPTER!
YOU HAVE ONE HOUR!!

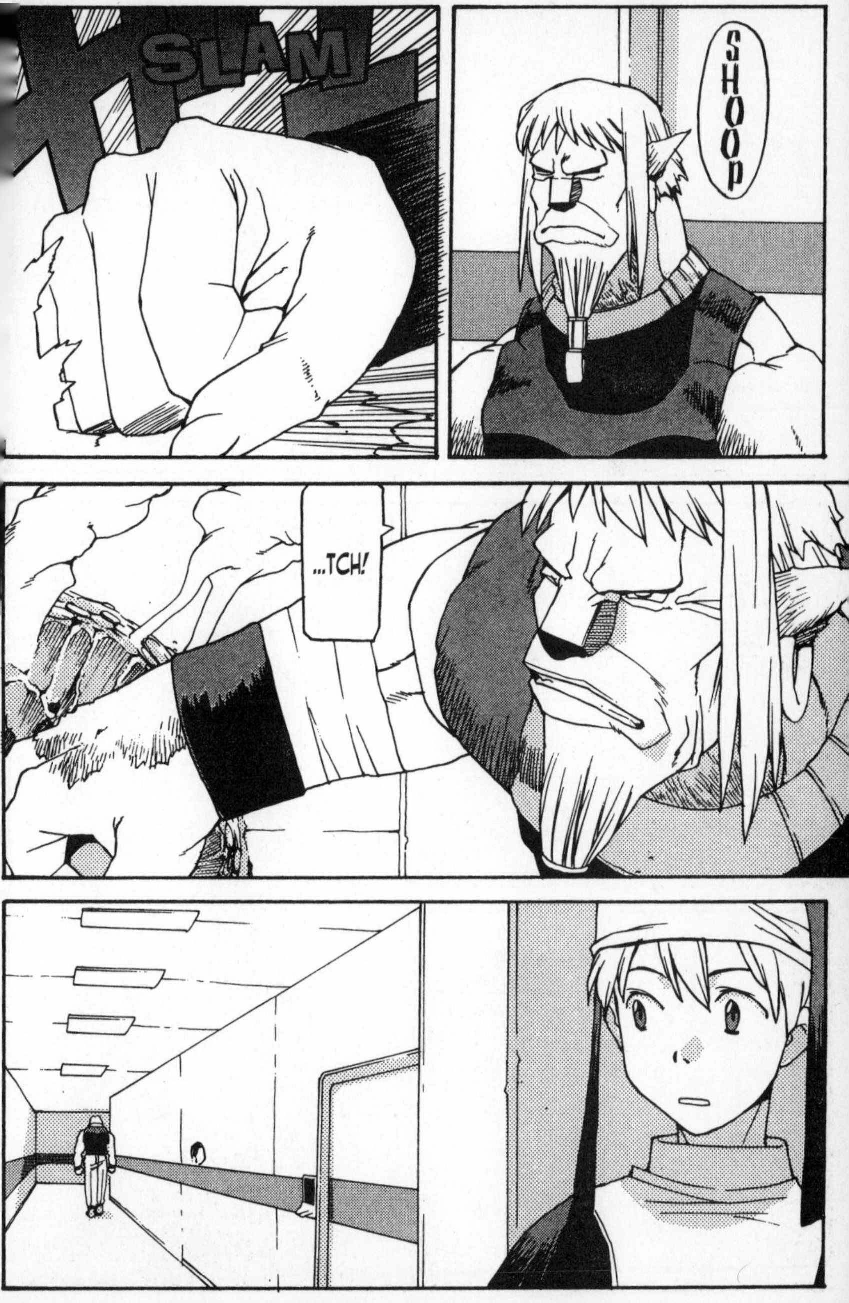
SHOOP
SLAM
...TCH!

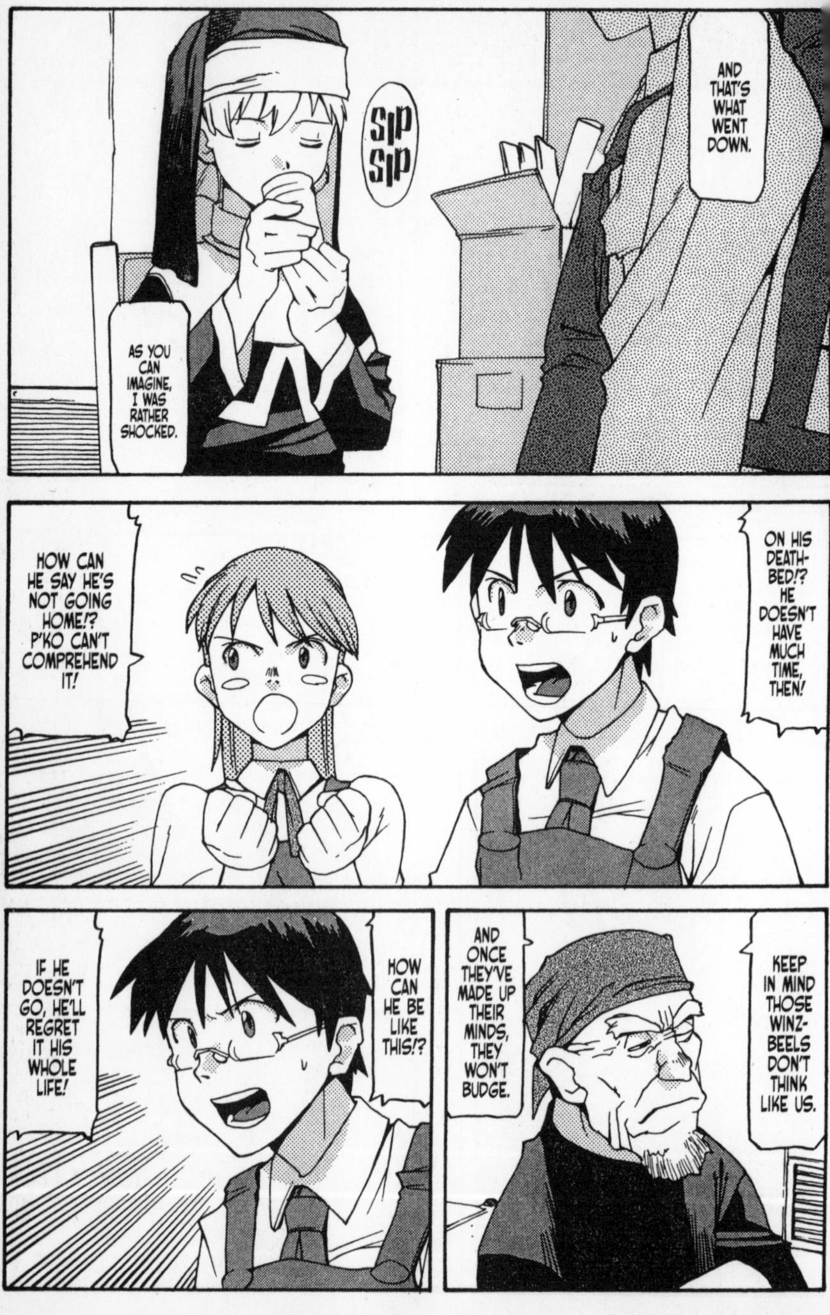
AND THAT'S WHAT WENT DOWN.
SIP SIP
AS YOU CAN IMAGINE, I WAS RATHER SHOCKED.
ON HIS DEATH-BED!? HE DOESN'T HAVE MUCH TIME, THEN!
HOW CAN HE SAY HE'S NOT GOING HOME!? P'KO CAN'T COMPREHEND IT!
KEEP IN MIND THOSE WINZ-BEELS DON'T THINK LIKE US.
AND ONCE THEY'VE MADE UP THEIR MINDS, THEY WON'T BUDGE.
HOW CAN HE BE LIKE THIS!?
IF HE DOESN'T GO, HE'LL REGRET IT HIS WHOLE LIFE!

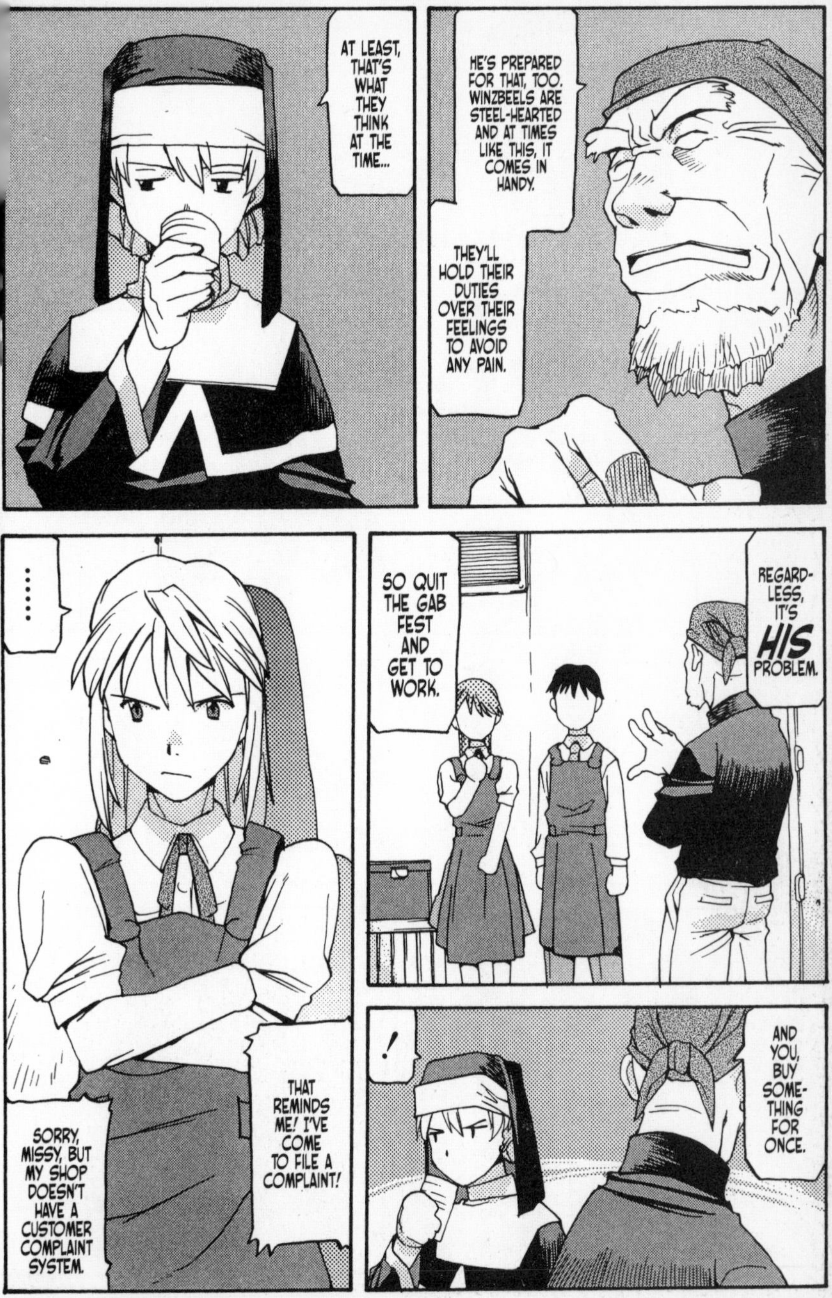
HE'S PREPARED FOR THAT, TOO. WINZBEELS ARE STEEL-HEARTED AND AT TIMES LIKE THIS, IT COMES IN HANDY.
THEY'LL HOLD THEIR DUTIES OVER THEIR FEELINGS TO AVOID ANY PAIN.
AT LEAST, THAT'S WHAT THEY THINK AT THE TIME...
REGARDLESS, IT'S HIS PROBLEM.
SO QUIT THE GAB FEST AND GET TO WORK.
AND YOU, BUY SOMETHING FOR ONCE.
!
......
THAT REMINDS ME! I'VE COME TO FILE A COMPLAINT!
SORRY, MISSY, BUT MY SHOP DOESN'T HAVE A CUSTOMER COMPLAINT SYSTEM.

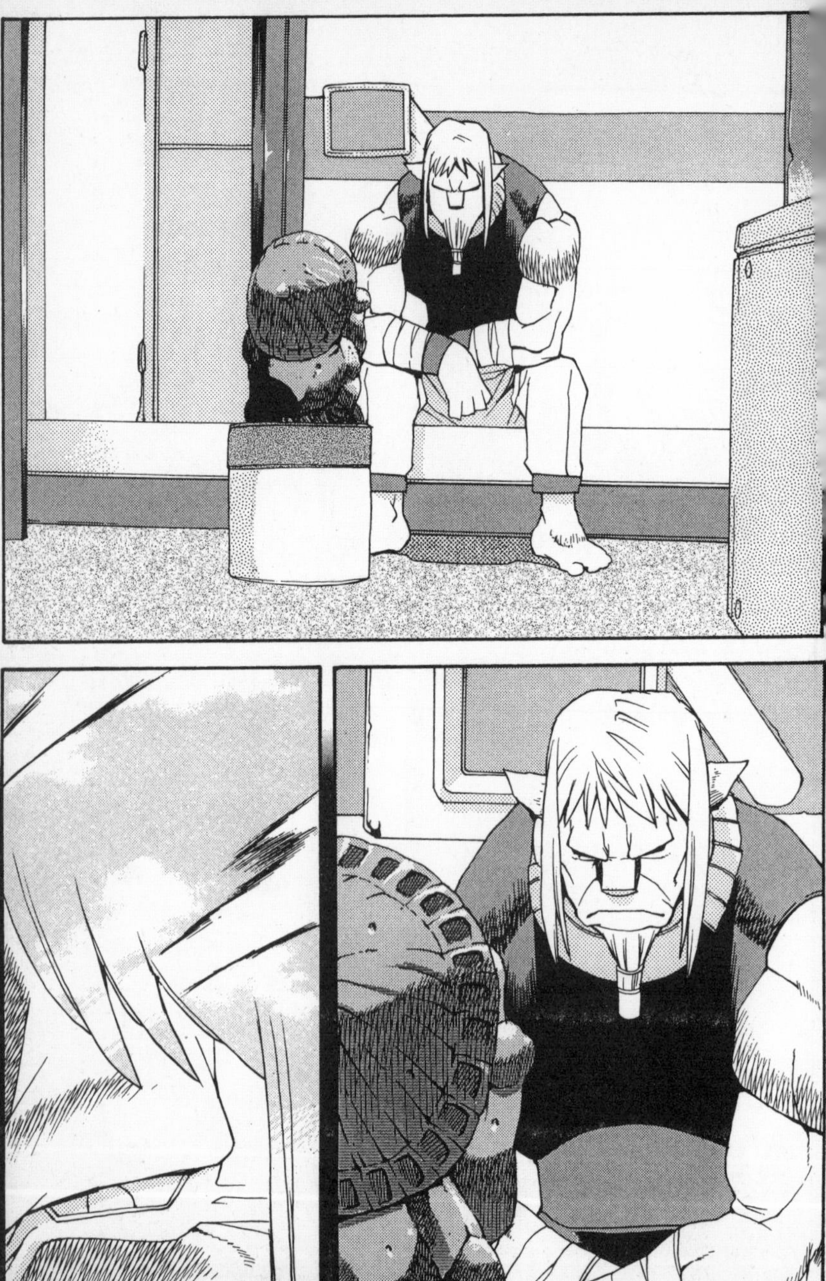

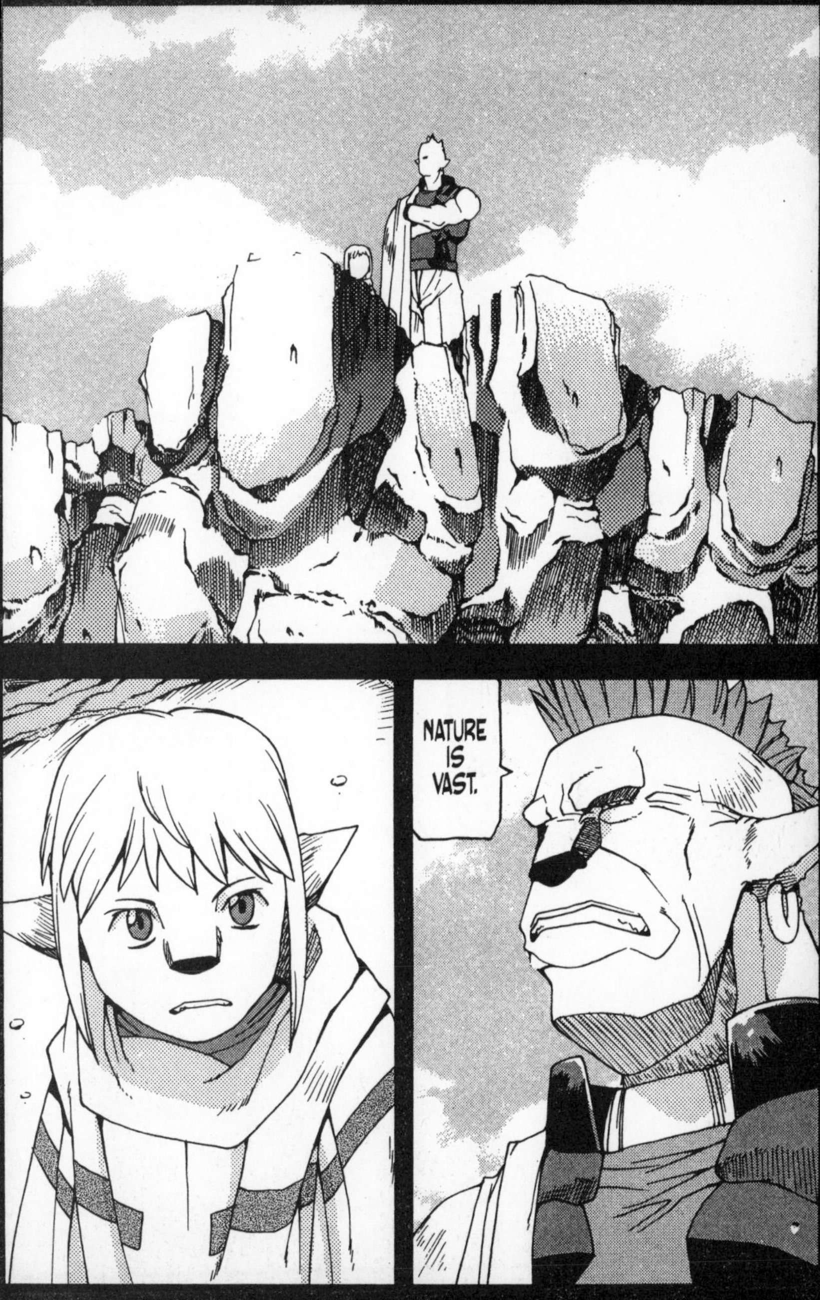
NATURE IS VAST.

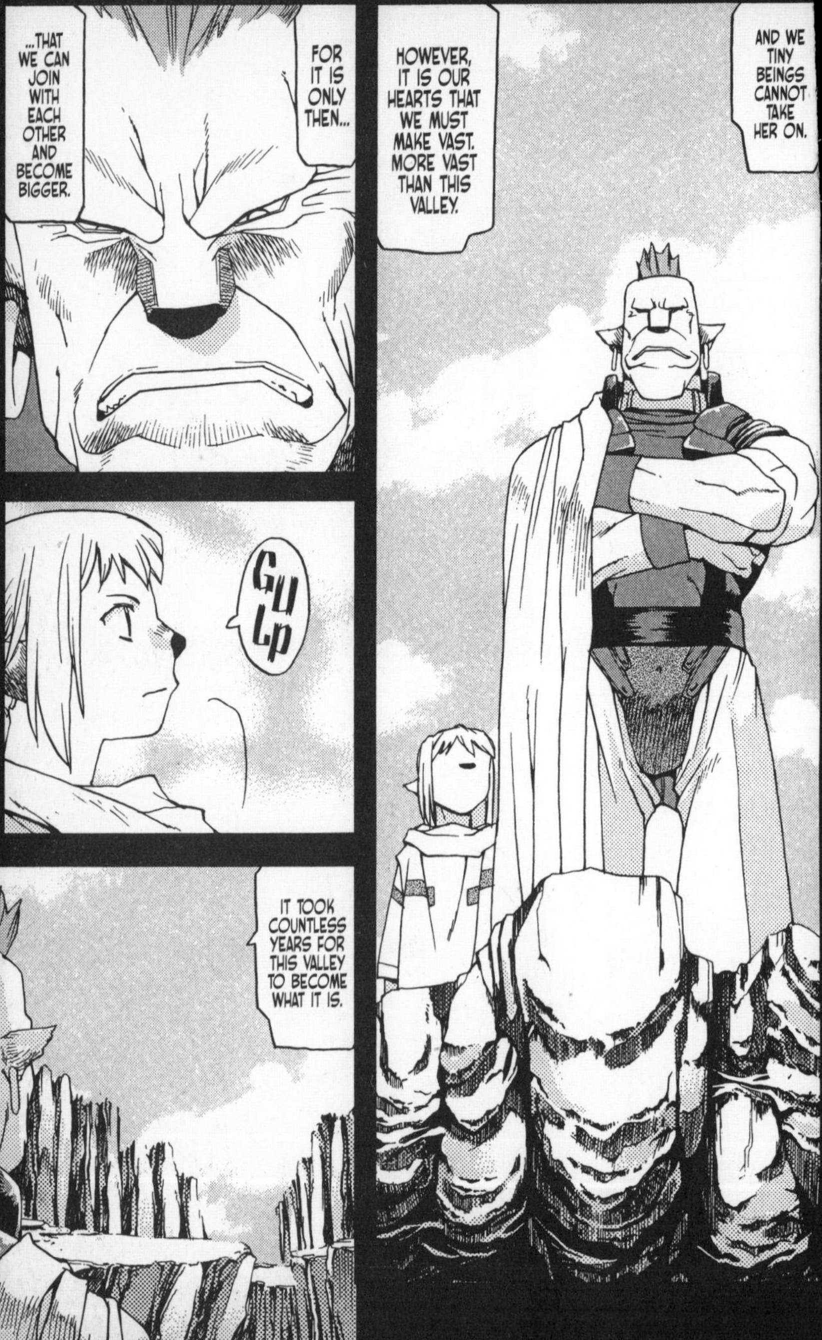
AND WE TINY BEINGS CANNOT TAKE HER ON.
HOWEVER, IT IS OUR HEARTS THAT WE MUST MAKE VAST. MORE VAST THAN THIS VALLEY.
FOR IT IS ONLY THEN...
...THAT WE CAN JOIN WITH EACH OTHER AND BECOME BIGGER.
GULP
IT TOOK COUNTLESS YEARS FOR THIS VALLEY TO BECOME WHAT IT IS.

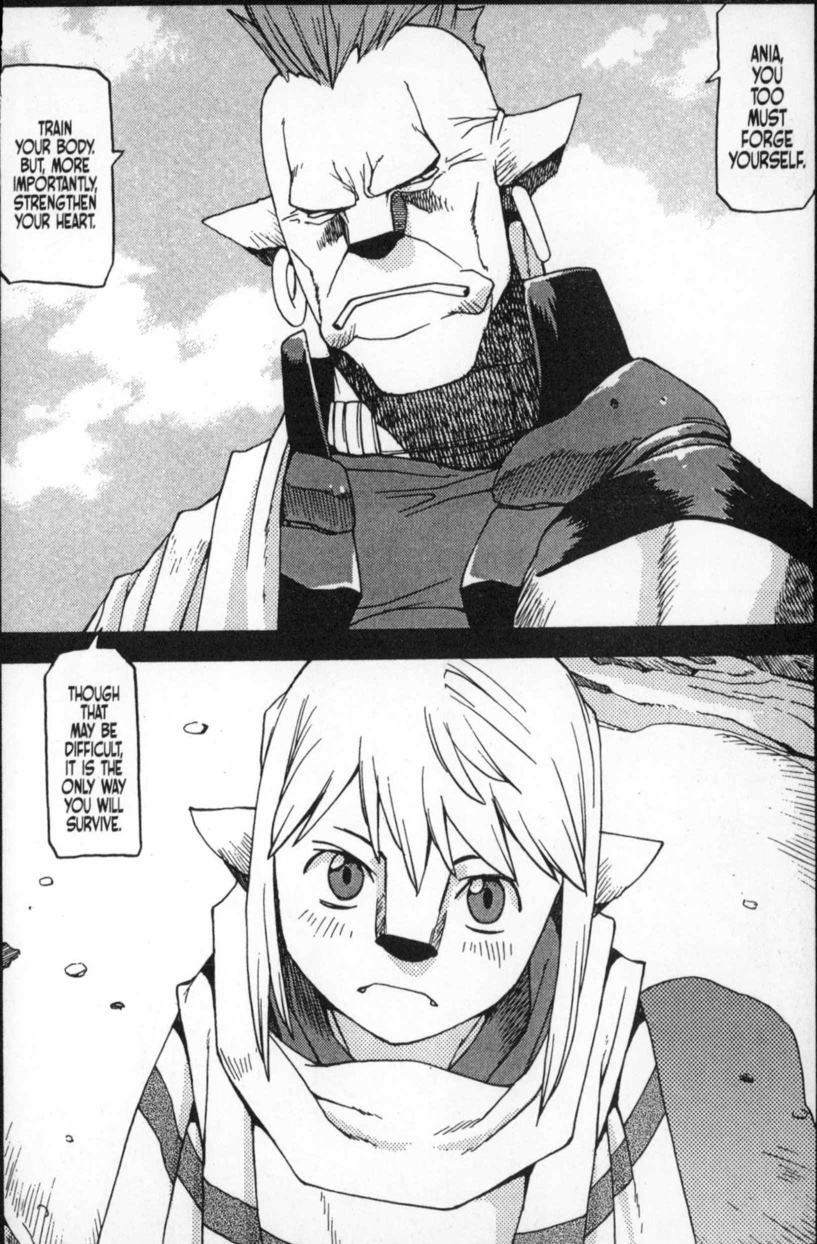
ANIA, YOU TOO MUST FORGE YOURSELF.
TRAIN YOUR BODY. BUT, MORE IMPORTANTLY, STRENGTHEN YOUR HEART.
THOUGH THAT MAY BE DIFFICULT, IT IS THE ONLY WAY YOU WILL SURVIVE.

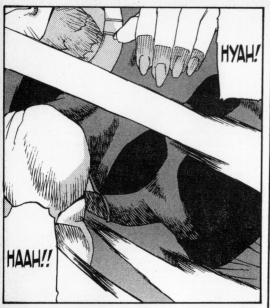

HYAH!

HAAH!!

HIYA AAH!

GOT A MINUTE?

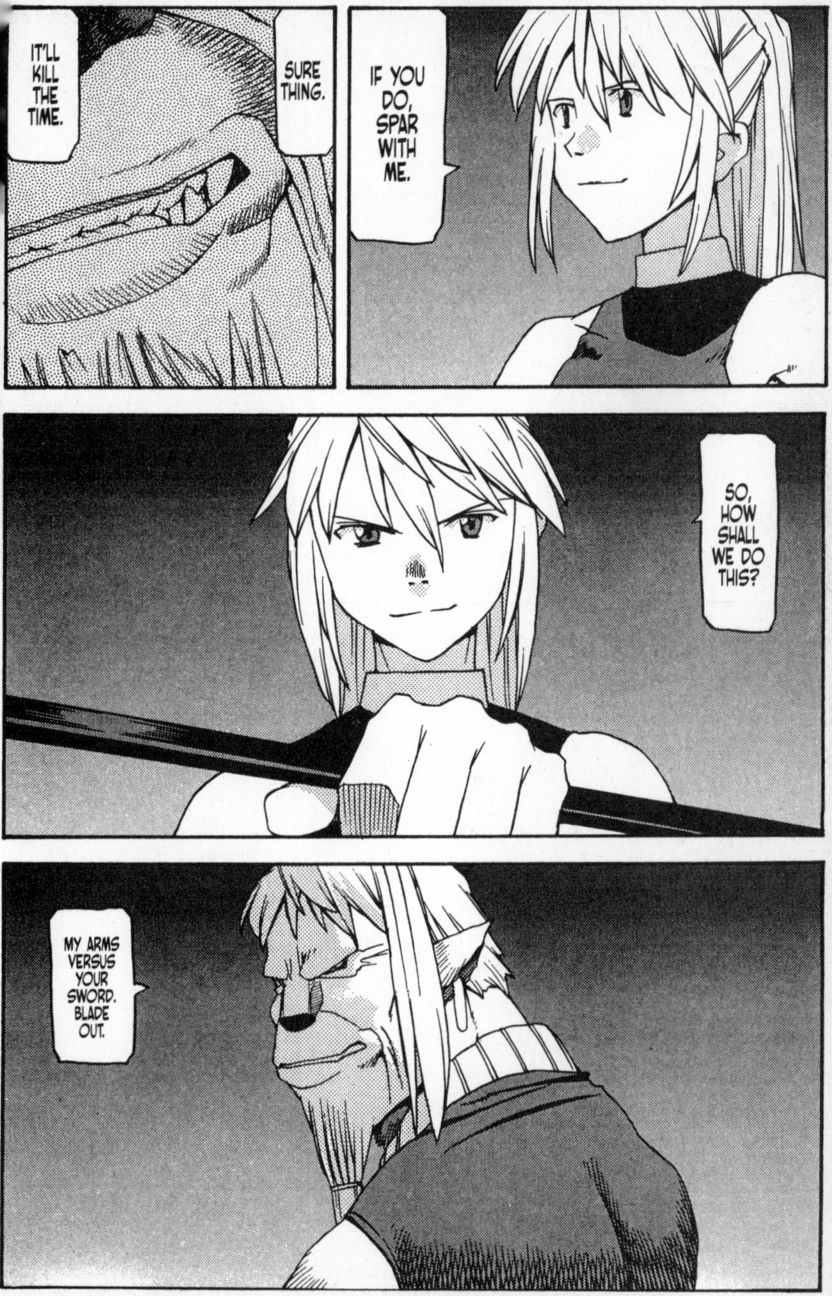
IF YOU DO, SPAR WITH ME.
SURE THING.
IT'LL KILL THE TIME.
SO, HOW SHALL WE DO THIS?
MY ARMS VERSUS YOUR SWORD. BLADE OUT.

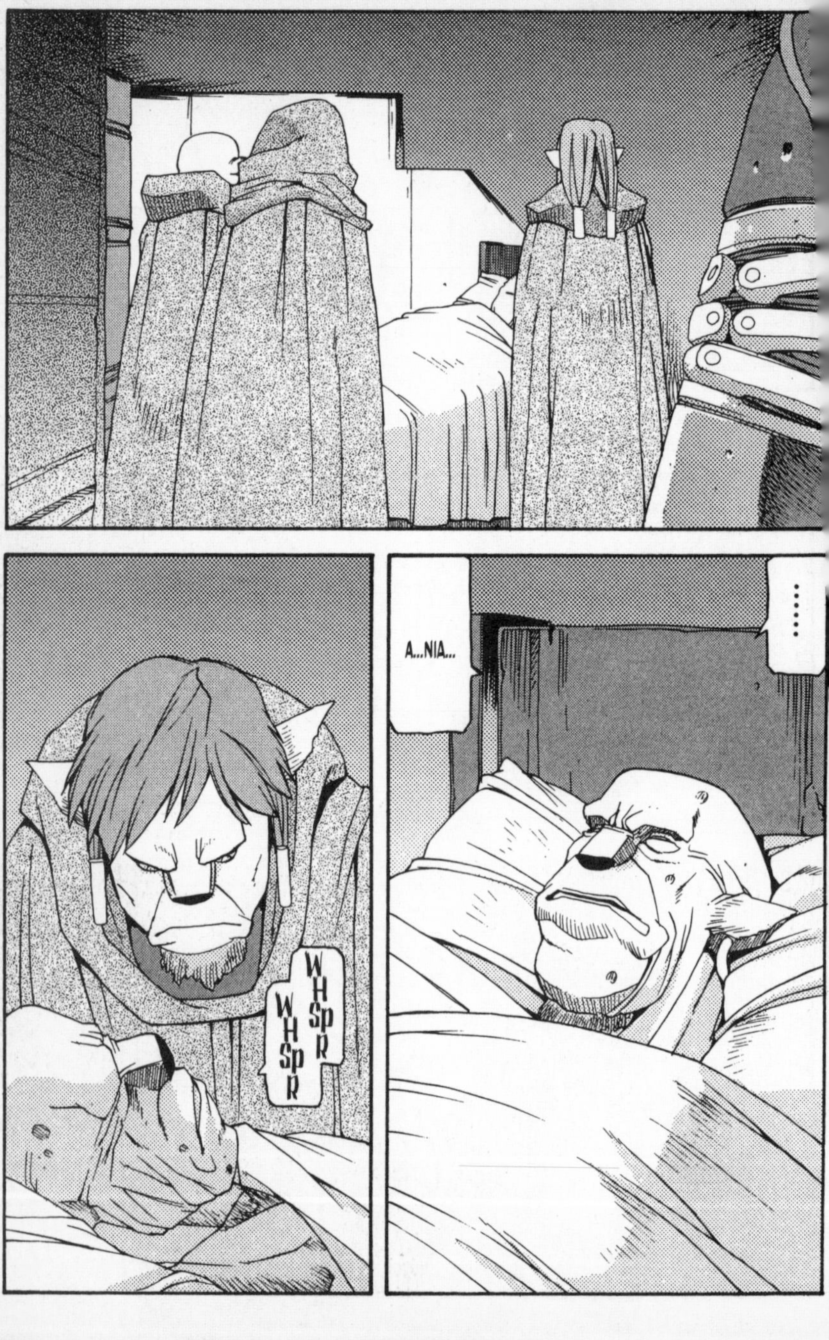
......
A...NIA...
WHSpR
WHSpR

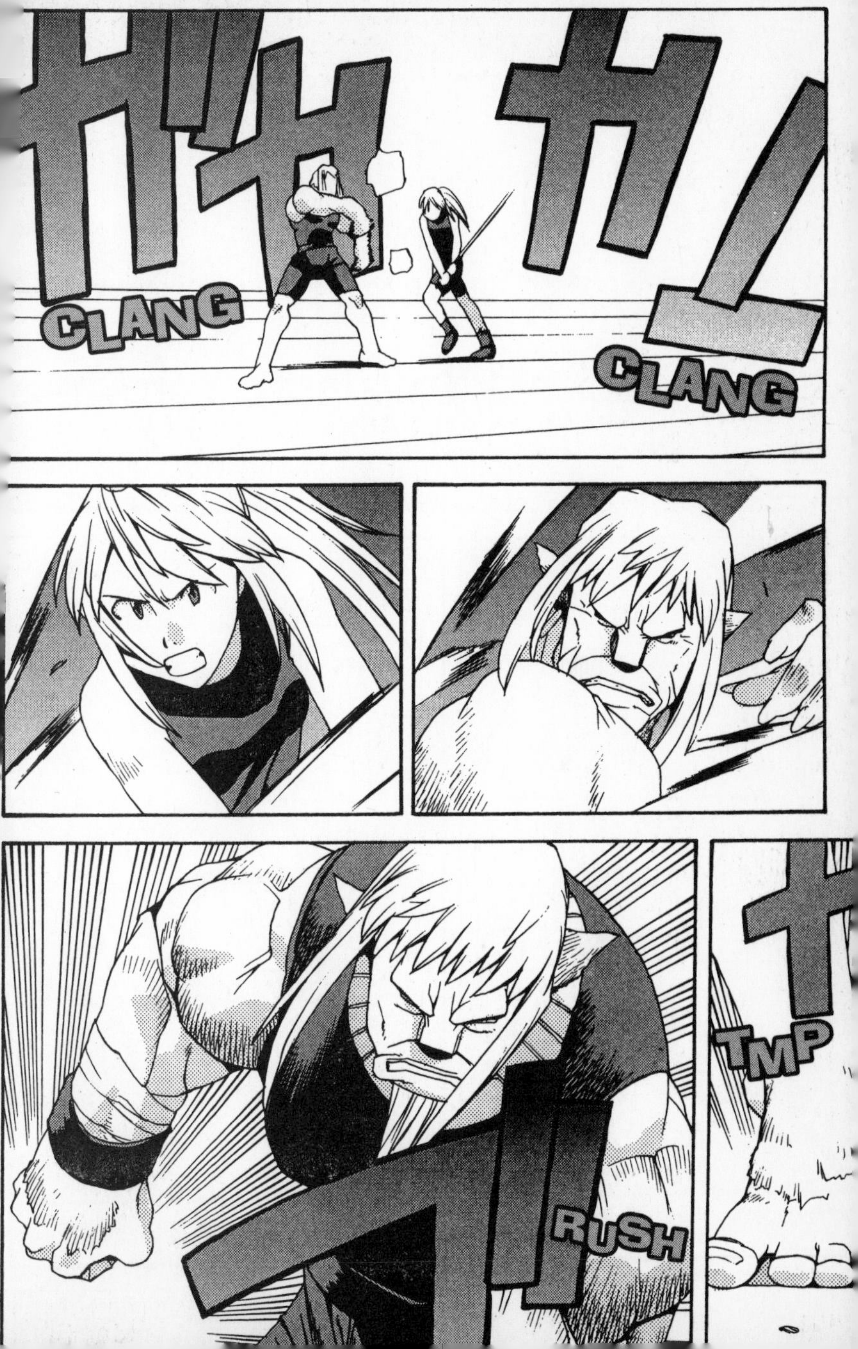
CLANG
CLANG
TMP
RUSH

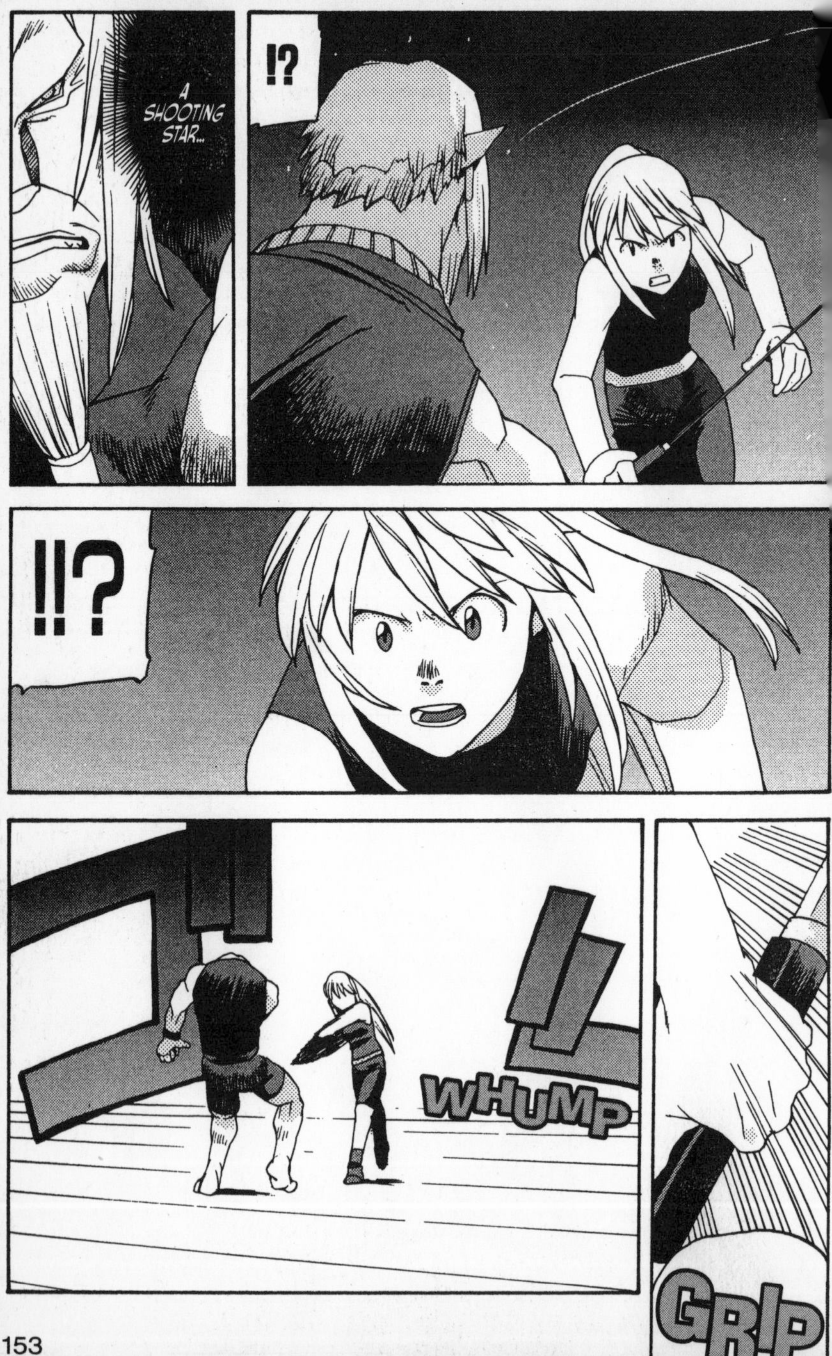
!?
A SHOOTING STAR...
!!?
GRIP
WHUMP

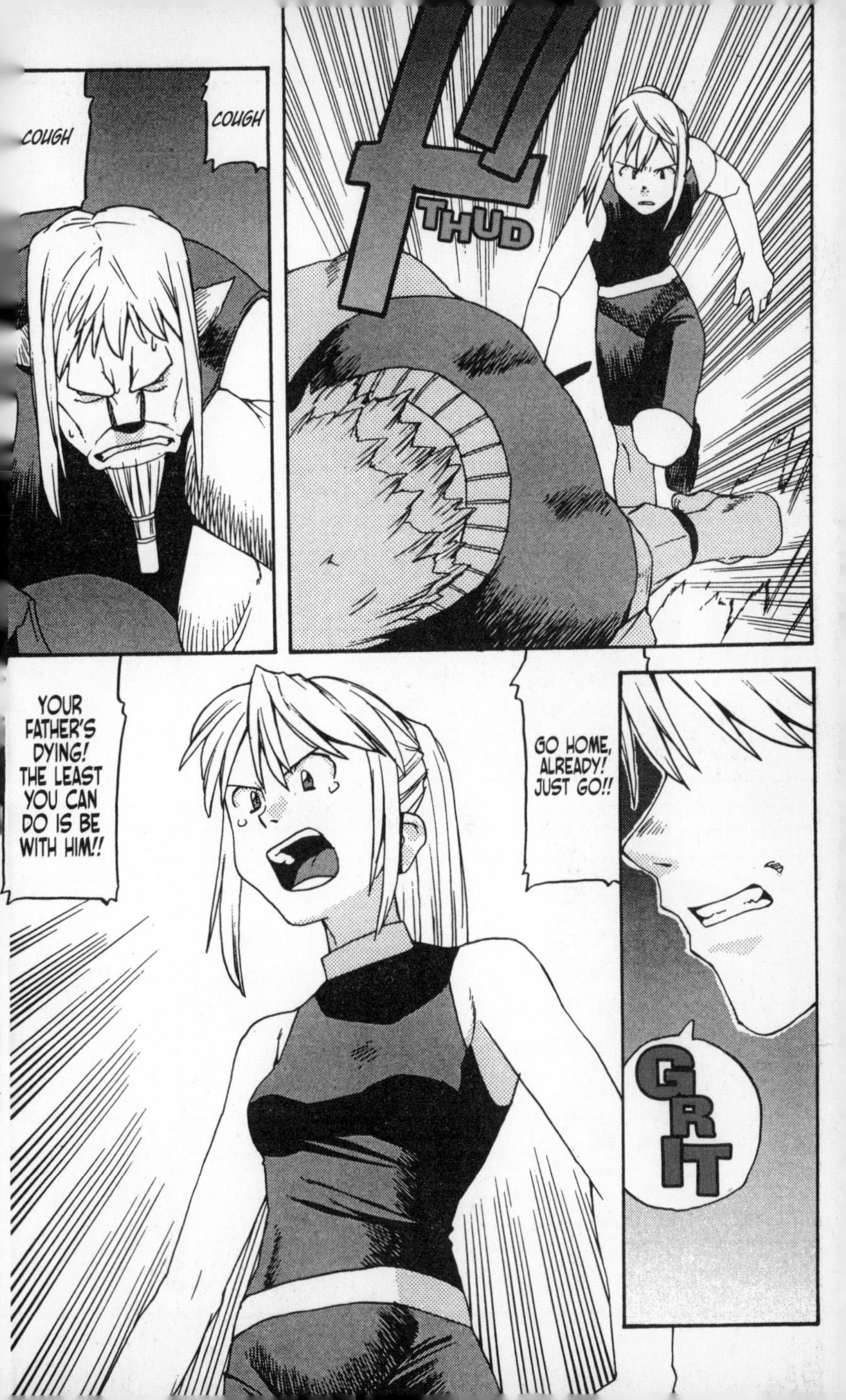
THUD
COUGH
COUGH
GO HOME, ALREADY! JUST GO!!
GRIT
YOUR FATHER'S DYING! THE LEAST YOU CAN DO IS BE WITH HIM!!

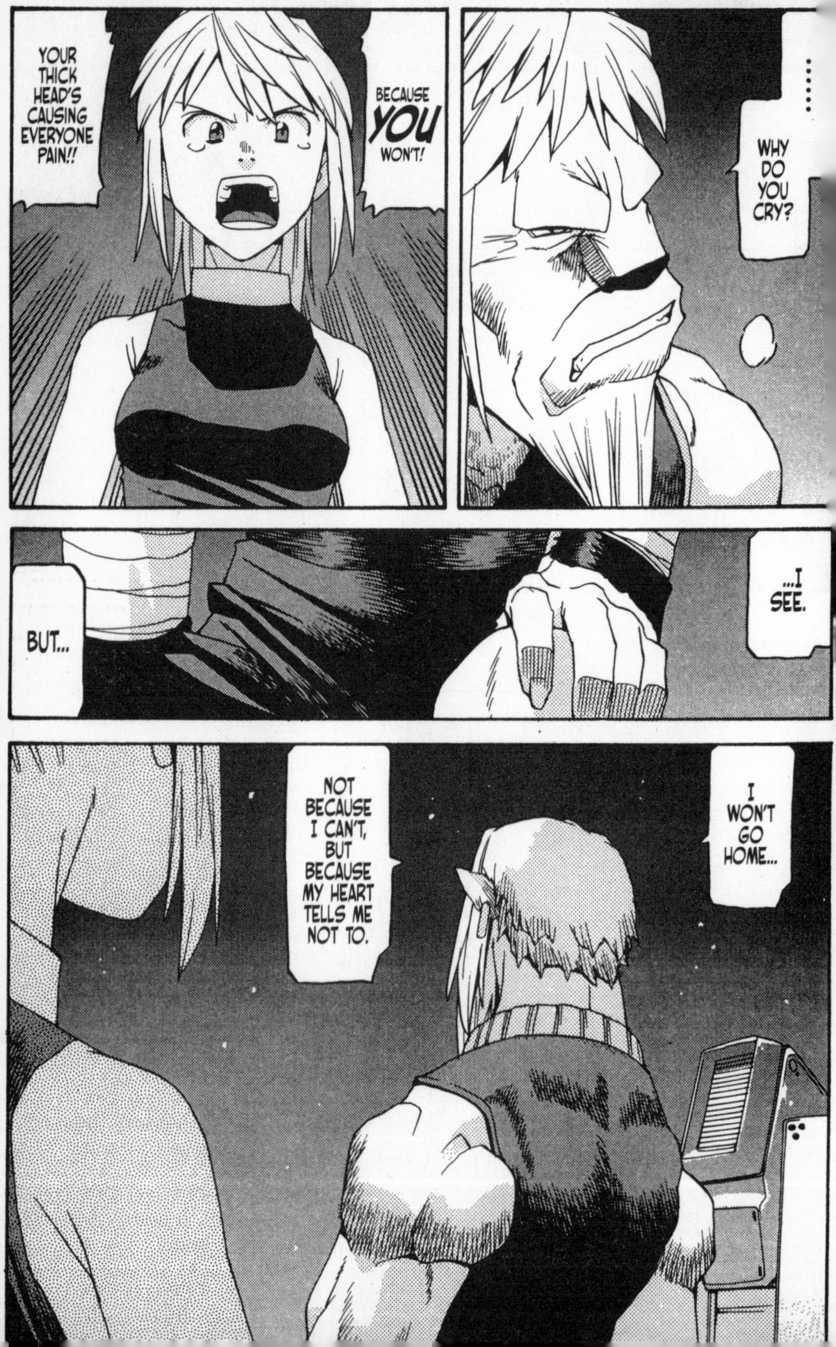
......
WHY DO YOU CRY?
BECAUSE YOU WON'T!
YOUR THICK HEAD'S CAUSING EVERYONE PAIN!!
...I SEE.
BUT...
I WON'T GO HOME...
NOT BECAUSE I CAN'T, BUT BECAUSE MY HEART TELLS ME NOT TO.

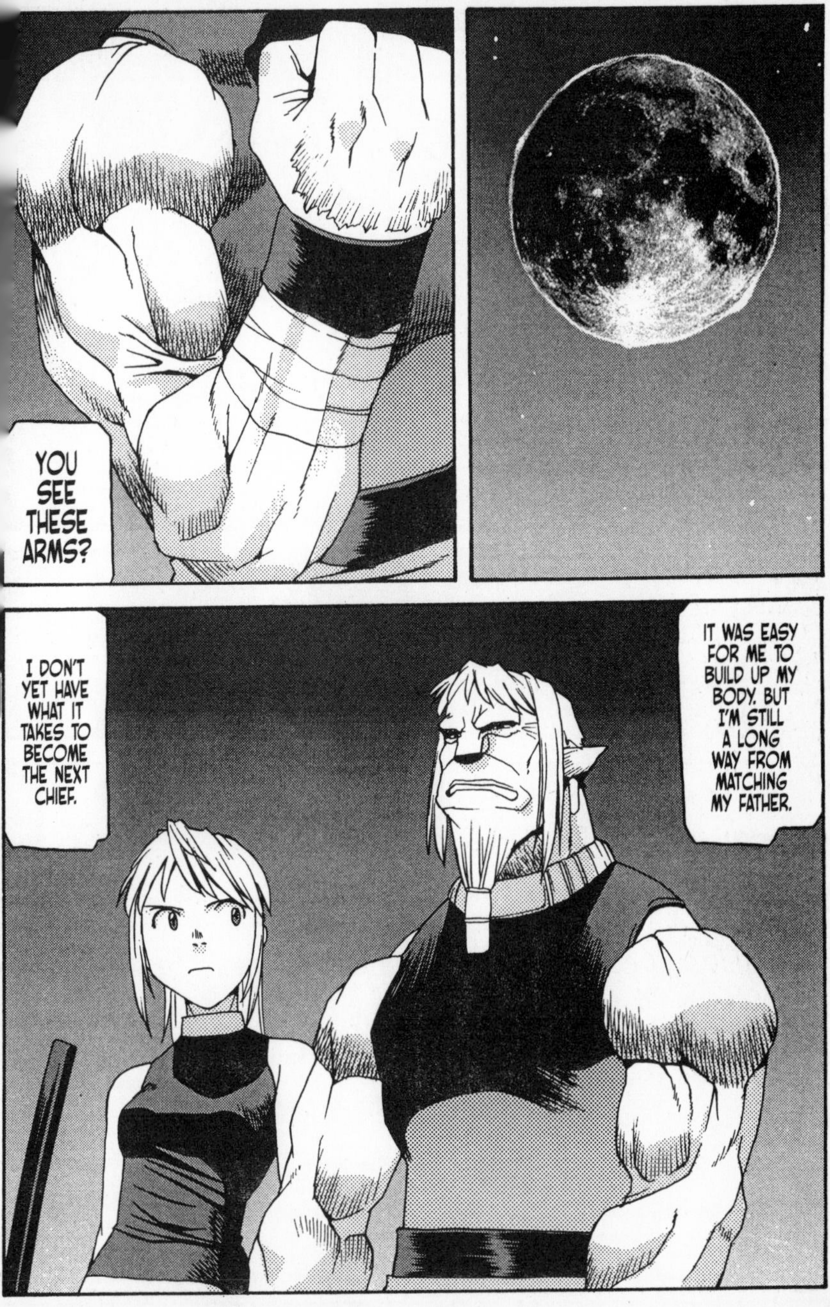
YOU SEE THESE ARMS?
IT WAS EASY FOR ME TO BUILD UP MY BODY. BUT I'M STILL A LONG WAY FROM MATCHING MY FATHER.
I DON'T YET HAVE WHAT IT TAKES TO BECOME THE NEXT CHIEF.

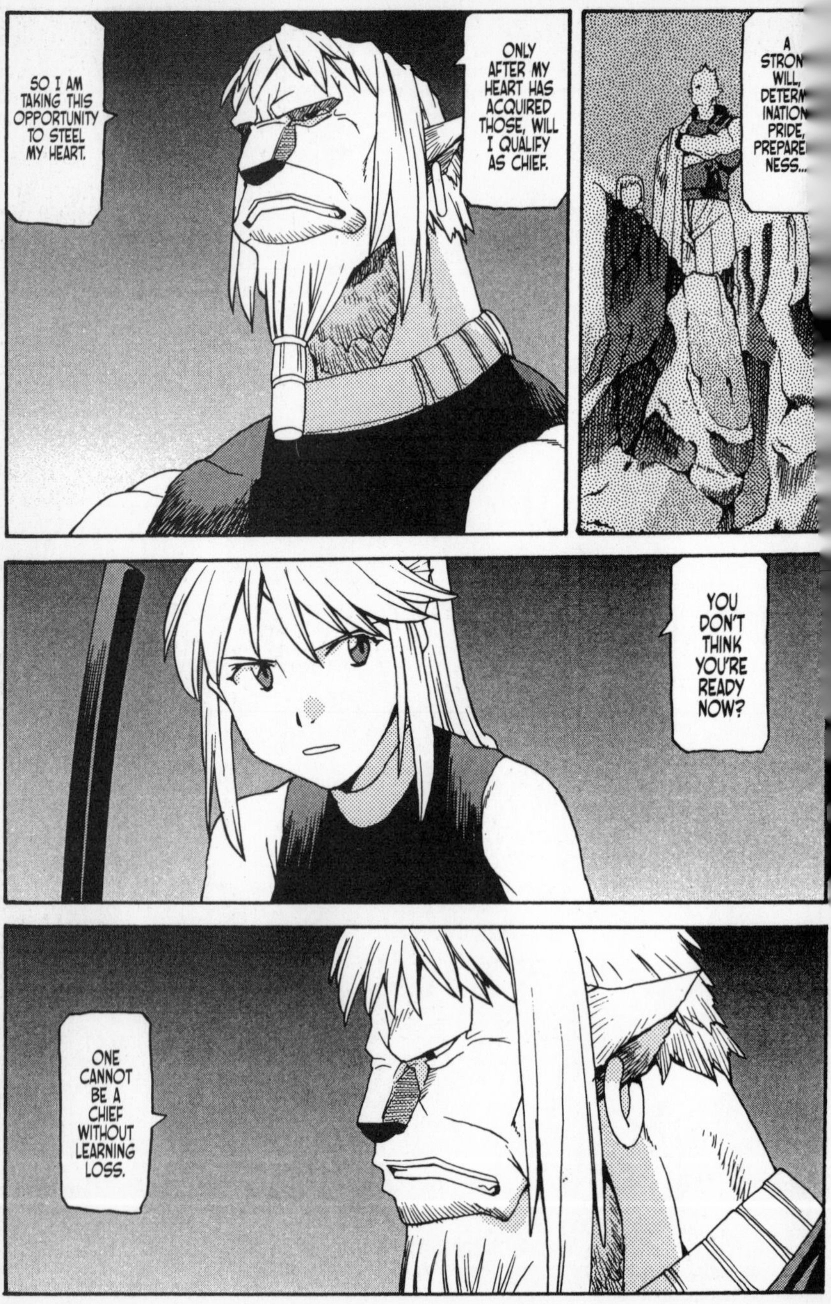
A STRON WILL, DETERM INATION PRIDE, PREPARE NESS...
ONLY AFTER MY HEART HAS ACQUIRED THOSE, WILL I QUALIFY AS CHIEF.
SO I AM TAKING THIS OPPORTUNITY TO STEEL MY HEART.
YOU DON'T THINK YOU'RE READY NOW?
ONE CANNOT BE A CHIEF WITHOUT LEARNING LOSS.

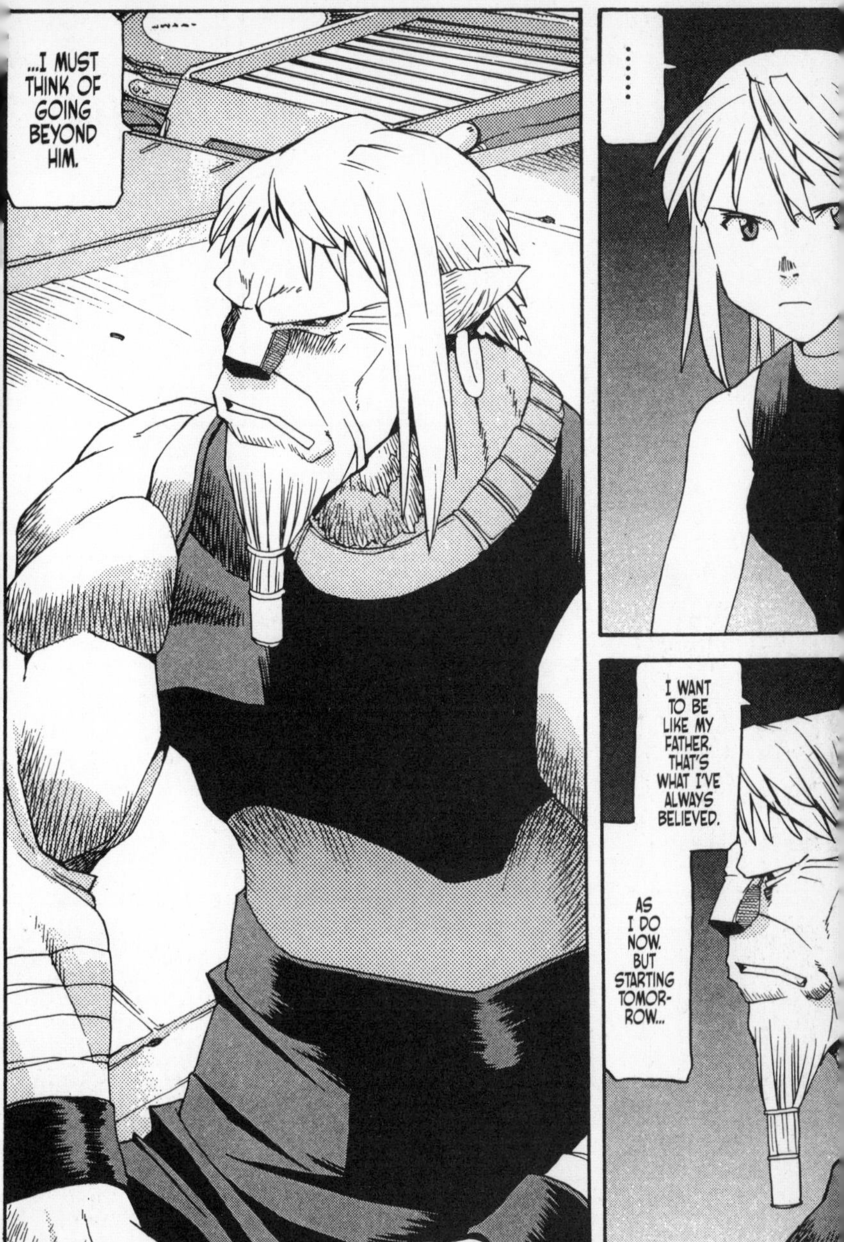
......
I WANT TO BE LIKE MY FATHER. THAT'S WHAT I'VE ALWAYS BELIEVED.
AS I DO NOW. BUT STARTING TOMORROW...
...I MUST THINK OF GOING BEYOND HIM.

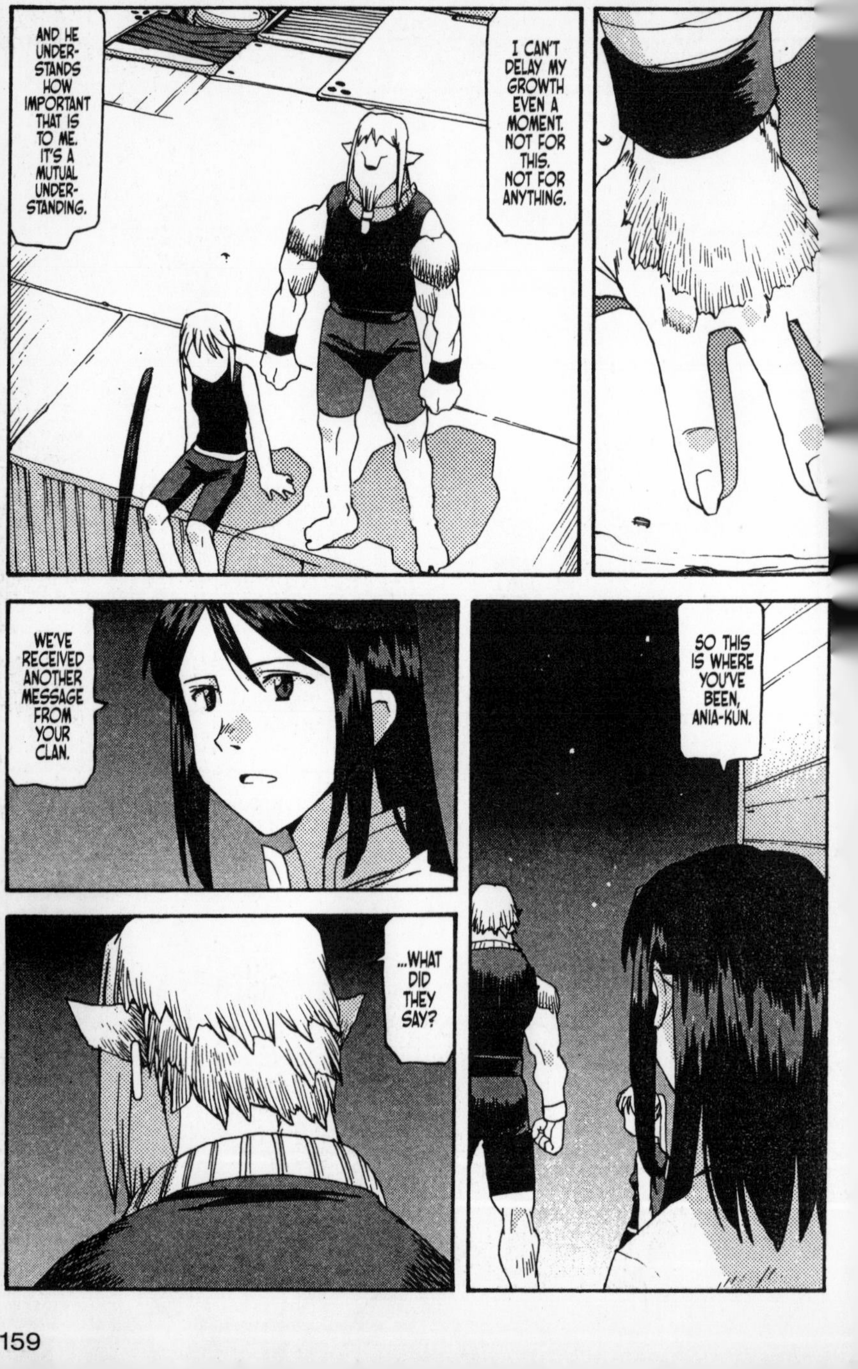
I CAN'T DELAY MY GROWTH EVEN A MOMENT. NOT FOR THIS. NOT FOR ANYTHING.
AND HE UNDERSTANDS HOW IMPORTANT THAT IS TO ME. IT'S A MUTUAL UNDERSTANDING.
SO THIS IS WHERE YOU'VE BEEN, ANIA-KUN.
WE'VE RECEIVED ANOTHER MESSAGE FROM YOUR CLAN.
...WHAT DID THEY SAY?

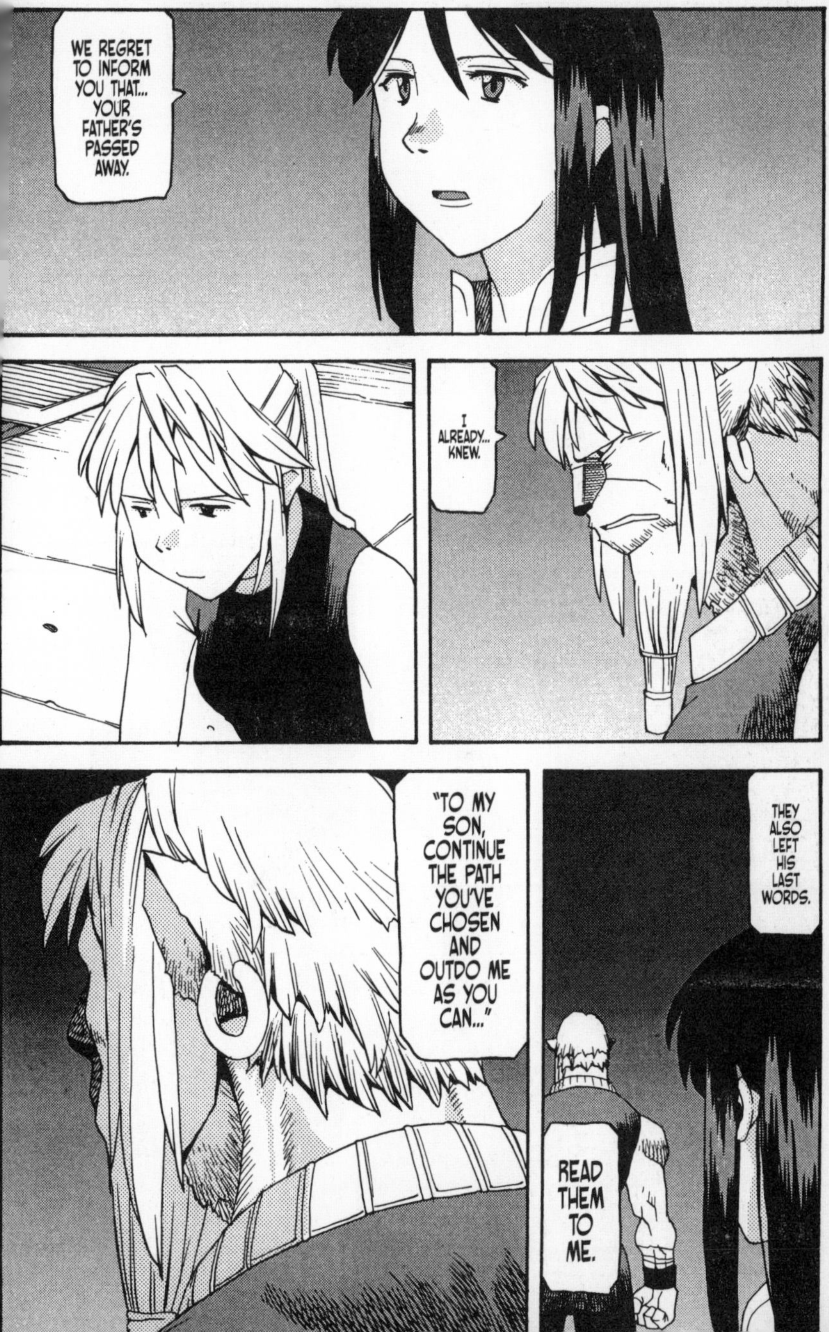
WE REGRET TO INFORM YOU THAT... YOUR FATHER'S PASSED AWAY.
I ALREADY... KNEW.
THEY ALSO LEFT HIS LAST WORDS.
READ THEM TO ME.
"TO MY SON, CONTINUE THE PATH YOU'VE CHOSEN AND OUTDO ME AS YOU CAN..."

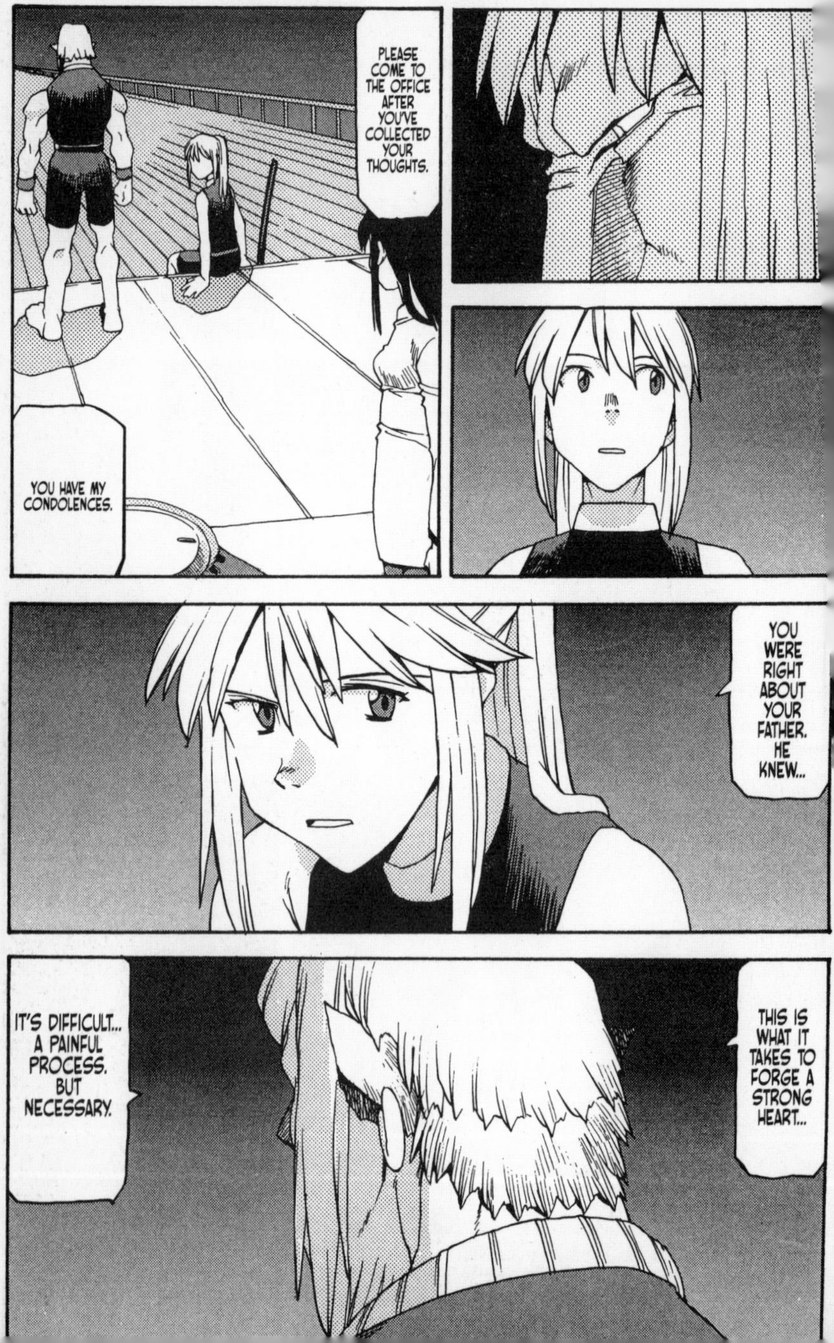
PLEASE COME TO THE OFFICE AFTER YOU'VE COLLECTED YOUR THOUGHTS.
YOU HAVE MY CONDOLENCES.
YOU WERE RIGHT ABOUT YOUR FATHER. HE KNEW...
THIS IS WHAT IT TAKES TO FORGE A STRONG HEART...
IT'S DIFFICULT... A PAINFUL PROCESS. BUT NECESSARY.

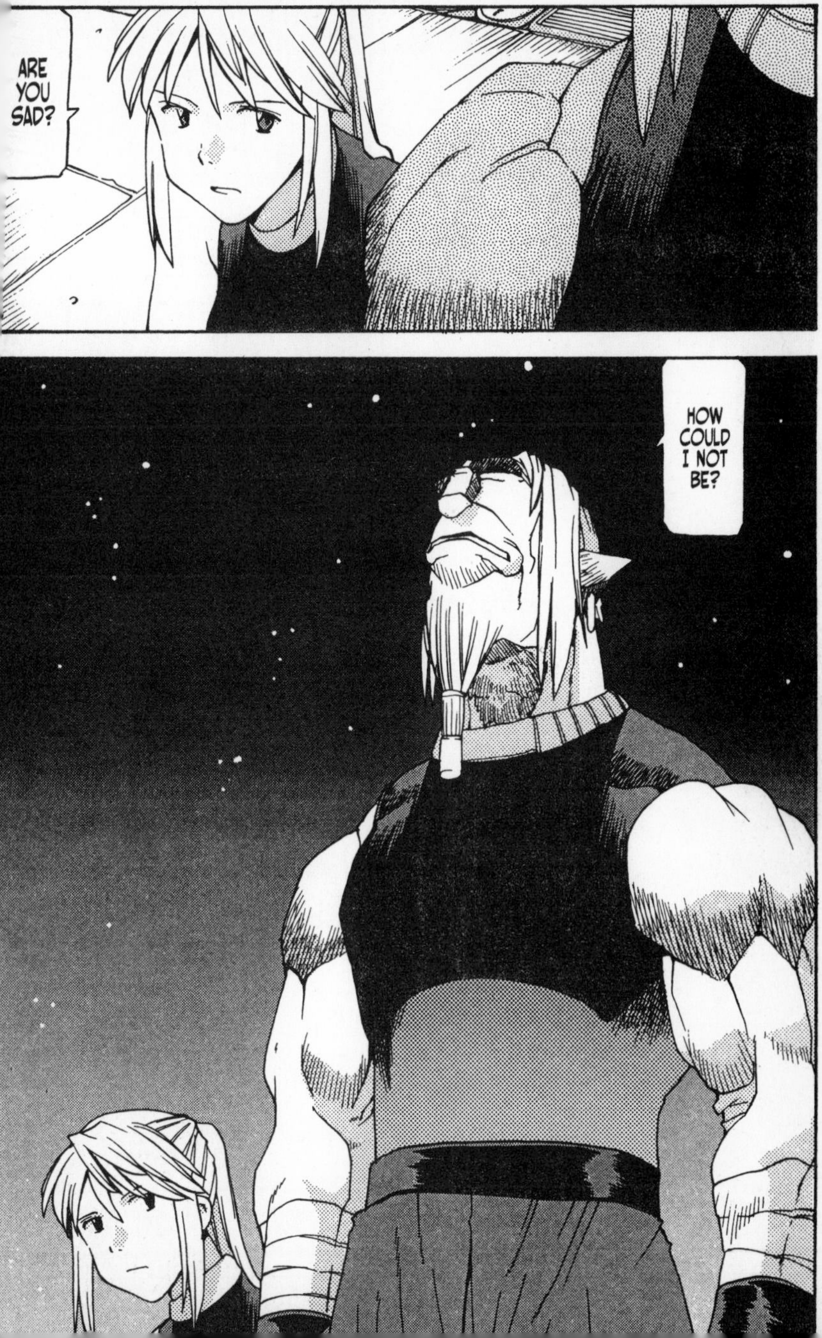
ARE YOU SAD?
HOW COULD I NOT BE?

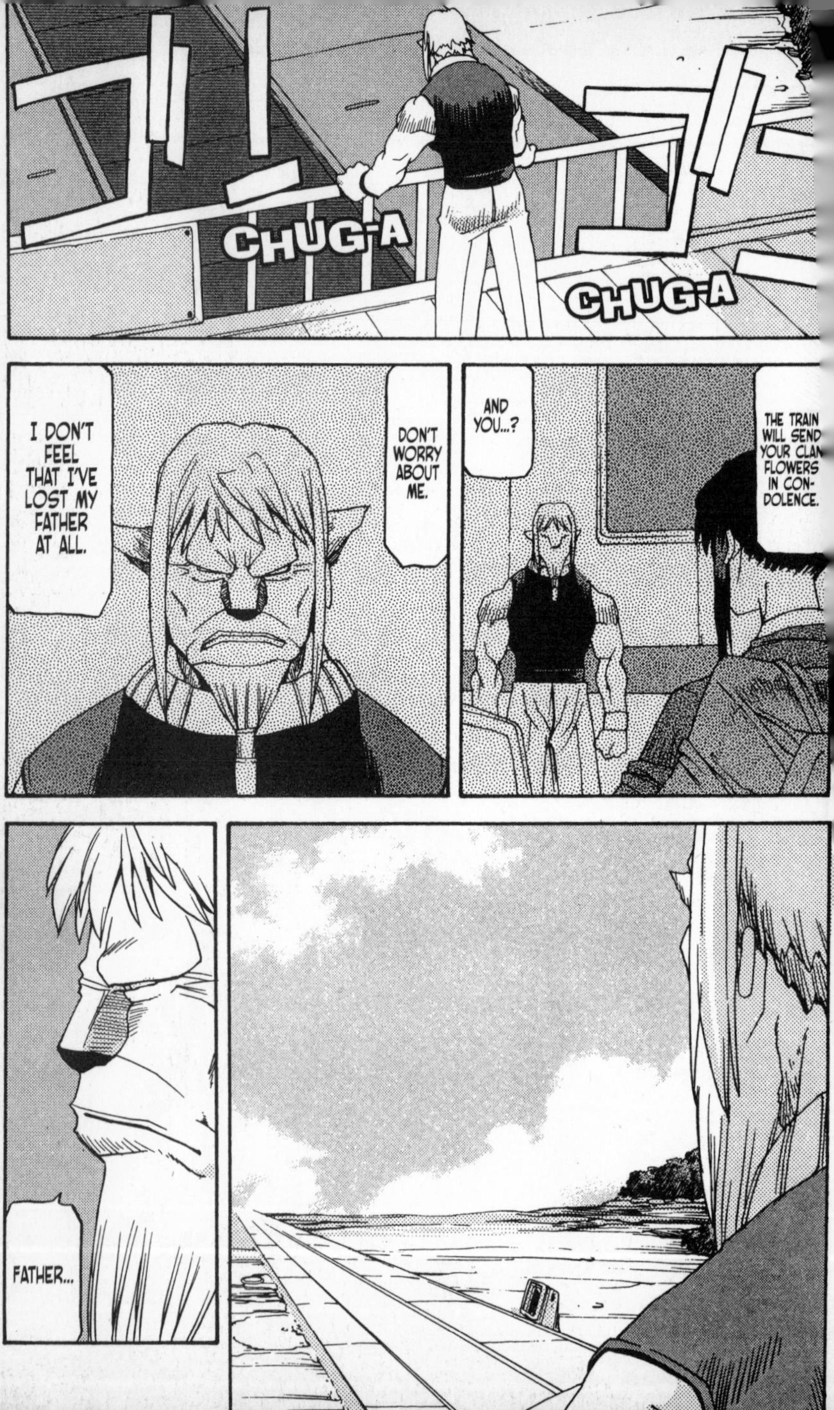
CHUG-A
CHUG-A
THE TRAIN WILL SEND YOUR CLAN FLOWERS IN CON-DOLENCE.
AND YOU...?
DON'T WORRY ABOUT ME.
I DON'T FEEL THAT I'VE LOST MY FATHER AT ALL.
FATHER...

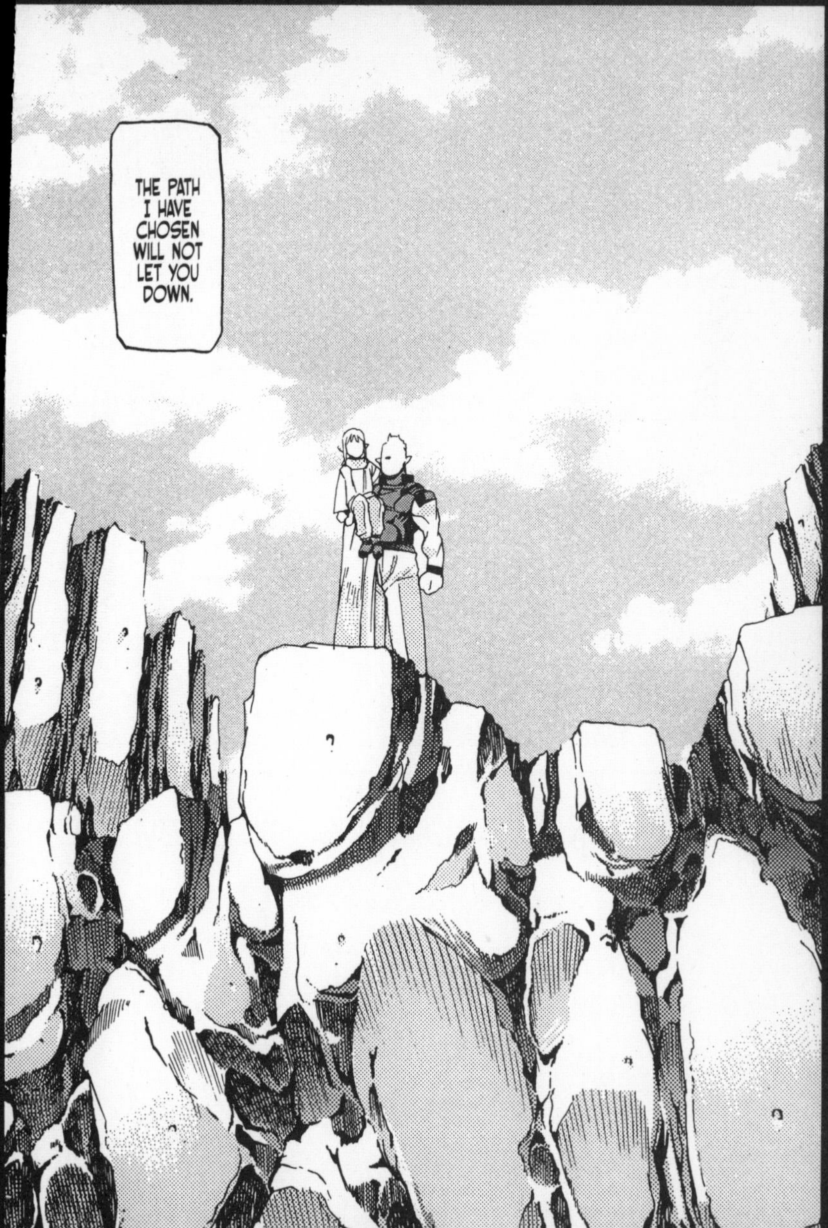
THE PATH I HAVE CHOSEN WILL NOT LET YOU DOWN.

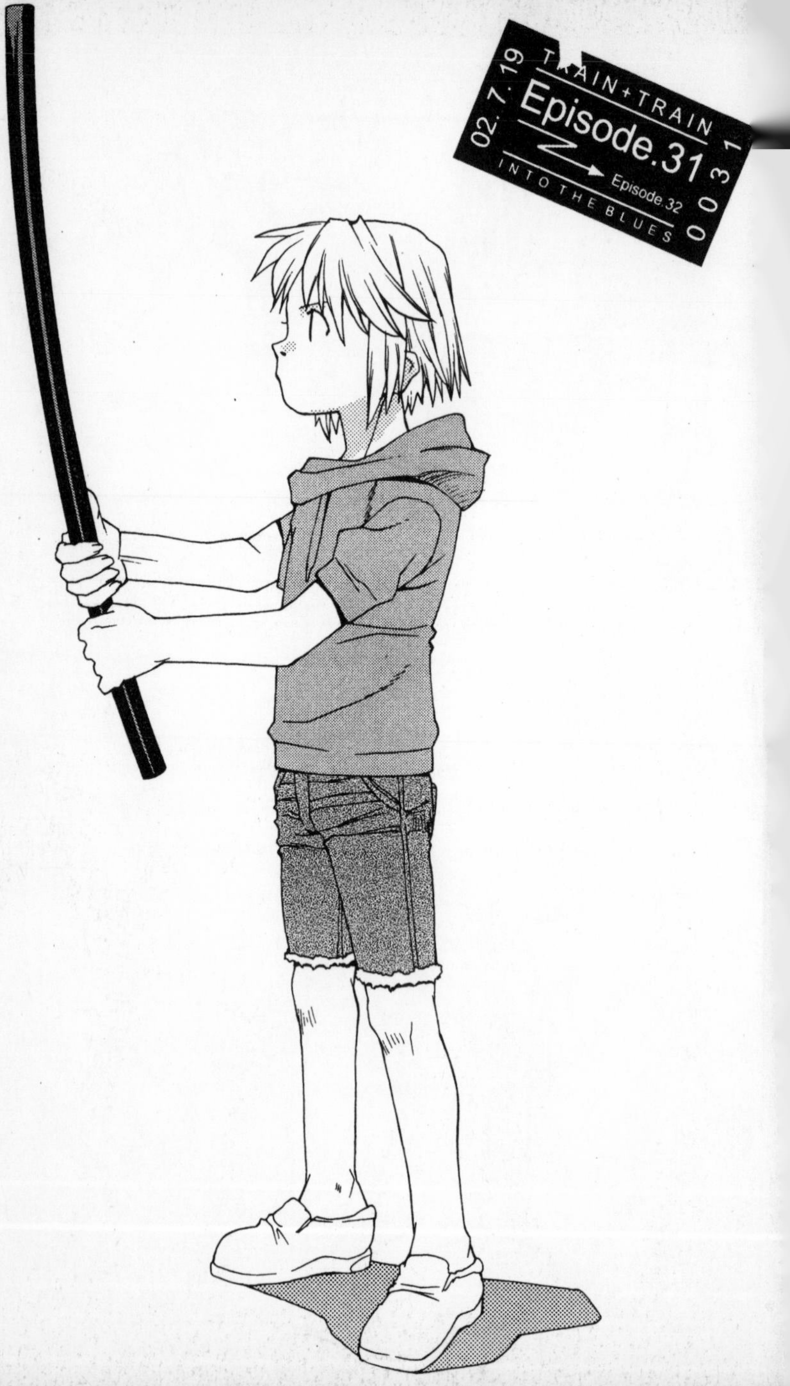
02. 7. 19
TRAIN+TRAIN
Episode.31
INTO THE BLUES
Episode.32
0031

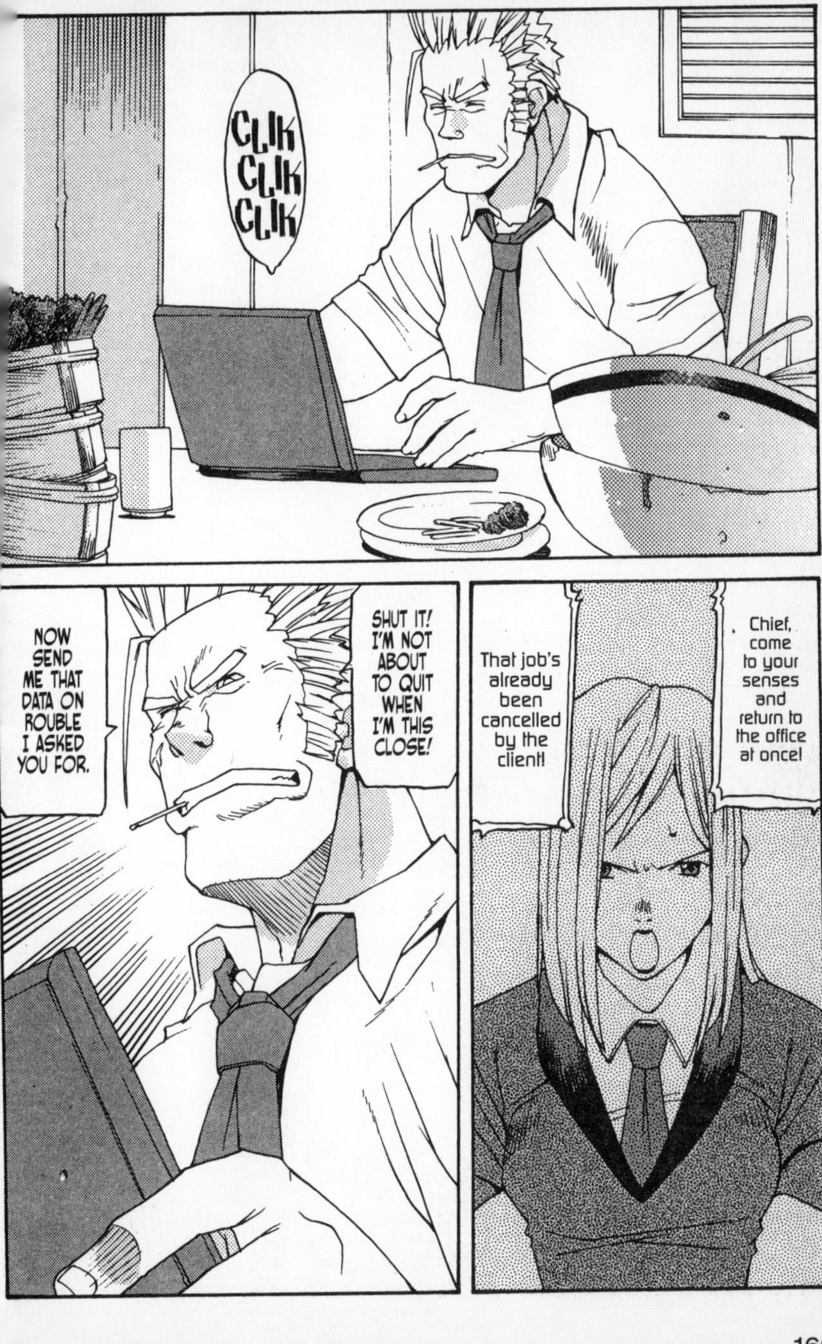
CLIK CLIK CLIK
Chief, come to your senses and return to the office at once!
That job's already been cancelled by the client!
SHUT IT! I'M NOT ABOUT TO QUIT WHEN I'M THIS CLOSE!
NOW SEND ME THAT DATA ON ROUBLE I ASKED YOU FOR.

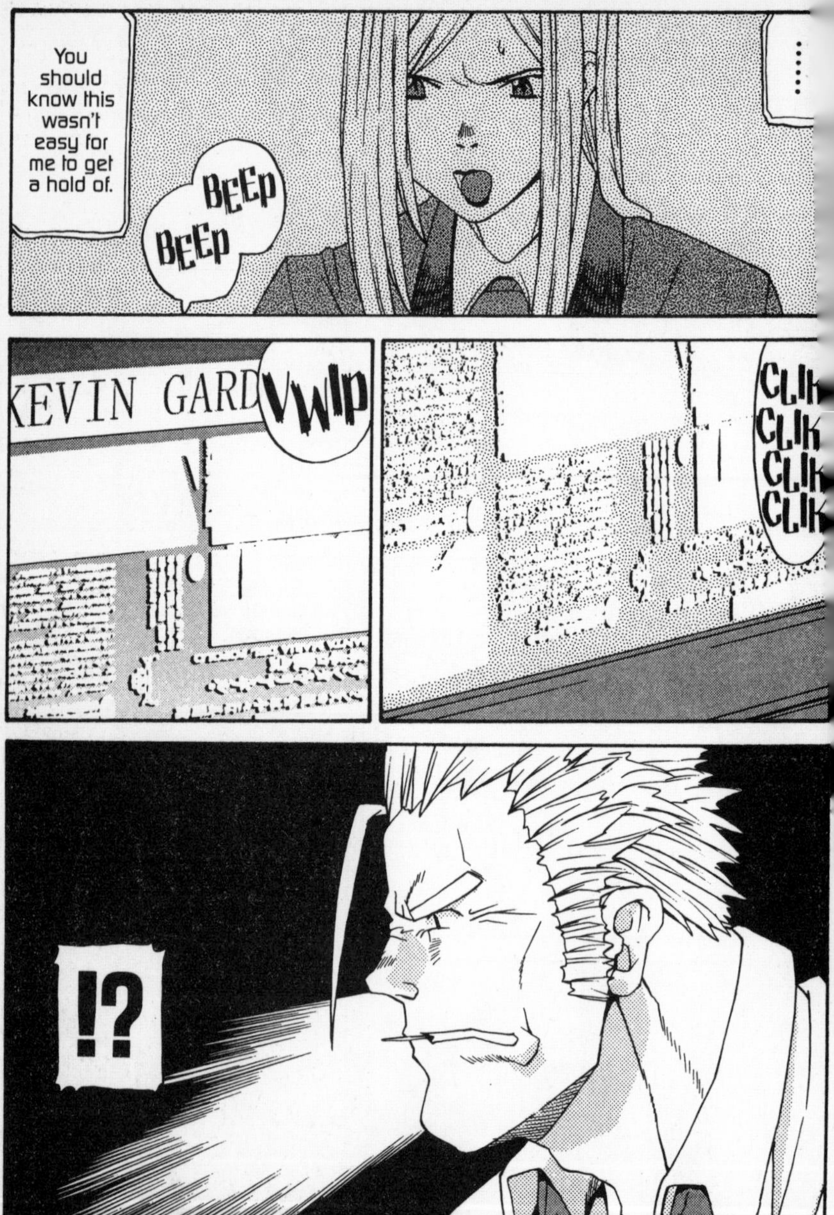
……
You should know this wasn't easy for me to get a hold of.
BEEP BEEP
CLIK CLIK CLIK CLIK
KEVIN GARD
VWIP
!?

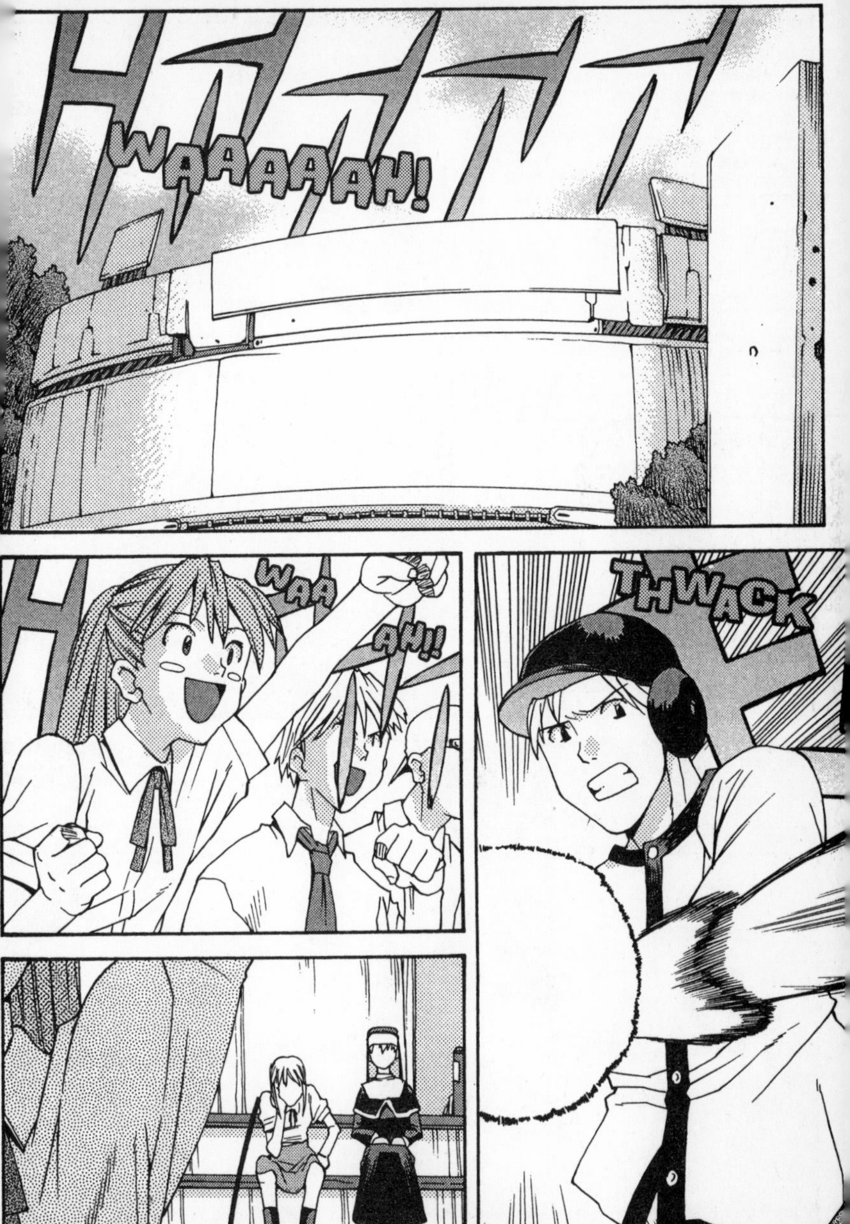
WAAAAAAH!
THWACK
WAA AH!!

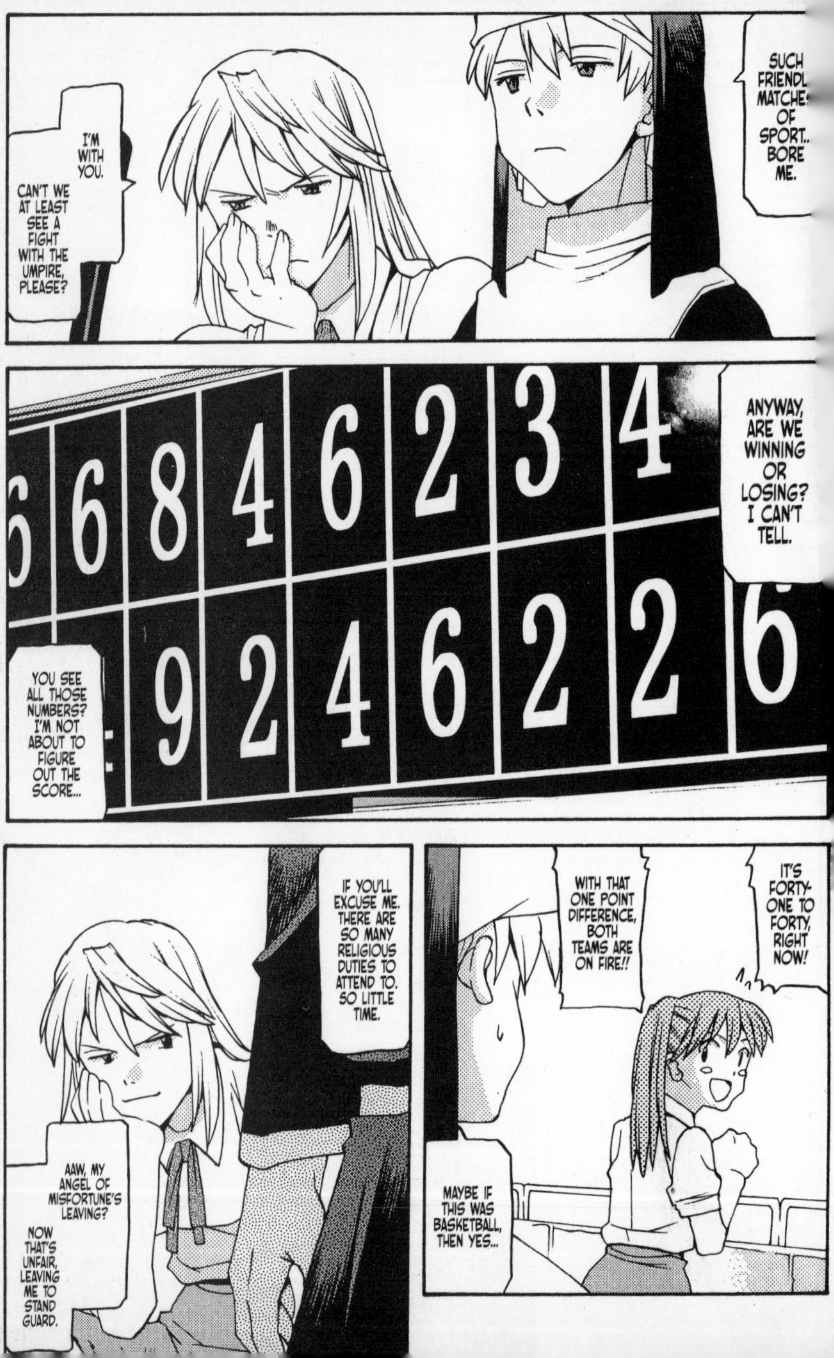
SUCH FRIENDL MATCHES OF SPORT.. BORE ME.
I'M WITH YOU.
CAN'T WE AT LEAST SEE A FIGHT WITH THE UMPIRE, PLEASE?
6 6 8 4 6 2 3 4
9 2 4 6 2 2 6
ANYWAY, ARE WE WINNING OR LOSING? I CAN'T TELL.
YOU SEE ALL THOSE NUMBERS? I'M NOT ABOUT TO FIGURE OUT THE SCORE...
IT'S FORTY-ONE TO FORTY, RIGHT NOW!
WITH THAT ONE POINT DIFFERENCE, BOTH TEAMS ARE ON FIRE!!
MAYBE IF THIS WAS BASKETBALL, THEN YES...
IF YOU'LL EXCUSE ME. THERE ARE SO MANY RELIGIOUS DUTIES TO ATTEND TO. SO LITTLE TIME.
AAW, MY ANGEL OF MISFORTUNE'S LEAVING?
NOW THAT'S UNFAIR, LEAVING ME TO STAND GUARD.

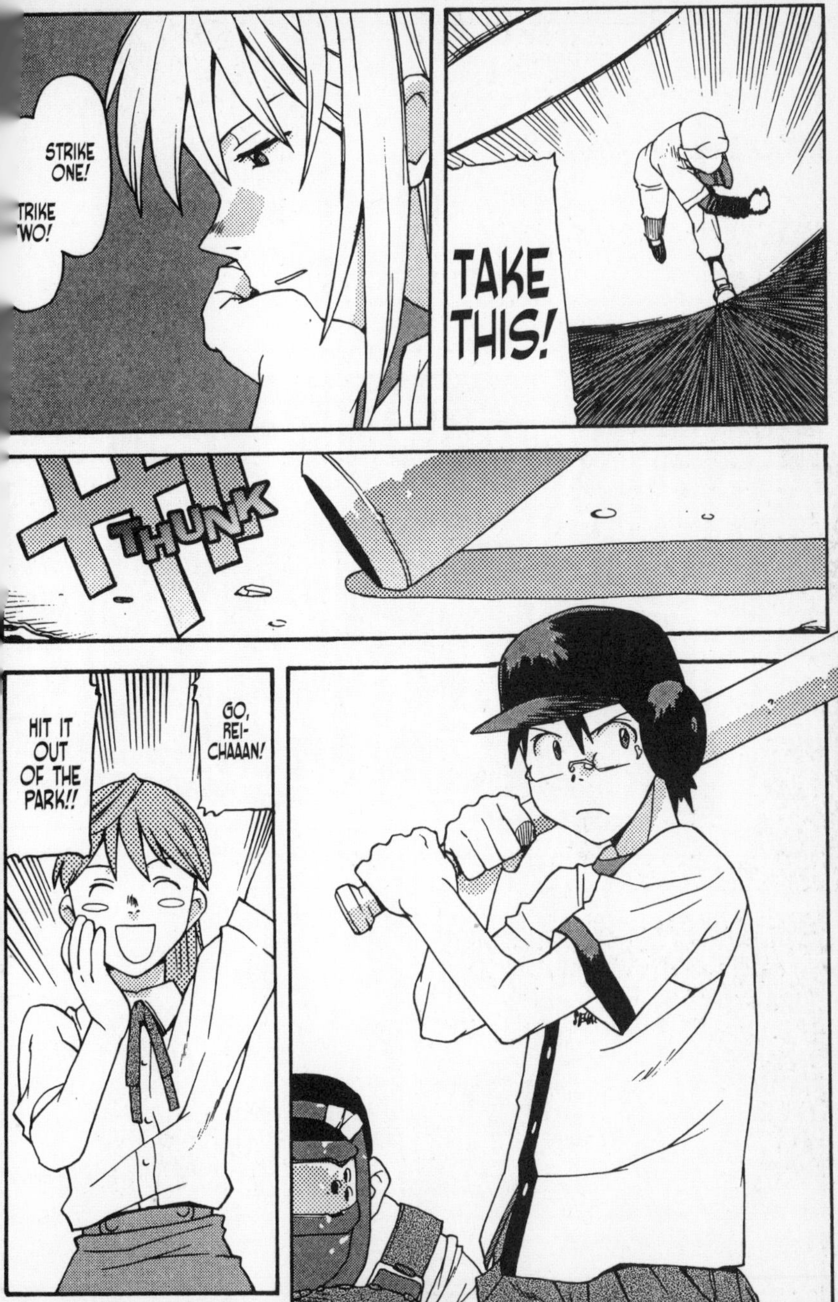
TAKE THIS!
STRIKE ONE!
TRIKE TWO!
THUNK
GO, REI-CHAAAN!
HIT IT OUT OF THE PARK!!

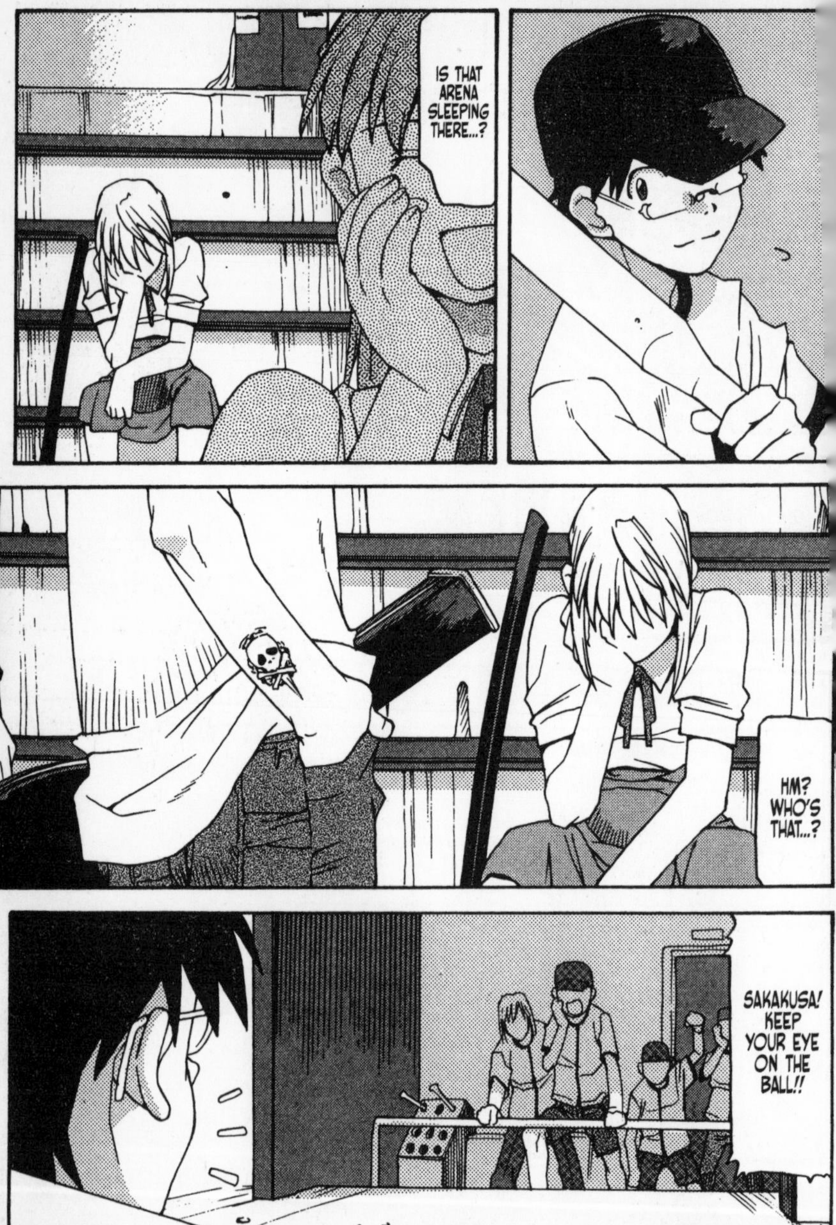
IS THAT ARENA SLEEPING THERE...?
HM? WHO'S THAT...?
SAKAKUSA! KEEP YOUR EYE ON THE BALL!!

STEEERIKE THREE!

PoOMF

4	6	2
2	4	6

...-CHAN... ARENA-CHAN.

LET'S GET GOING, ARENA-CHAN.

OH, IT'S OVER...? DID WE WIN?

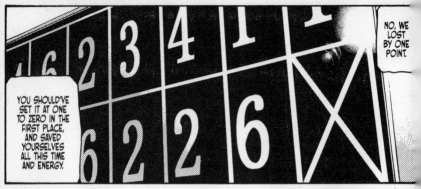

NO, WE LOST BY ONE POINT.
YOU SHOULD'VE SET IT AT ONE TO ZERO IN THE FIRST PLACE, AND SAVED YOURSELVES ALL THIS TIME AND ENERGY.
WE HAD A GOOD TIME.
IT'S BEEN TOO LONG SINCE WE HAD A CHANCE TO MOVE AROUND LIKE THAT.
SP
I SE-
WHAT'S THE MATTER?
MY SWORD! IT'S GONE...!
SOMEBODY STOLE IT!!

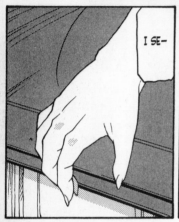

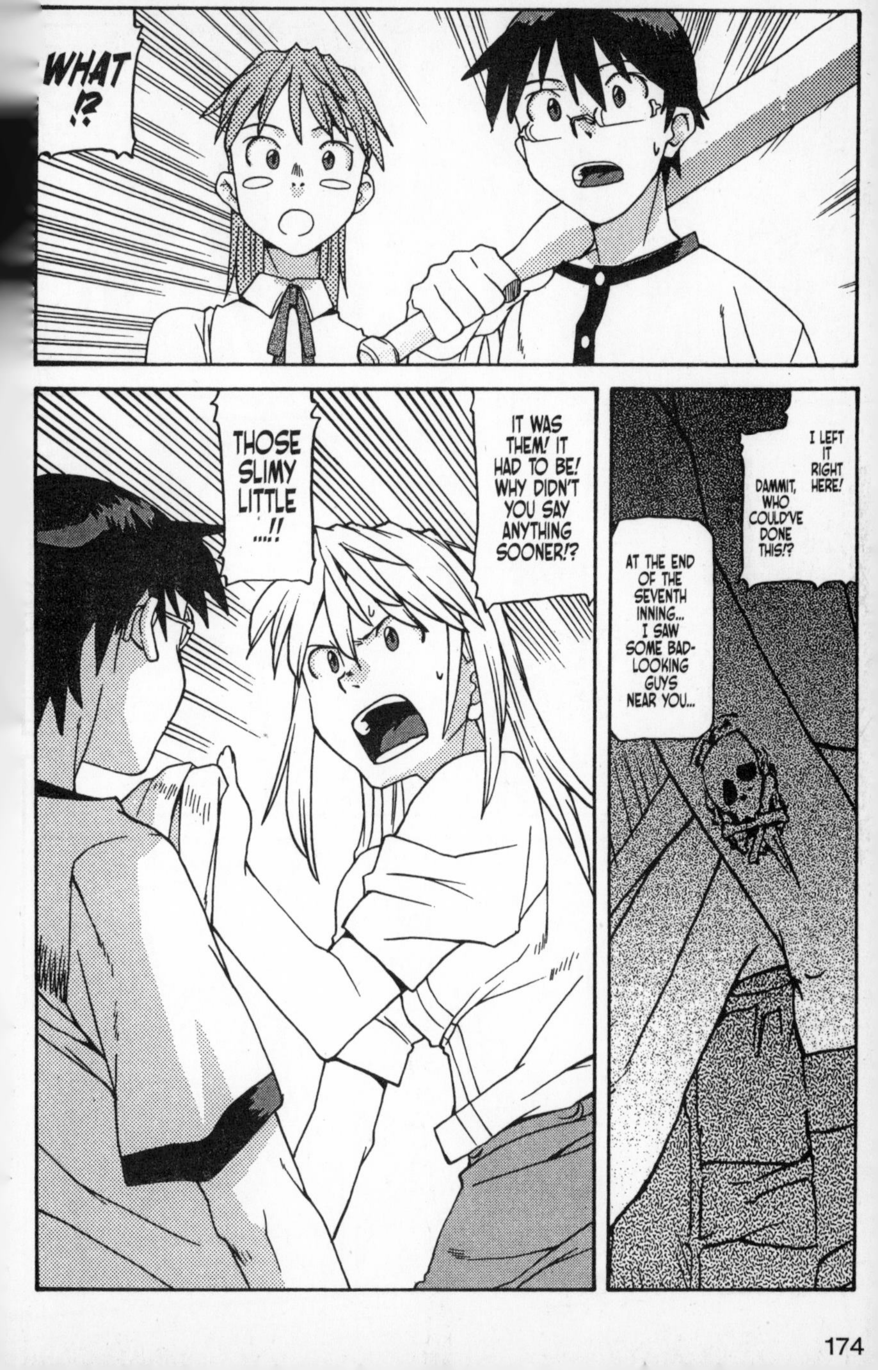
WHAT!?
I LEFT IT RIGHT HERE!
DAMMIT, WHO COULD'VE DONE THIS!?
AT THE END OF THE SEVENTH INNING... I SAW SOME BAD-LOOKING GUYS NEAR YOU...
IT WAS THEM! IT HAD TO BE! WHY DIDN'T YOU SAY ANYTHING SOONER!?
THOSE SLIMY LITTLE ...!!

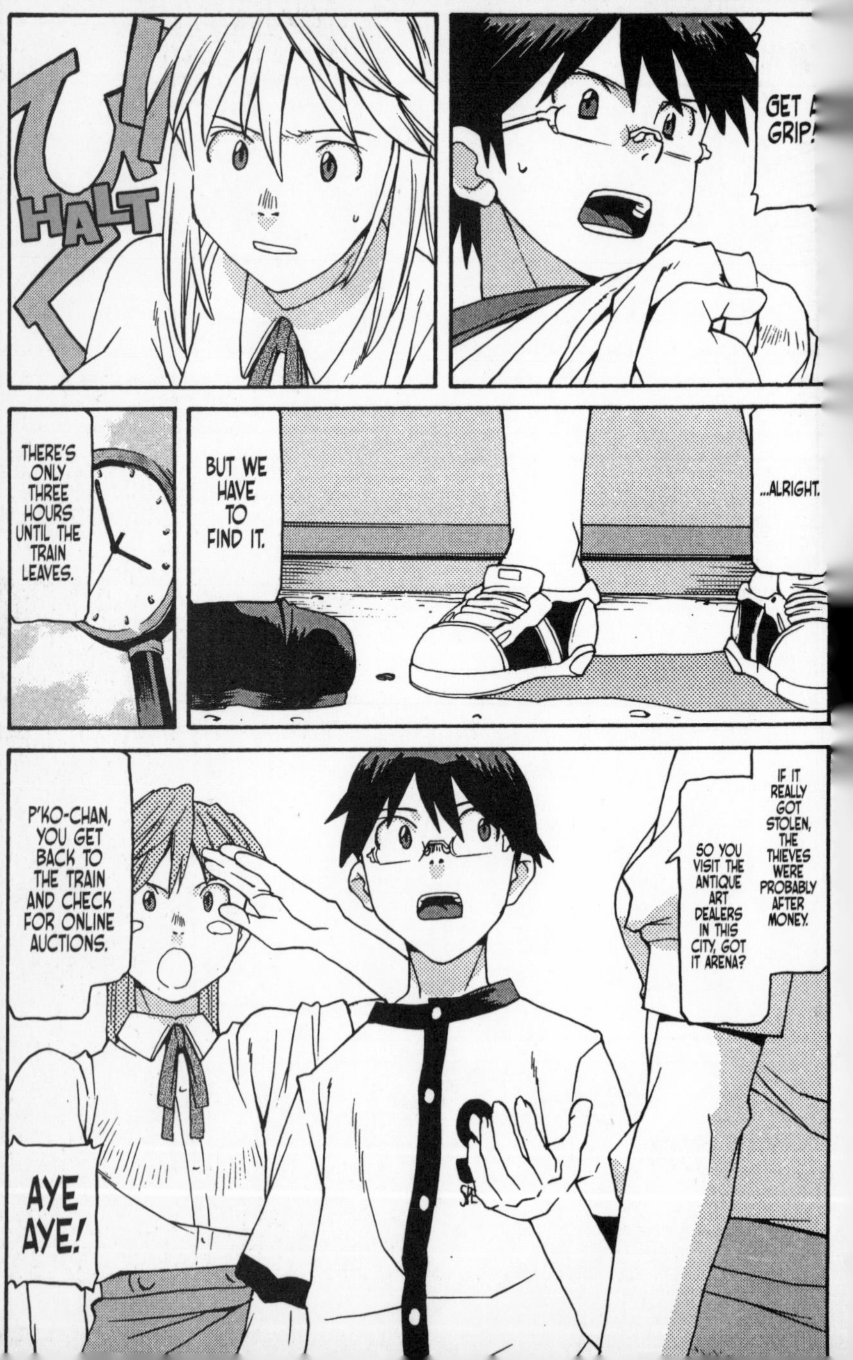
GET A GRIP!
HALT
...ALRIGHT.
BUT WE HAVE TO FIND IT.
THERE'S ONLY THREE HOURS UNTIL THE TRAIN LEAVES.
IF IT REALLY GOT STOLEN, THE THIEVES WERE PROBABLY AFTER MONEY.
SO YOU VISIT THE ANTIQUE ART DEALERS IN THIS CITY, GOT IT ARENA?
P'KO-CHAN, YOU GET BACK TO THE TRAIN AND CHECK FOR ONLINE AUCTIONS.
AYE AYE!

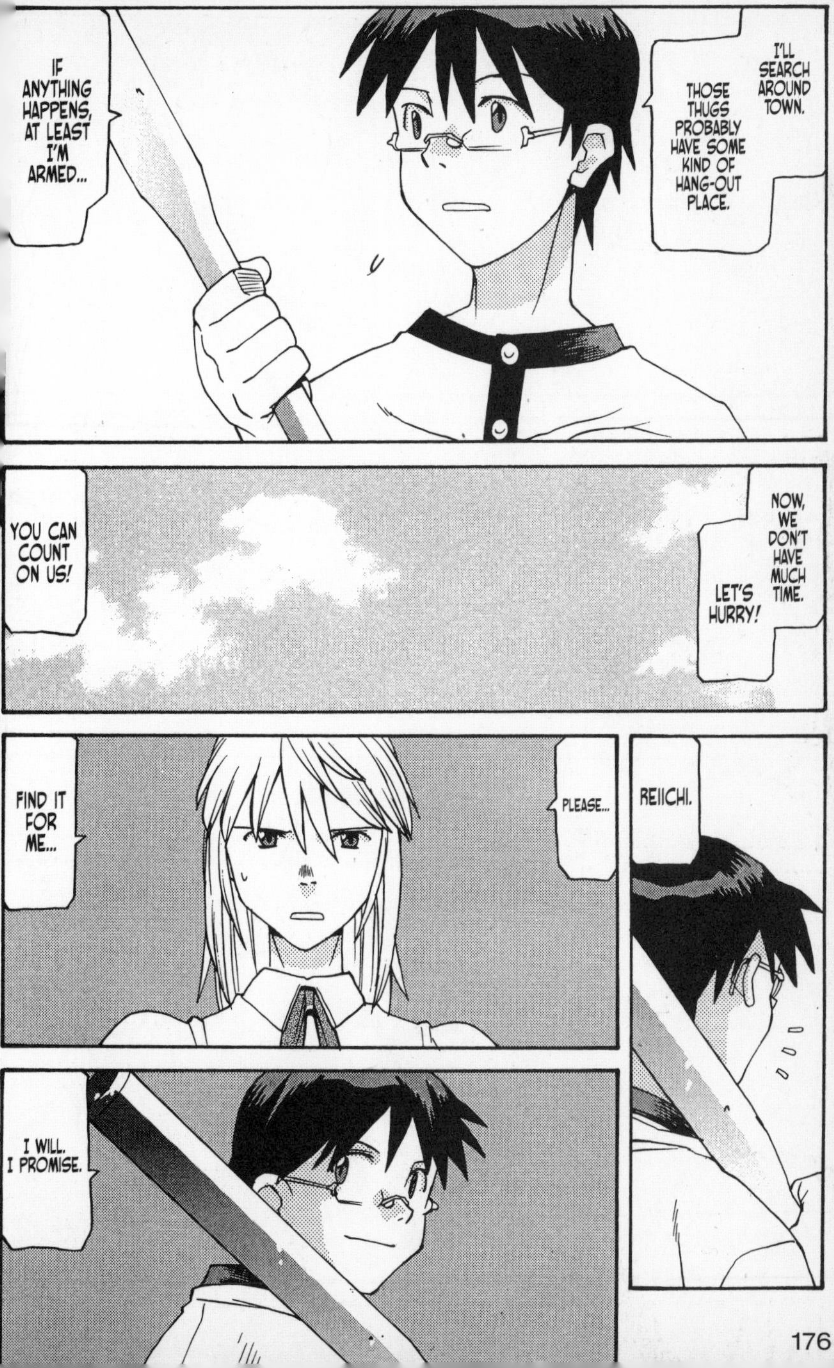
I'LL SEARCH AROUND TOWN.
THOSE THUGS PROBABLY HAVE SOME KIND OF HANG-OUT PLACE.
IF ANYTHING HAPPENS, AT LEAST I'M ARMED...
NOW, WE DON'T HAVE MUCH TIME.
LET'S HURRY!
YOU CAN COUNT ON US!
REIICHI.
PLEASE...
FIND IT FOR ME...
I WILL. I PROMISE.

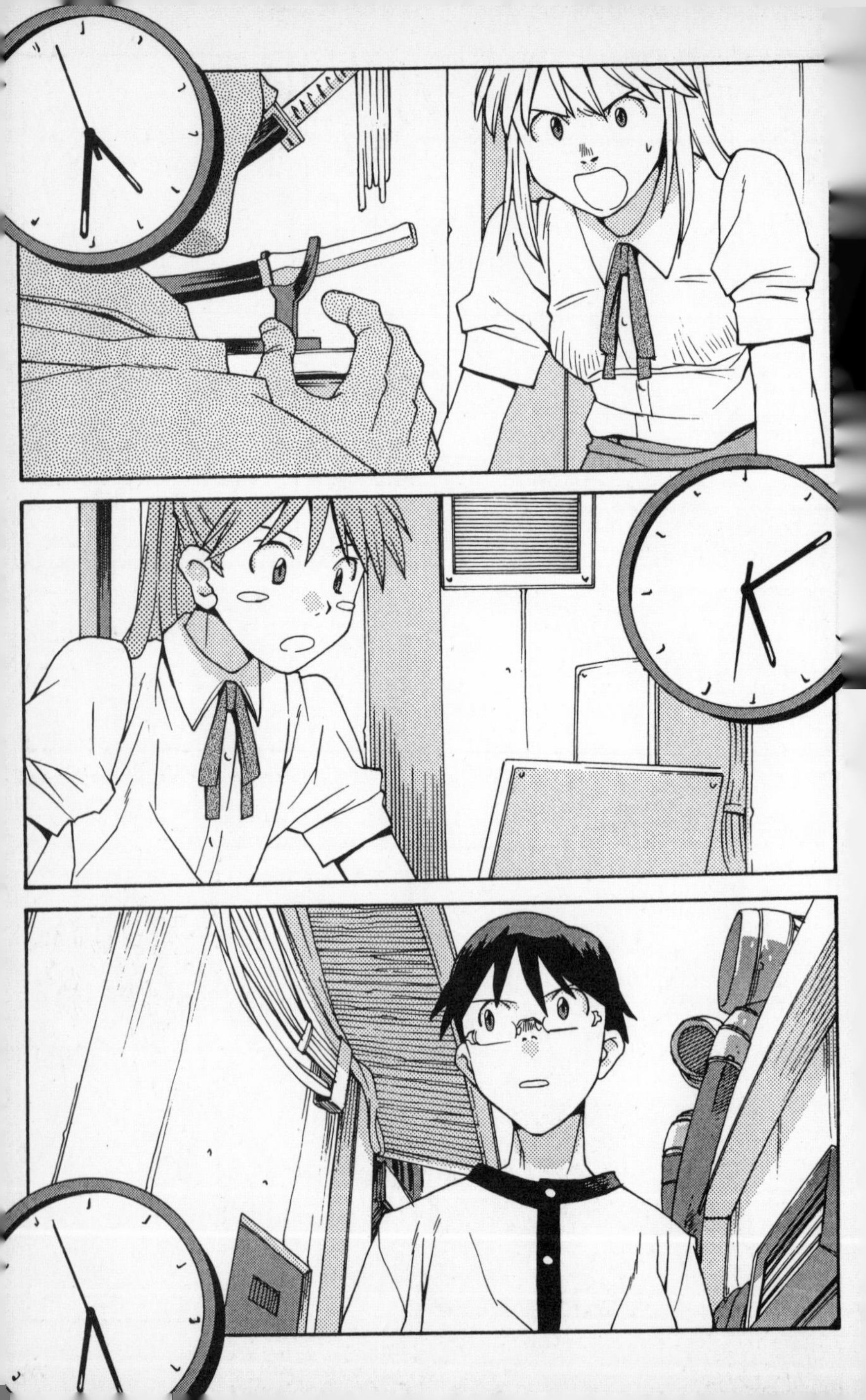

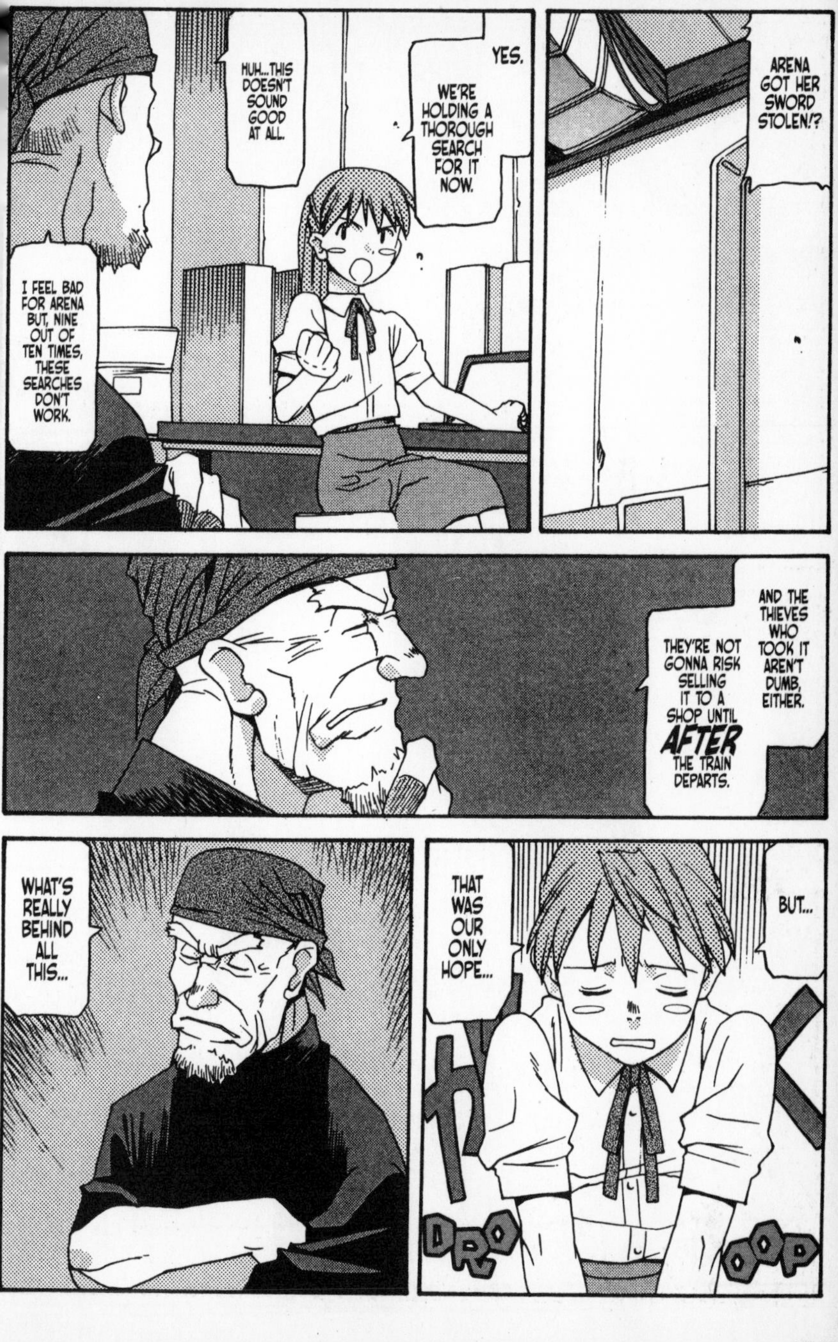
ARENA GOT HER SWORD STOLEN!?
YES.
WE'RE HOLDING A THOROUGH SEARCH FOR IT NOW.
HUH...THIS DOESN'T SOUND GOOD AT ALL.
I FEEL BAD FOR ARENA BUT, NINE OUT OF TEN TIMES, THESE SEARCHES DON'T WORK.
AND THE THIEVES WHO TOOK IT AREN'T DUMB, EITHER.
THEY'RE NOT GONNA RISK SELLING IT TO A SHOP UNTIL AFTER THE TRAIN DEPARTS.
BUT...
THAT WAS OUR ONLY HOPE...
DROOOP
WHAT'S REALLY BEHIND ALL THIS...

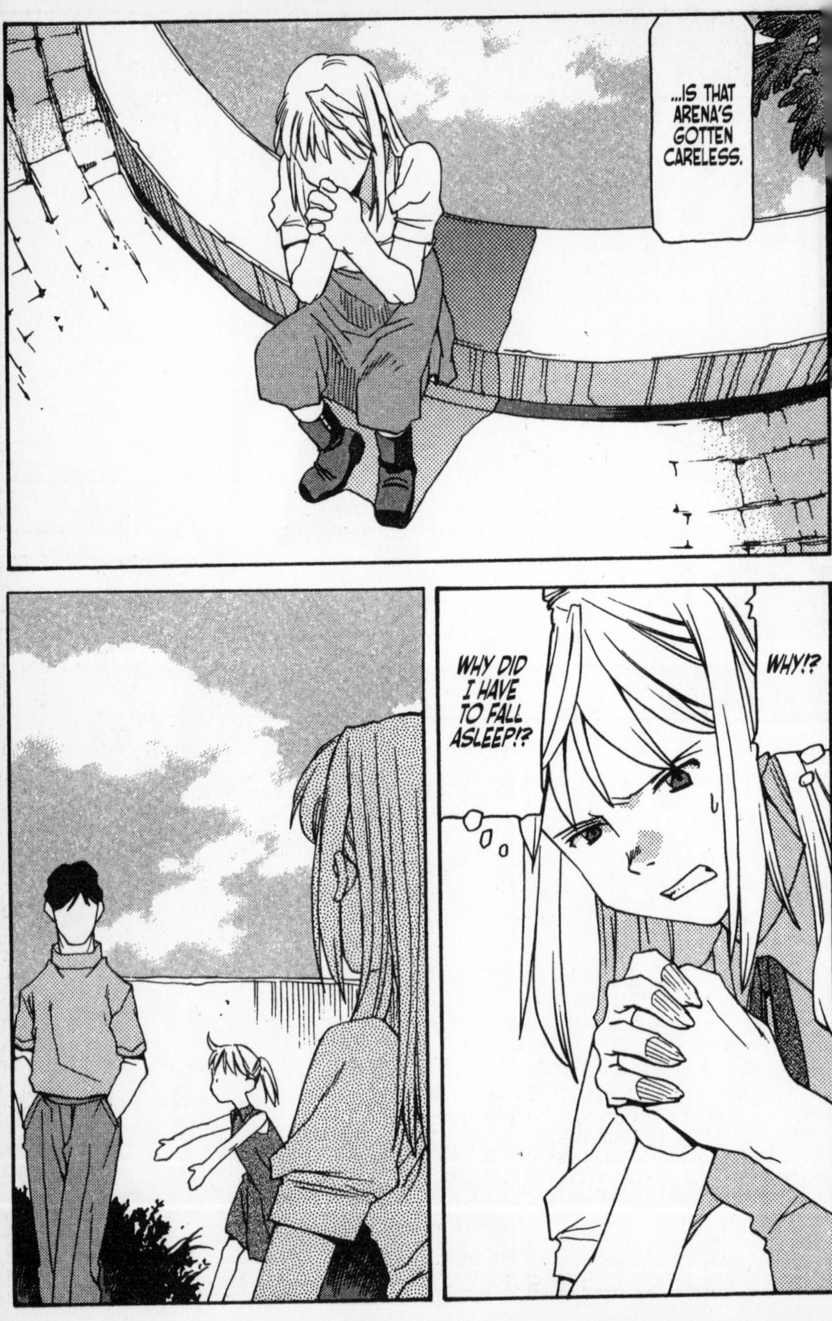
...IS THAT ARENA'S GOTTEN CARELESS.
WHY!?
WHY DID I HAVE TO FALL ASLEEP!?

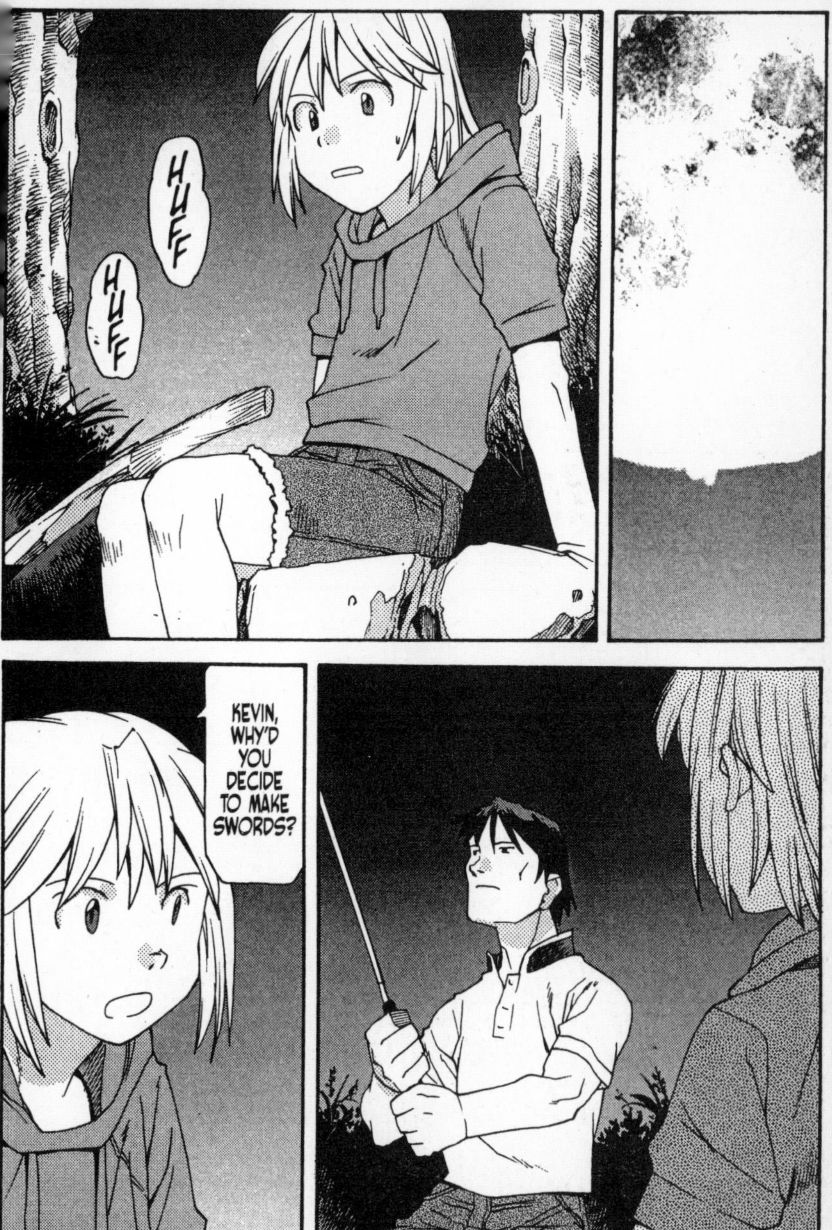
HUFF
HUFF
KEVIN, WHY'D YOU DECIDE TO MAKE SWORDS?

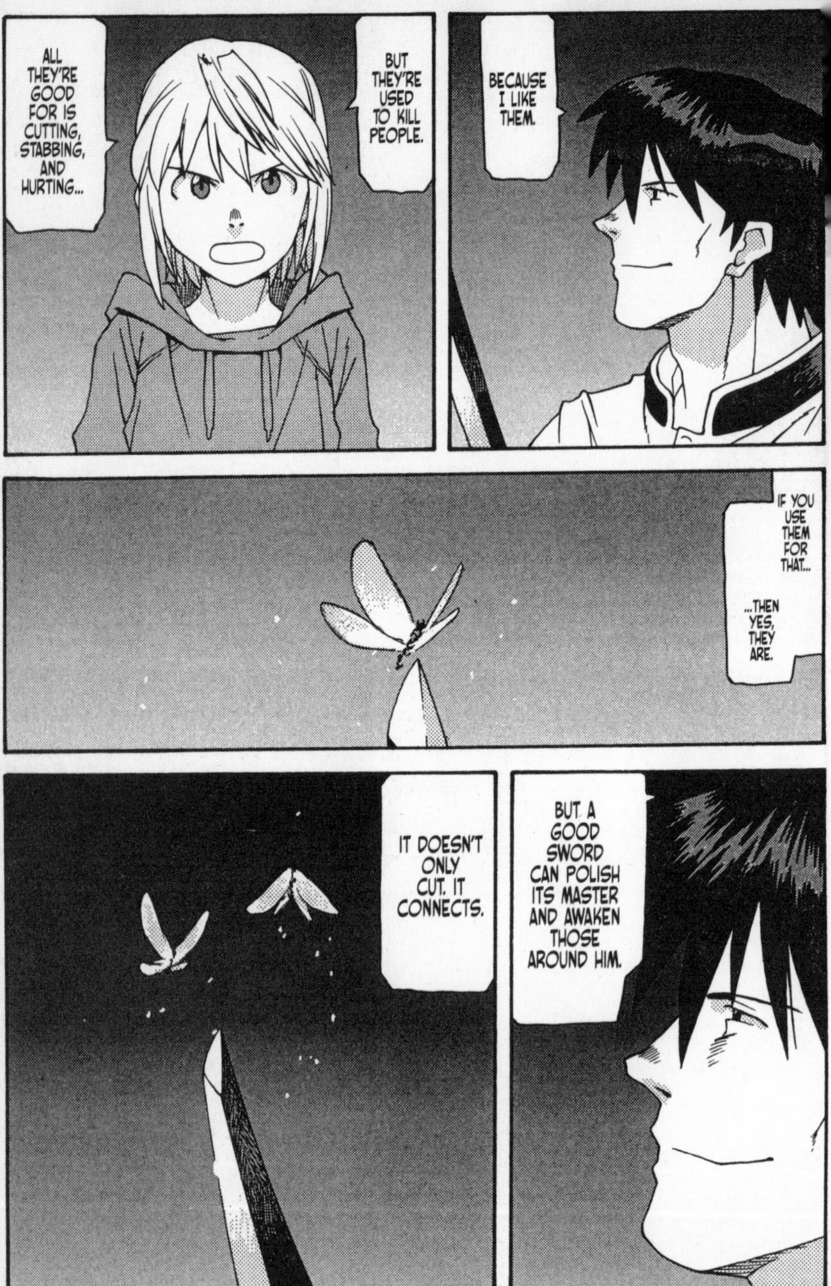
BECAUSE I LIKE THEM.
BUT THEY'RE USED TO KILL PEOPLE.
ALL THEY'RE GOOD FOR IS CUTTING, STABBING, AND HURTING...
IF YOU USE THEM FOR THAT...
...THEN YES, THEY ARE.
BUT A GOOD SWORD CAN POLISH ITS MASTER AND AWAKEN THOSE AROUND HIM.
IT DOESN'T ONLY CUT. IT CONNECTS.

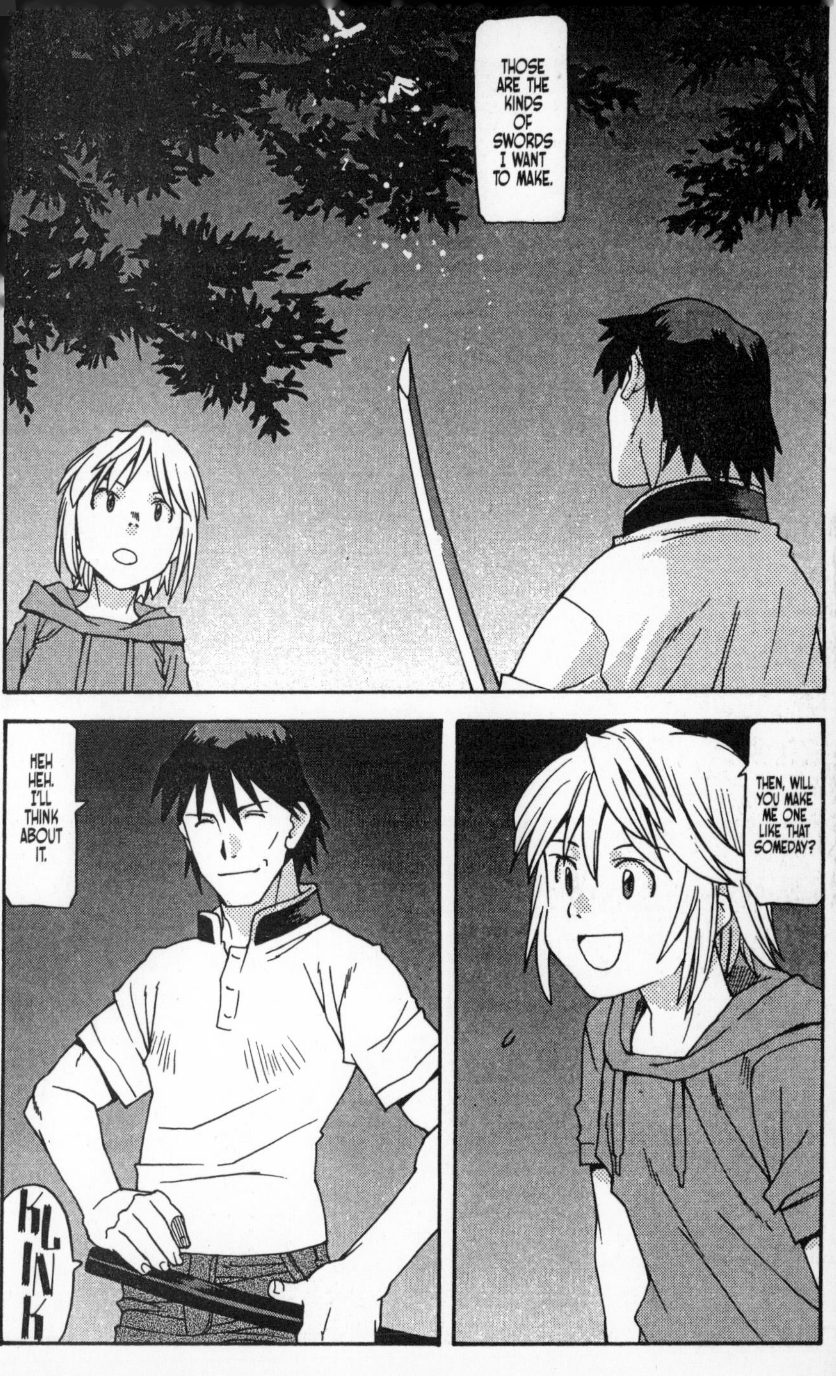
THOSE ARE THE KINDS OF SWORDS I WANT TO MAKE.
THEN, WILL YOU MAKE ME ONE LIKE THAT SOMEDAY?
HEH HEH. I'LL THINK ABOUT IT.
KLINK

OKAY.

LET'S GO HOME.

COME ON. YOU'RE PROBABLY TIRED.

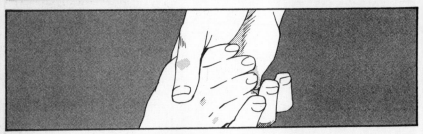

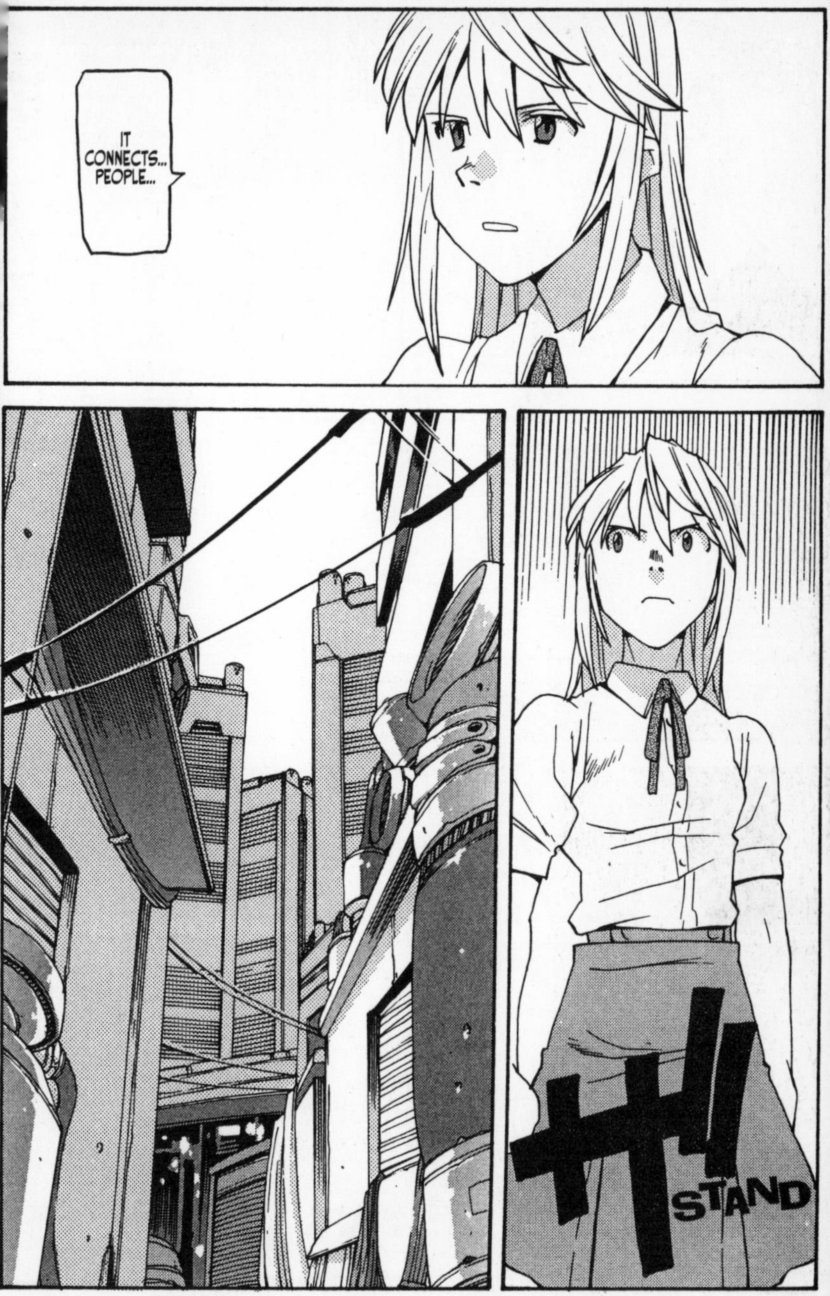
IT CONNECTS... PEOPLE...
STAND

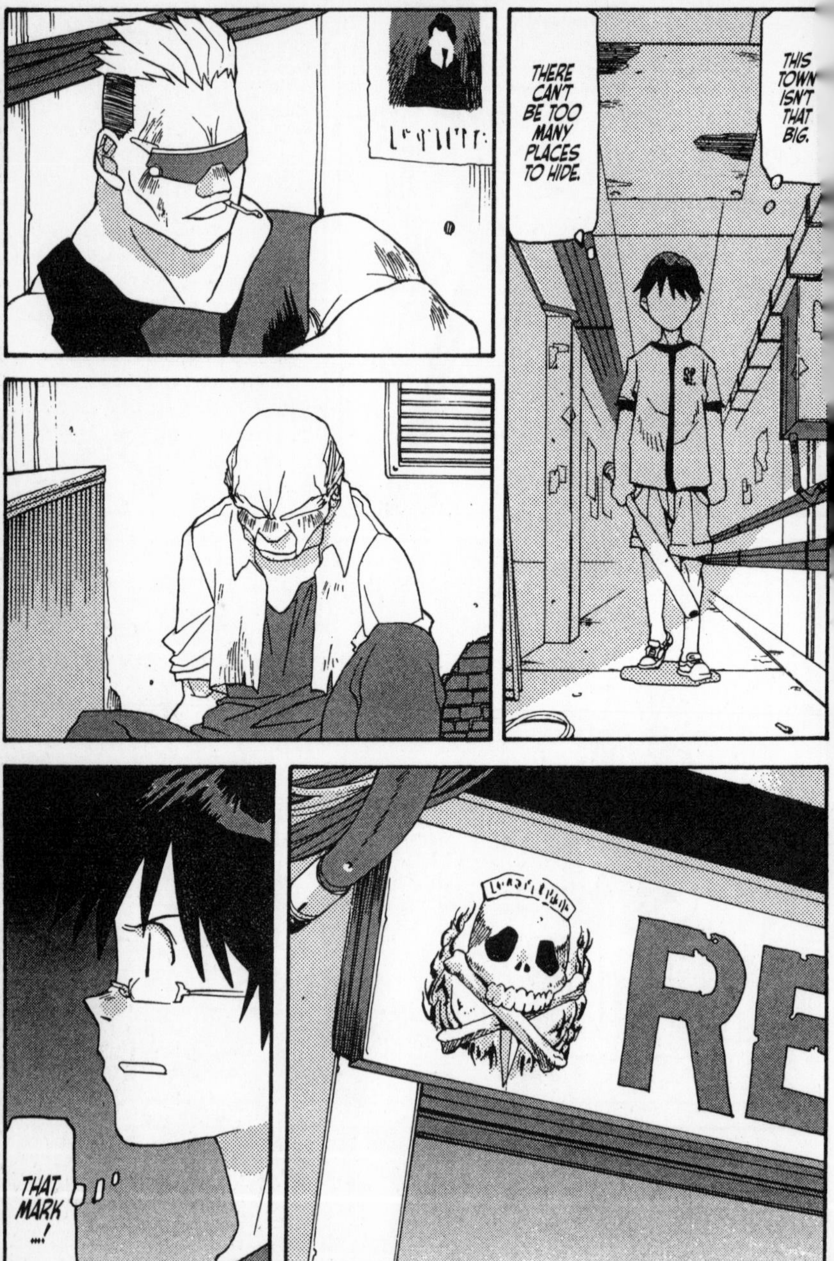
THIS TOWN ISN'T THAT BIG.
THERE CAN'T BE TOO MANY PLACES TO HIDE.
RE
THAT MARK ...!

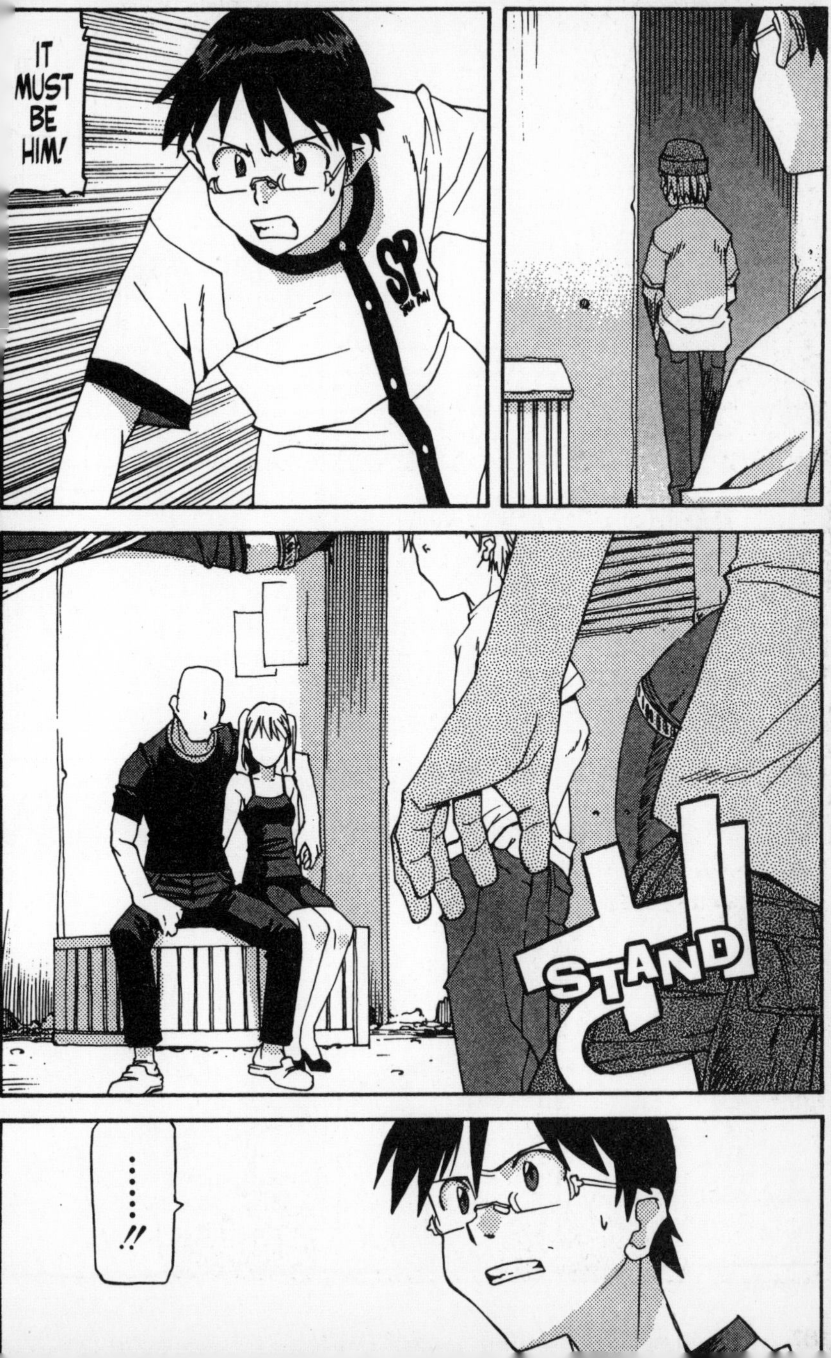
IT MUST BE HIM!
STAND
......!!

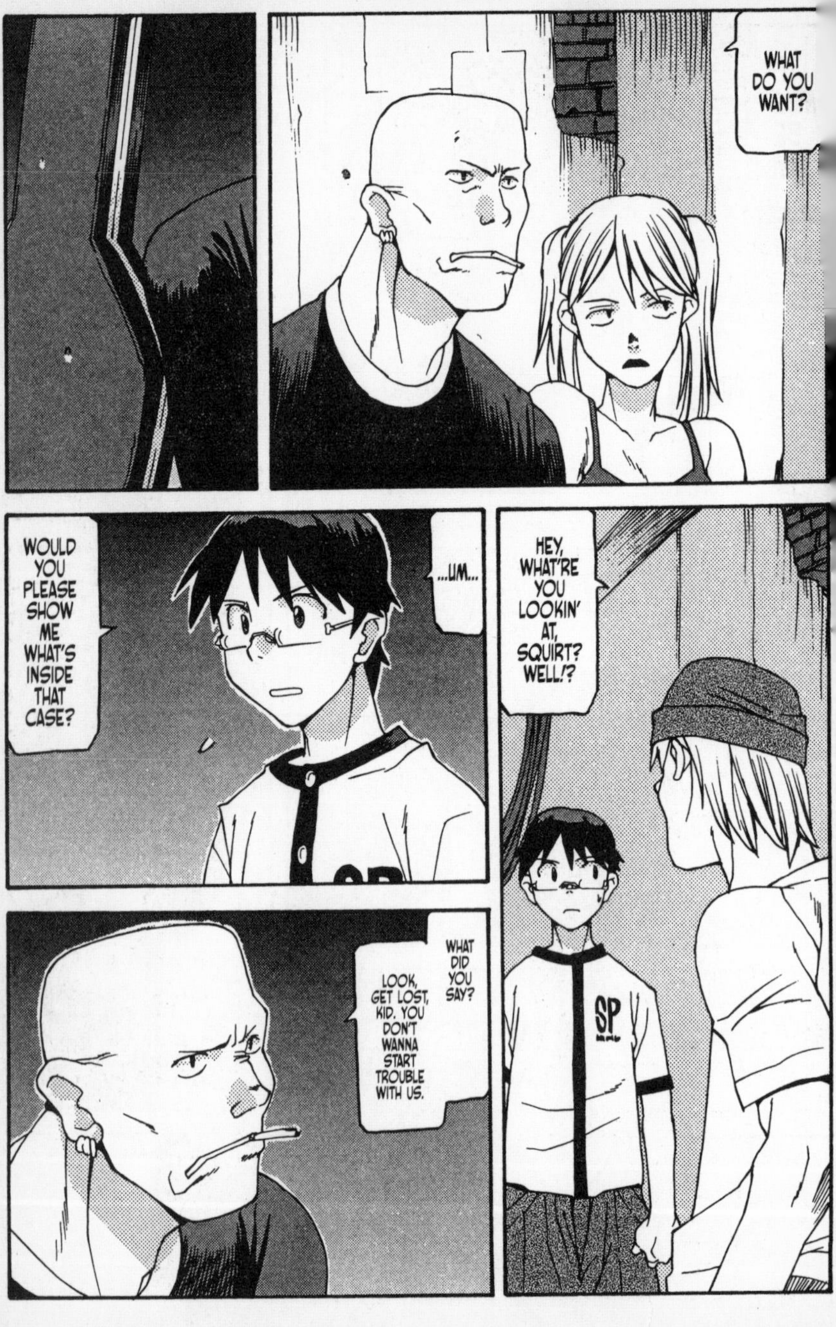
WHAT DO YOU WANT?
HEY, WHAT'RE YOU LOOKIN' AT, SQUIRT? WELL!?
...UM...
WOULD YOU PLEASE SHOW ME WHAT'S INSIDE THAT CASE?
WHAT DID YOU SAY?
LOOK, GET LOST, KID. YOU DON'T WANNA START TROUBLE WITH US.
SP

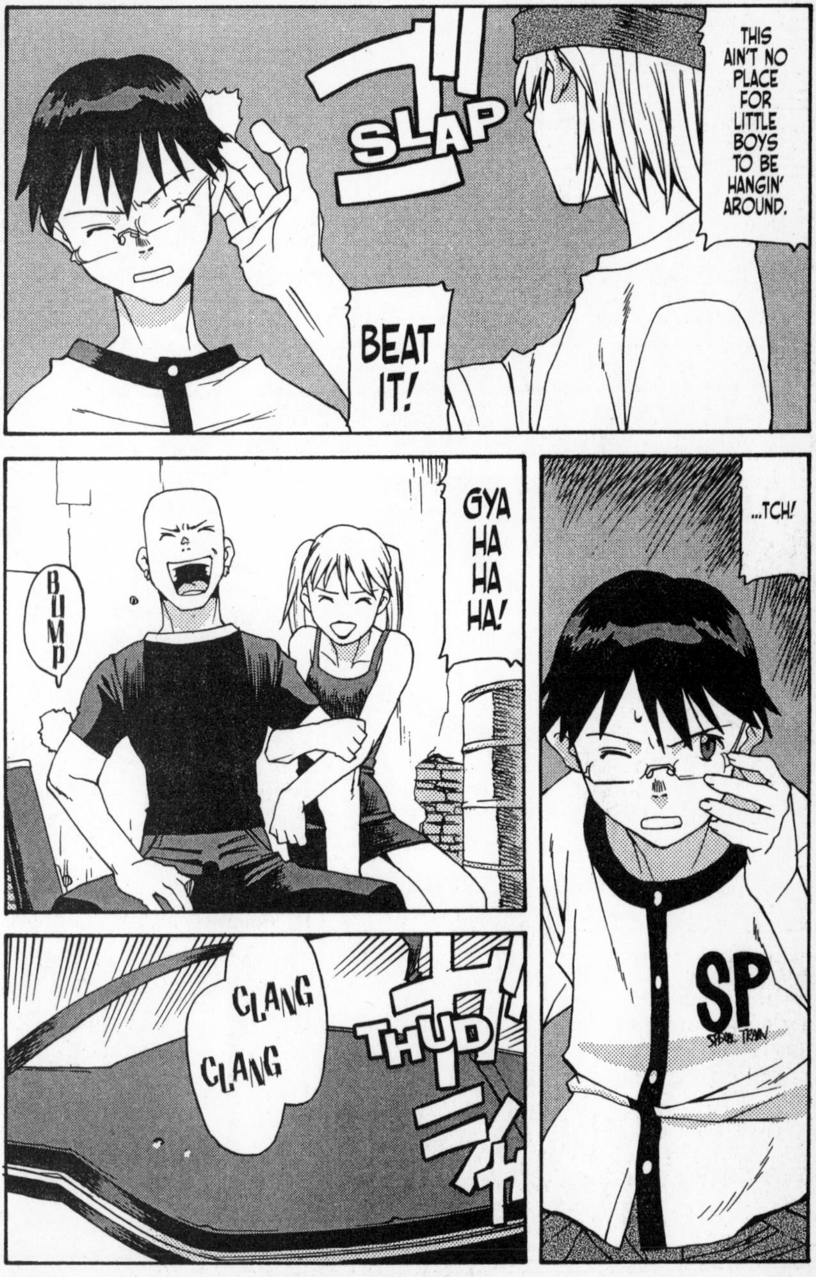
THIS AIN'T NO PLACE FOR LITTLE BOYS TO BE HANGIN' AROUND.
SLAP
BEAT IT!
...TCH!
SP
GYA HA HA HA!
BUMP
THUD
CLANG
CLANG

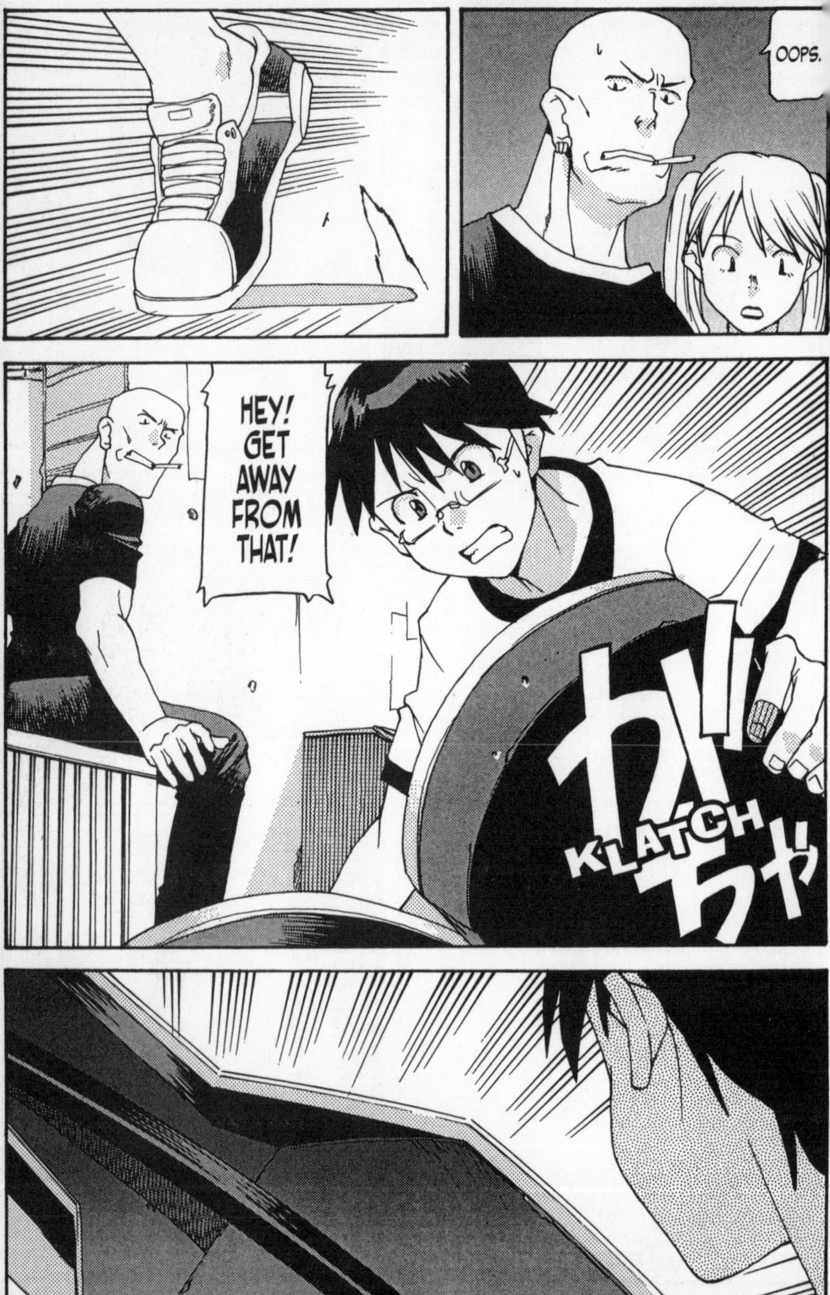
OOPS.
HEY! GET AWAY FROM THAT!
KLATCH
ガチャ

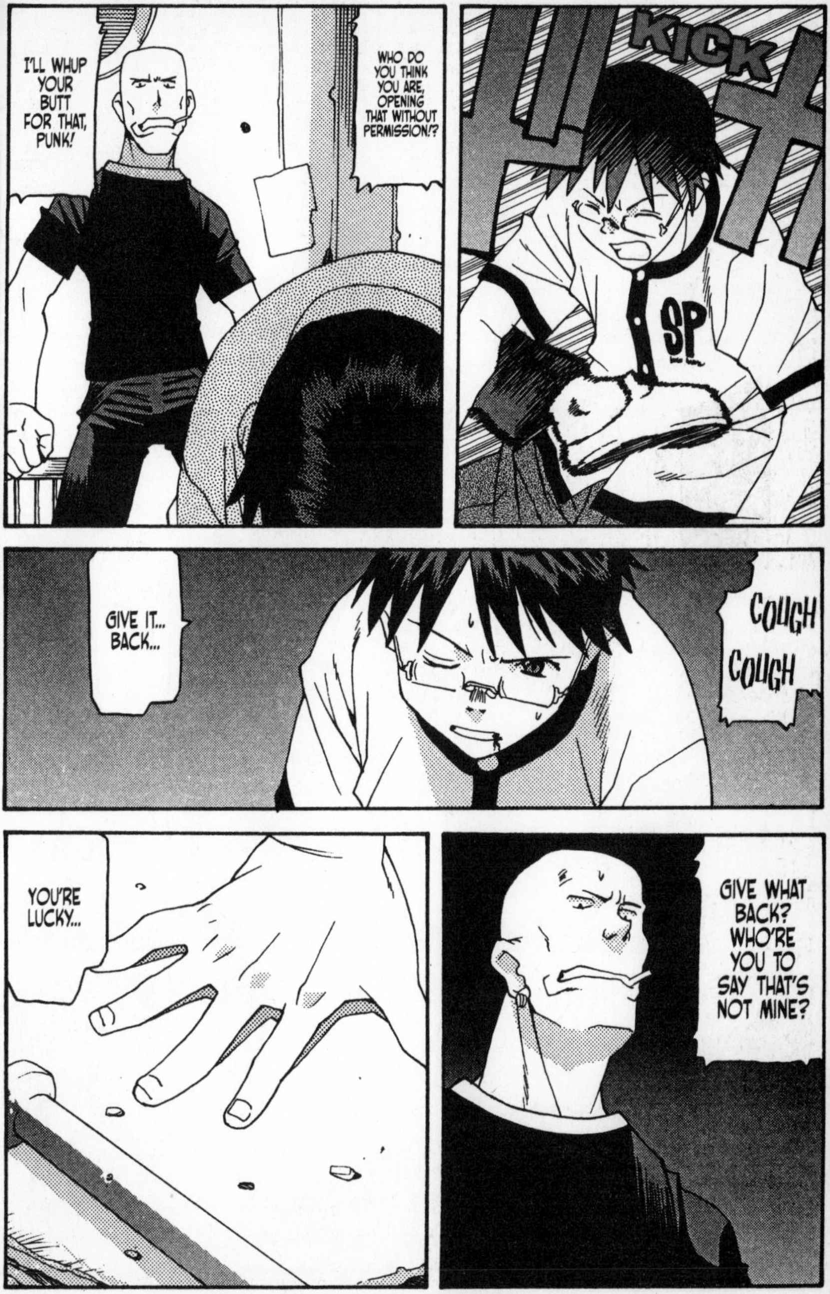
KICK
WHO DO YOU THINK YOU ARE, OPENING THAT WITHOUT PERMISSION!?
I'LL WHUP YOUR BUTT FOR THAT, PUNK!
COUGH
COUGH
GIVE IT... BACK...
GIVE WHAT BACK? WHO'RE YOU TO SAY THAT'S NOT MINE?
YOU'RE LUCKY...

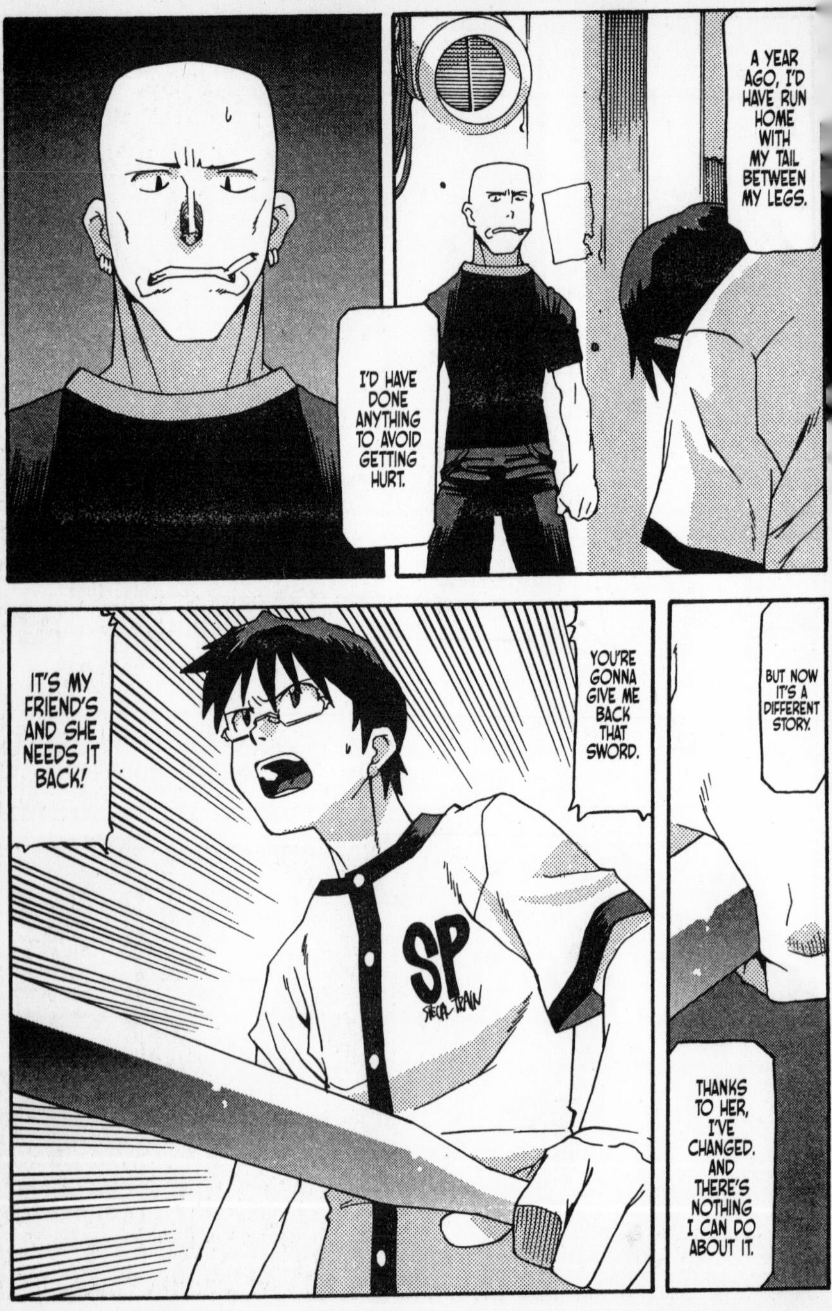
A YEAR AGO, I'D HAVE RUN HOME WITH MY TAIL BETWEEN MY LEGS.
I'D HAVE DONE ANYTHING TO AVOID GETTING HURT.
BUT NOW IT'S A DIFFERENT STORY.
THANKS TO HER, I'VE CHANGED. AND THERE'S NOTHING I CAN DO ABOUT IT.
YOU'RE GONNA GIVE ME BACK THAT SWORD.
IT'S MY FRIEND'S AND SHE NEEDS IT BACK!
SP

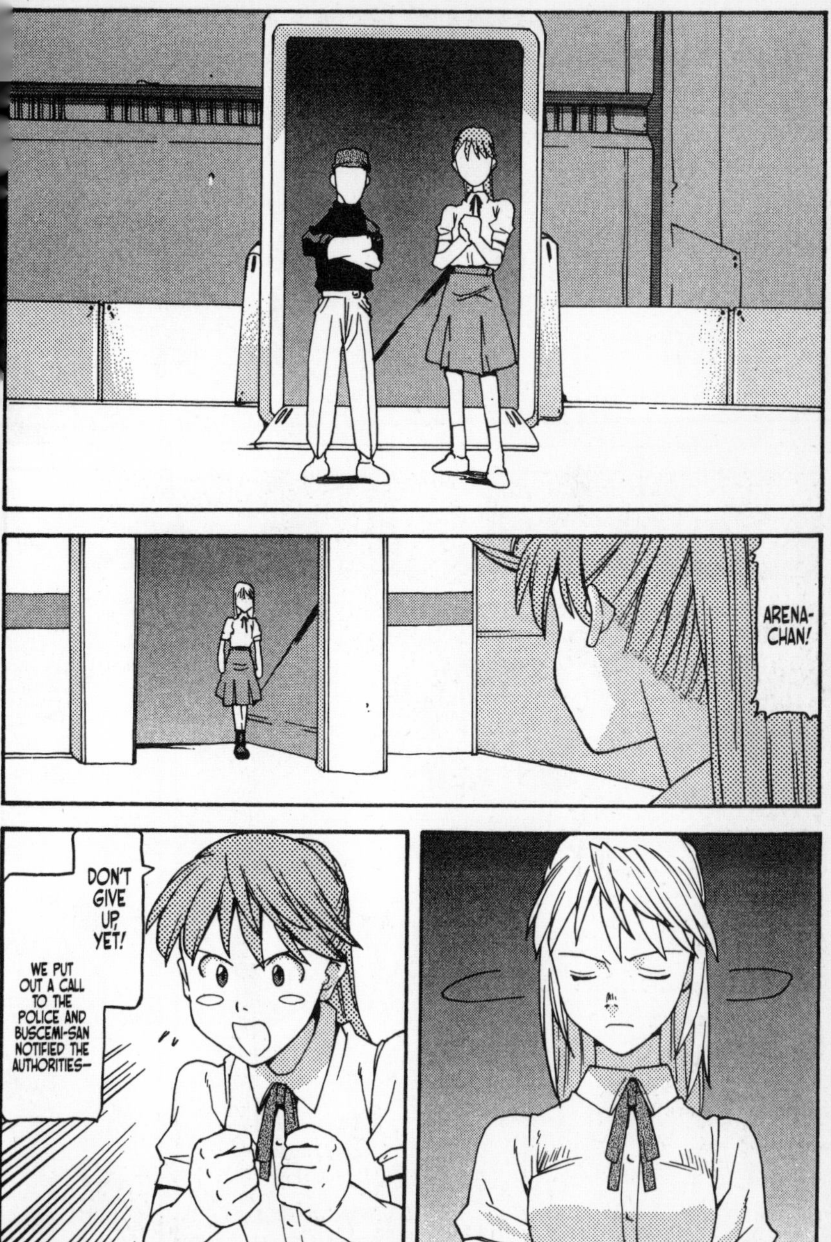
ARENA-CHAN!
DON'T GIVE UP, YET!
WE PUT OUT A CALL TO THE POLICE AND BUSCEMI-SAN NOTIFIED THE AUTHORITIES—

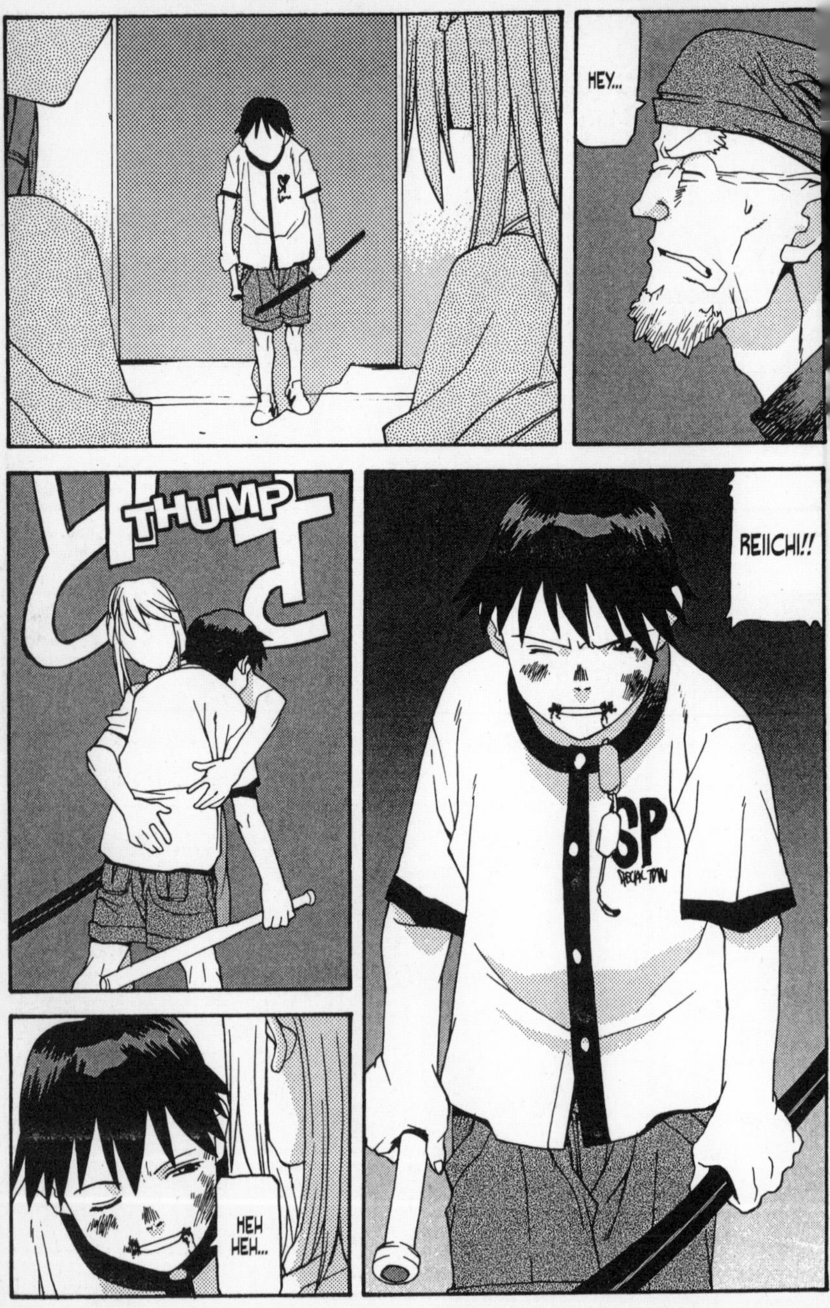
HEY...
REIICHI!!
THUMP
HEH HEH...

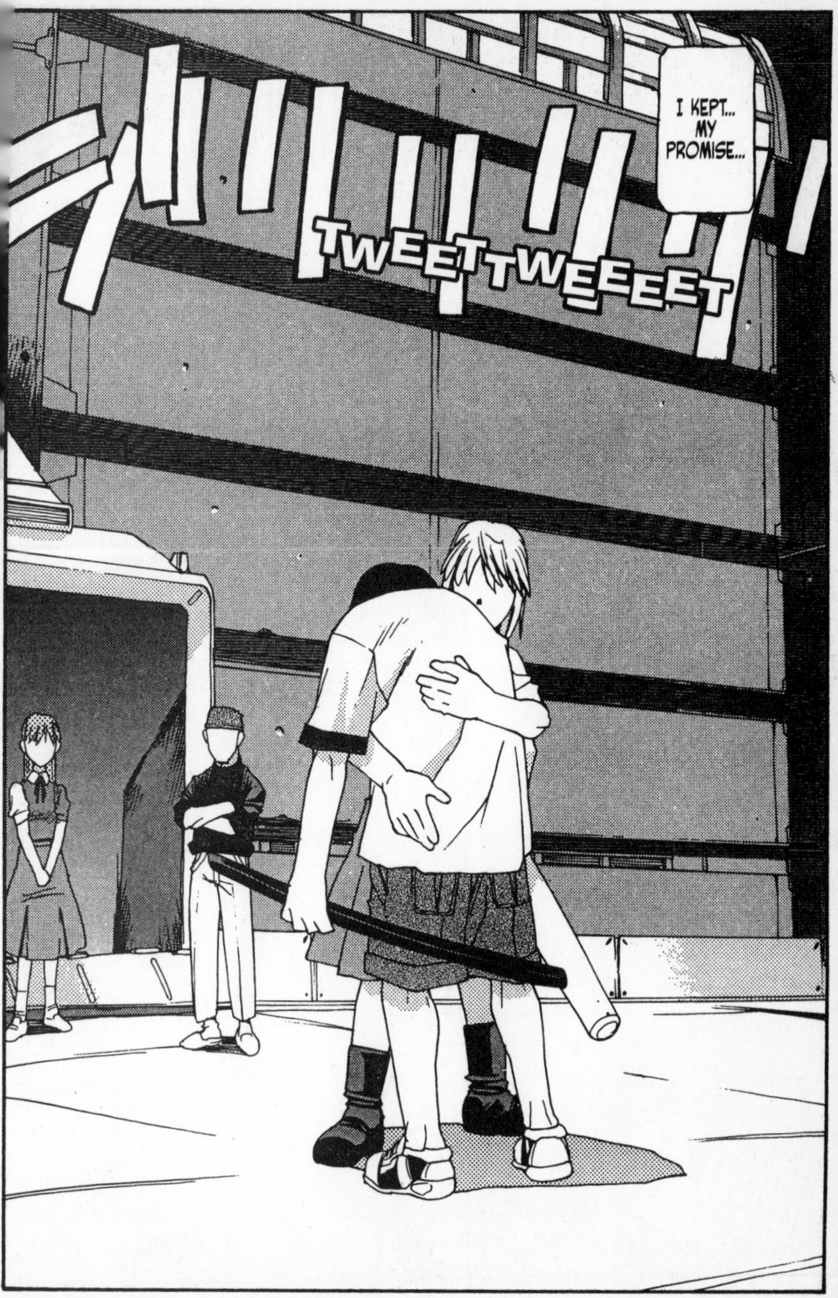
I KEPT... MY PROMISE...
TWEETTWEEEEET

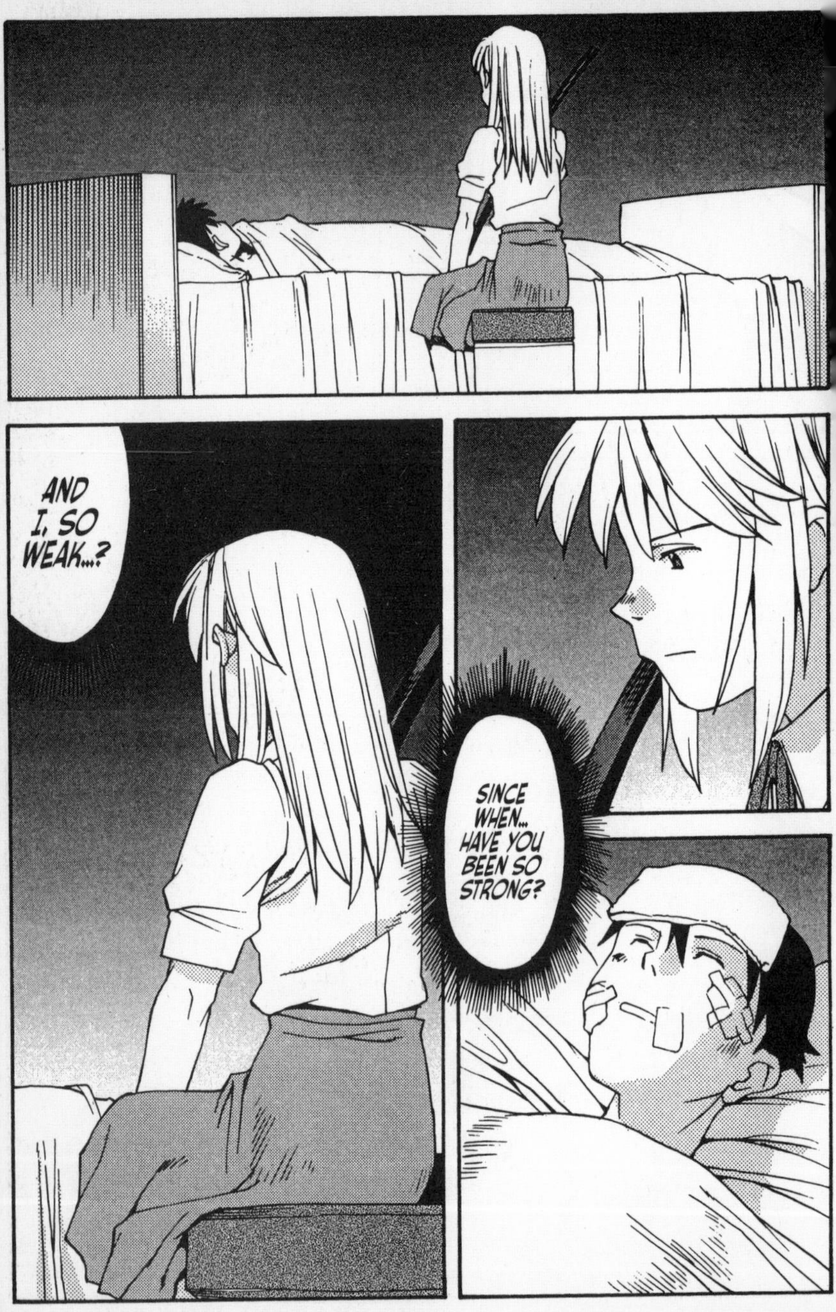
SINCE WHEN... HAVE YOU BEEN SO STRONG?
AND I, SO WEAK...?

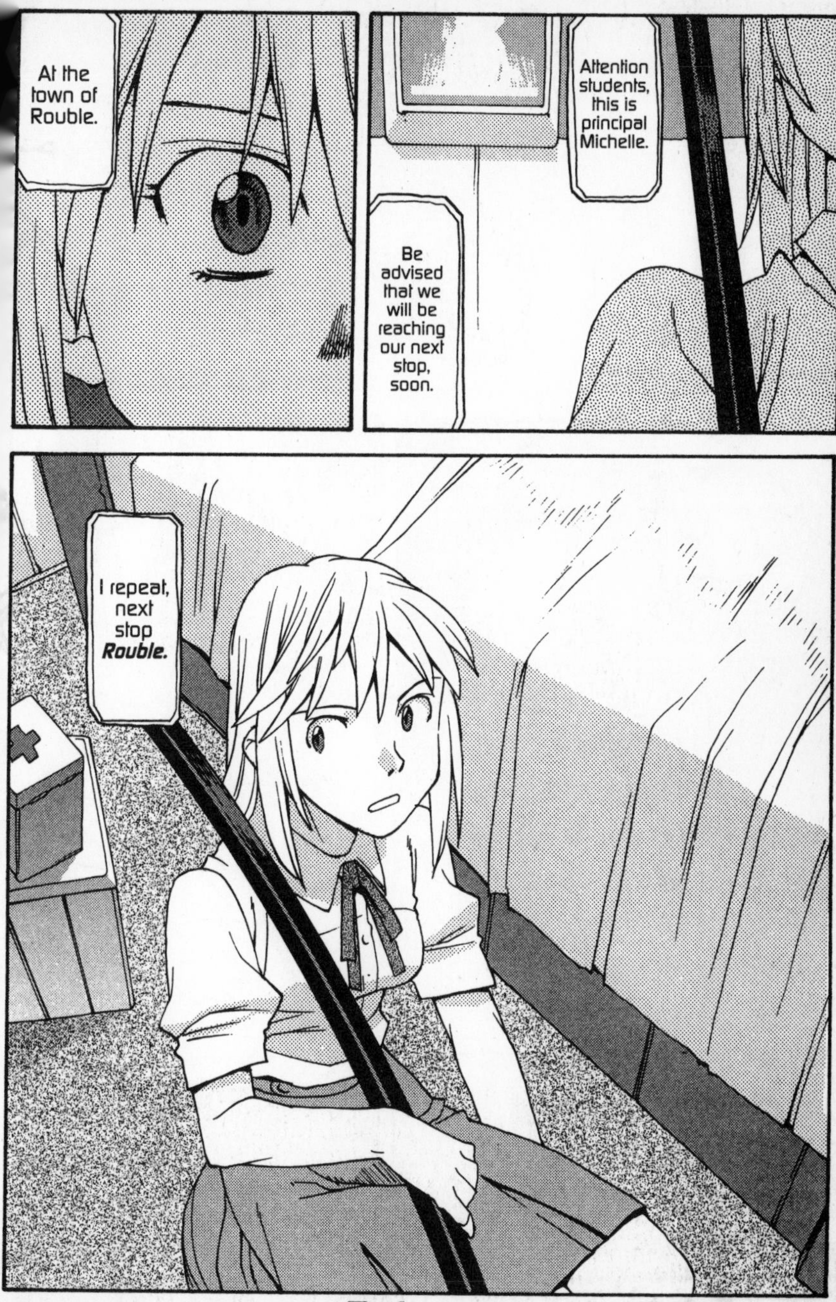
Attention students, this is principal Michelle.
Be advised that we will be reaching our next stop, soon.
At the town of Rouble.
I repeat, next stop *Rouble.*

To be continued NEXT ISSUE

Illustration by TOMOMASA TAKUMA
Text by HIDEYUKI KURATA

TRAIN+TRAIN PLOT WRITER'S NOTE
FILE NO. 008

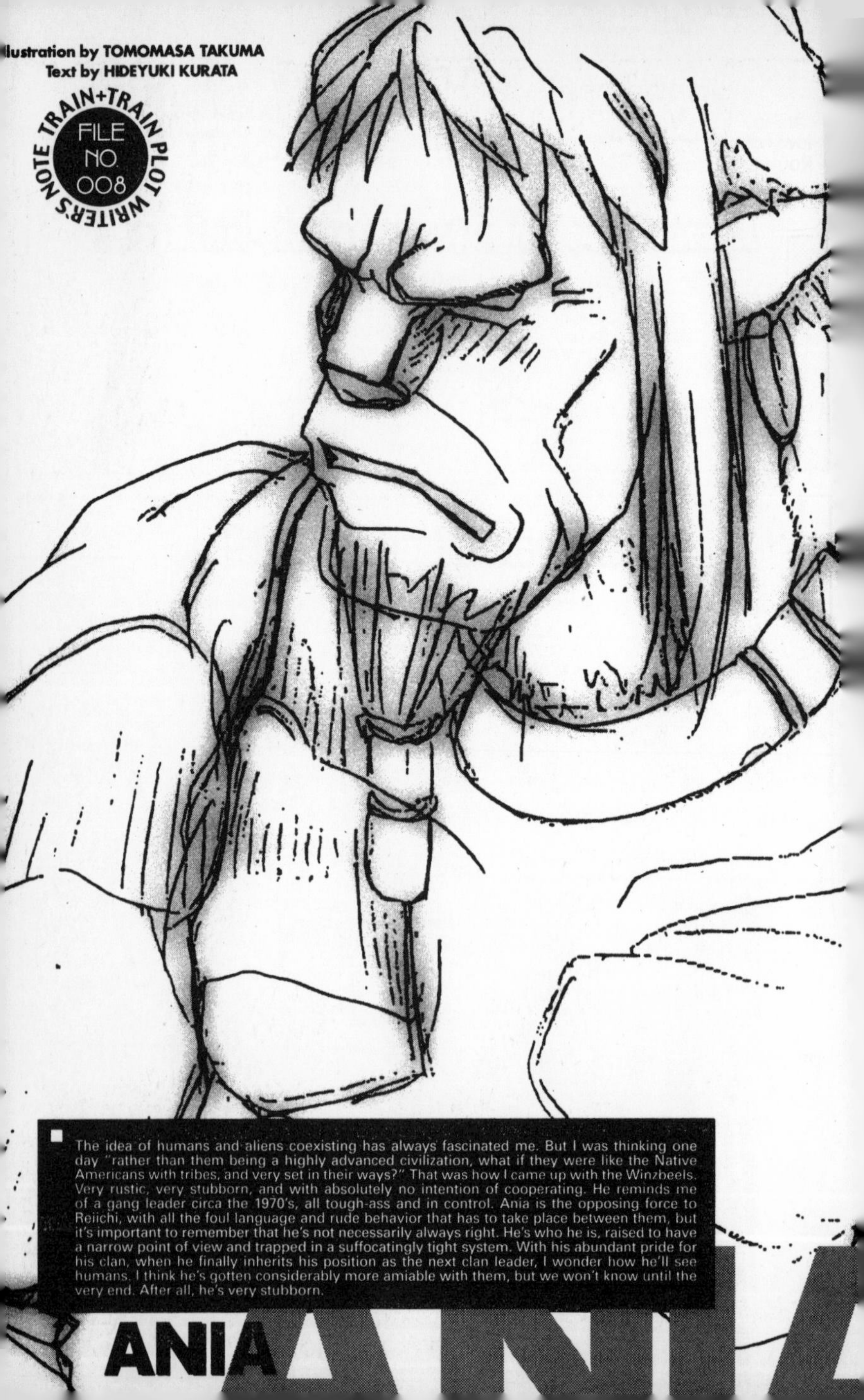

The idea of humans and aliens coexisting has always fascinated me. But I was thinking one day "rather than them being a highly advanced civilization, what if they were like the Native Americans with tribes, and very set in their ways?" That was how I came up with the Winzbeels. Very rustic, very stubborn, and with absolutely no intention of cooperating. He reminds me of a gang leader circa the 1970's, all tough-ass and in control. Ania is the opposing force to Reiichi, with all the foul language and rude behavior that has to take place between them, but it's important to remember that he's not necessarily always right. He's who he is, raised to have a narrow point of view and trapped in a suffocatingly tight system. With his abundant pride for his clan, when he finally inherits his position as the next clan leader, I wonder how he'll see humans. I think he's gotten considerably more amiable with them, but we won't know until the very end. After all, he's very stubborn.

ANIA

In the final volume of **TRAIN + TRAIN**

Arena's been in tough spots before...

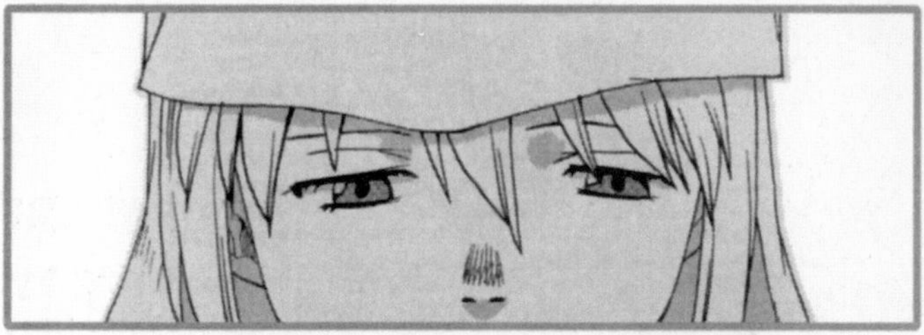

...but nothing like this!

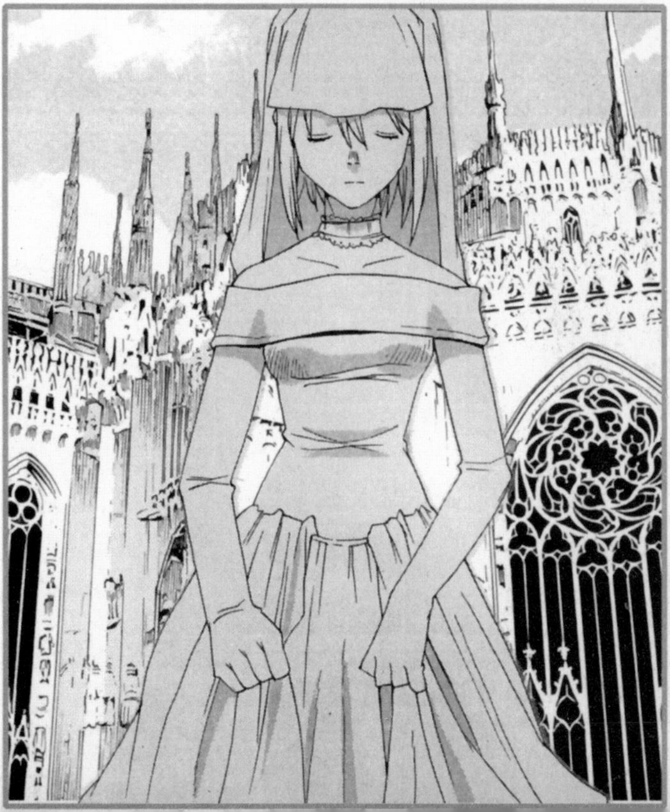

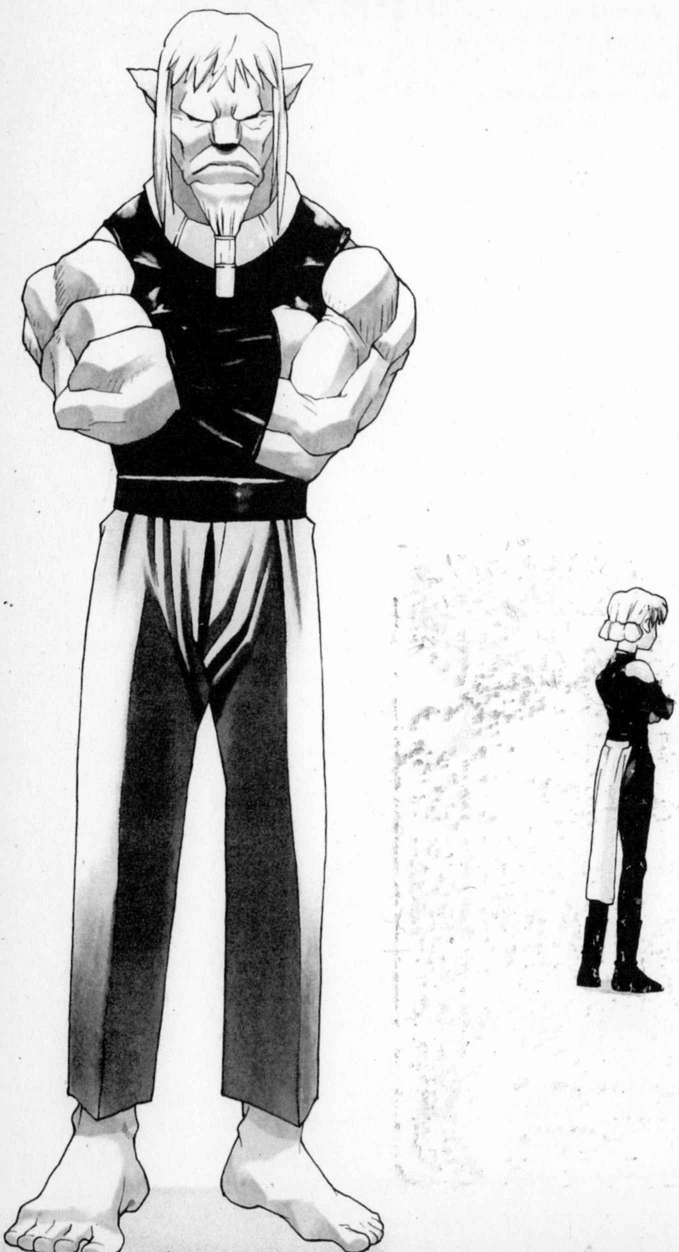

Translation and Adaptation – Christine Schilling
Editorial Assistant – Mallory Reaves
Lettering – TeamPokopen
Production Manager – James Dashiell
Editor – Brynne Chandler

A Go! Comi manga

Published by Go! Media Entertainment, LLC

Train + Train Volume 5
© HIDEYUKI KURATA - TOMOMASA TAKUMA 2002
First published in 2002 by Media Works inc., Tokyo, Japan.
English translation rights arranged with Media Works inc.

Visit us online at www.gocomi.com
e-mail: info@gocomi.com

ISBN 978-1-933617-51-0

First printed in January 2008

1 2 3 4 5 6 7 8 9

Manufactured in the United States of America

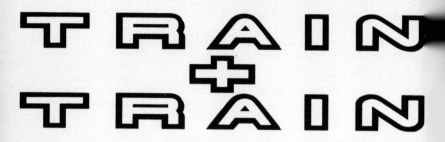

TRAIN + TRAIN

Volume 5

Original Story by

HIDEYUKI KURATA

Art by

TOMOMASA TAKUMA

go!comi

Concerning Honorifics

At Go! Comi, we do our best to ensure that our translations read seamlessly in English while respecting the original Japanese language and culture. To this end, the original honorifics (the suffixes found at the end of characters' names) remain intact. in Japan, where politeness and formality are more integrated into every aspect of the language, honorifics give a better understanding of character relationships. They can be used to indicate both respect and affection. Whether a person addresses someone by first name or last name also indicates how close their relationship is.

Here are some of the honorifics you might encounter in reading this book:

-san: This is the most common and neutral of honorifics. The polite way to address someone you're not on close terms with is to use "-san." it's kind of like Mr. or Ms., except you can use "-san" with first names as easily as family names.

-chan: Used for friendly familiarity, mostly applied towards young girls. "-chan" also carries a connotation of cuteness with it, so it is frequently used with nick-names towards both boys and girls (such as "Na-chan" for "Natsu").

-kun: Like "-chan," it's an informal suffix for friends and classmates, only "-kun" is usually associated with boys. it can also be used in a professional environment by someone addressing a subordinate.

-sama: indicates a great deal of respect or admiration.

Sempai: in school, "sempai" is used to refer to an upperclassman or club leader. it can also be used in the workplace by a new employee to address a mentor or staff member with seniority.

Sensei: Teachers, doctors, writers or any master of a trade are referred to as "sensei." When addressing a manga creator, the polite thing to do is attach "-sensei" to the manga-ka's name (as in Takuma-sensei).

Onii: This is the more casual term for an older brother. Usually you'll see it with an honorific attached, such as "onii-chan."

Onee: The casual term for older sister, it's used like "onii" with honorifics.

[blank]: Not using an honorific when addressing someone indicates that the speaker has permission to speak intimately with the other person. This relationship is usually reserved for close friends and family.

T R A I N

TRAIN + TRAIN
VOLUME 5

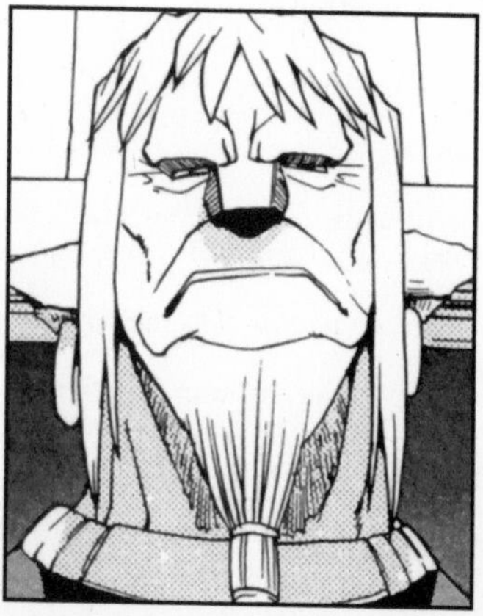

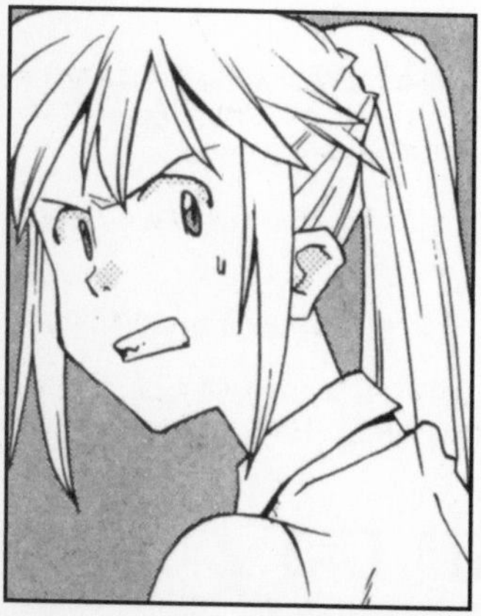

T R A I N

TRAIN
+
TRAIN

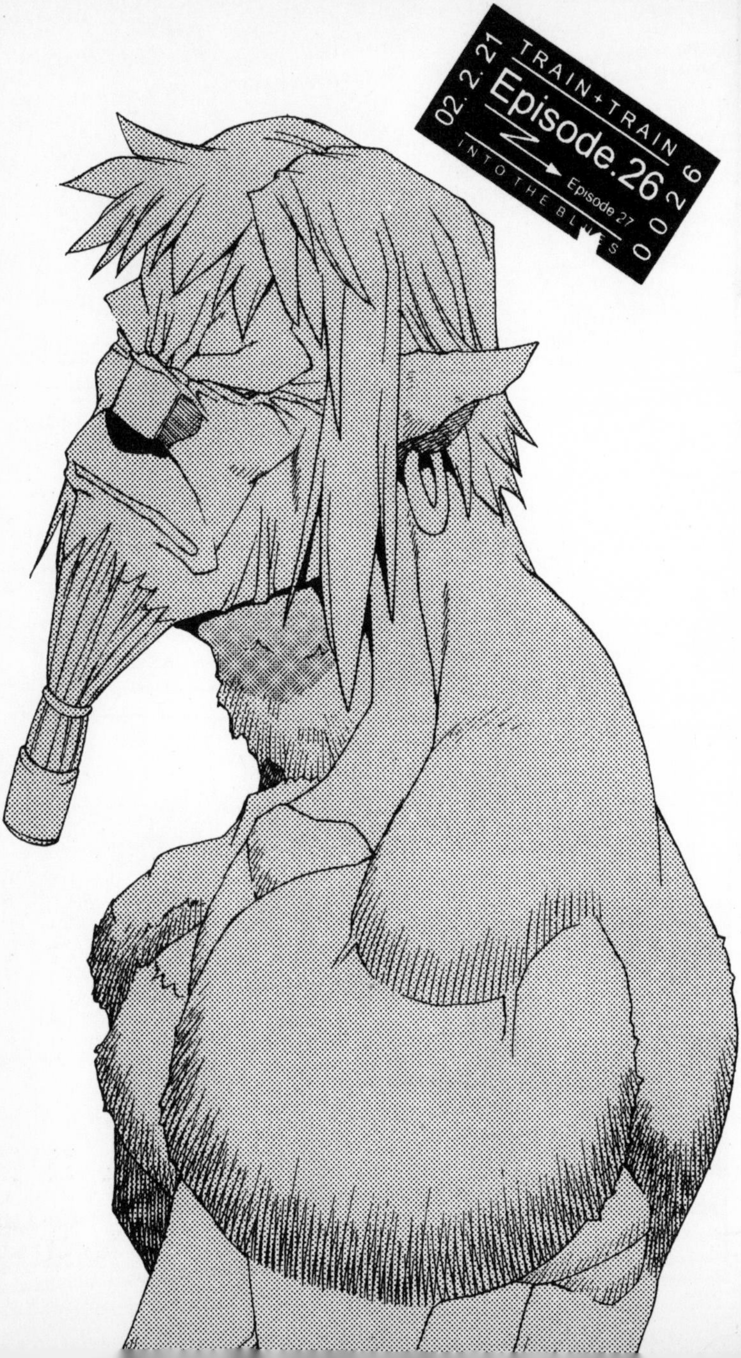
02.2.21
TRAIN+TRAIN
Episode.26
Episode 27
INTO THE BLUES
0026

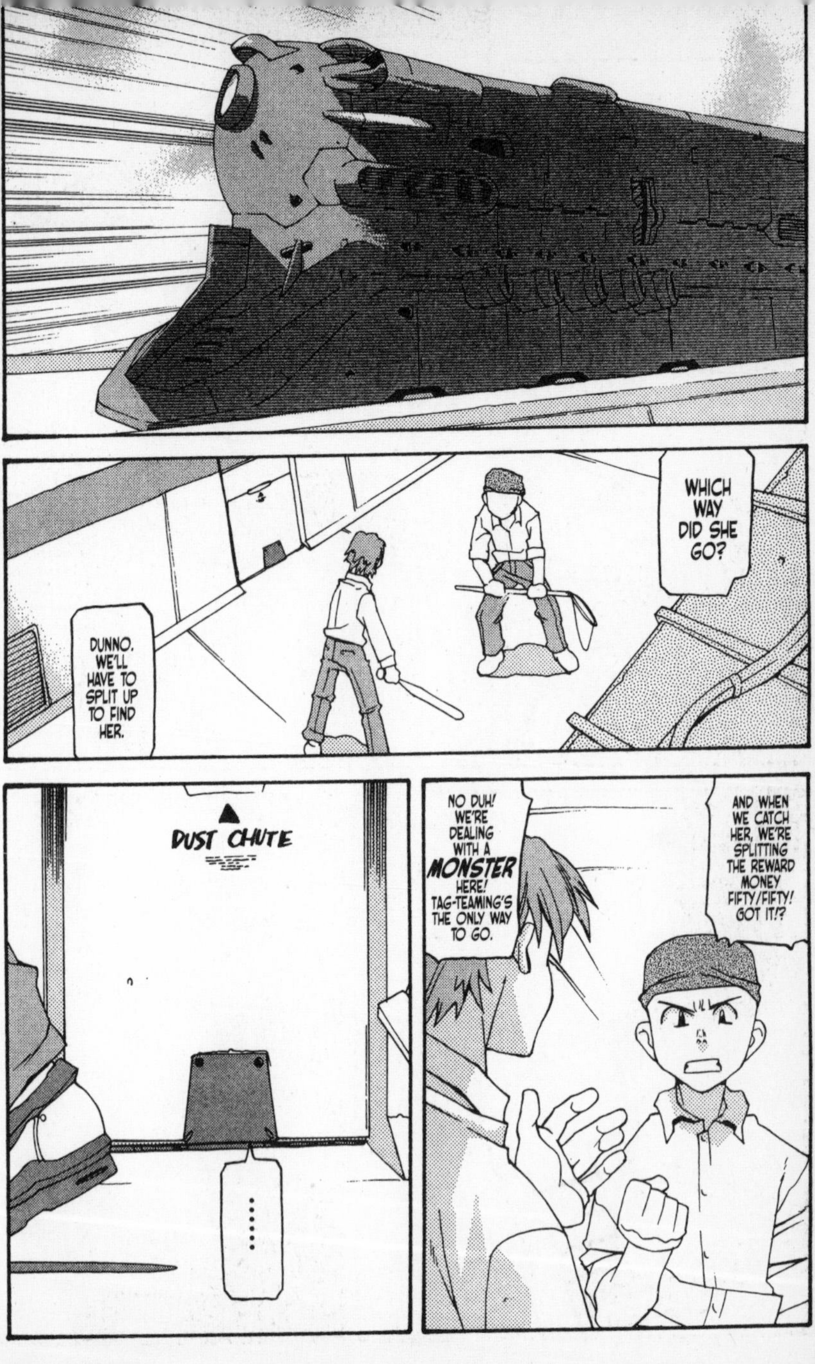
WHICH WAY DID SHE GO?
DUNNO. WE'LL HAVE TO SPLIT UP TO FIND HER.
AND WHEN WE CATCH HER, WE'RE SPLITTING THE REWARD MONEY FIFTY/FIFTY! GOT IT!?
NO DUH! WE'RE DEALING WITH A MONSTER HERE! TAG-TEAMING'S THE ONLY WAY TO GO.
DUST CHUTE
......

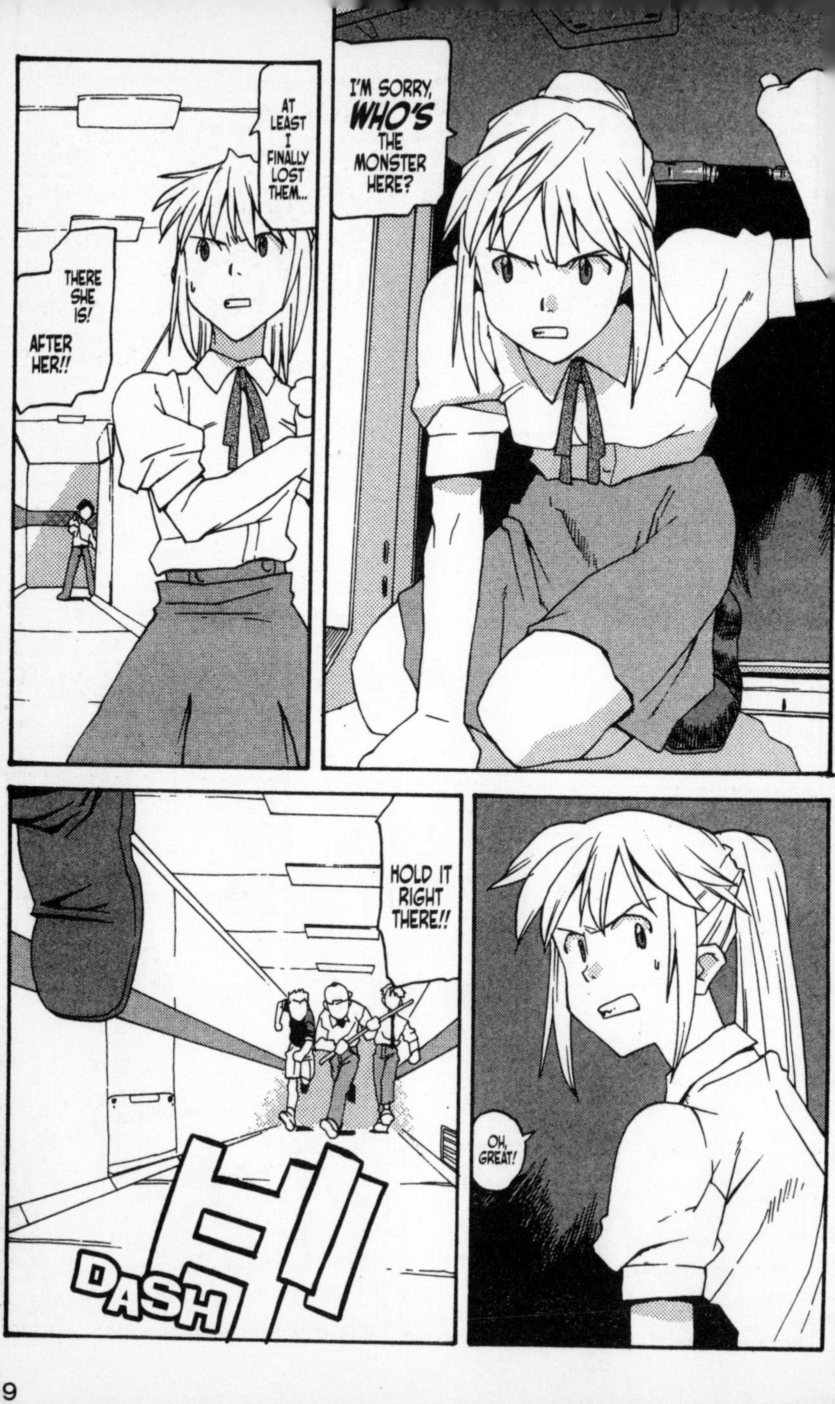
I'M SORRY, WHO'S THE MONSTER HERE?
AT LEAST I FINALLY LOST THEM...
THERE SHE IS!
AFTER HER!!
OH, GREAT!
HOLD IT RIGHT THERE!!
DASH

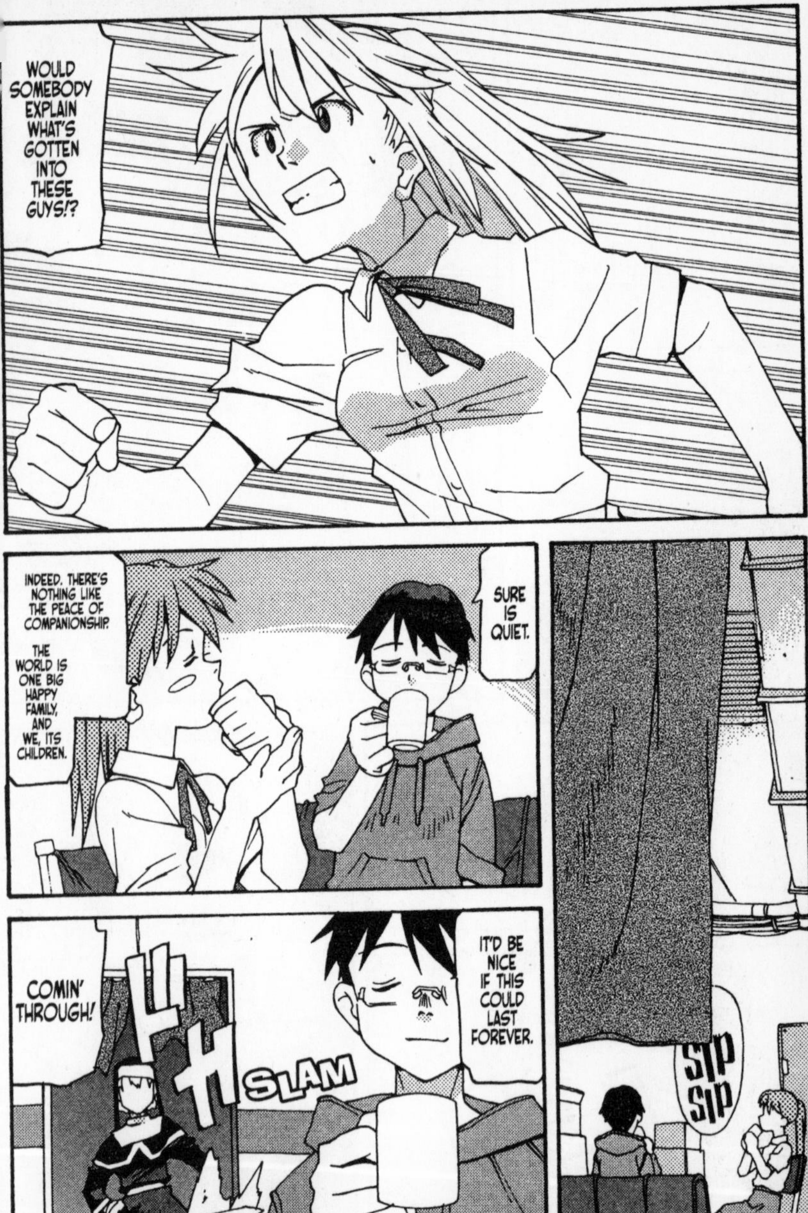
WOULD SOMEBODY EXPLAIN WHAT'S GOTTEN INTO THESE GUYS!?
SIP SIP
SURE IS QUIET.
INDEED. THERE'S NOTHING LIKE THE PEACE OF COMPANIONSHIP.
THE WORLD IS ONE BIG HAPPY FAMILY, AND WE, ITS CHILDREN.
IT'D BE NICE IF THIS COULD LAST FOREVER.
SLAM
COMIN' THROUGH!

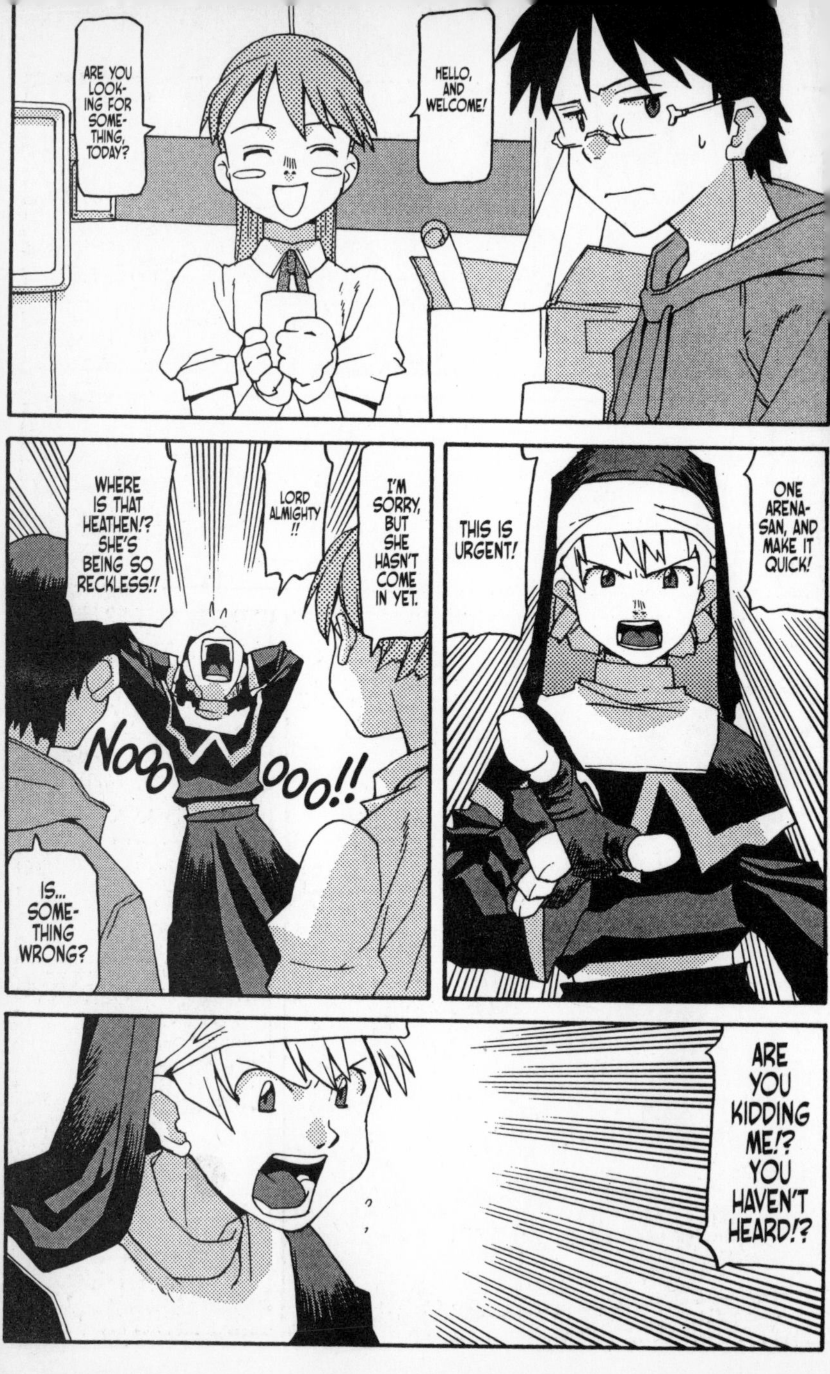
HELLO, AND WELCOME!
ARE YOU LOOKING FOR SOMETHING, TODAY?
ONE ARENA-SAN, AND MAKE IT QUICK!
THIS IS URGENT!
I'M SORRY, BUT SHE HASN'T COME IN YET.
LORD ALMIGHTY!!
WHERE IS THAT HEATHEN!? SHE'S BEING SO RECKLESS!!
NOOOOOOO!!
IS... SOMETHING WRONG?
ARE YOU KIDDING ME!? YOU HAVEN'T HEARD!?

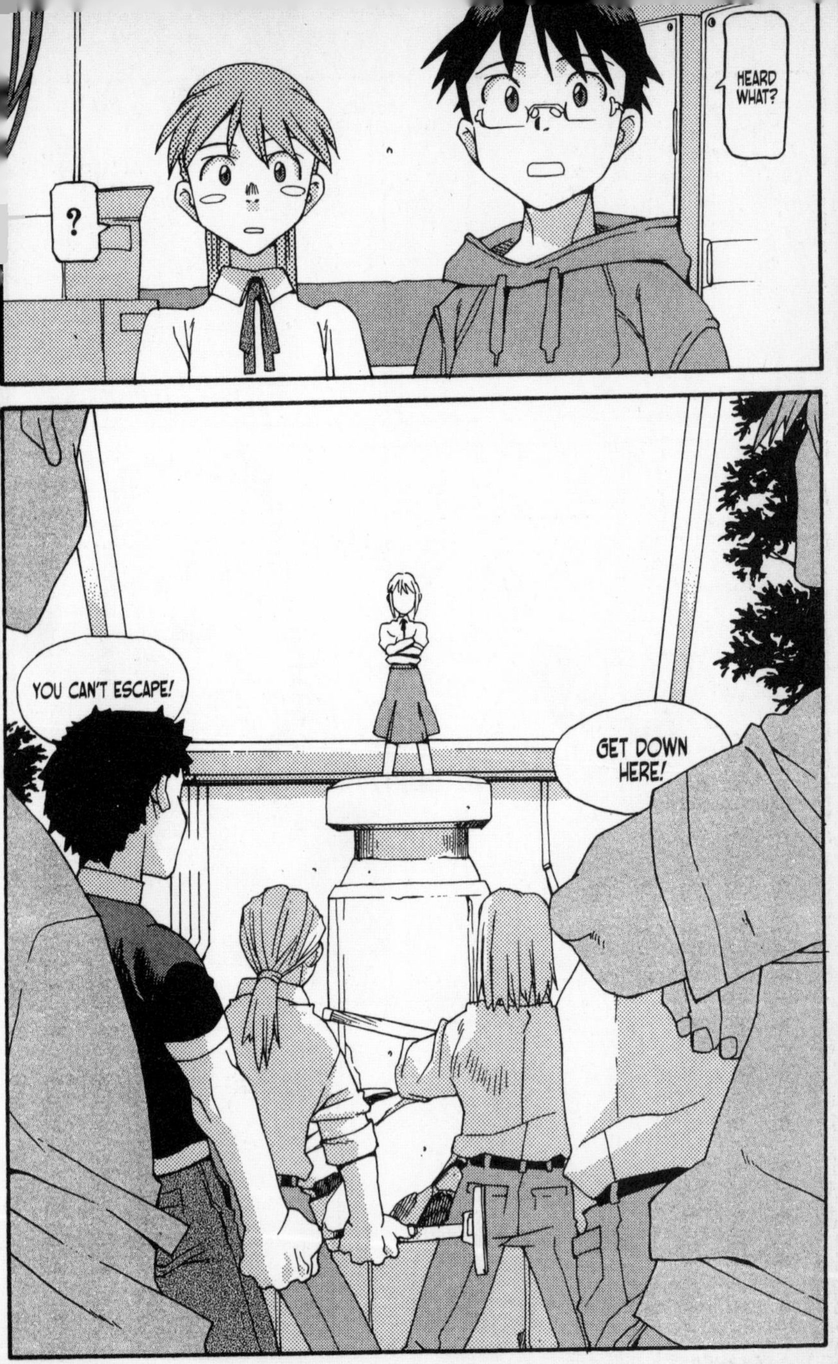
HEARD WHAT?
?
GET DOWN HERE!
YOU CAN'T ESCAPE!

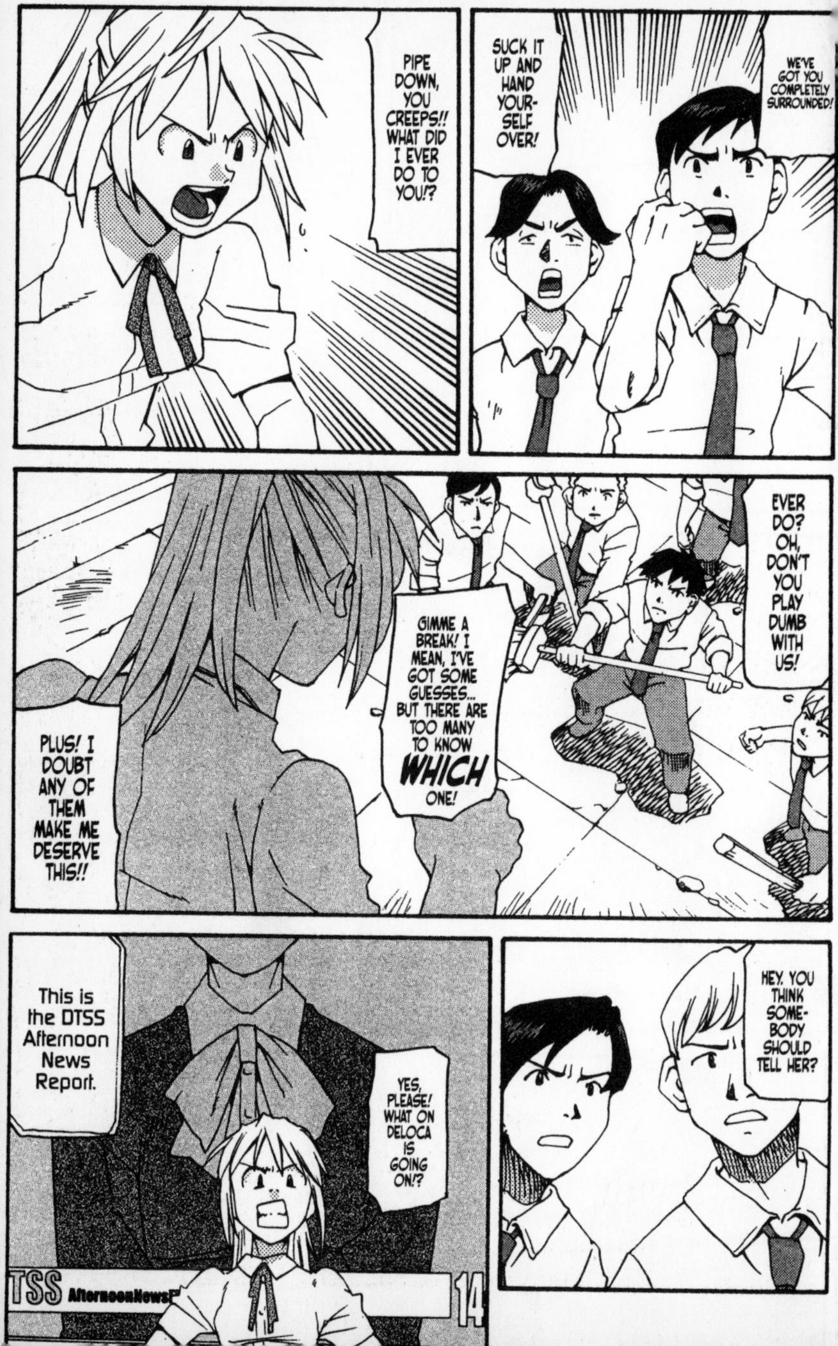
WE'VE GOT YOU COMPLETELY SURROUNDED!
SUCK IT UP AND HAND YOURSELF OVER!
PIPE DOWN, YOU CREEPS!! WHAT DID I EVER DO TO YOU!?
EVER DO? OH, DON'T YOU PLAY DUMB WITH US!
GIMME A BREAK! I MEAN, I'VE GOT SOME GUESSES... BUT THERE ARE TOO MANY TO KNOW WHICH ONE!
PLUS! I DOUBT ANY OF THEM MAKE ME DESERVE THIS!!
HEY. YOU THINK SOMEBODY SHOULD TELL HER?
This is the DTSS Afternoon News Report.
YES, PLEASE! WHAT ON DELOCA IS GOING ON!?
TSS AfternoonNews
14

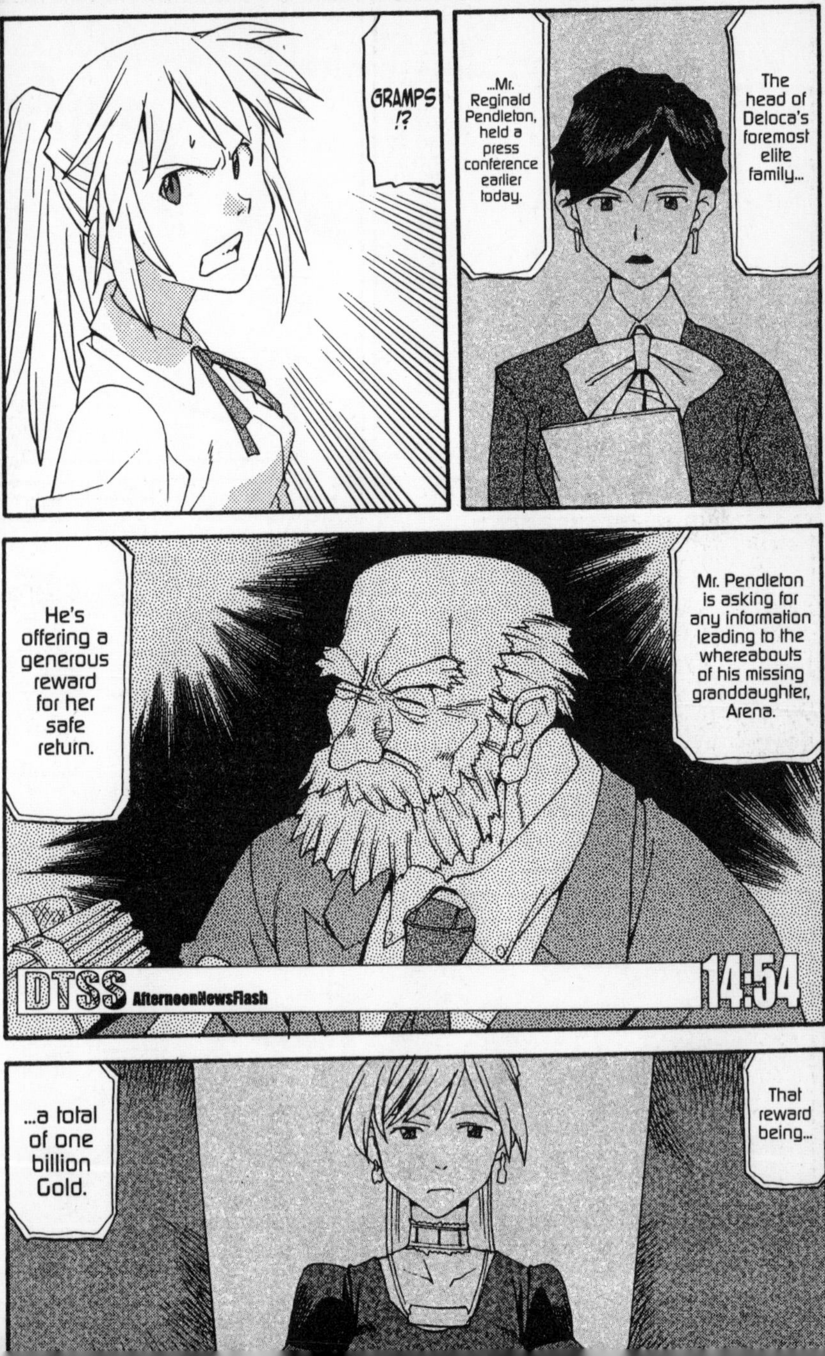
The head of Deloca's foremost elite family...
...Mr. Reginald Pendleton, held a press conference earlier today.
GRAMPS !?
Mr. Pendleton is asking for any information leading to the whereabouts of his missing granddaughter, Arena.
He's offering a generous reward for her safe return.
DTSS AfternoonNewsFlash
14:54
That reward being...
...a total of one billion Gold.

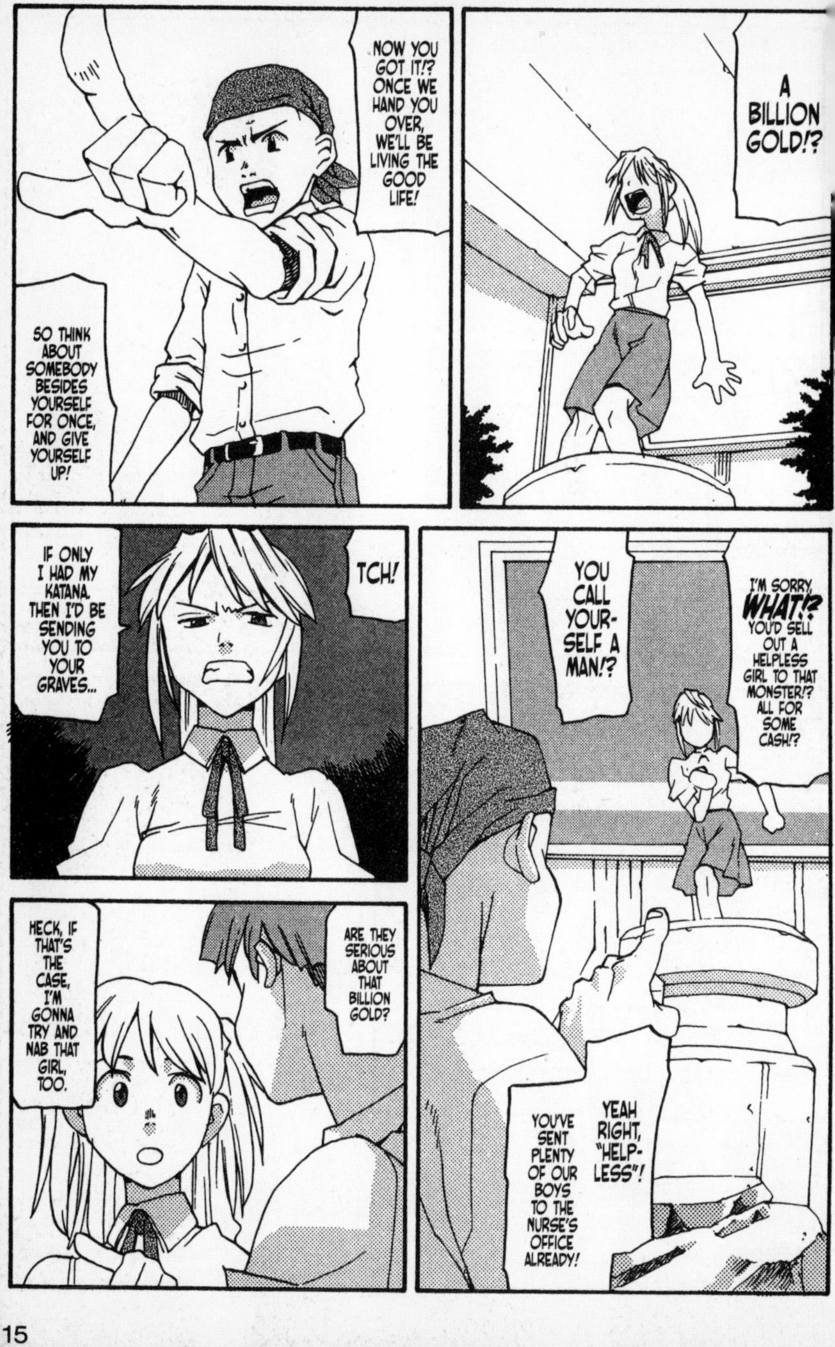
A BILLION GOLD!?
NOW YOU GOT IT!? ONCE WE HAND YOU OVER, WE'LL BE LIVING THE GOOD LIFE!
SO THINK ABOUT SOMEBODY BESIDES YOURSELF FOR ONCE, AND GIVE YOURSELF UP!
I'M SORRY, WHAT!? YOU'D SELL OUT A HELPLESS GIRL TO THAT MONSTER!? ALL FOR SOME CASH!?
YOU CALL YOURSELF A MAN!?
YEAH RIGHT, "HELPLESS"!
YOU'VE SENT PLENTY OF OUR BOYS TO THE NURSE'S OFFICE ALREADY!
TCH!
IF ONLY I HAD MY KATANA. THEN I'D BE SENDING YOU TO YOUR GRAVES...
ARE THEY SERIOUS ABOUT THAT BILLION GOLD?
HECK, IF THAT'S THE CASE, I'M GONNA TRY AND NAB THAT GIRL, TOO.

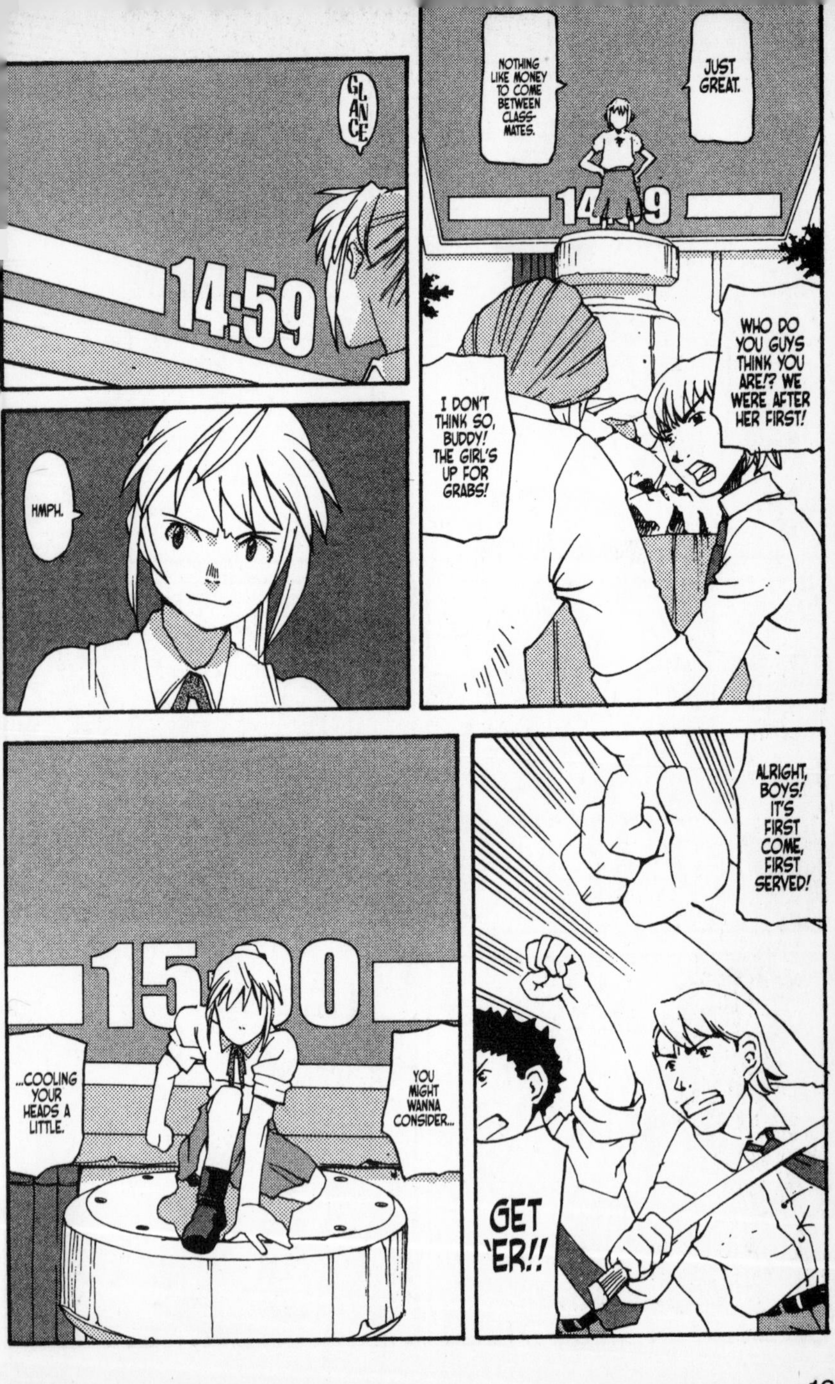
JUST GREAT.
NOTHING LIKE MONEY TO COME BETWEEN CLASS-MATES.
WHO DO YOU GUYS THINK YOU ARE!? WE WERE AFTER HER FIRST!
I DON'T THINK SO, BUDDY! THE GIRL'S UP FOR GRABS!
GLANCE
14:59
HMPH.
ALRIGHT, BOYS! IT'S FIRST COME, FIRST SERVED!
GET 'ER!!
YOU MIGHT WANNA CONSIDER...
...COOLING YOUR HEADS A LITTLE.

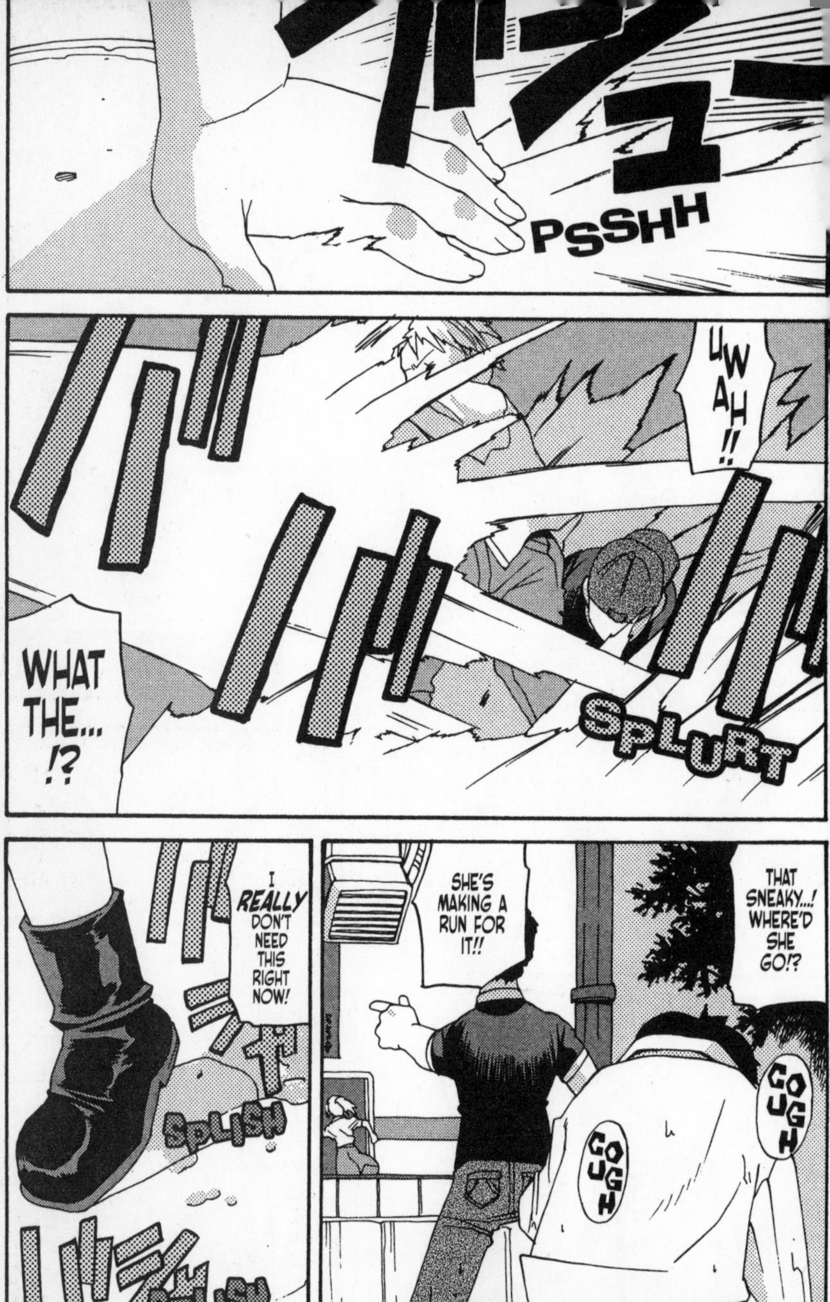
PSSHH
UWAH!!
SPLURT
WHAT THE...!?
THAT SNEAKY...! WHERE'D SHE GO!?
COUGH
COUGH
SHE'S MAKING A RUN FOR IT!!
I *REALLY* DON'T NEED THIS RIGHT NOW!
SPLISH
SPLISH

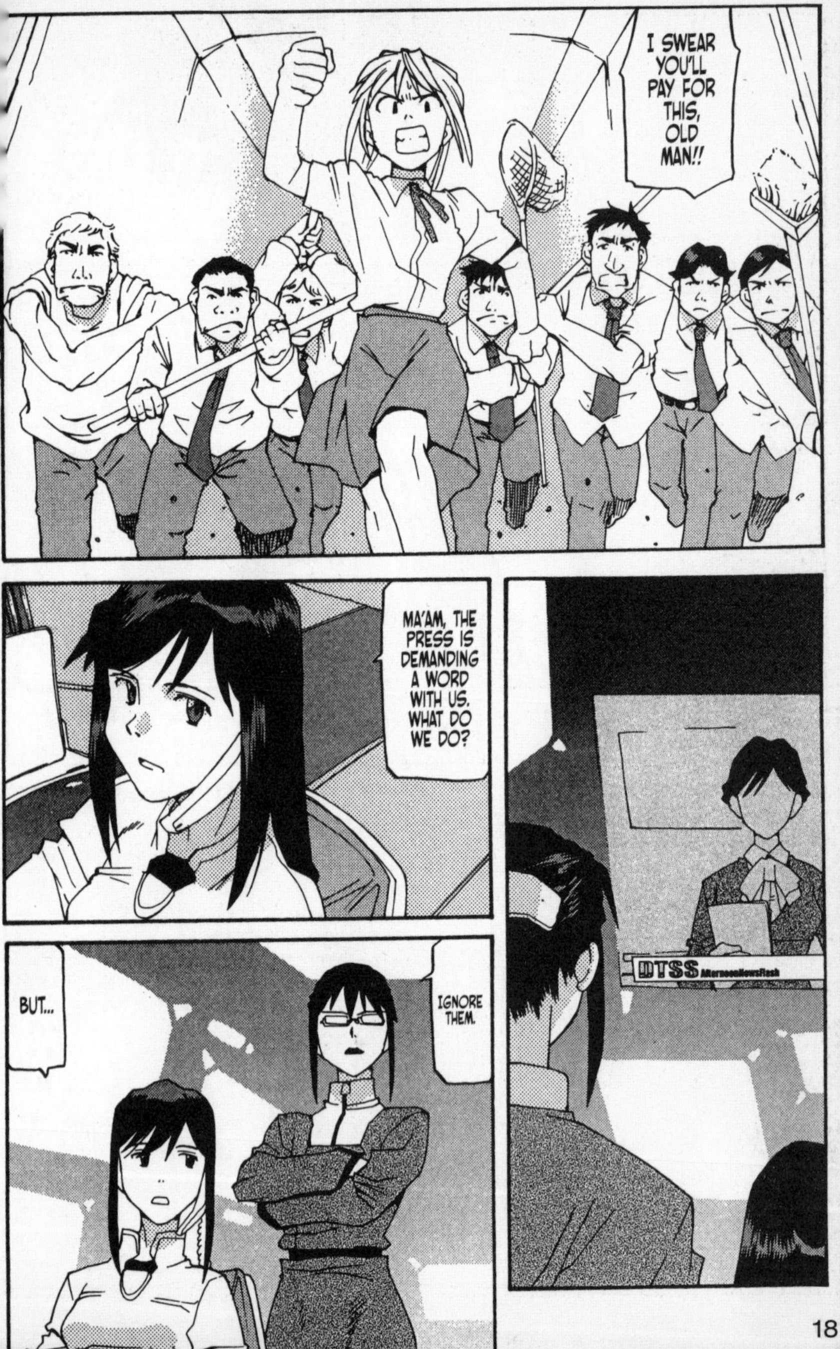
I SWEAR YOU'LL PAY FOR THIS, OLD MAN!!
DTSS
MA'AM, THE PRESS IS DEMANDING A WORD WITH US. WHAT DO WE DO?
IGNORE THEM.
BUT...

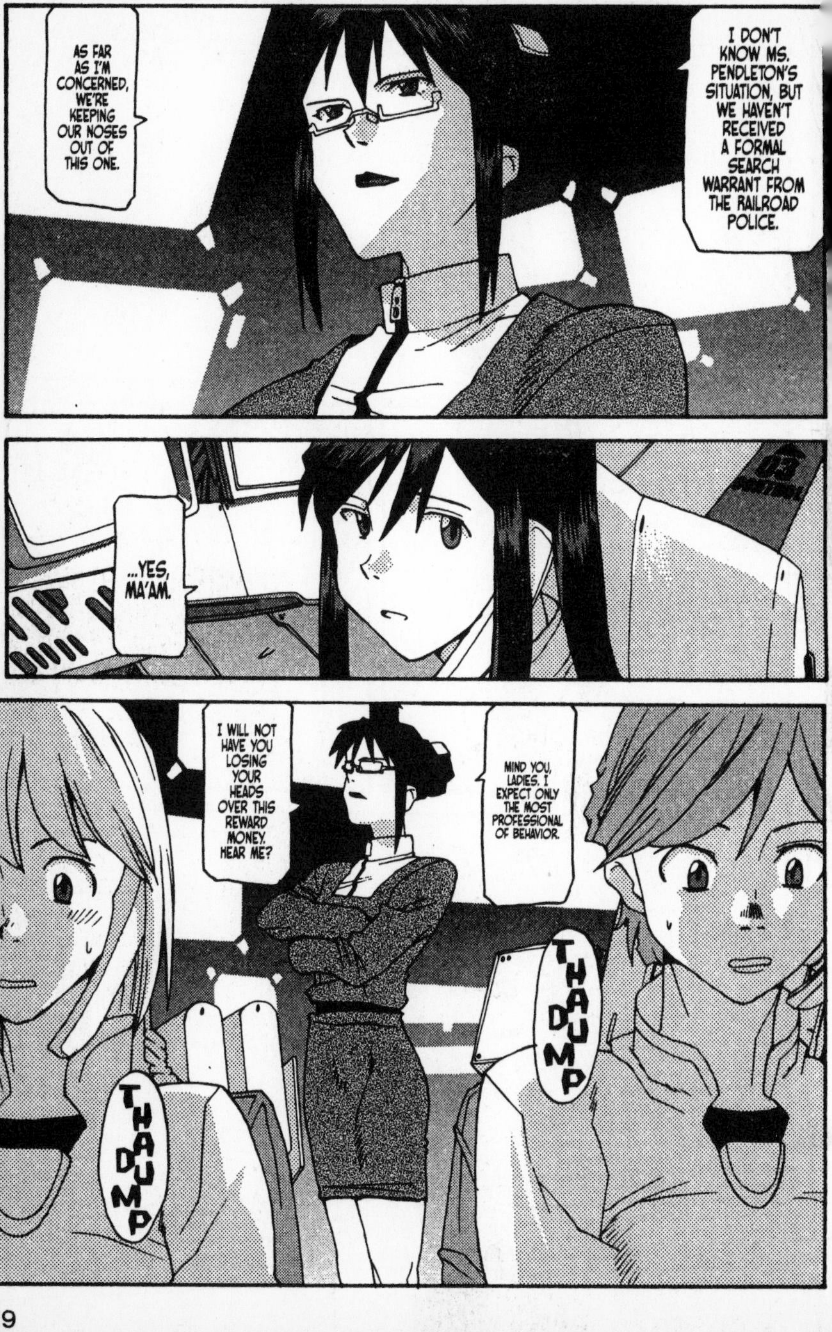
I DON'T KNOW MS. PENDLETON'S SITUATION, BUT WE HAVEN'T RECEIVED A FORMAL SEARCH WARRANT FROM THE RAILROAD POLICE.
AS FAR AS I'M CONCERNED, WE'RE KEEPING OUR NOSES OUT OF THIS ONE.
...YES, MA'AM.
MIND YOU, LADIES. I EXPECT ONLY THE MOST PROFESSIONAL OF BEHAVIOR.
I WILL NOT HAVE YOU LOSING YOUR HEADS OVER THIS REWARD MONEY. HEAR ME?
THADUMP
THADUMP

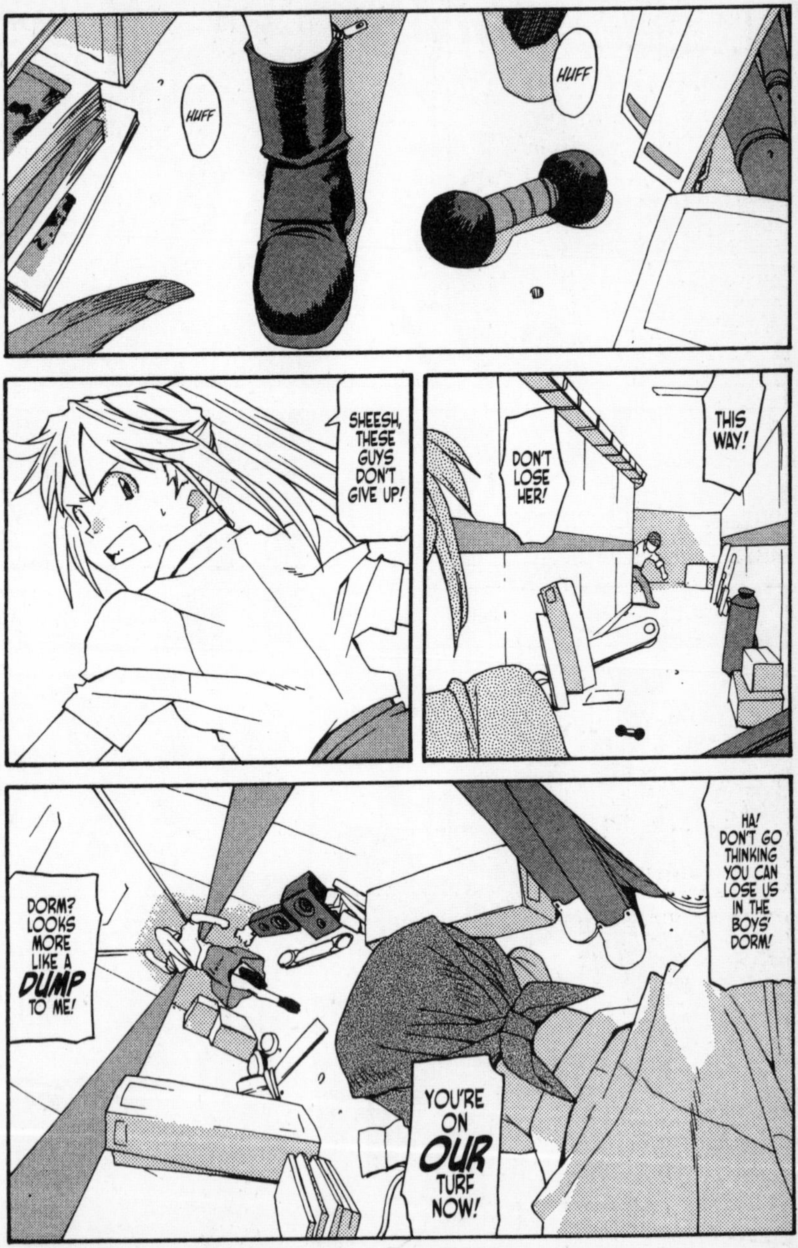
HUFF
HUFF
THIS WAY!
DON'T LOSE HER!
SHEESH, THESE GUYS DON'T GIVE UP!
HA! DON'T GO THINKING YOU CAN LOSE US IN THE BOYS' DORM!
YOU'RE ON OUR TURF NOW!
DORM? LOOKS MORE LIKE A DUMP TO ME!

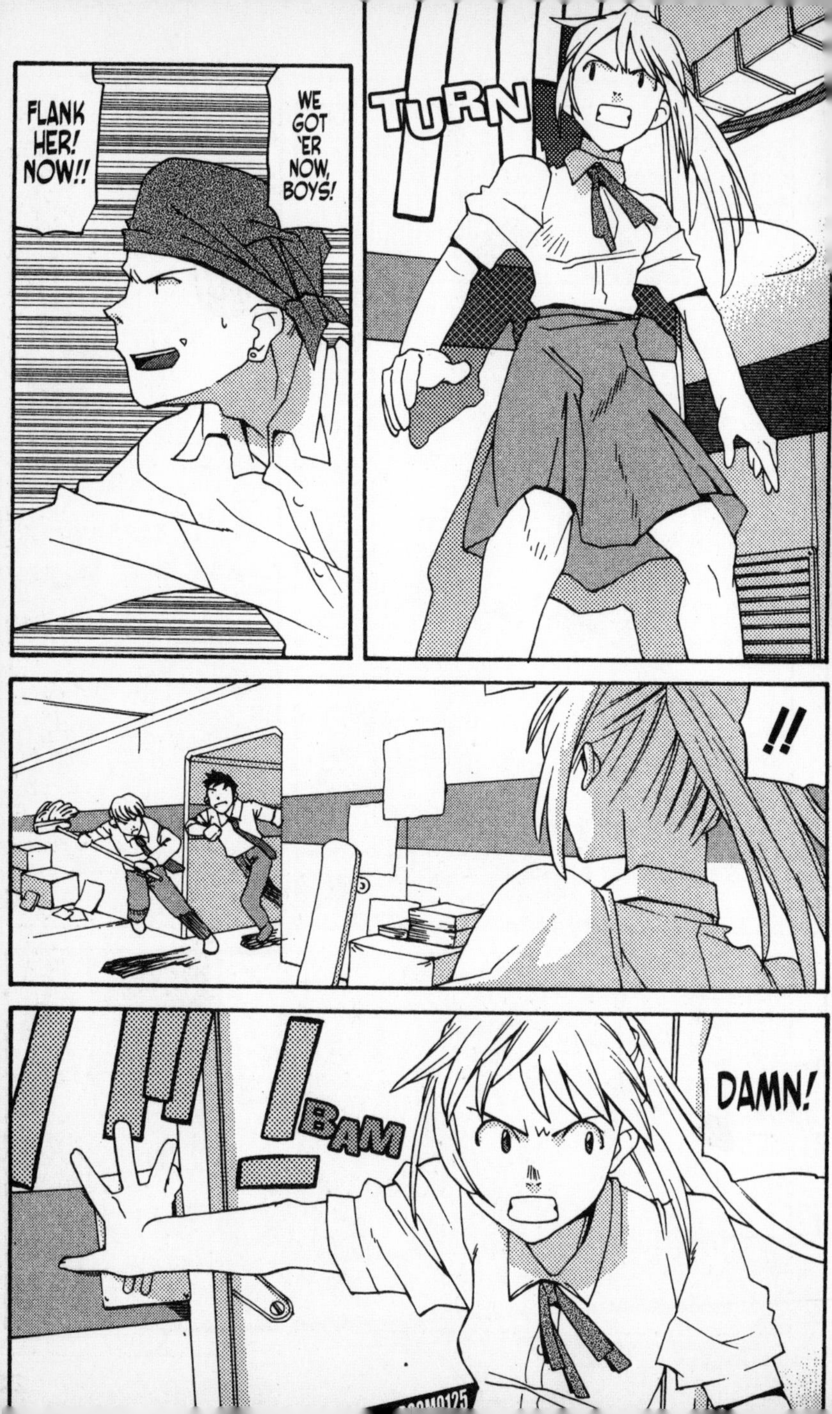
TURN
WE GOT 'ER NOW, BOYS!
FLANK HER! NOW!!
!!
DAMN!
BAM

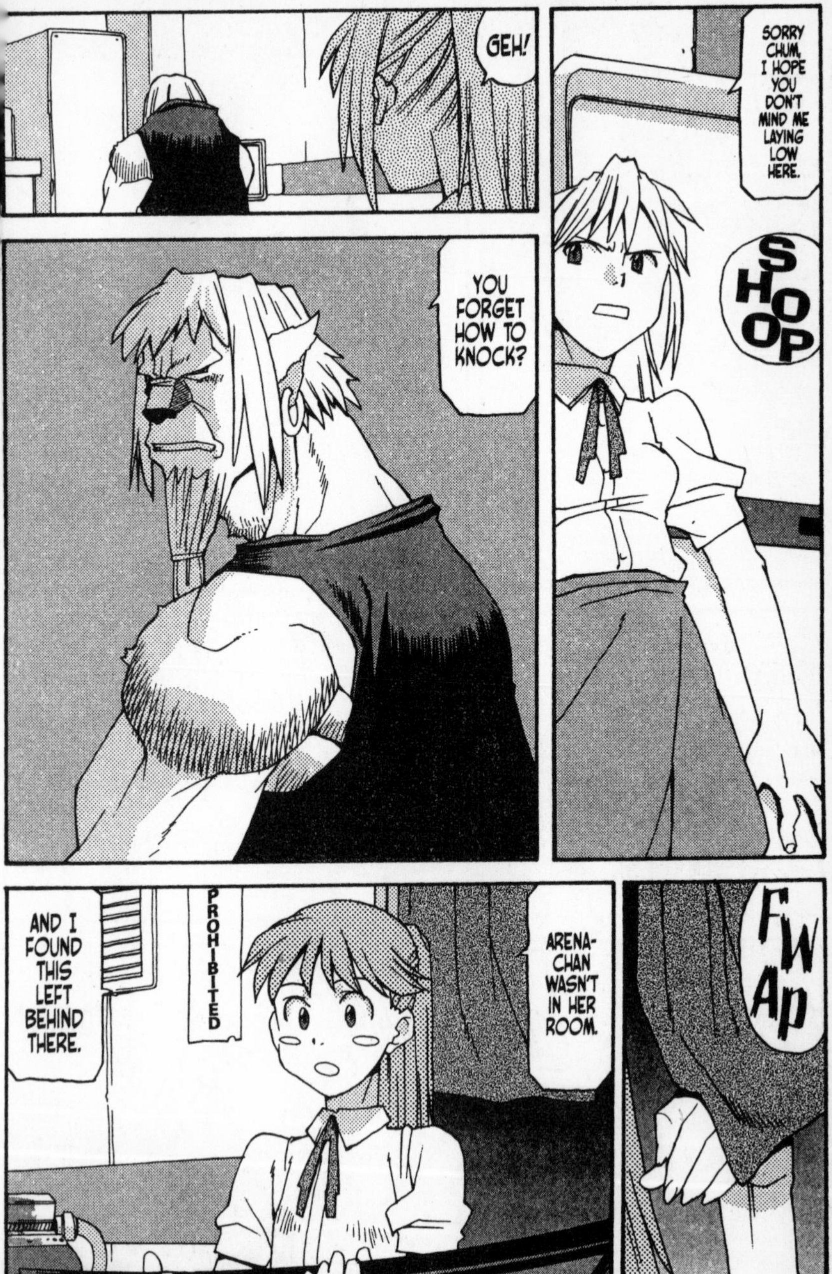
SORRY CHUM, I HOPE YOU DON'T MIND ME LAYING LOW HERE.
SHOOP
GEH!
YOU FORGET HOW TO KNOCK?
FWAp
ARENA-CHAN WASN'T IN HER ROOM.
PROHIBITED
AND I FOUND THIS LEFT BEHIND THERE.

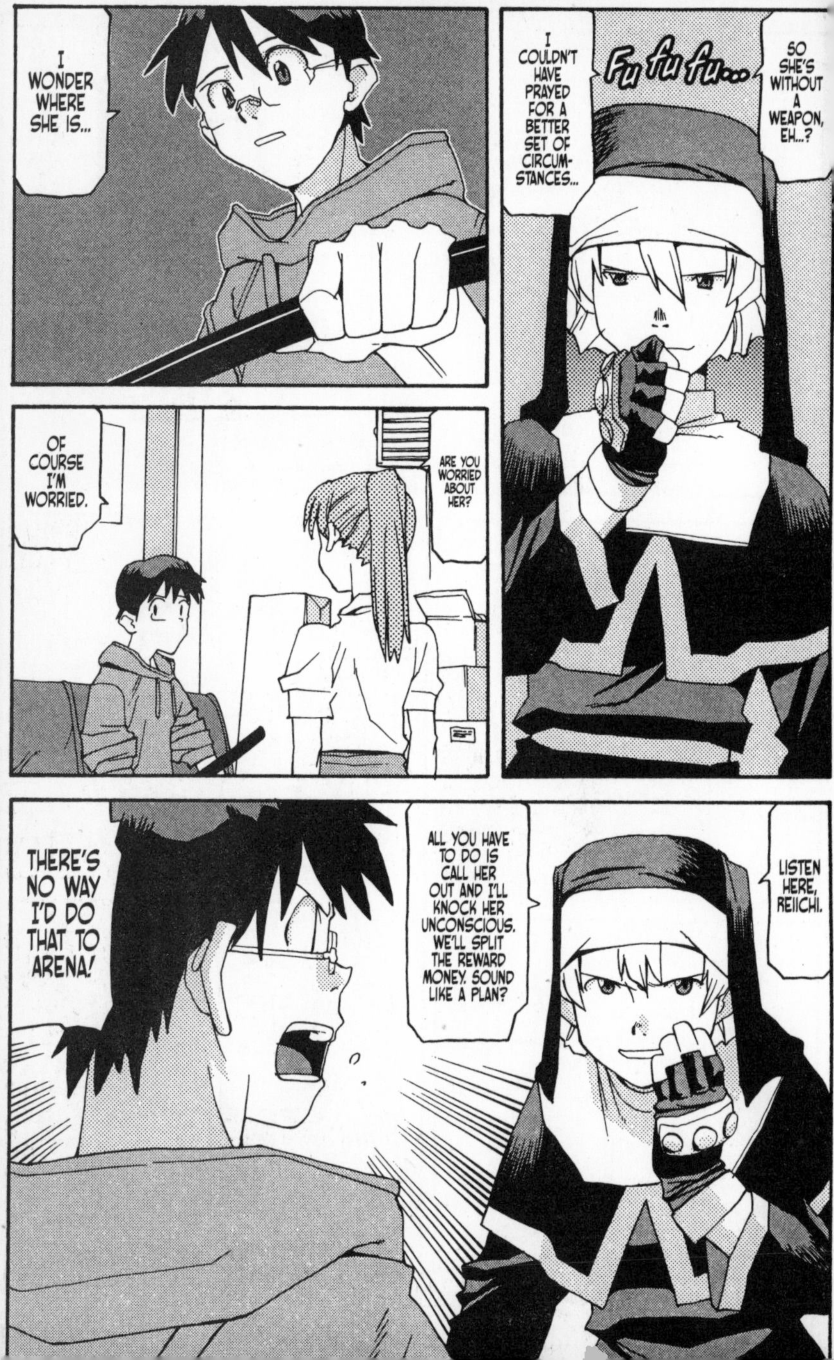
SO SHE'S WITHOUT A WEAPON, EH...?
Fu fu fu...
I COULDN'T HAVE PRAYED FOR A BETTER SET OF CIRCUMSTANCES...
I WONDER WHERE SHE IS...
ARE YOU WORRIED ABOUT HER?
OF COURSE I'M WORRIED.
LISTEN HERE, REIICHI.
ALL YOU HAVE TO DO IS CALL HER OUT AND I'LL KNOCK HER UNCONSCIOUS. WE'LL SPLIT THE REWARD MONEY. SOUND LIKE A PLAN?
THERE'S NO WAY I'D DO THAT TO ARENA!

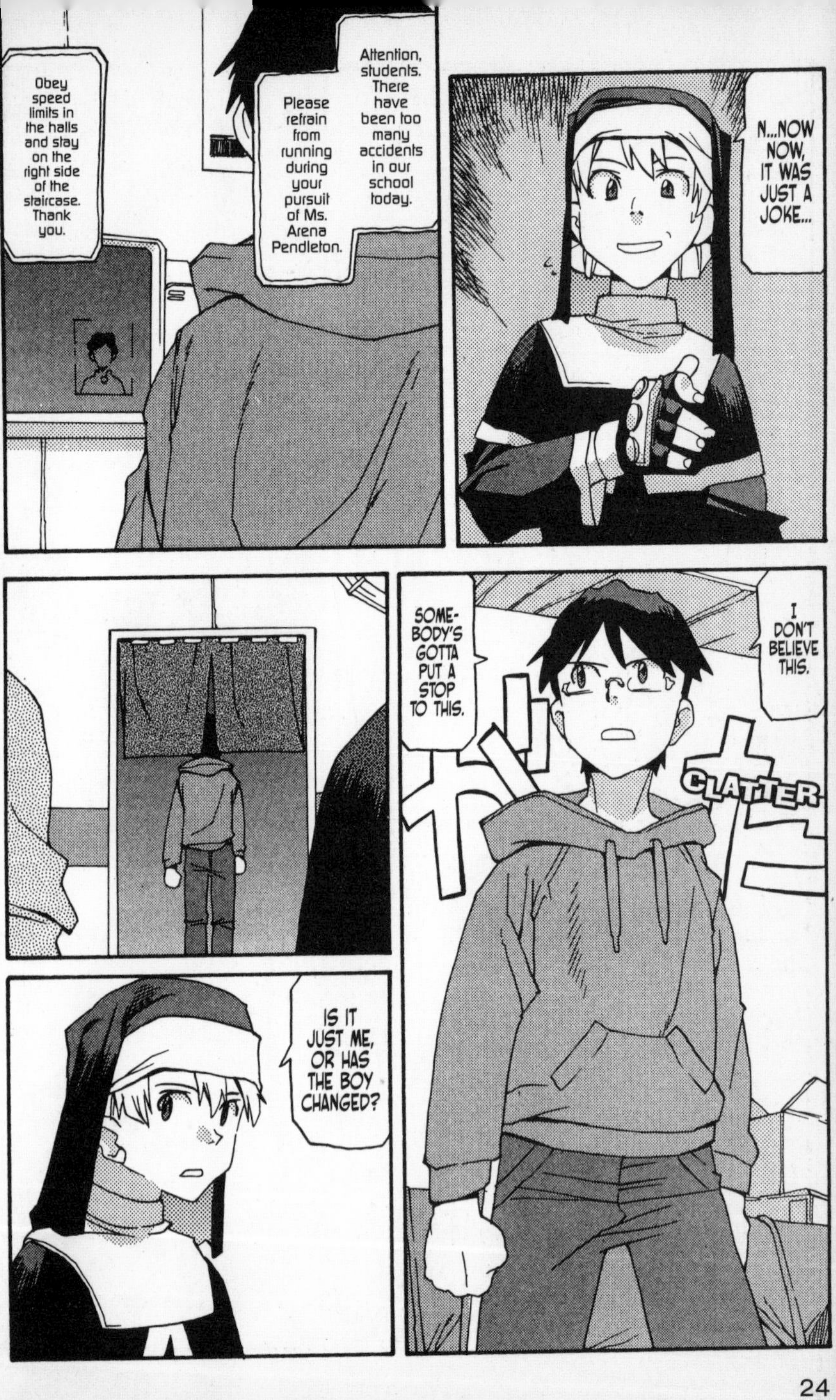
N...NOW NOW, IT WAS JUST A JOKE...
Attention, students. There have been too many accidents in our school today.
Please refrain from running during your pursuit of Ms. Arena Pendleton.
Obey speed limits in the halls and stay on the right side of the staircase. Thank you.
I DON'T BELIEVE THIS.
SOME-BODY'S GOTTA PUT A STOP TO THIS.
CLATTER
IS IT JUST ME, OR HAS THE BOY CHANGED?

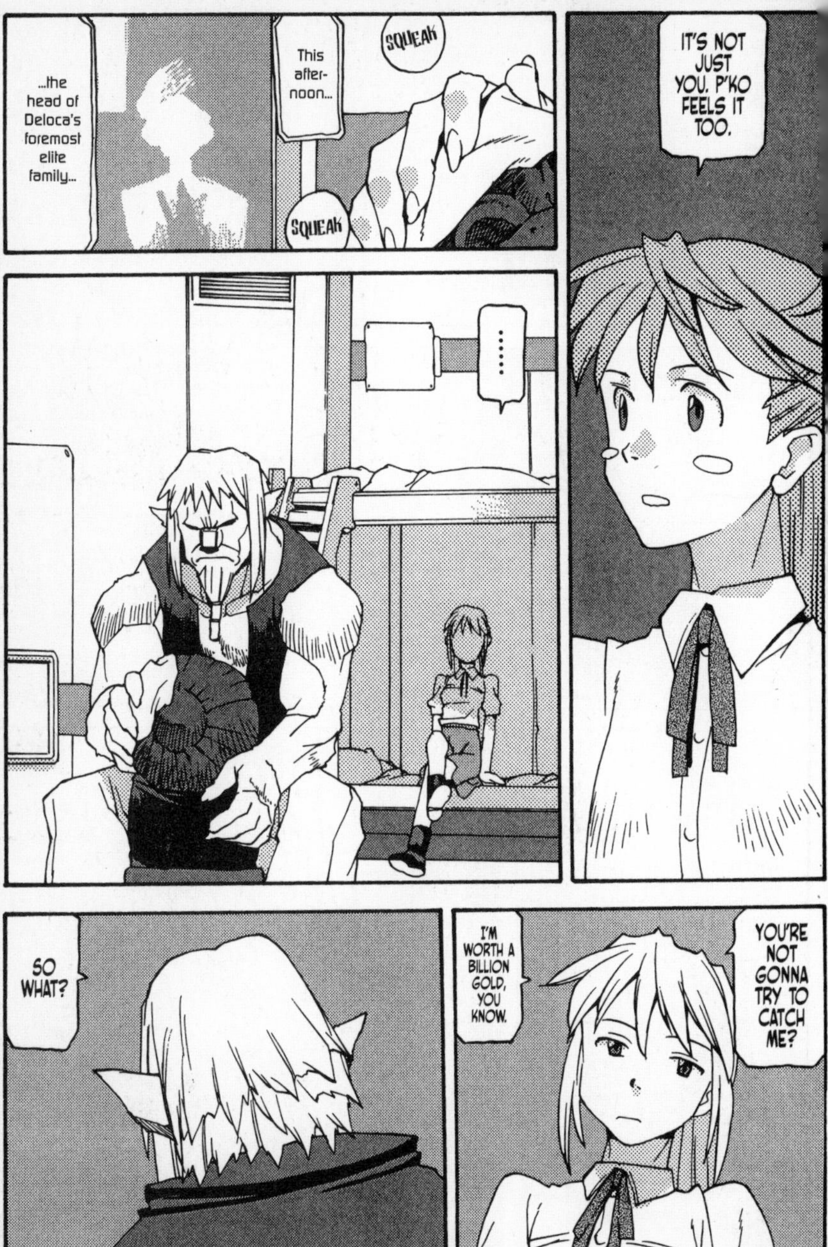
IT'S NOT JUST YOU. P'KO FEELS IT TOO.
SQUEAK
This after-noon...
SQUEAK
...the head of Deloca's foremost elite family...
......
YOU'RE NOT GONNA TRY TO CATCH ME?
I'M WORTH A BILLION GOLD, YOU KNOW.
SO WHAT?

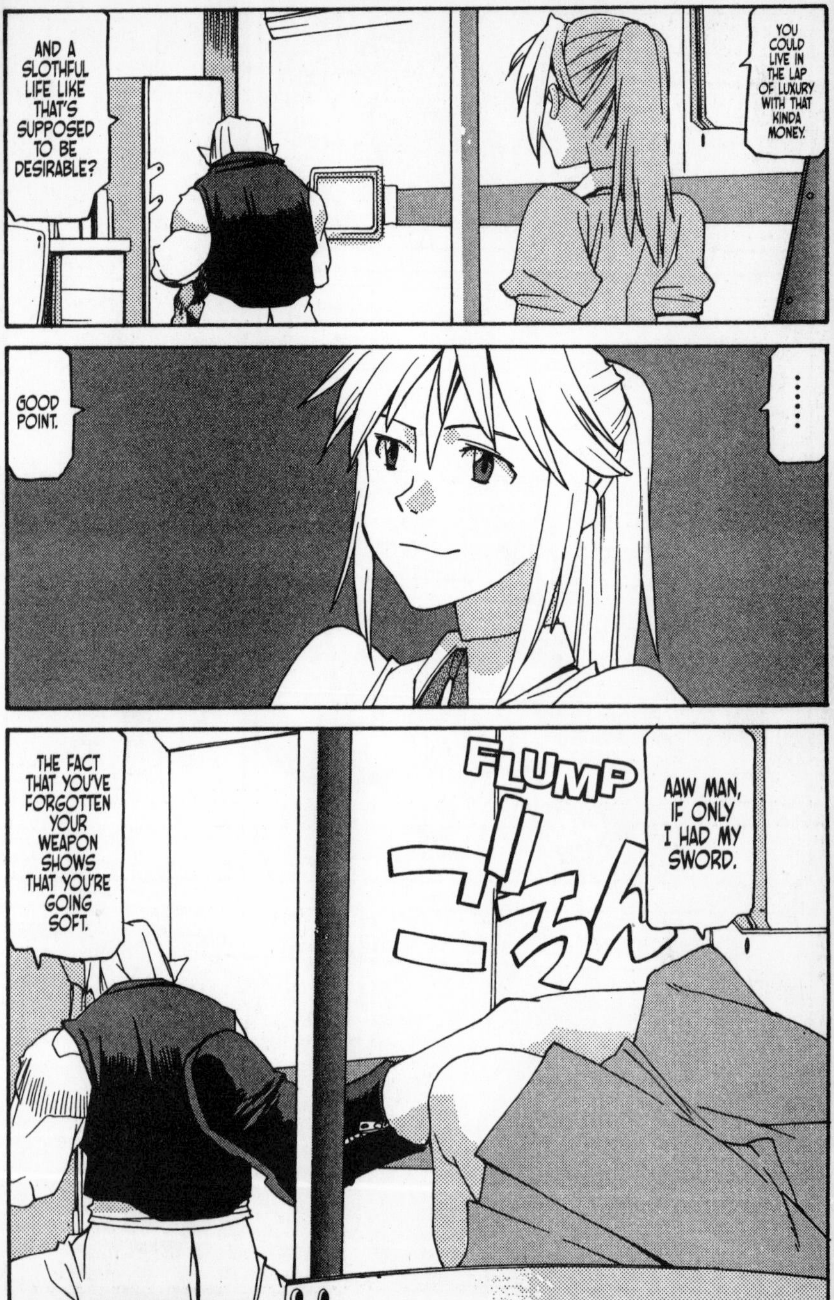
YOU COULD LIVE IN THE LAP OF LUXURY WITH THAT KINDA MONEY.
AND A SLOTHFUL LIFE LIKE THAT'S SUPPOSED TO BE DESIRABLE?
......
GOOD POINT.
AAW MAN, IF ONLY I HAD MY SWORD.
FLUMP
ごろん
THE FACT THAT YOU'VE FORGOTTEN YOUR WEAPON SHOWS THAT YOU'RE GOING SOFT.

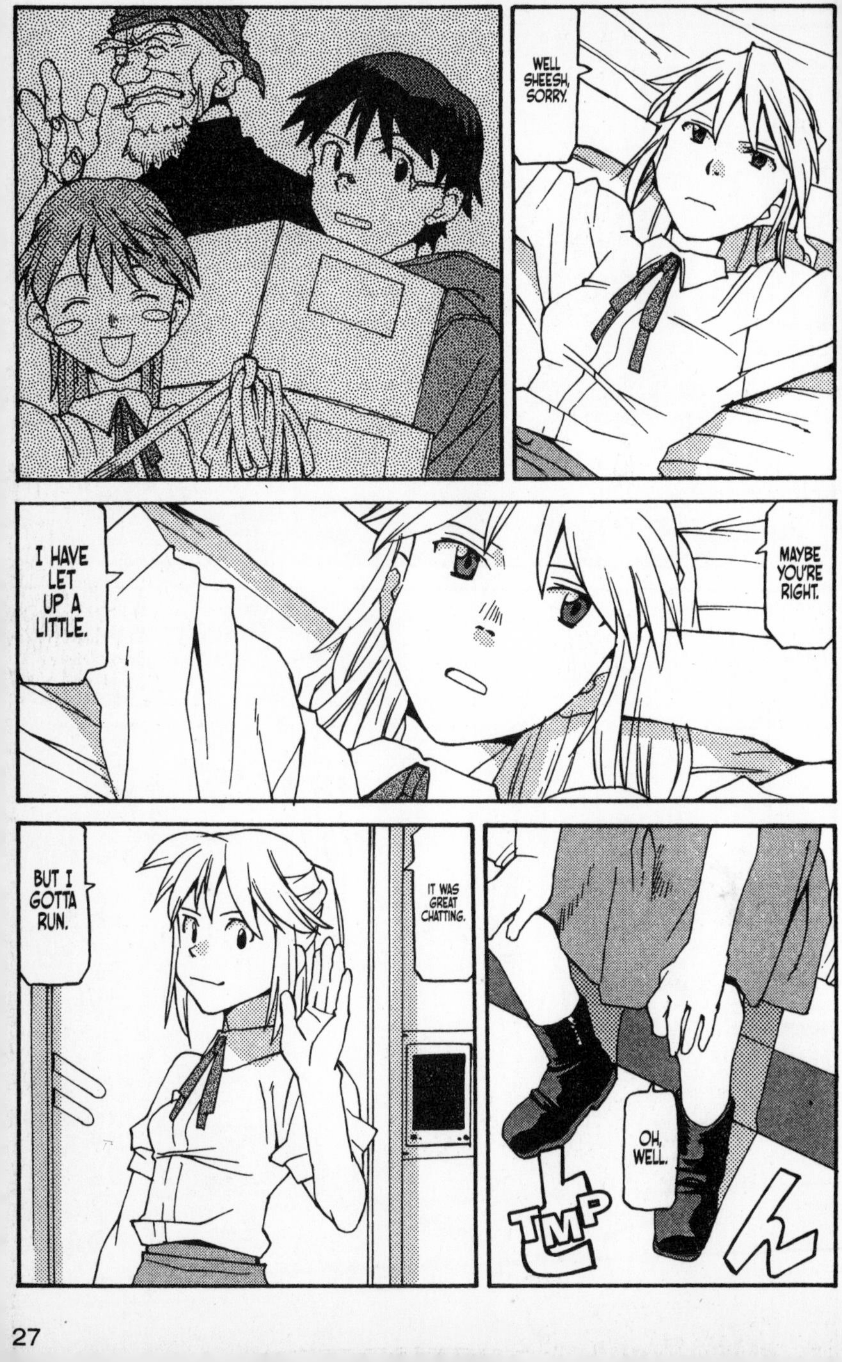
WELL SHEESH, SORRY.
MAYBE YOU'RE RIGHT.
I HAVE LET UP A LITTLE.
OH, WELL.
TMP
IT WAS GREAT CHATTING.
BUT I GOTTA RUN.

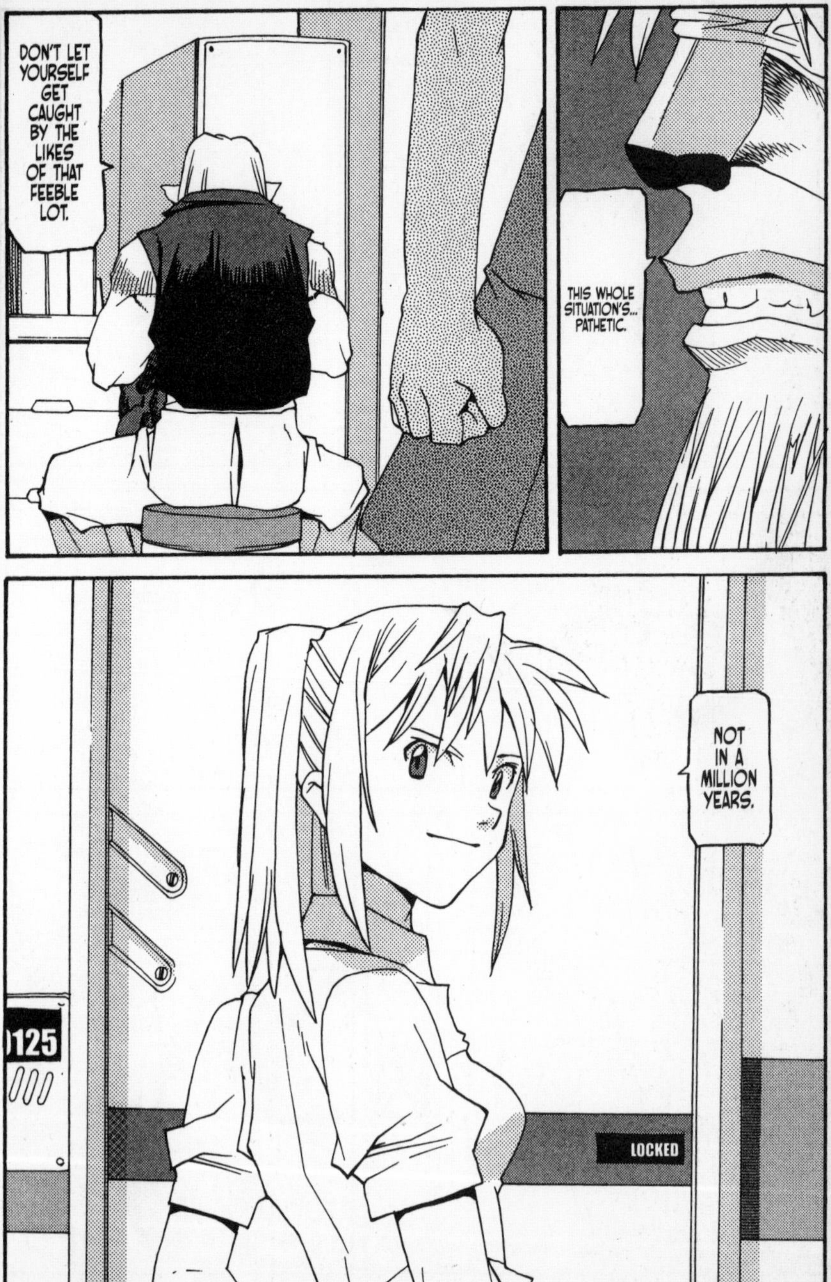
THIS WHOLE SITUATION'S... PATHETIC.
DON'T LET YOURSELF GET CAUGHT BY THE LIKES OF THAT FEEBLE LOT.
NOT IN A MILLION YEARS.
LOCKED

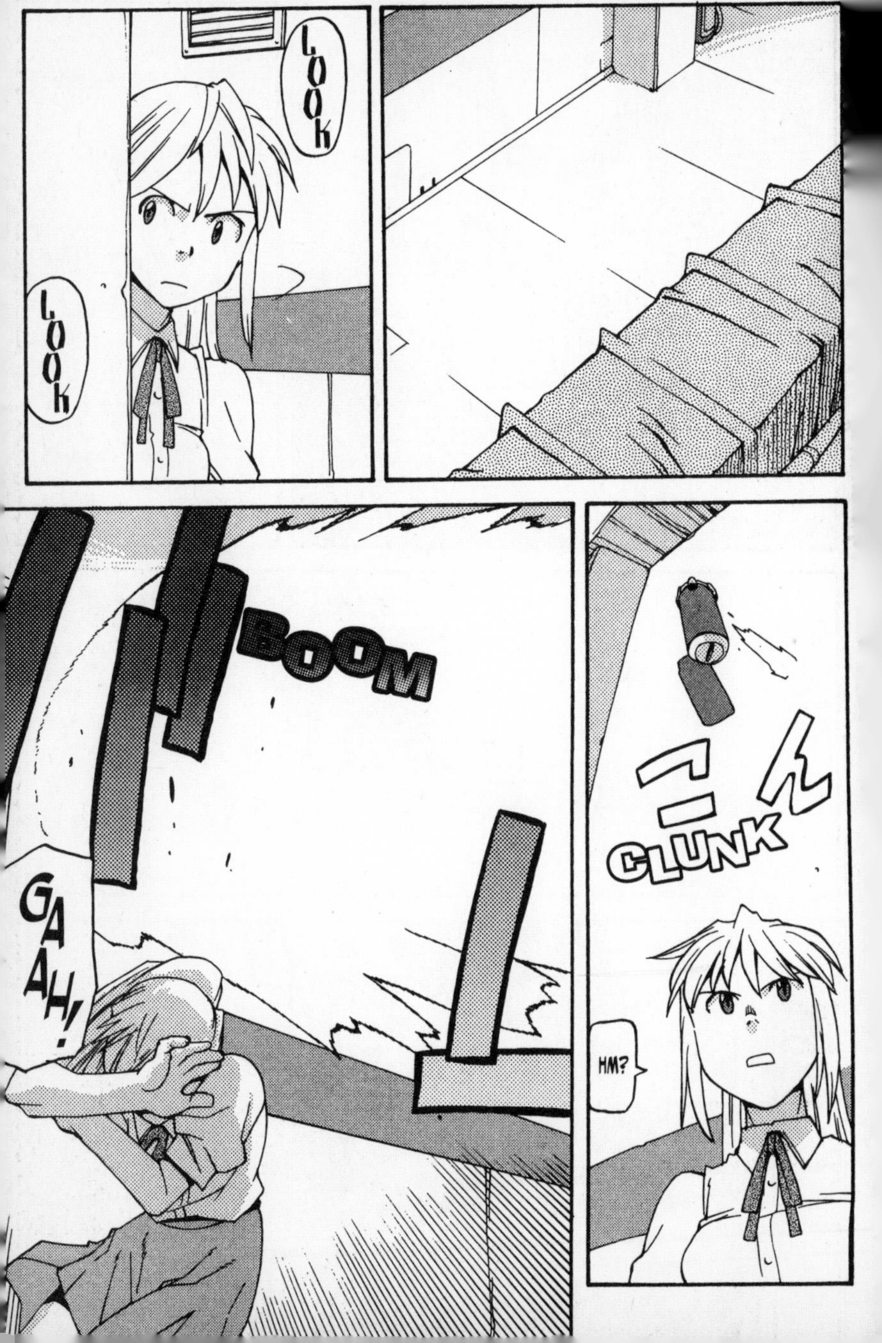
LOOK
LOOK
CLUNK
HM?
BOOM
GAAAH!

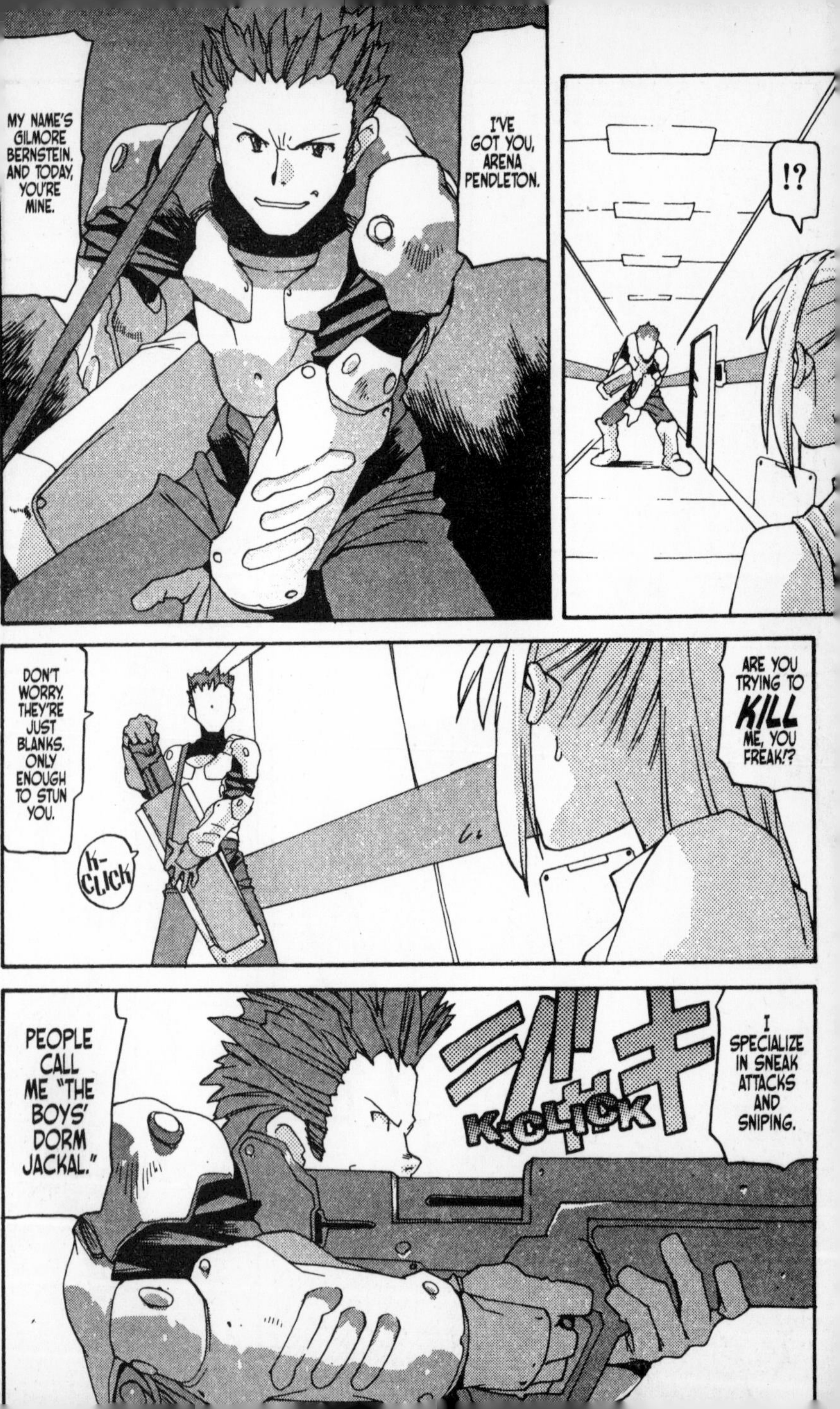
!?
I'VE GOT YOU, ARENA PENDLETON.
MY NAME'S GILMORE BERNSTEIN. AND TODAY, YOU'RE MINE.
ARE YOU TRYING TO KILL ME, YOU FREAK!?
DON'T WORRY. THEY'RE JUST BLANKS. ONLY ENOUGH TO STUN YOU.
K-CLICK
I SPECIALIZE IN SNEAK ATTACKS AND SNIPING.
ジャキ
K-CLICK
PEOPLE CALL ME "THE BOYS' DORM JACKAL."

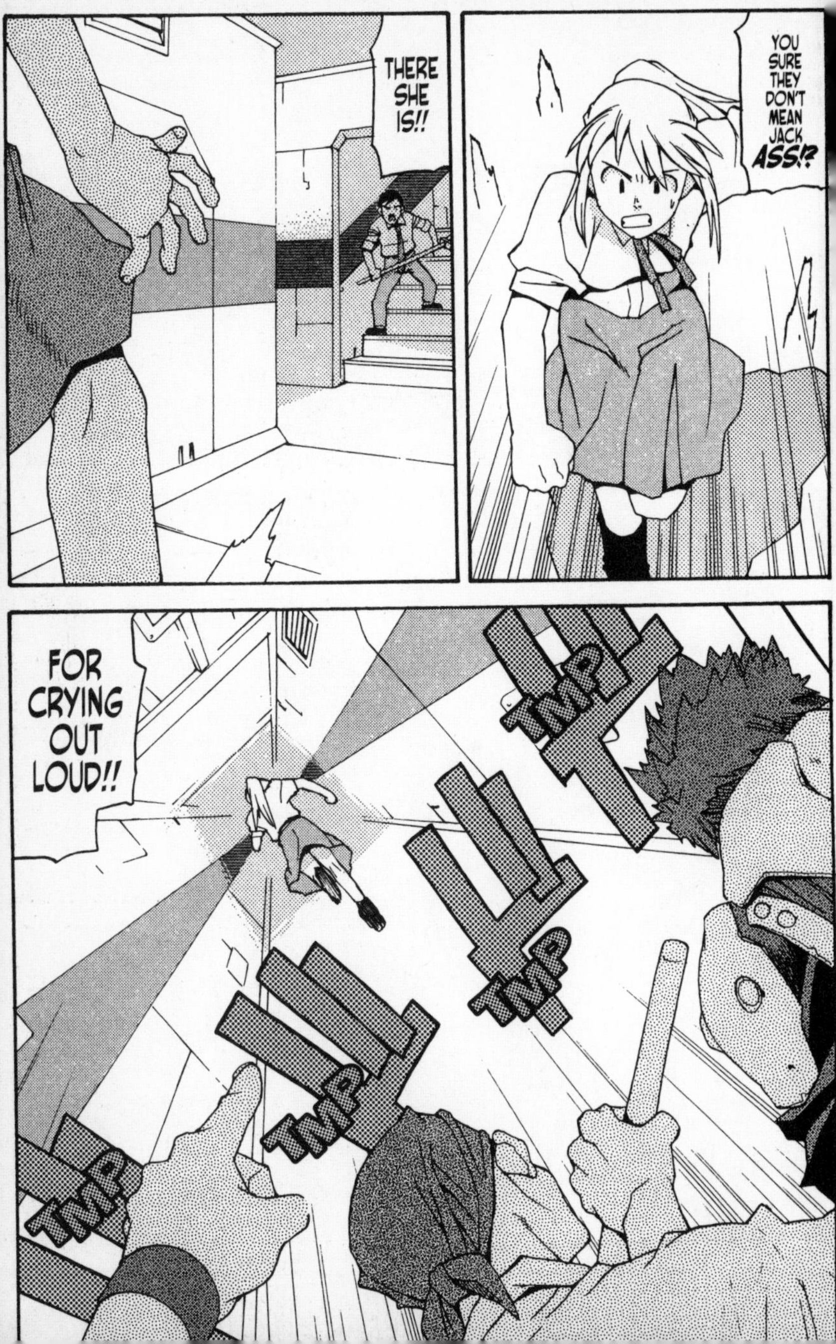
YOU SURE THEY DON'T MEAN JACK ASS!?
THERE SHE IS!!
FOR CRYING OUT LOUD!!
TMP
TMP
TMP
TMP

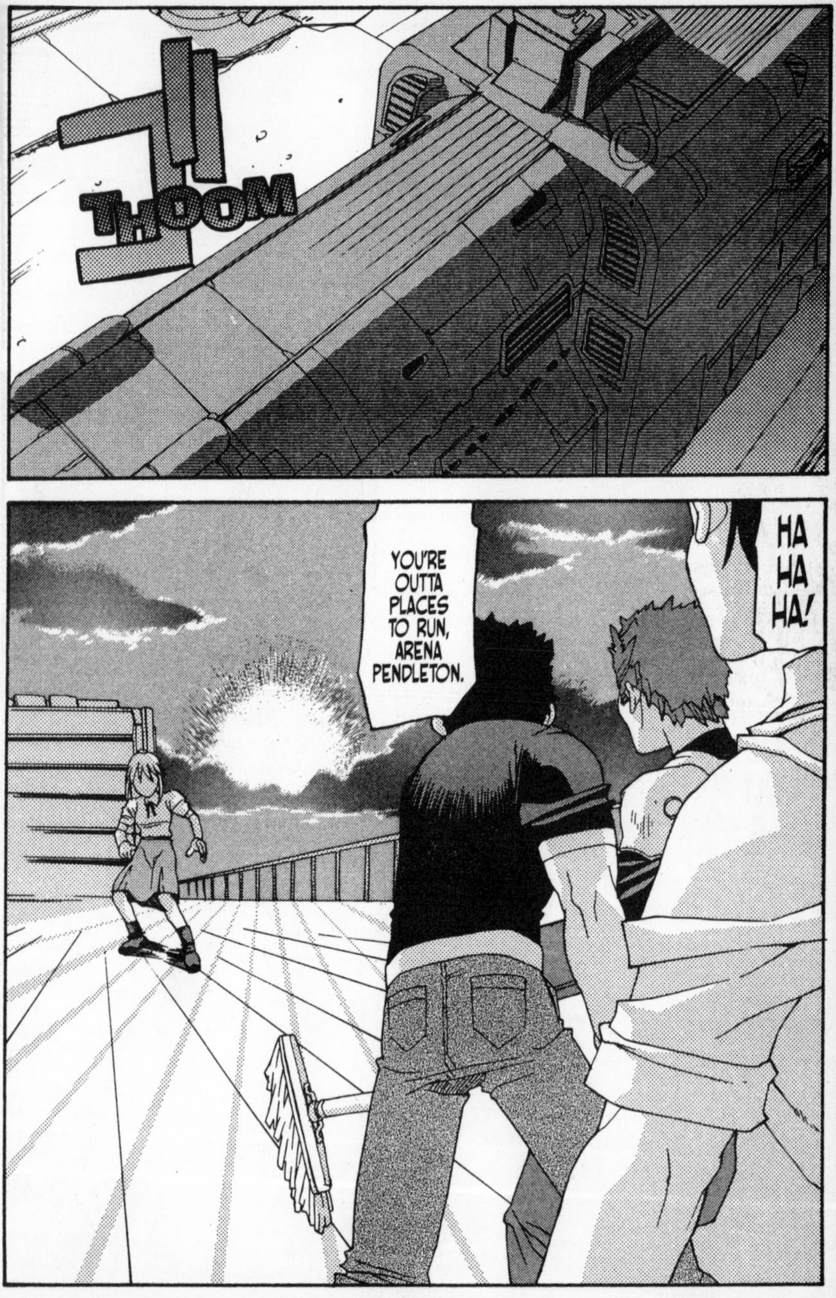
THOOM
HA HA HA!
YOU'RE OUTTA PLACES TO RUN, ARENA PENDLETON.

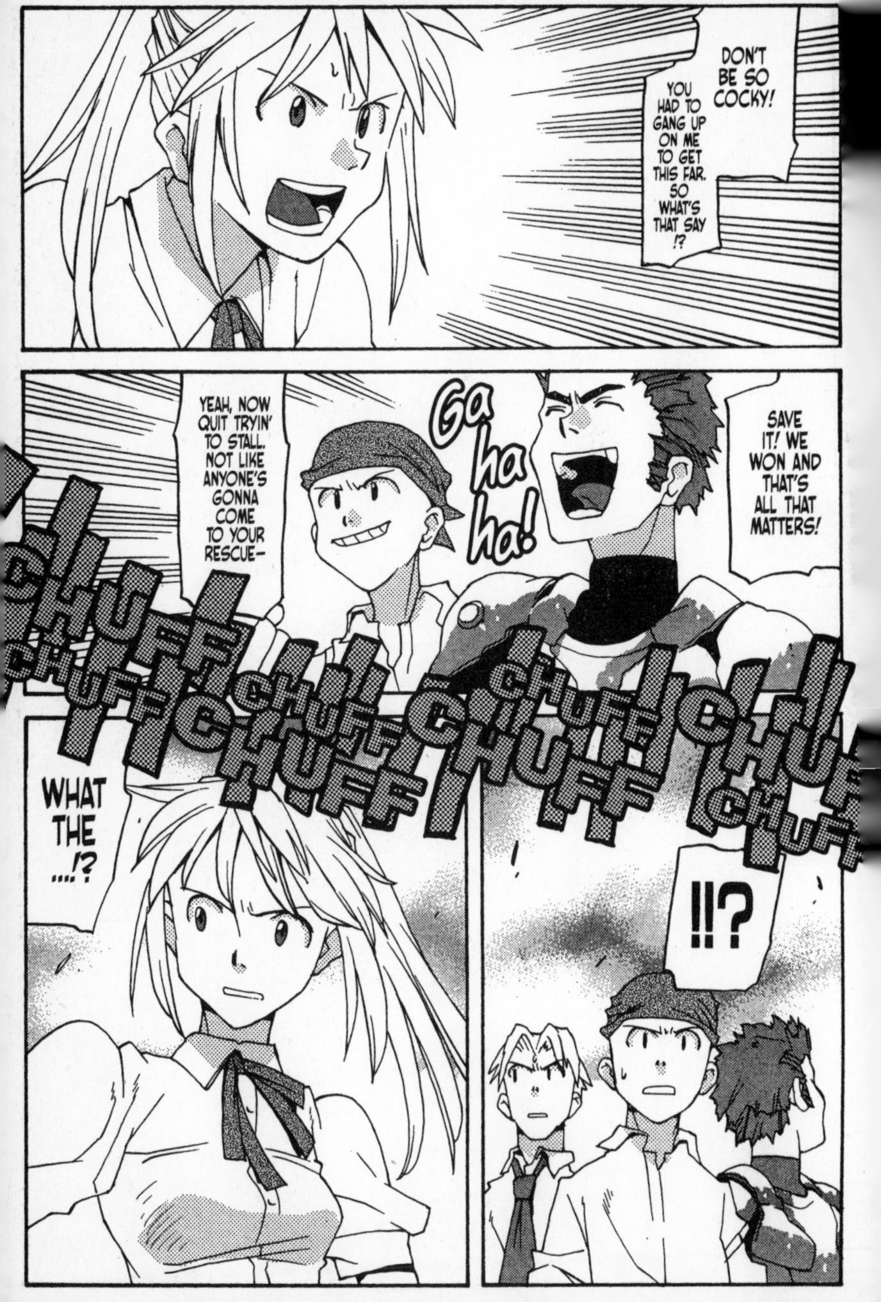
DON'T BE SO COCKY!
YOU HAD TO GANG UP ON ME TO GET THIS FAR. SO WHAT'S THAT SAY !?
SAVE IT! WE WON AND THAT'S ALL THAT MATTERS!
Ga ha ha!
YEAH, NOW QUIT TRYIN' TO STALL. NOT LIKE ANYONE'S GONNA COME TO YOUR RESCUE–
CHUFF CHUFF CHUFF CHUFF CHUFF CHUFF CHUFF CHUFF
!!?
WHAT THE ...!?

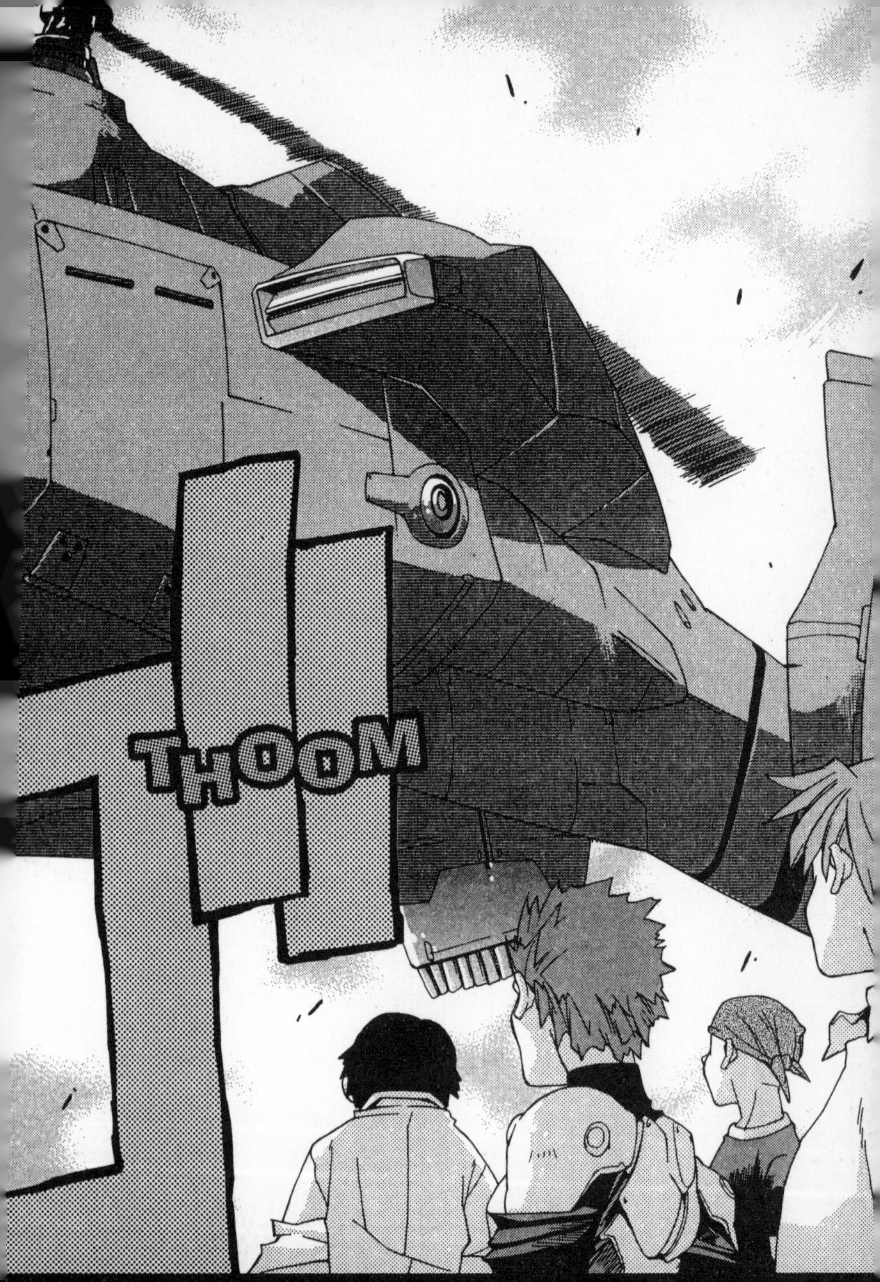
THOOM

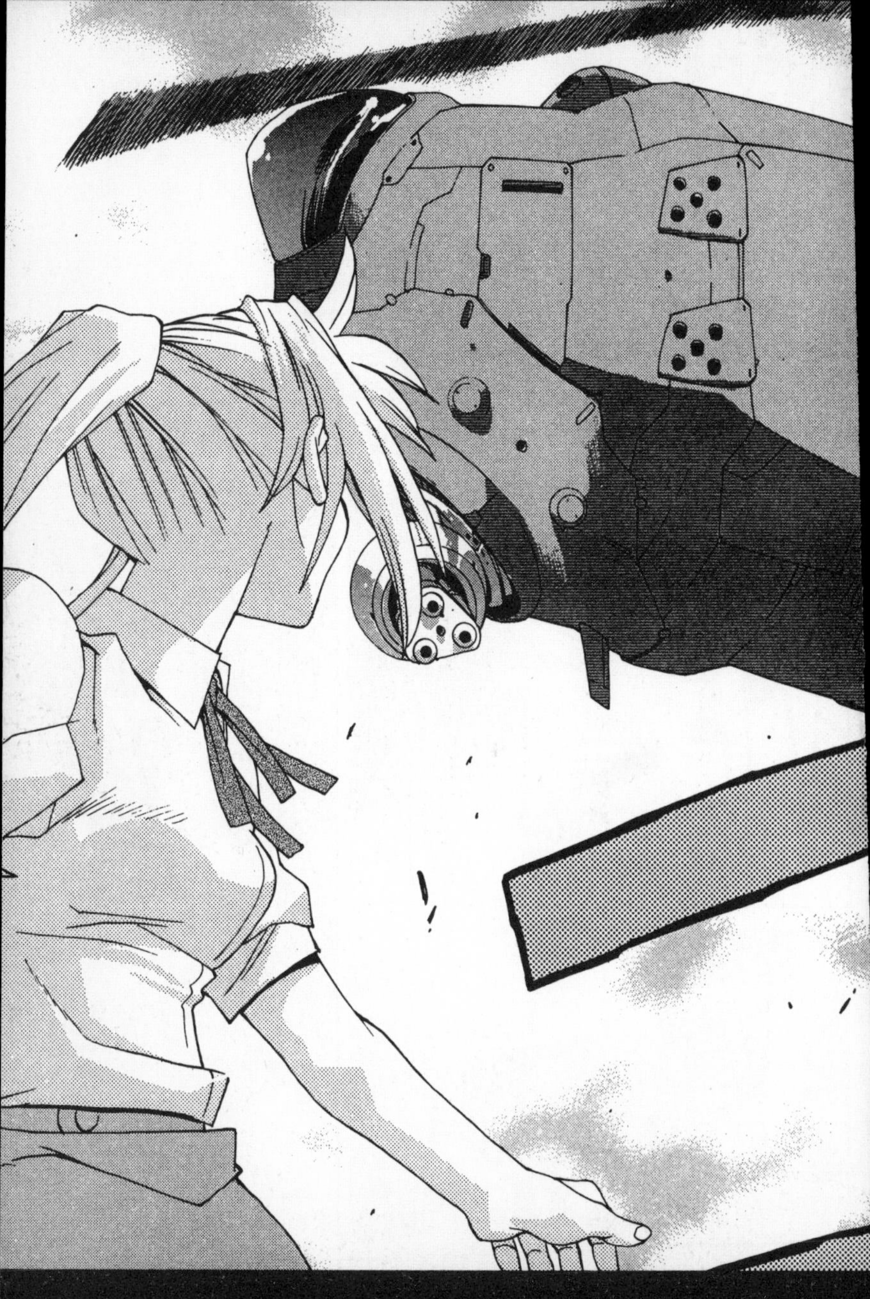

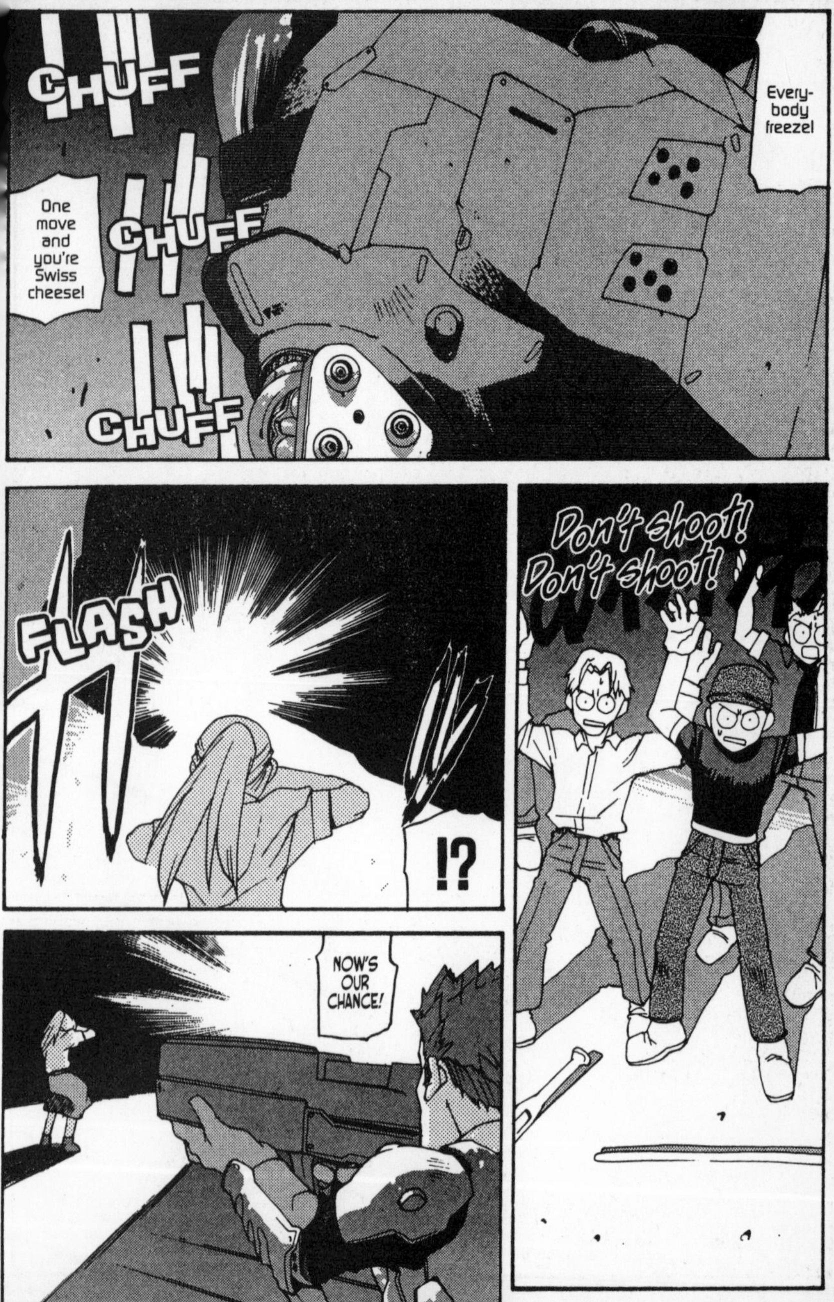
Every-body freeze!
CHUFF
One move and you're Swiss cheese!
CHUFF
CHUFF
Don't shoot! Don't shoot!
FLASH
!?
NOW'S OUR CHANCE!

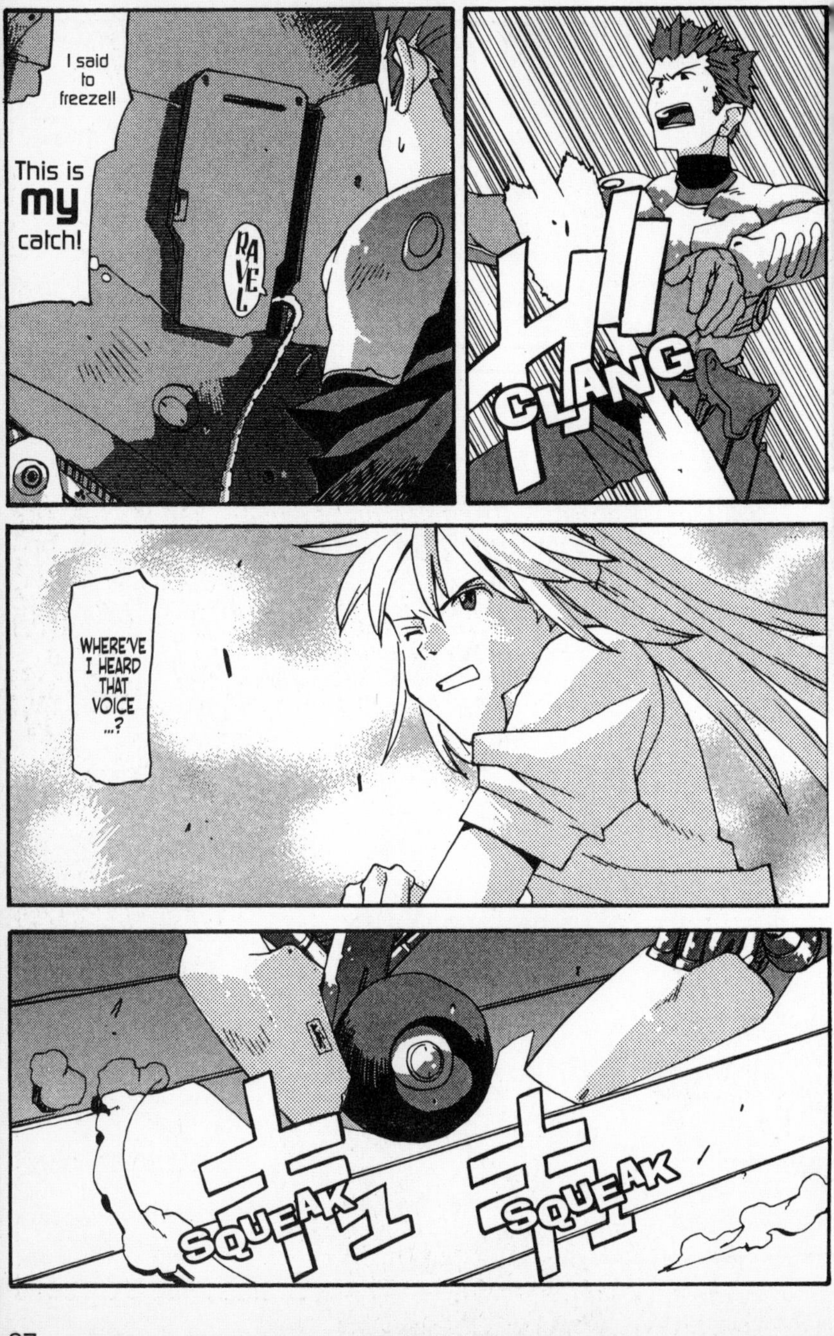
CLANG
I said to freeze!!
This is my catch!
RAVEL
WHERE'VE I HEARD THAT VOICE ...?
SQUEAK
SQUEAK

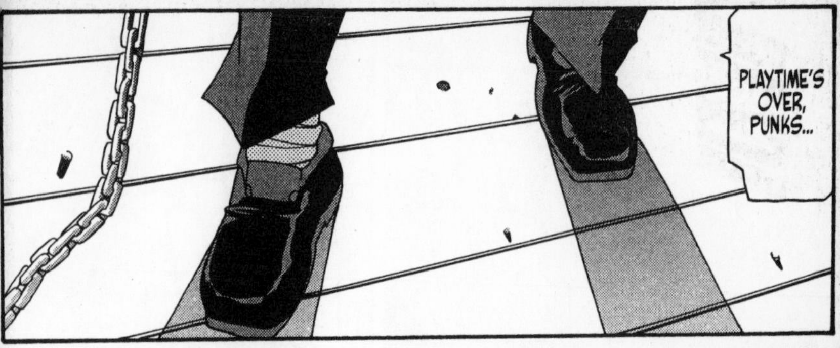
PLAYTIME'S OVER, PUNKS...

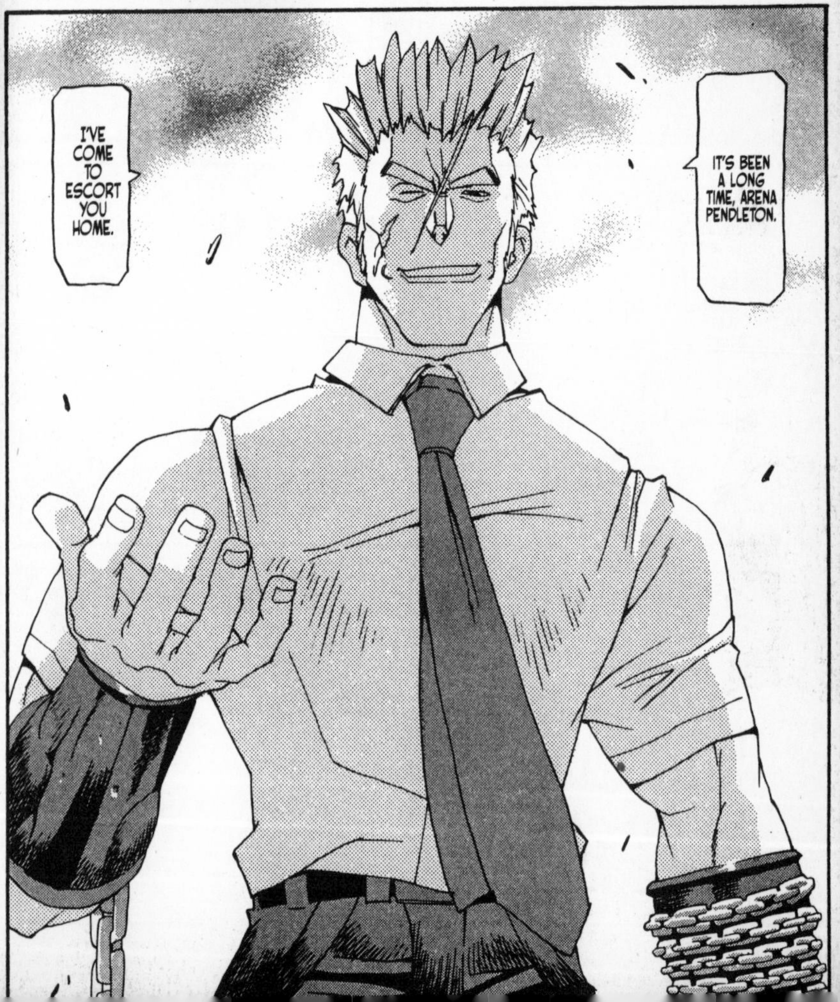
IT'S BEEN A LONG TIME, ARENA PENDLETON.
I'VE COME TO ESCORT YOU HOME.

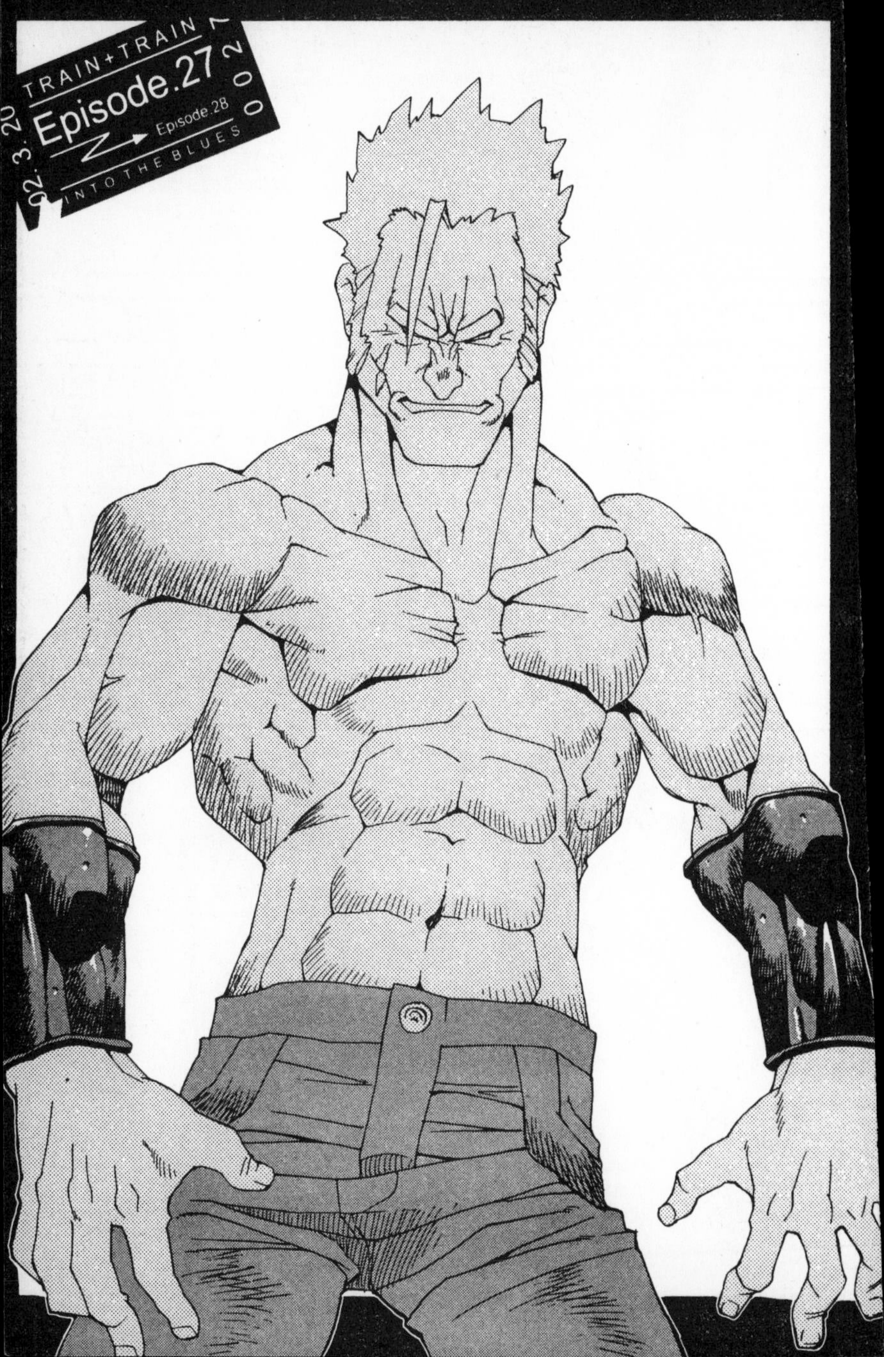
TRAIN+TRAIN
Episode.27
Episode.28
INTO THE BLUES
02. 3. 20
0027

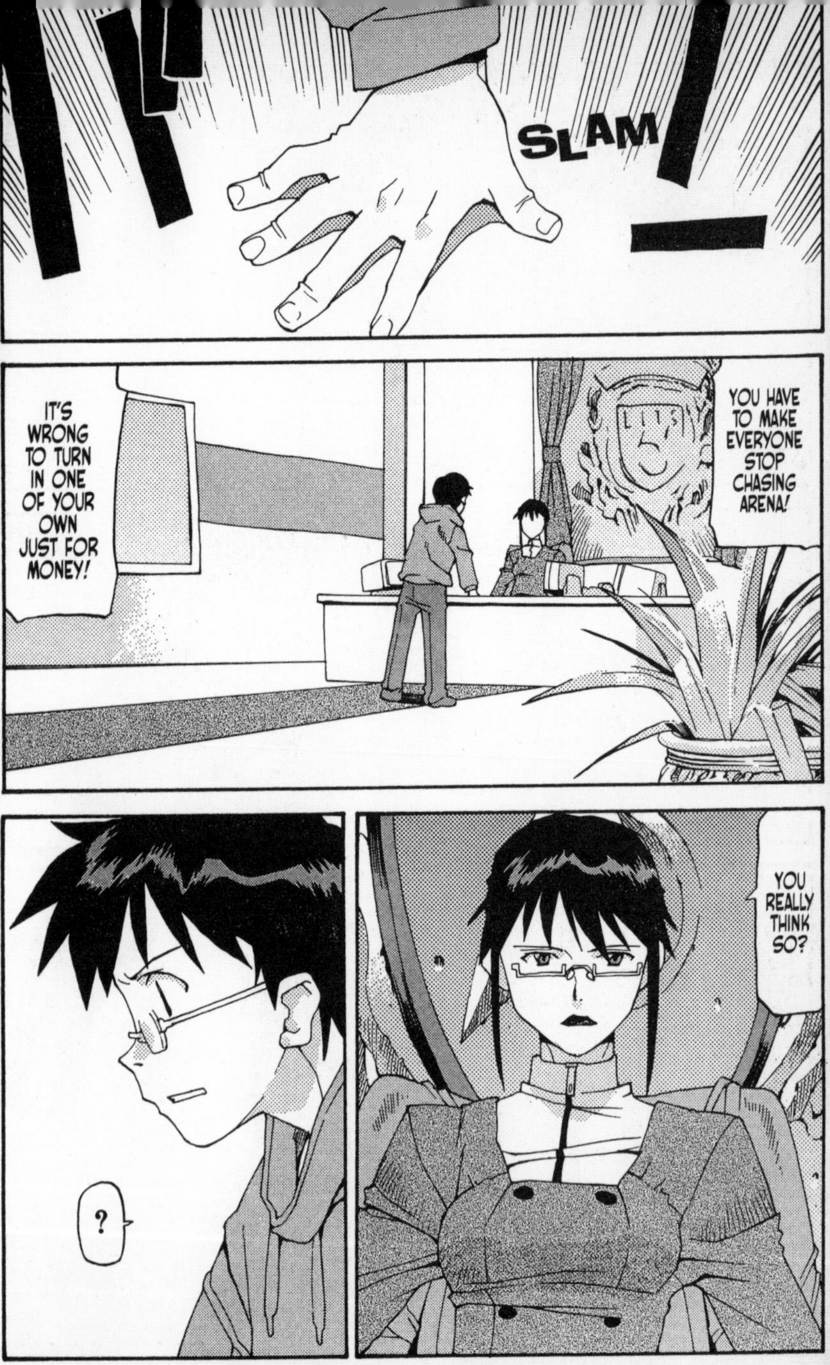
SLAM
YOU HAVE TO MAKE EVERYONE STOP CHASING ARENA!
IT'S WRONG TO TURN IN ONE OF YOUR OWN JUST FOR MONEY!
YOU REALLY THINK SO?
?

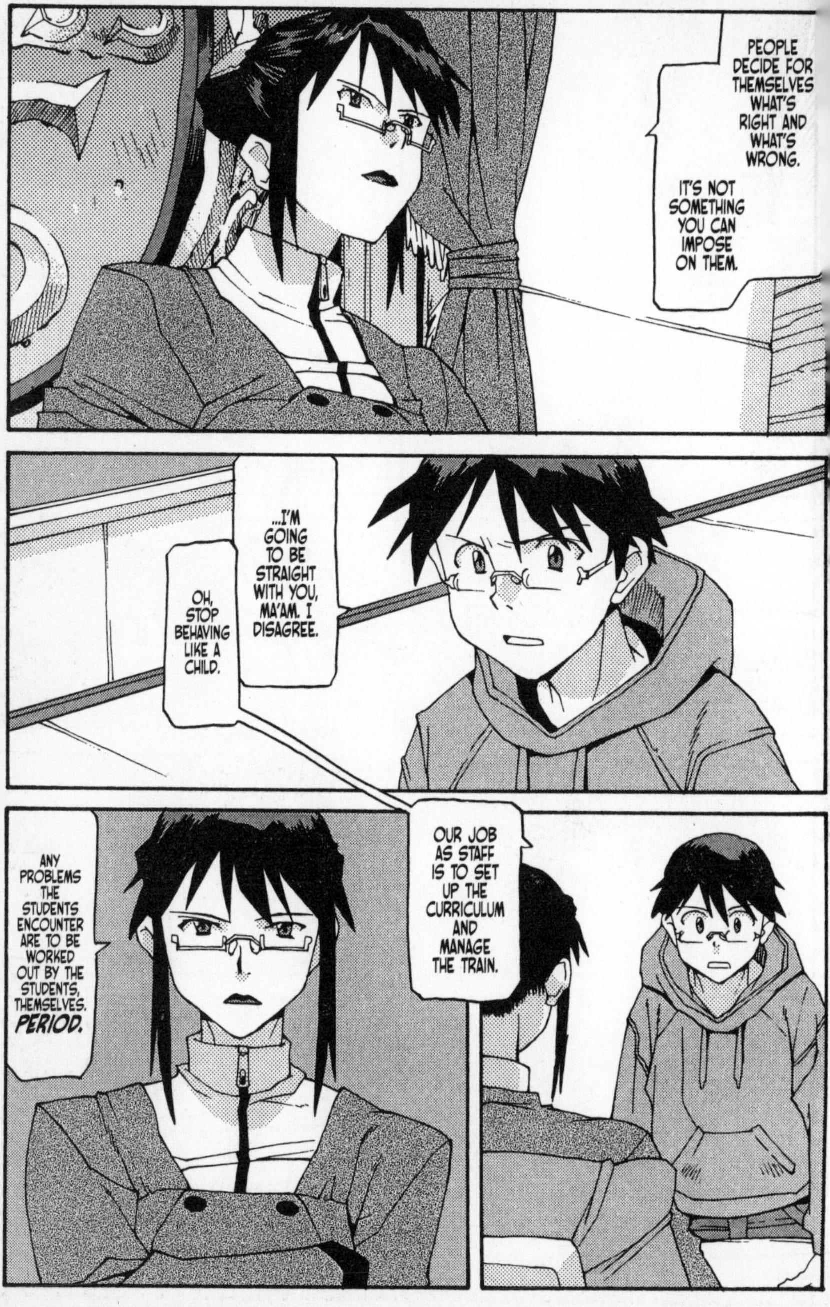
PEOPLE DECIDE FOR THEMSELVES WHAT'S RIGHT AND WHAT'S WRONG.
IT'S NOT SOMETHING YOU CAN IMPOSE ON THEM.
...I'M GOING TO BE STRAIGHT WITH YOU, MA'AM. I DISAGREE.
OH, STOP BEHAVING LIKE A CHILD.
OUR JOB AS STAFF IS TO SET UP THE CURRICULUM AND MANAGE THE TRAIN.
ANY PROBLEMS THE STUDENTS ENCOUNTER ARE TO BE WORKED OUT BY THE STUDENTS, THEMSELVES. *PERIOD.*

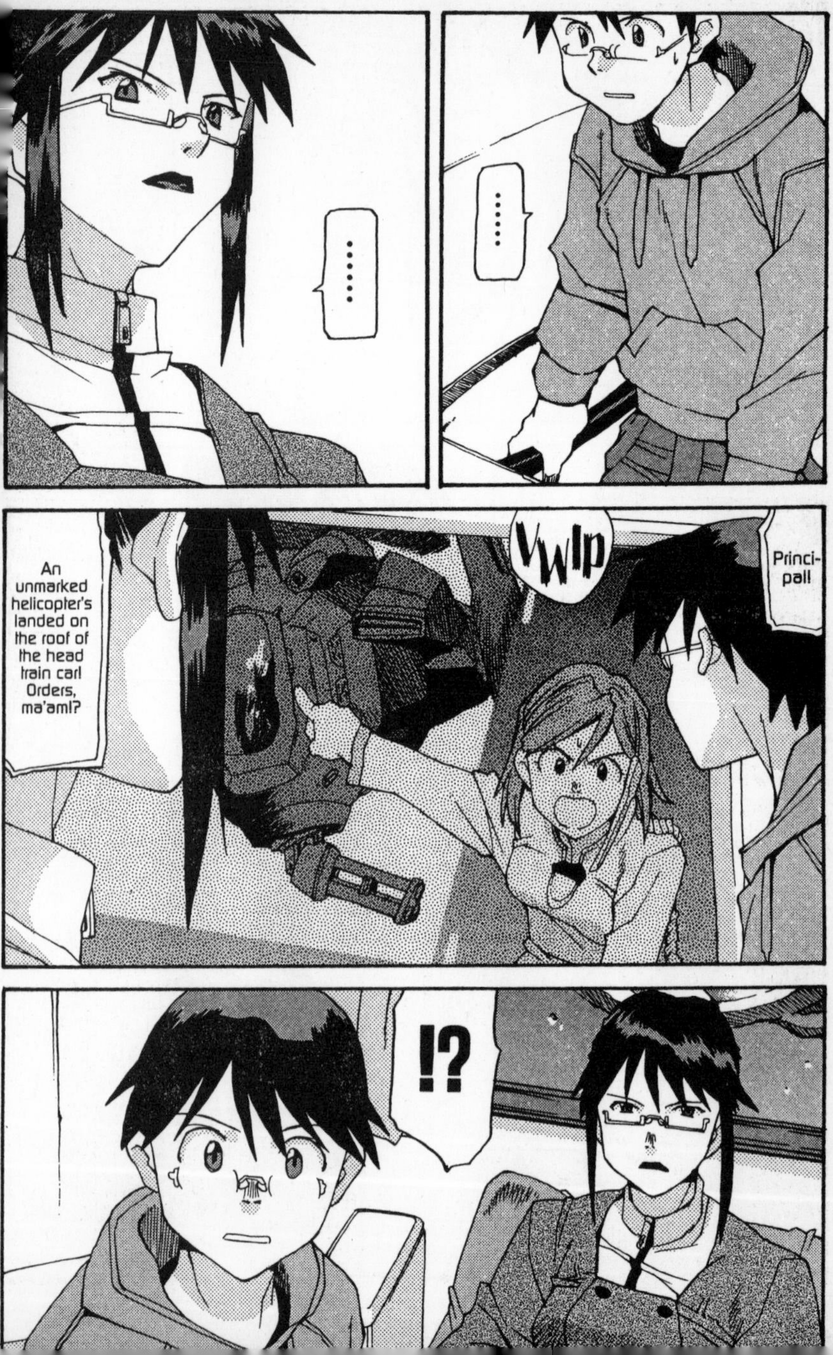
......
......
Princi-pal!
VWIP
An unmarked helicopter's landed on the roof of the head train car! Orders, ma'am!?
!?

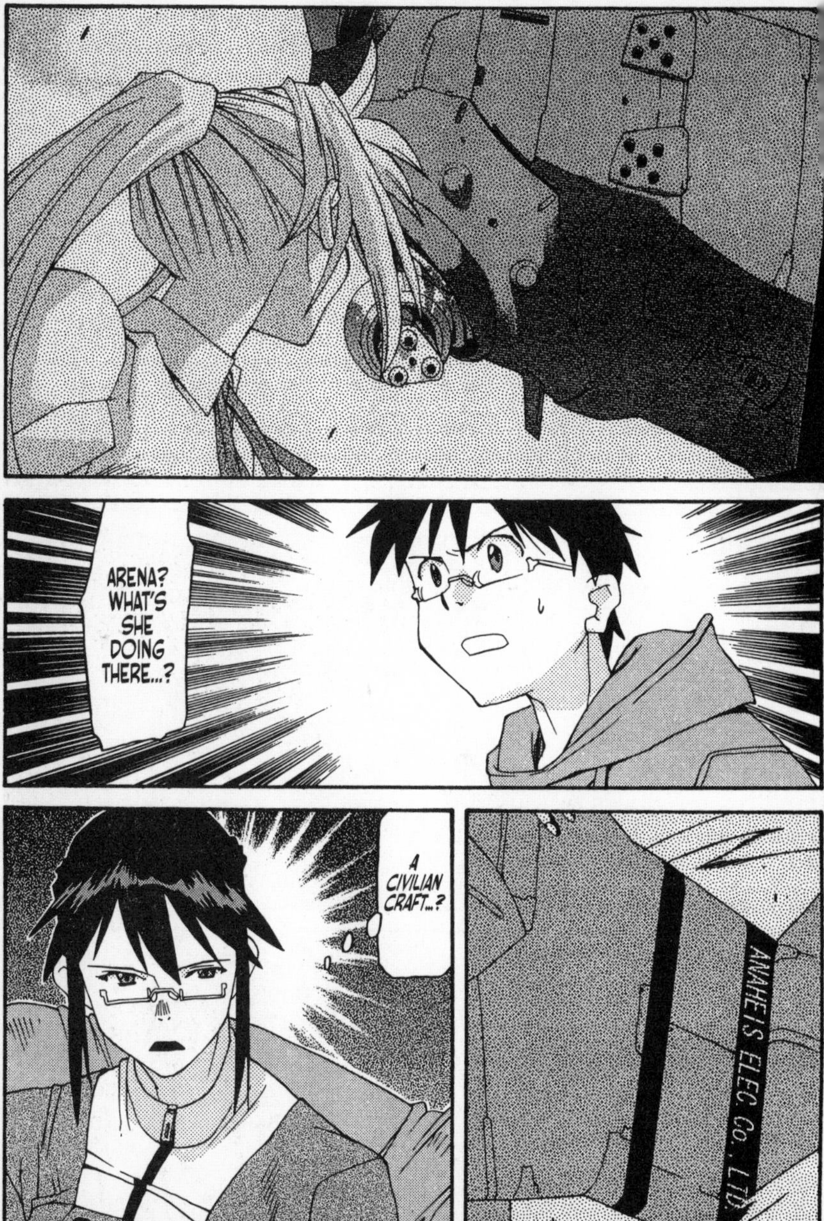
ARENA? WHAT'S SHE DOING THERE...?
ANAHEIS ELEC Co. LTD.
A CIVILIAN CRAFT...?

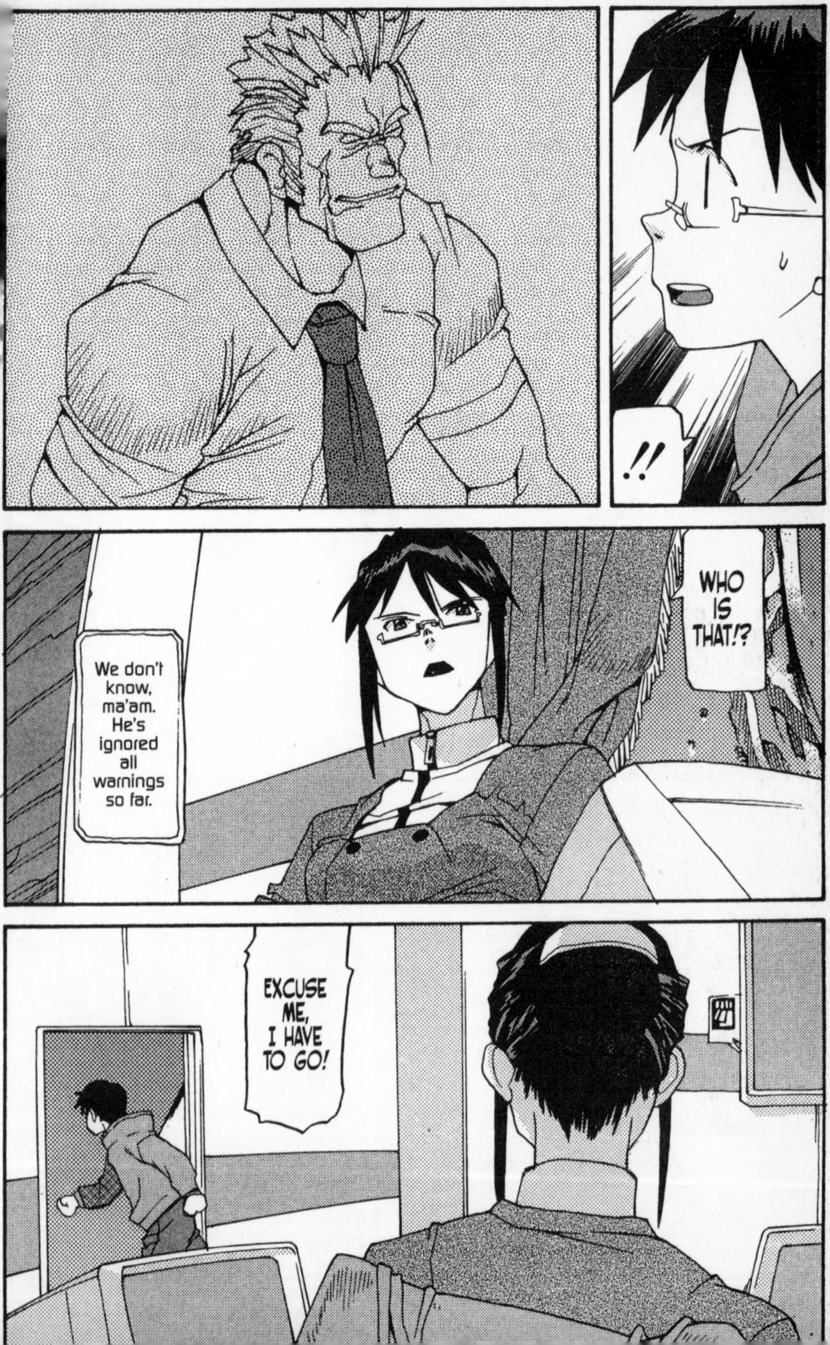
!!
WHO IS THAT!?
We don't know, ma'am. He's ignored all warnings so far.
EXCUSE ME, I HAVE TO GO!

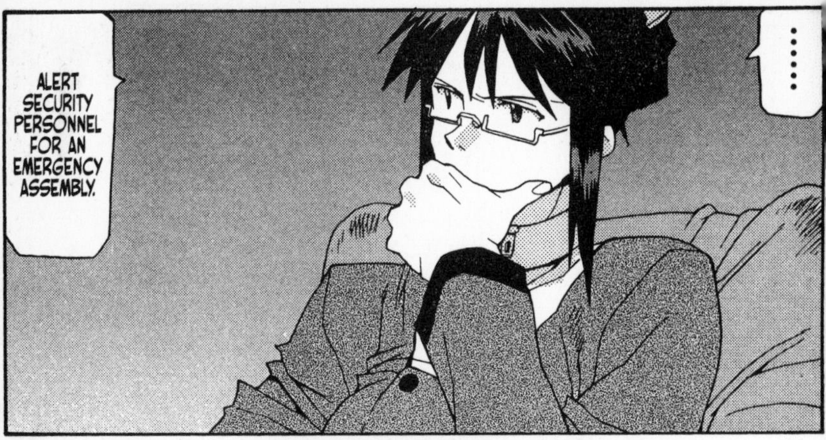
......
ALERT SECURITY PERSONNEL FOR AN EMERGENCY ASSEMBLY.

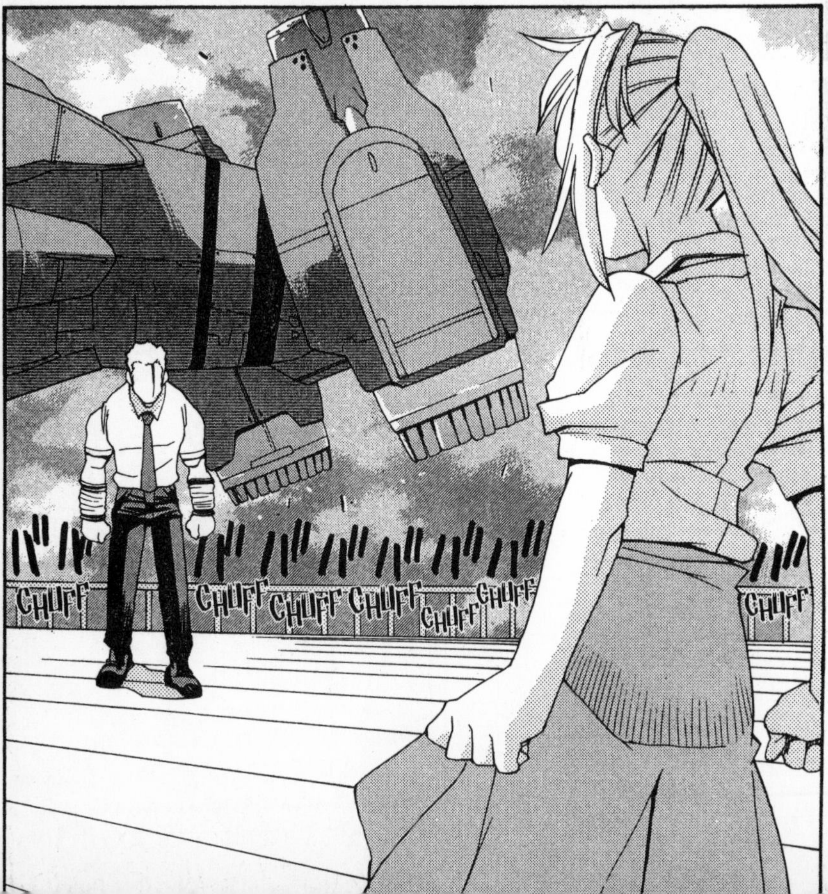
CHUFF
CHUFF
CHUFF
CHUFF
CHUFF
CHUFF
CHUFF

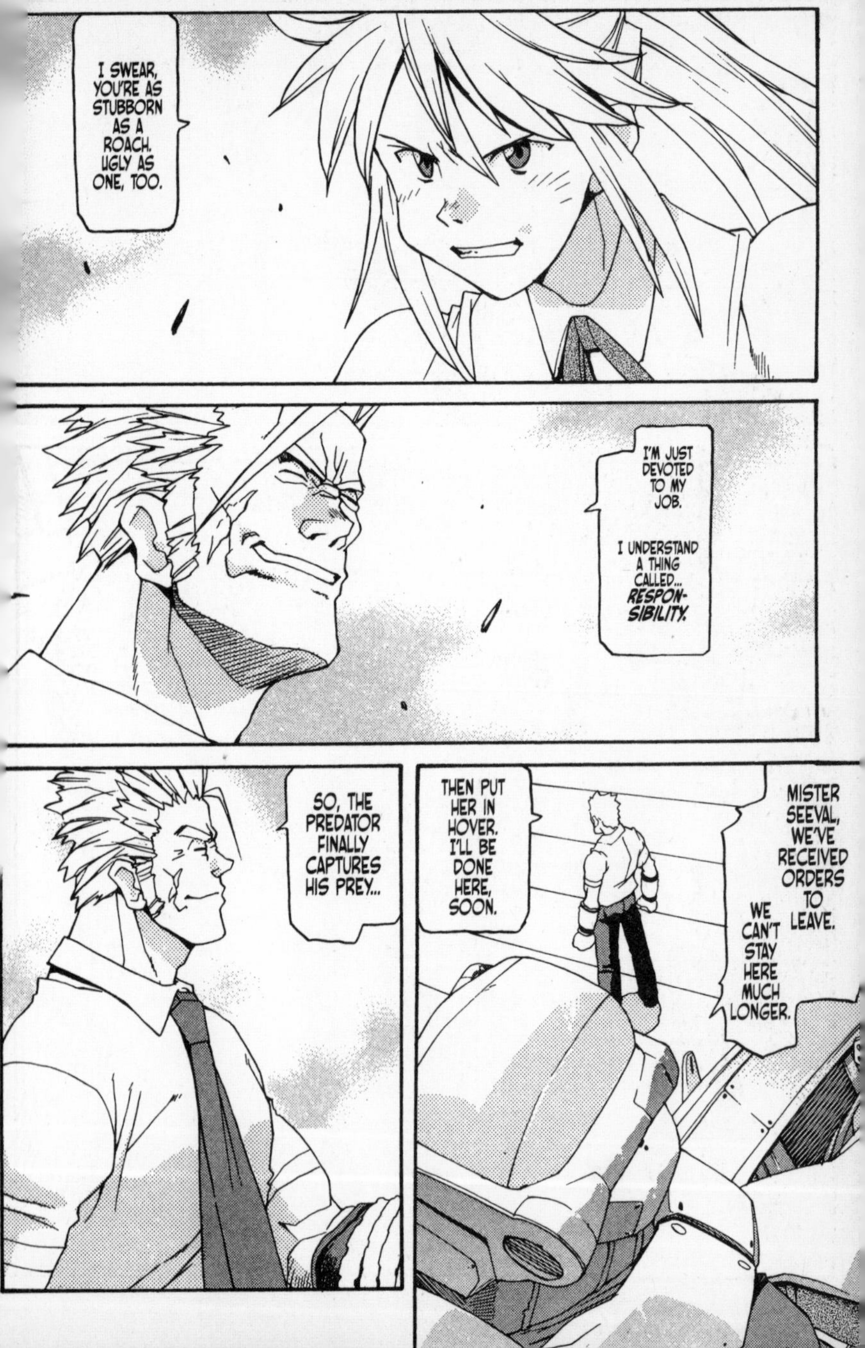
I SWEAR, YOU'RE AS STUBBORN AS A ROACH. UGLY AS ONE, TOO.
I'M JUST DEVOTED TO MY JOB.
I UNDERSTAND A THING CALLED... *RESPONSIBILITY.*
MISTER SEEVAL, WE'VE RECEIVED ORDERS TO LEAVE.
WE CAN'T STAY HERE MUCH LONGER.
THEN PUT HER IN HOVER. I'LL BE DONE HERE, SOON.
SO, THE PREDATOR FINALLY CAPTURES HIS PREY...

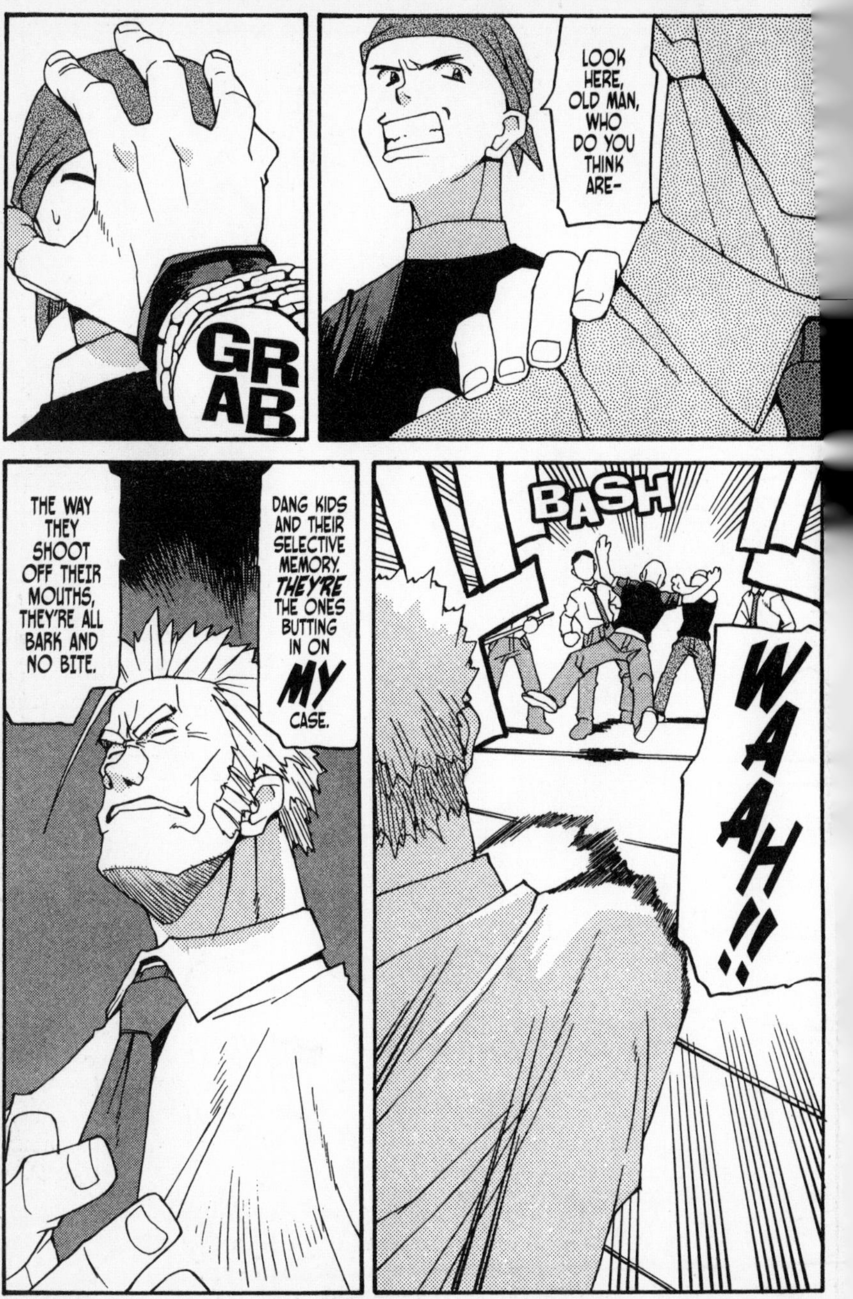
LOOK HERE, OLD MAN, WHO DO YOU THINK ARE-
GRAB
BASH
WAAH!!
DANG KIDS AND THEIR SELECTIVE MEMORY. THEY'RE THE ONES BUTTING IN ON MY CASE.
THE WAY THEY SHOOT OFF THEIR MOUTHS, THEY'RE ALL BARK AND NO BITE.

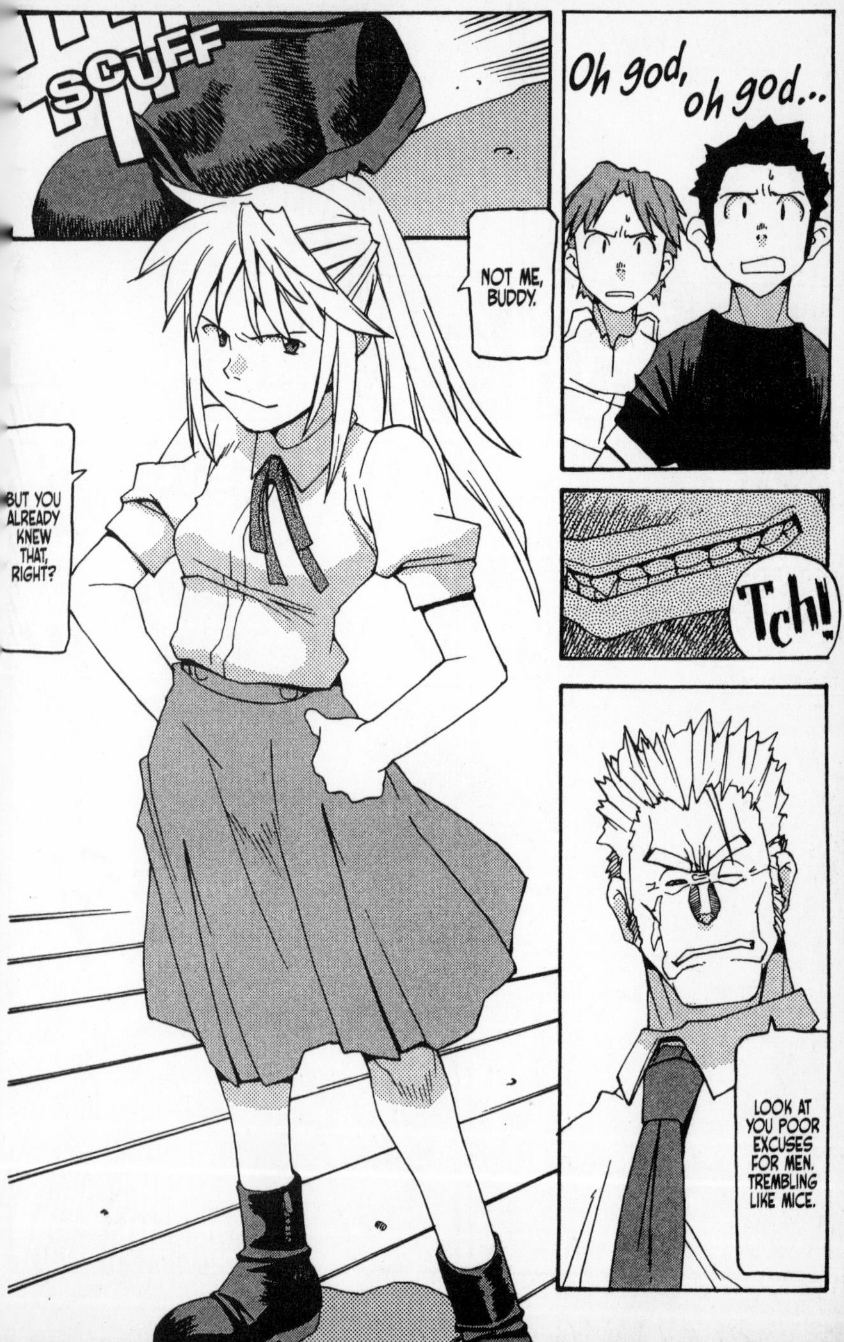
Oh god, oh god...
Tch!
LOOK AT YOU POOR EXCUSES FOR MEN. TREMBLING LIKE MICE.
SCUFF
NOT ME, BUDDY.
BUT YOU ALREADY KNEW THAT, RIGHT?

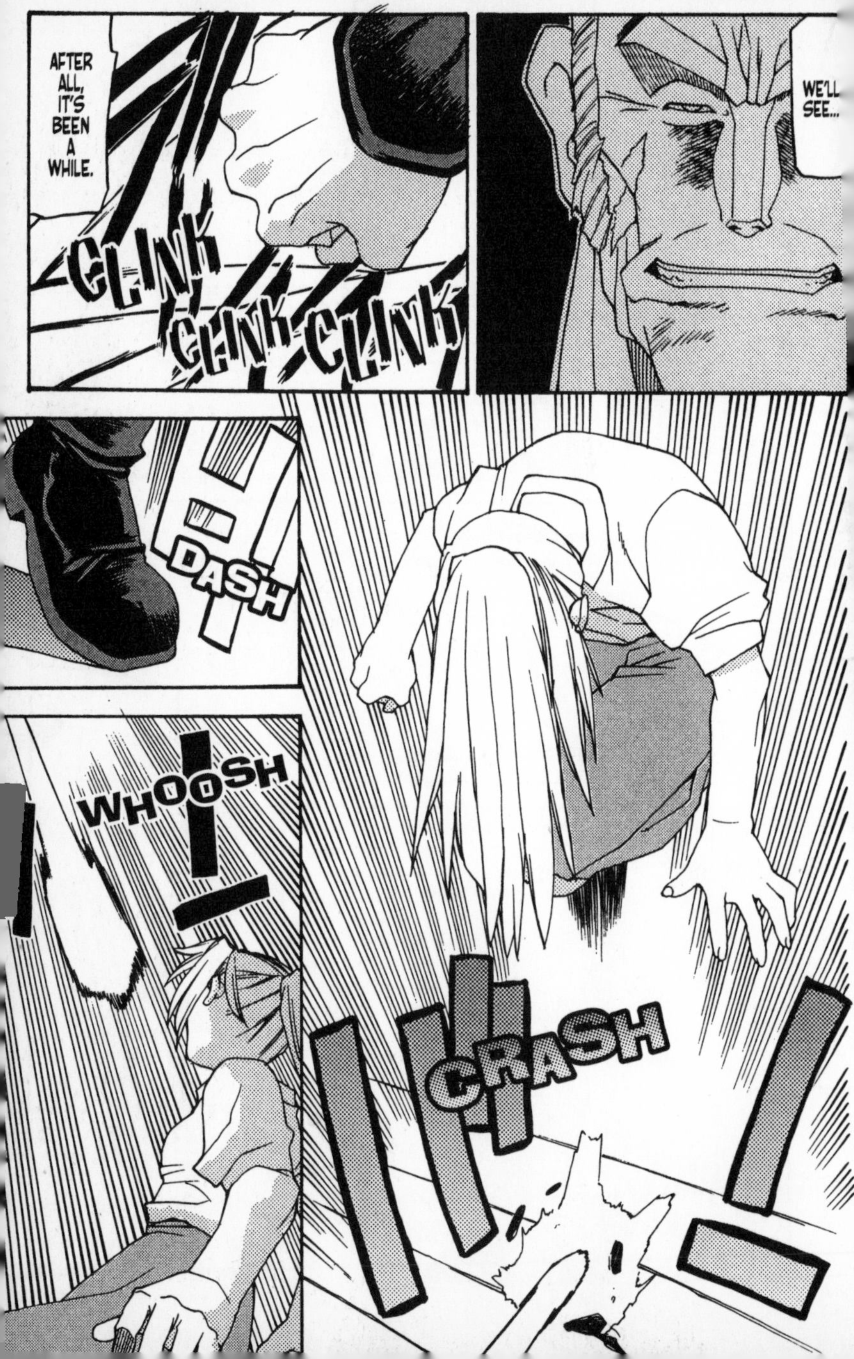
WE'LL SEE...
AFTER ALL, IT'S BEEN A WHILE.
CLINK CLINK CLINK
CRASH
DASH
WHOOSH

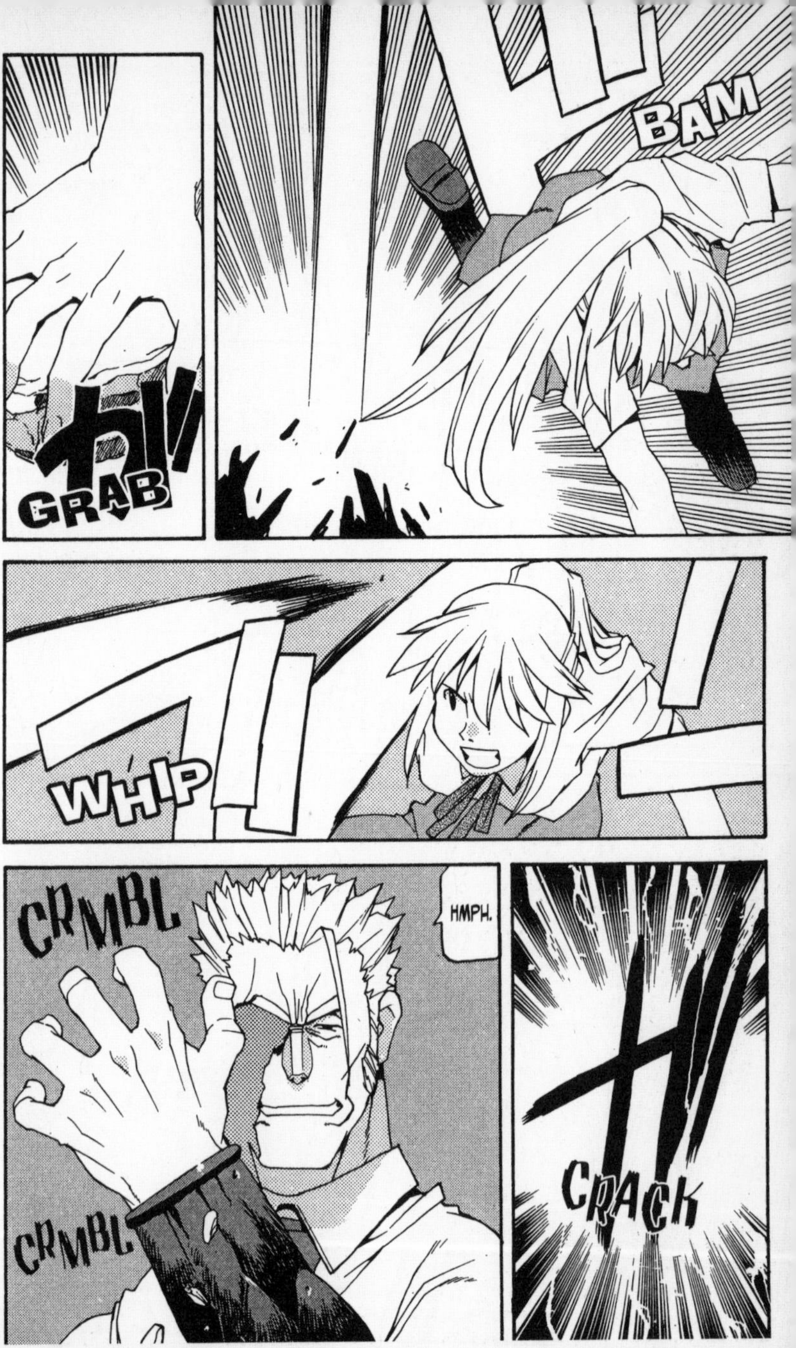
BAM
GRAB
WHIP
CRACK
CRMBL
HMPH.
CRMBL

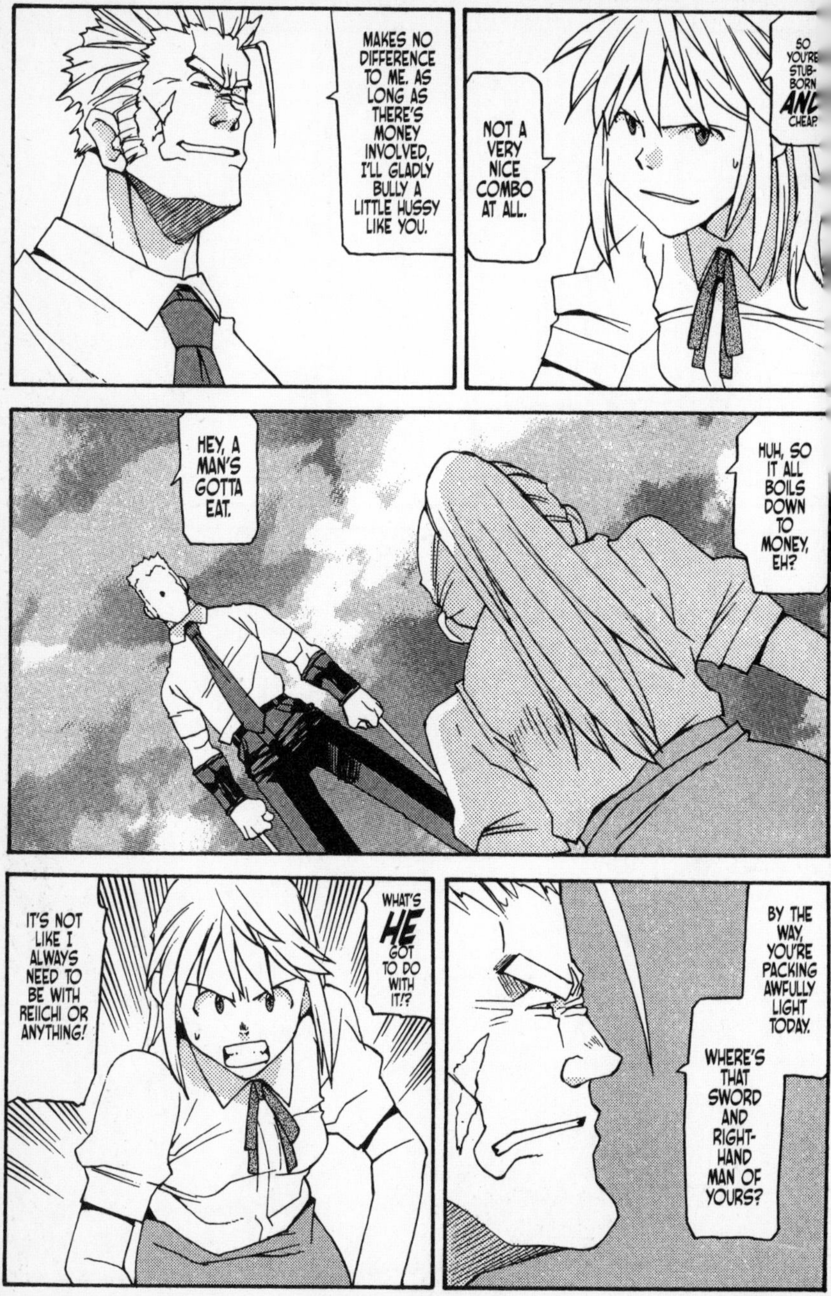
SO YOU'RE STUB-BORN AN CHEAP.
NOT A VERY NICE COMBO AT ALL.
MAKES NO DIFFERENCE TO ME. AS LONG AS THERE'S MONEY INVOLVED, I'LL GLADLY BULLY A LITTLE HUSSY LIKE YOU.
HUH, SO IT ALL BOILS DOWN TO MONEY, EH?
HEY, A MAN'S GOTTA EAT.
BY THE WAY, YOU'RE PACKING AWFULLY LIGHT TODAY.
WHERE'S THAT SWORD AND RIGHT-HAND MAN OF YOURS?
WHAT'S *HE* GOT TO DO WITH IT!?
IT'S NOT LIKE I ALWAYS NEED TO BE WITH REIICHI OR ANYTHING!

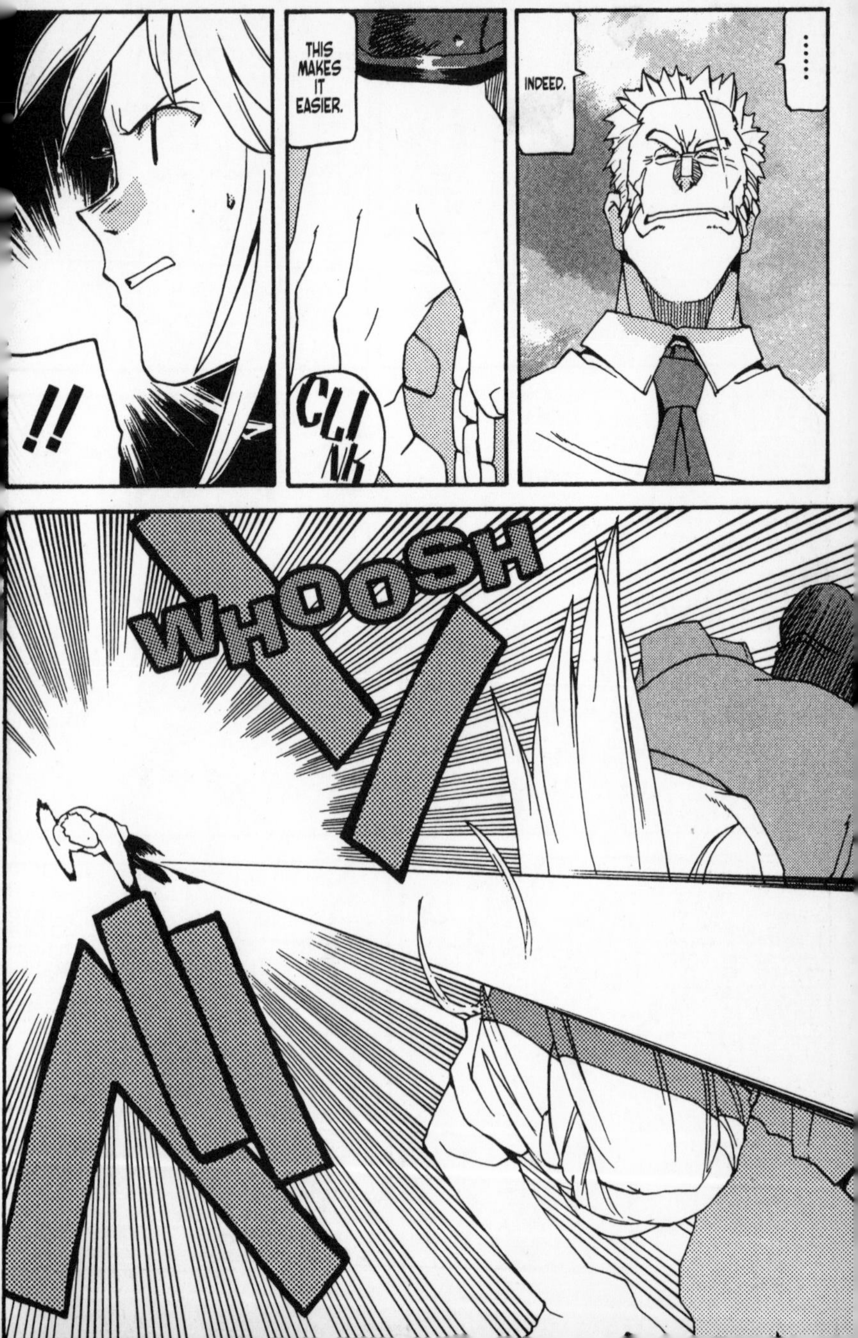
......
INDEED.
THIS MAKES IT EASIER.
CLINK
!!
WHOOSH

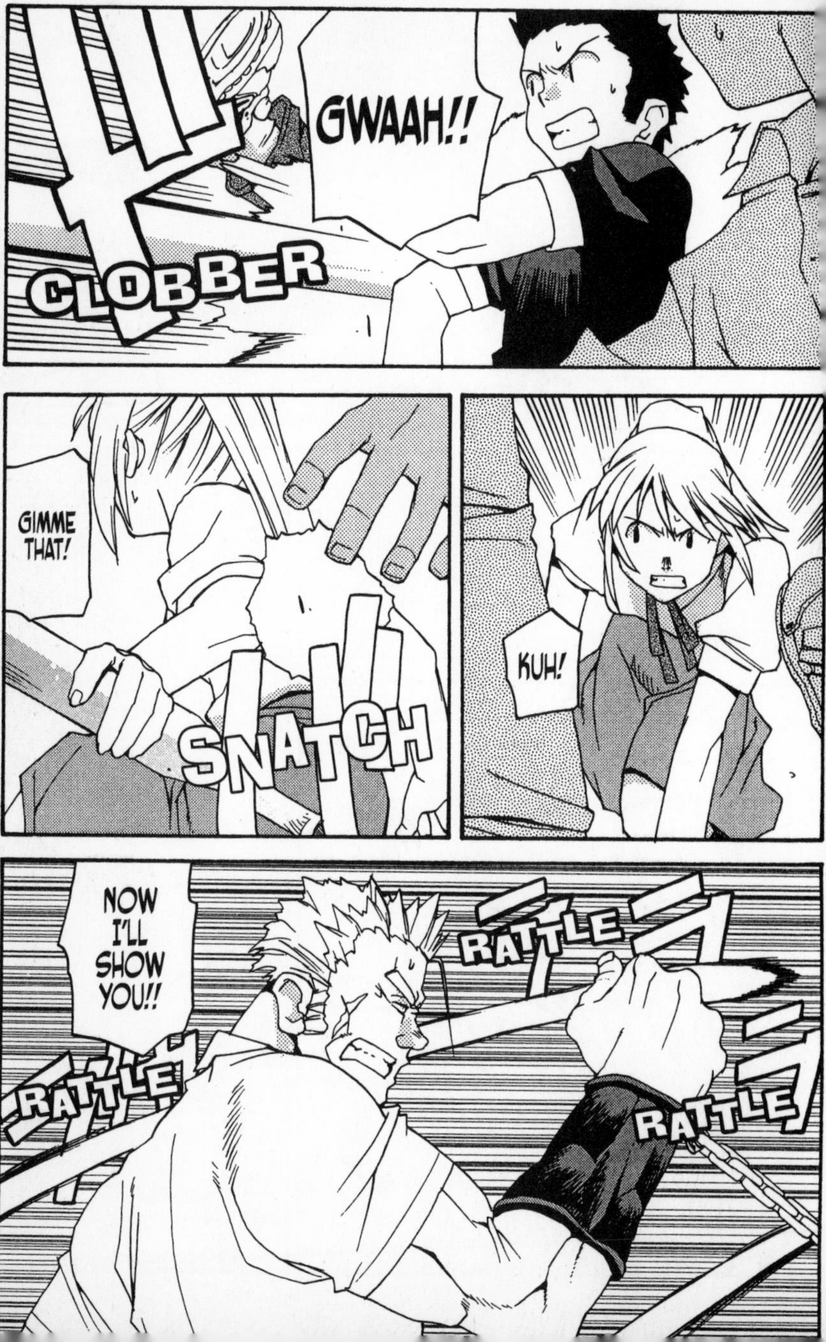
GWAAH!!
CLOBBER
KUH!
GIMME THAT!
SNATCH
RATTLE
NOW I'LL SHOW YOU!!
RATTLE
RATTLE

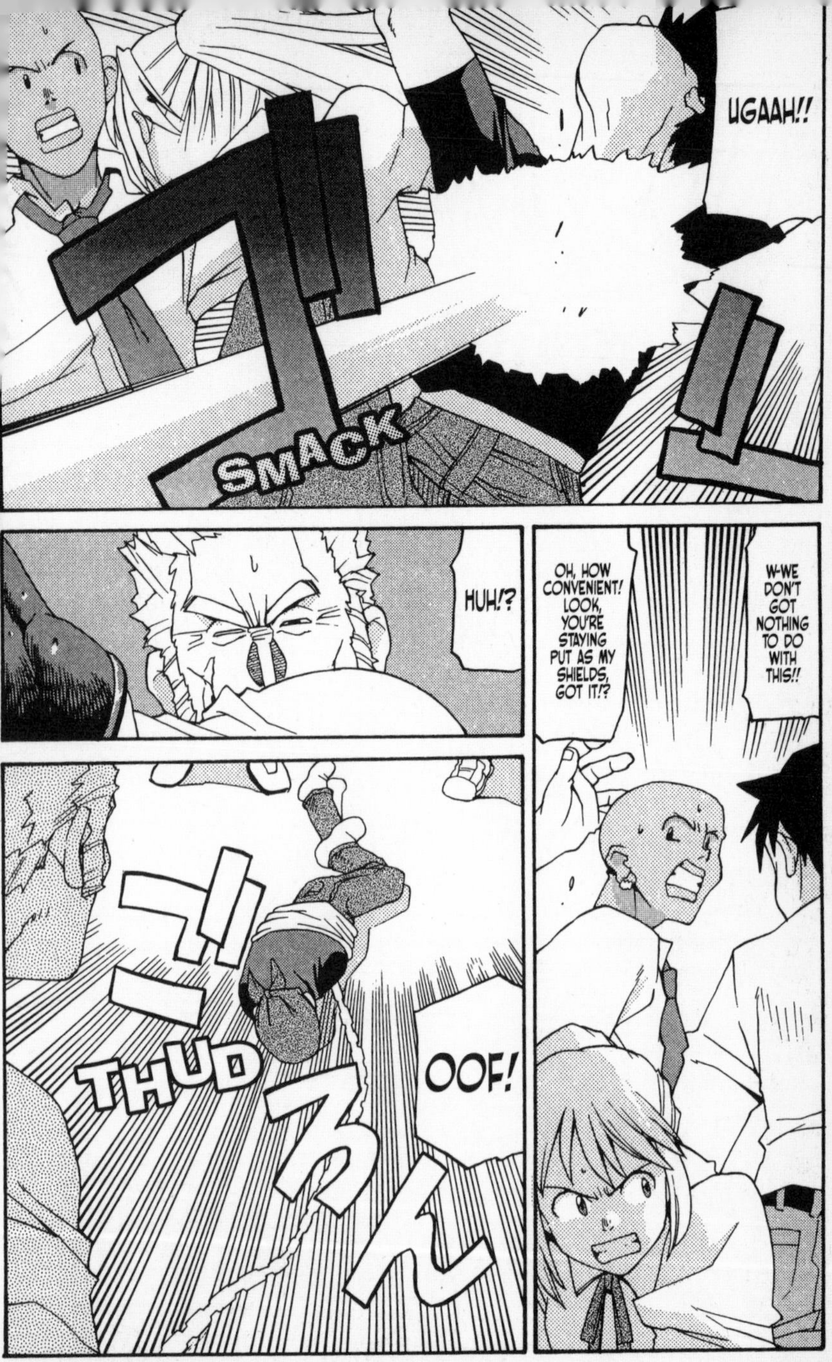
UGAAH!!
SMACK
W-WE DON'T GOT NOTHING TO DO WITH THIS!!
OH, HOW CONVENIENT! LOOK, YOU'RE STAYING PUT AS MY SHIELDS, GOT IT!?
HUH!?
OOF!
THUD

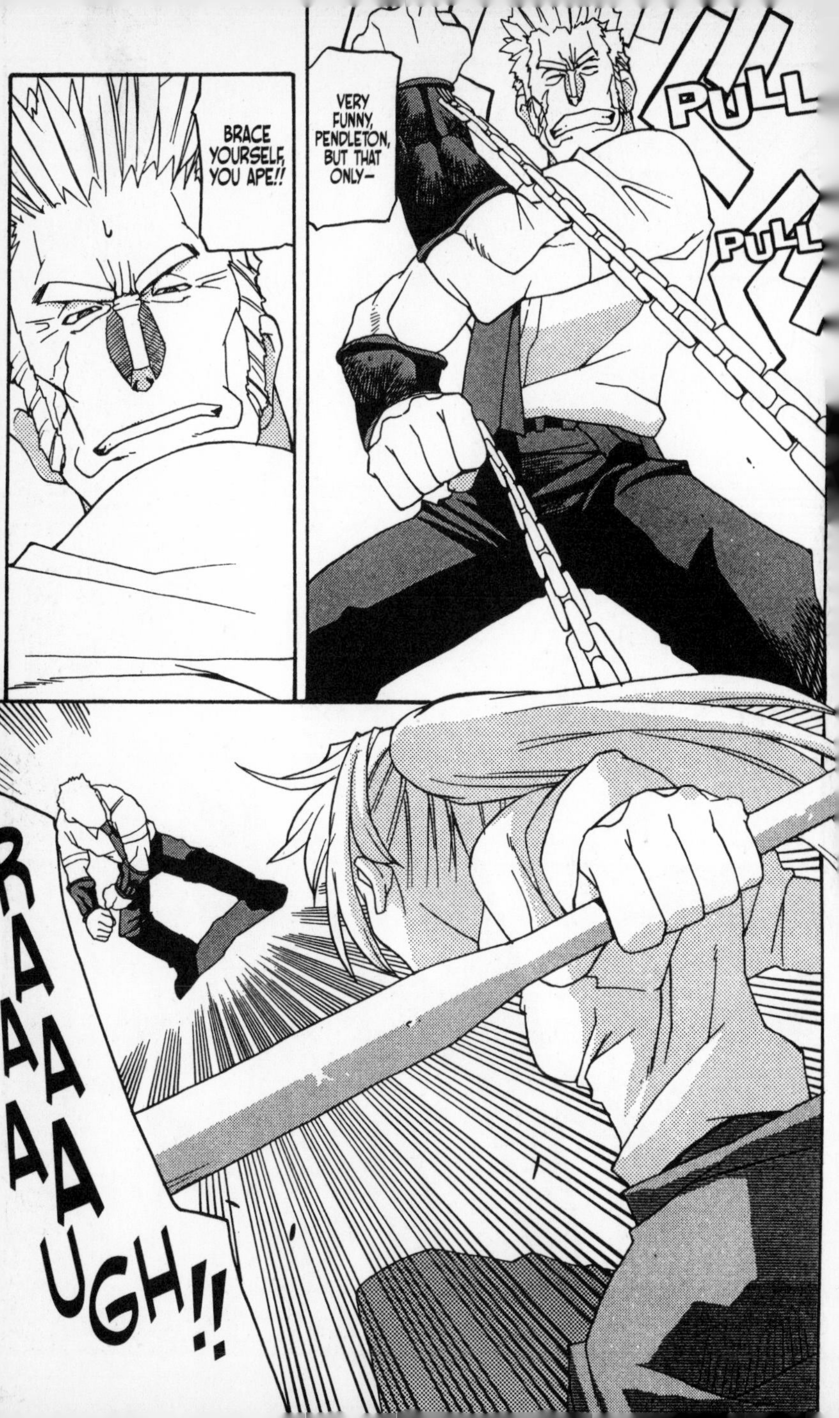
VERY FUNNY, PENDLETON, BUT THAT ONLY–
PULL
PULL
BRACE YOURSELF, YOU APE!!
RAAAAAUGH!!

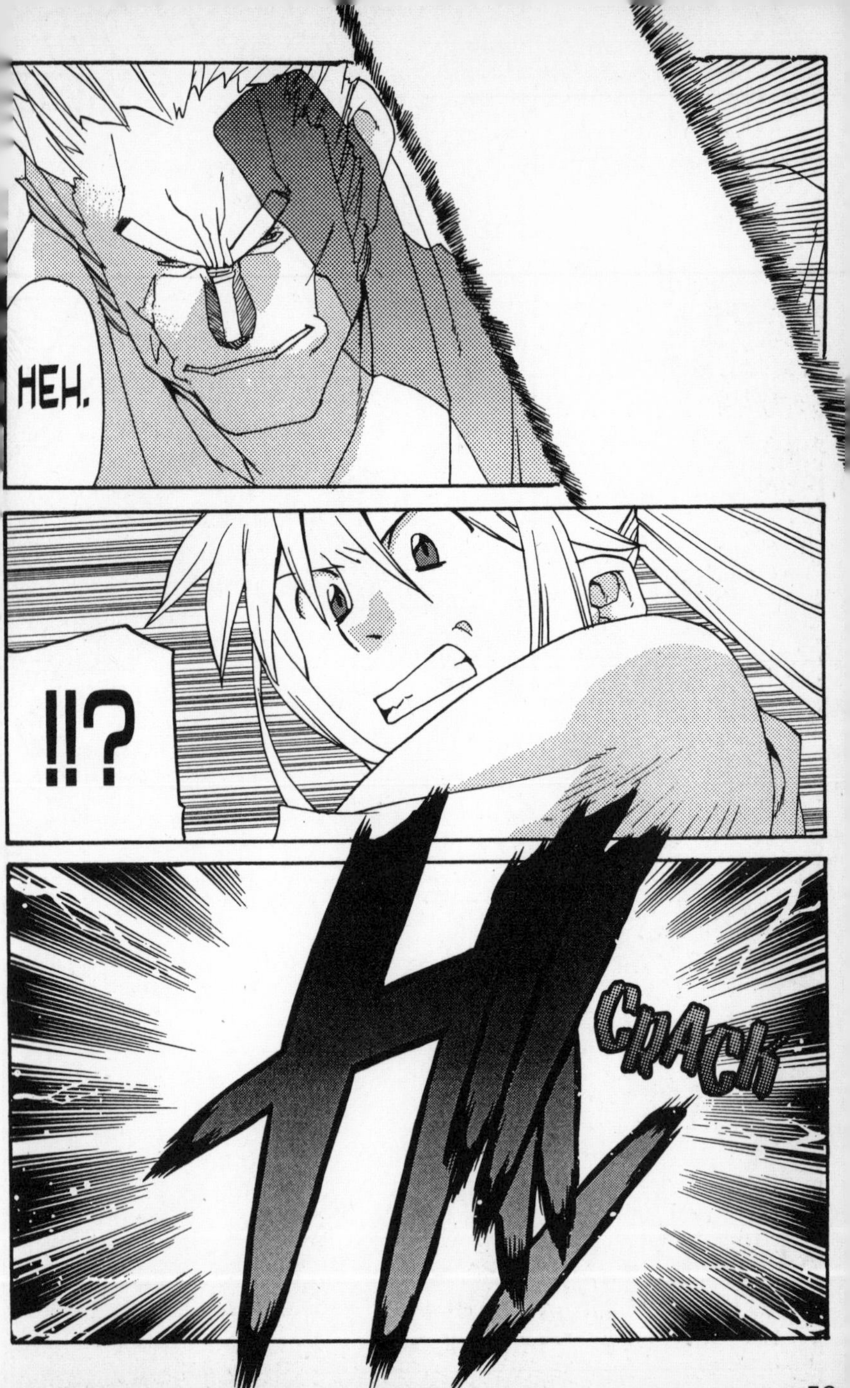
HEH.
!!?
CRACK

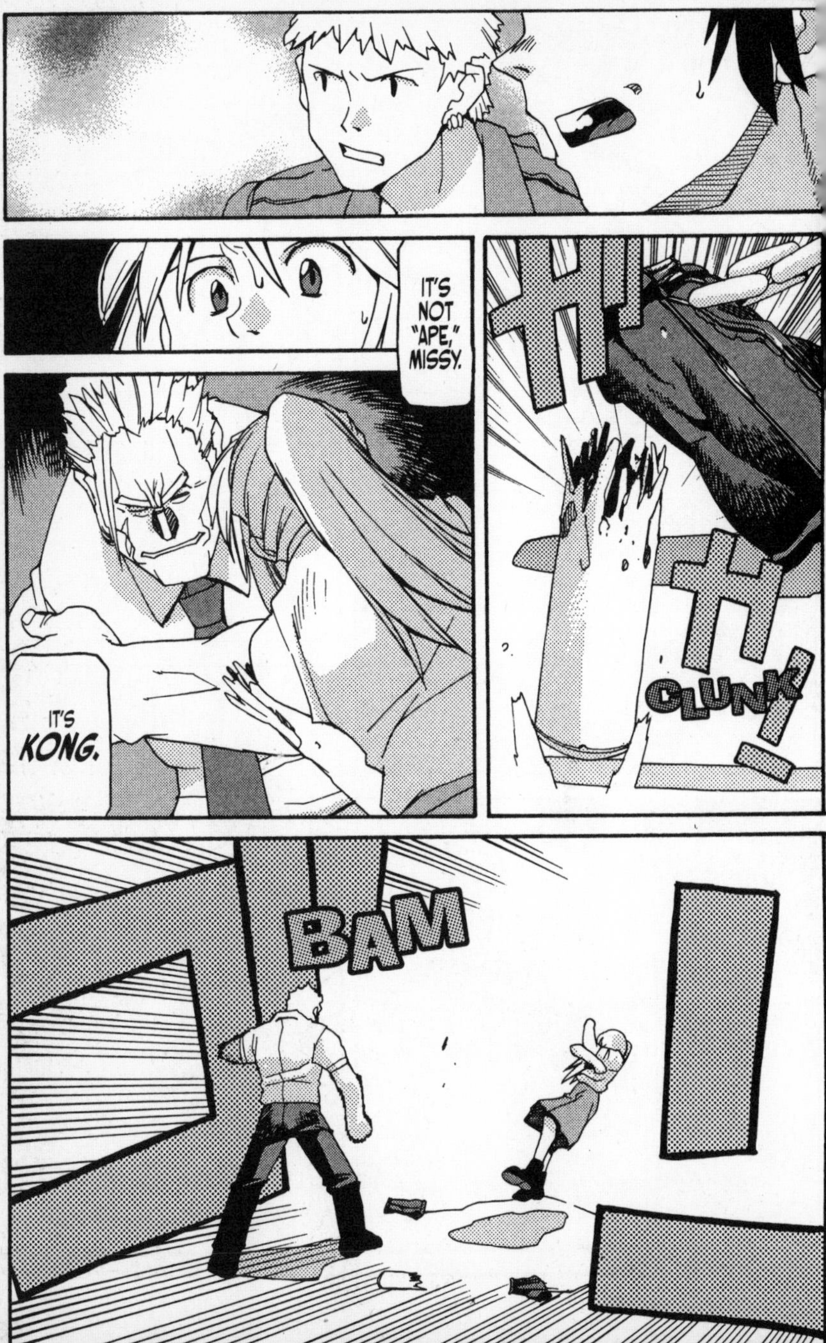
CLUNK
IT'S NOT "APE," MISSY.
IT'S KONG.
BAM

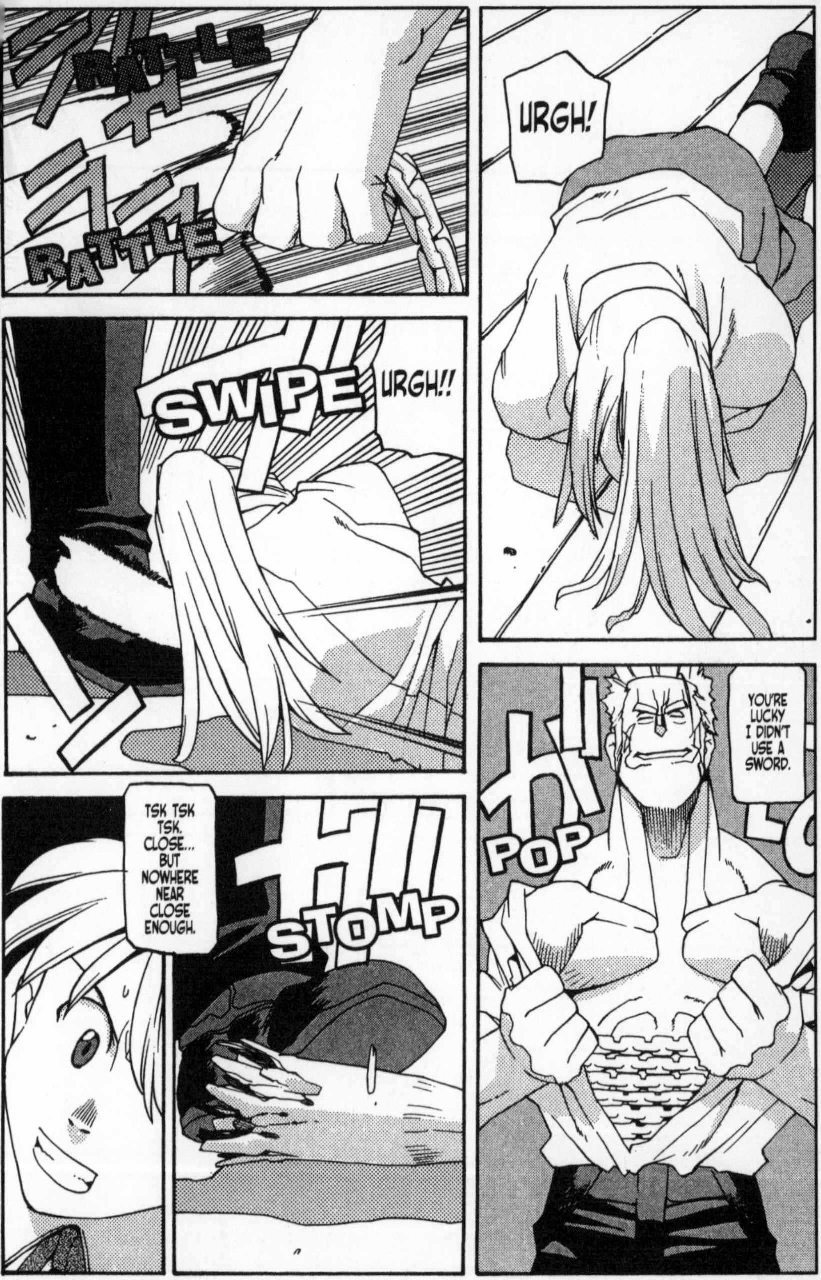
URGH!
RATTLE
RATTLE
SWIPE
URGH!!
YOU'RE LUCKY I DIDN'T USE A SWORD.
POP
TSK TSK TSK. CLOSE... BUT NOWHERE NEAR CLOSE ENOUGH.
STOMP

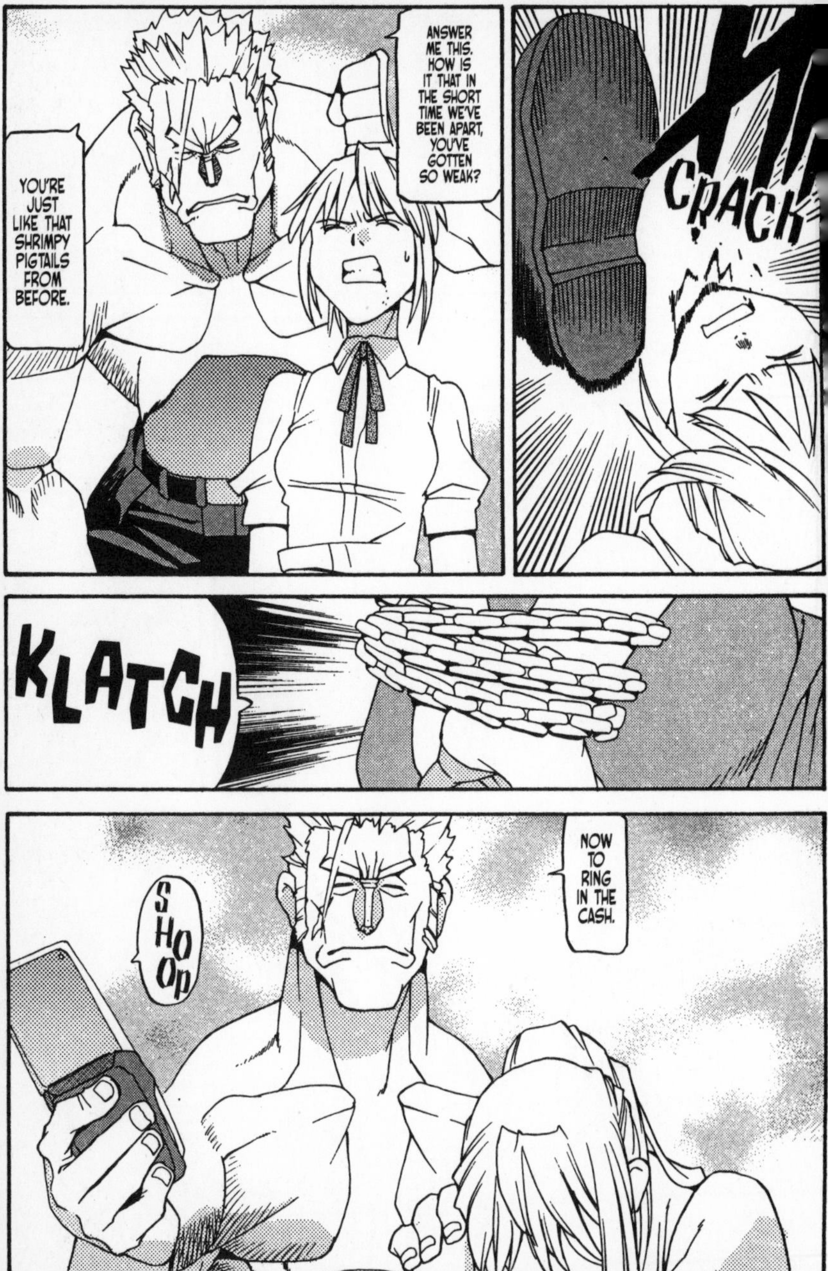
CRACK
ANSWER ME THIS. HOW IS IT THAT IN THE SHORT TIME WE'VE BEEN APART, YOU'VE GOTTEN SO WEAK?
YOU'RE JUST LIKE THAT SHRIMPY PIGTAILS FROM BEFORE.
KLATCH
NOW TO RING IN THE CASH.
SHOOp

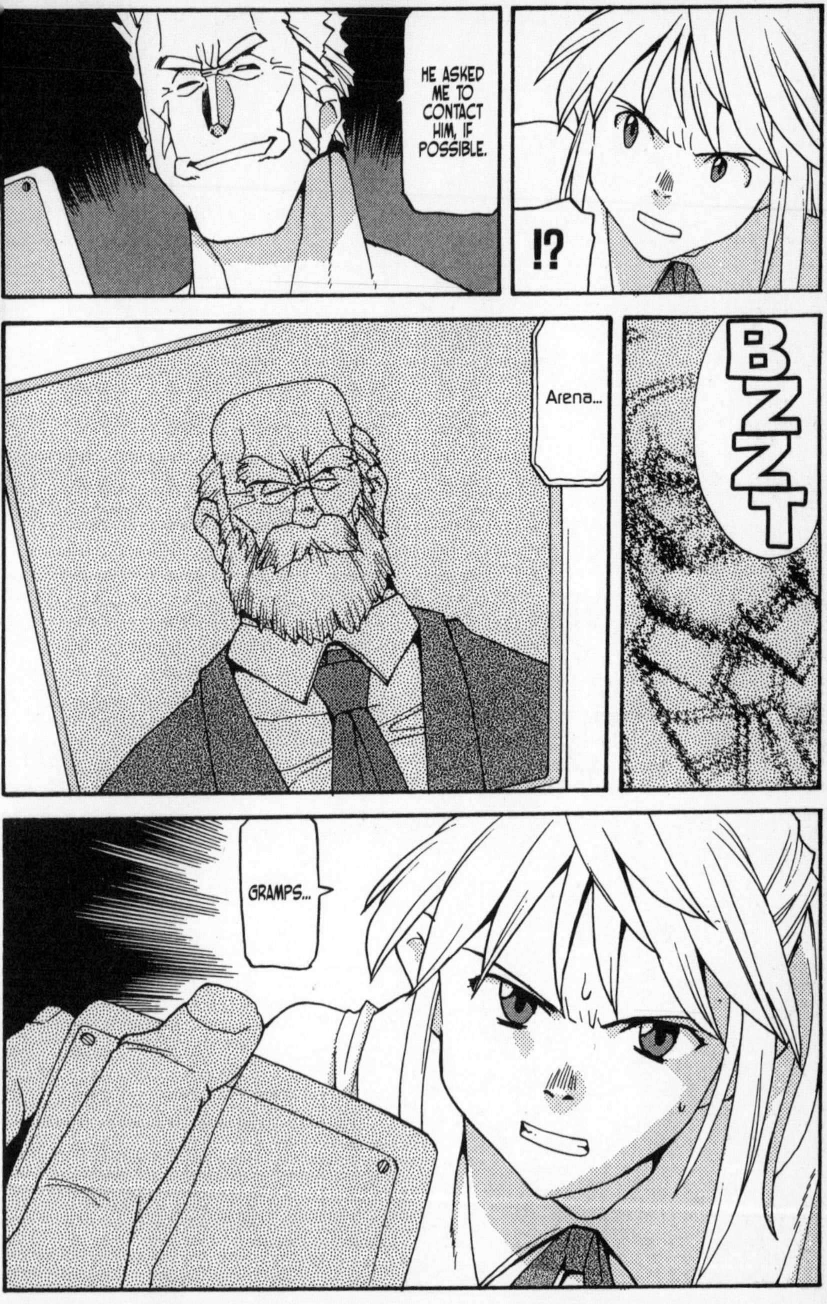
!?
HE ASKED ME TO CONTACT HIM, IF POSSIBLE.
BZZT
Arena...
GRAMPS...

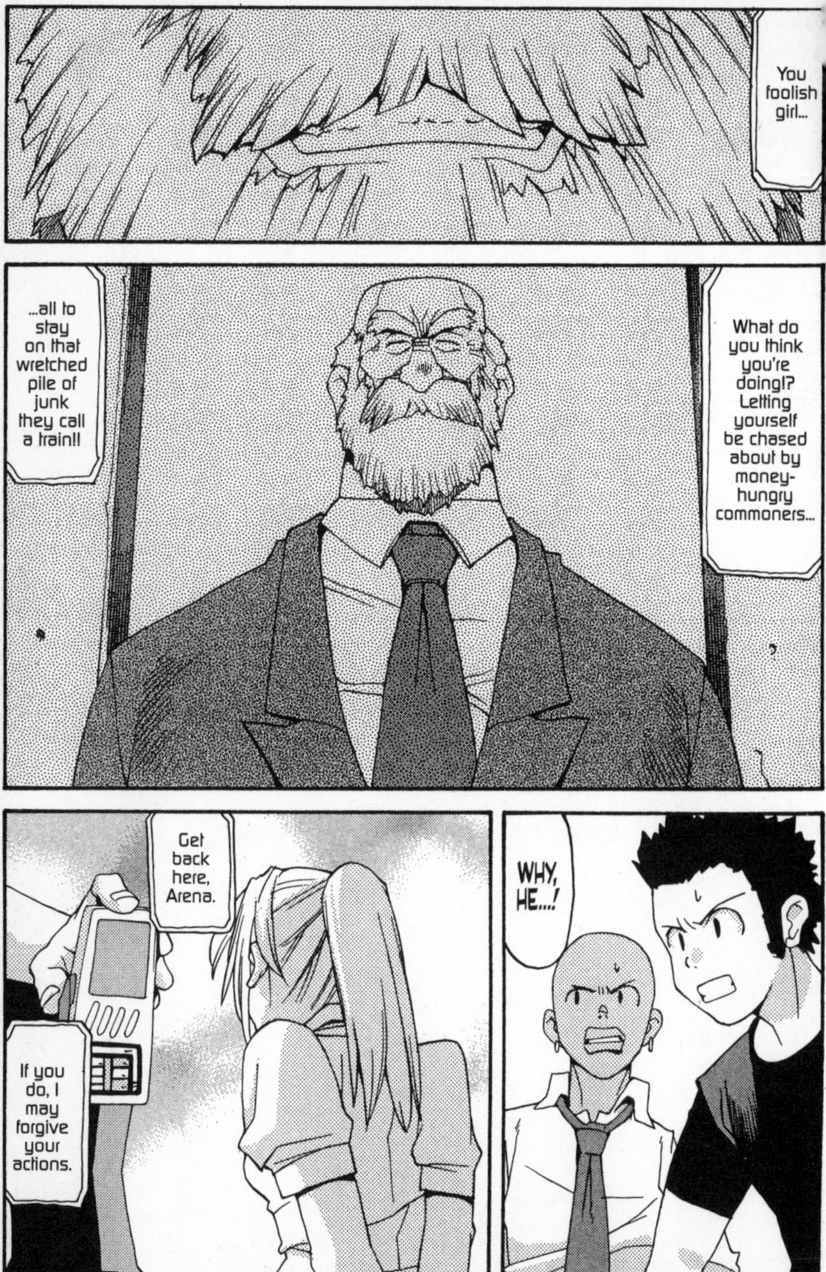
You foolish girl...
What do you think you're doing!? Letting yourself be chased about by money-hungry commoners...
...all to stay on that wretched pile of junk they call a train!!
WHY, HE...!
Get back here, Arena.
If you do, I may forgive your actions.

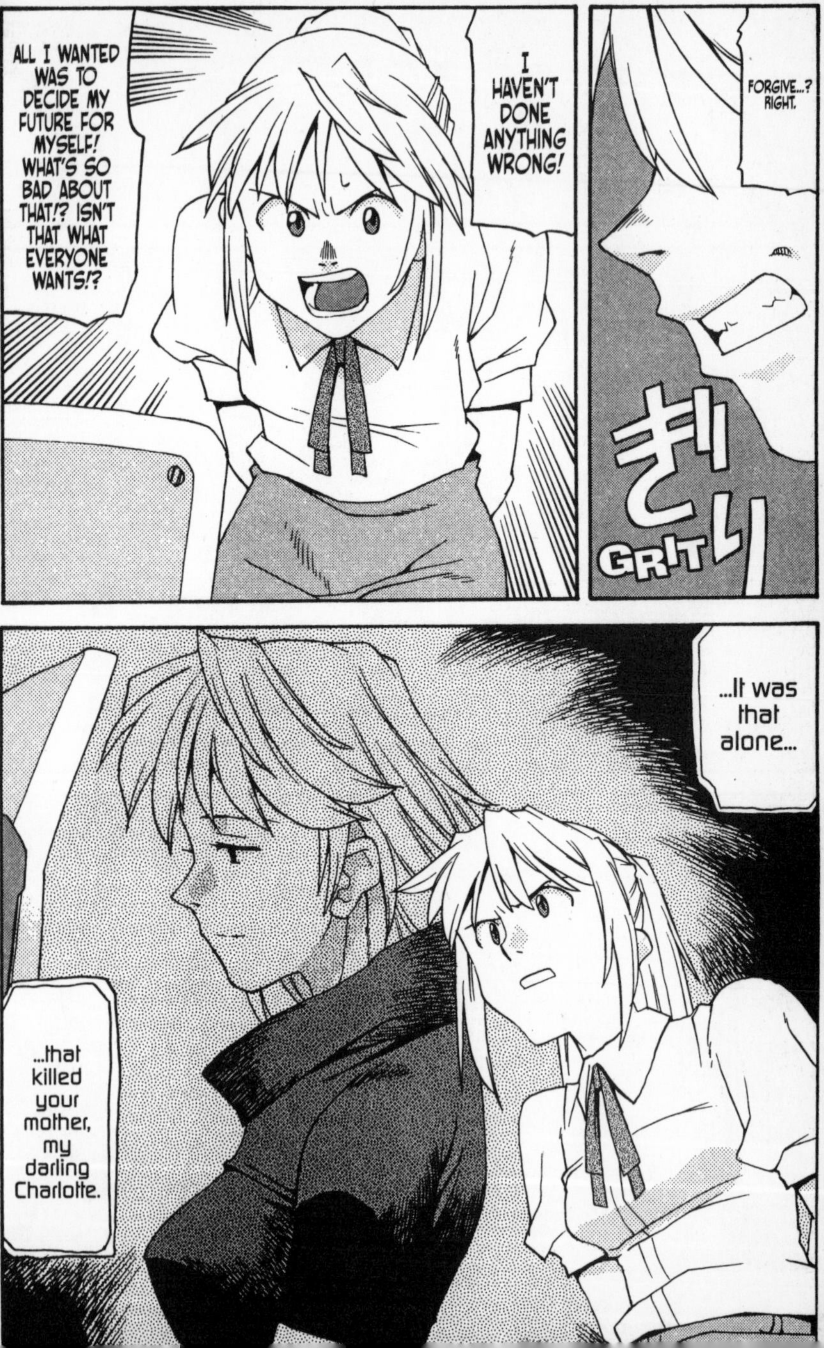
FORGIVE...? RIGHT.
ぎり
GRIT
I HAVEN'T DONE ANYTHING WRONG!
ALL I WANTED WAS TO DECIDE MY FUTURE FOR MYSELF! WHAT'S SO BAD ABOUT THAT!? ISN'T THAT WHAT EVERYONE WANTS!?
...It was that alone...
...that killed your mother, my darling Charlotte.

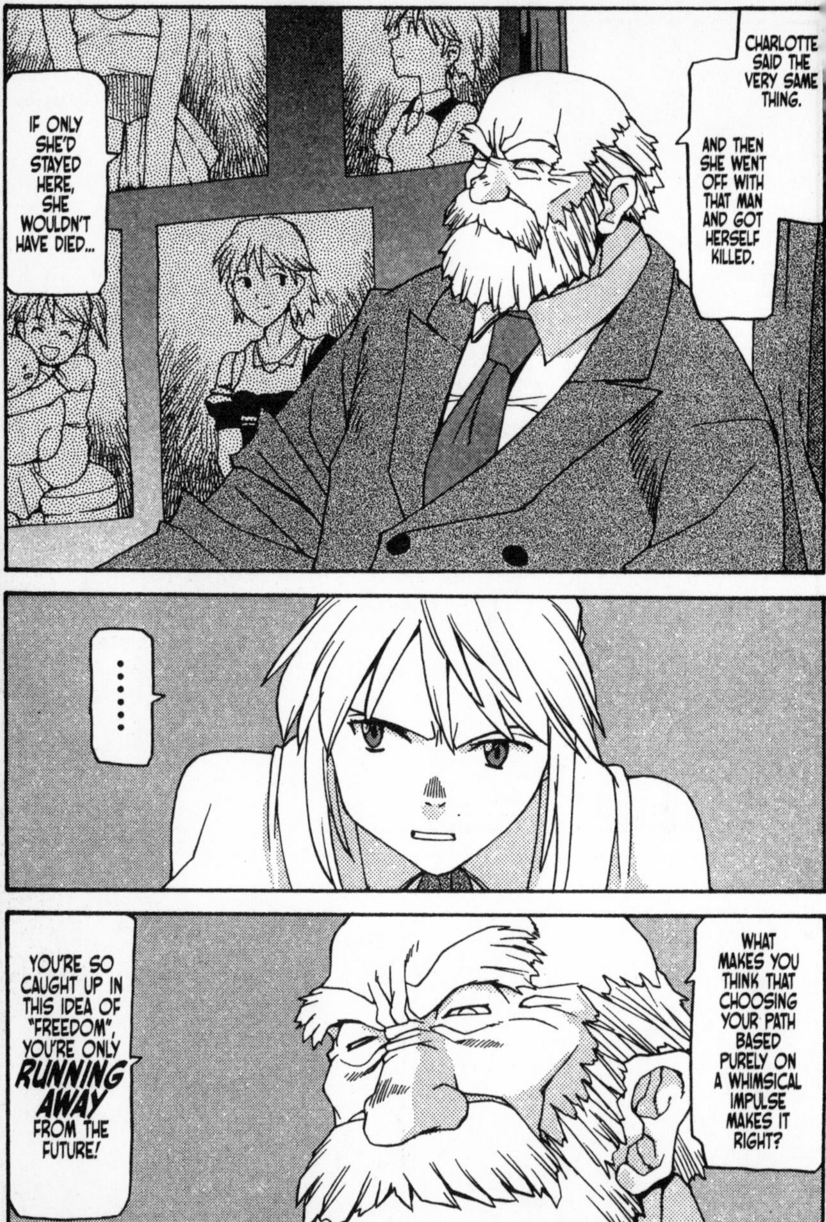
CHARLOTTE SAID THE VERY SAME THING.
AND THEN SHE WENT OFF WITH THAT MAN AND GOT HERSELF KILLED.
IF ONLY SHE'D STAYED HERE, SHE WOULDN'T HAVE DIED...
......
WHAT MAKES YOU THINK THAT CHOOSING YOUR PATH BASED PURELY ON A WHIMSICAL IMPULSE MAKES IT RIGHT?
YOU'RE SO CAUGHT UP IN THIS IDEA OF "FREEDOM", YOU'RE ONLY ***RUNNING AWAY*** FROM THE FUTURE!

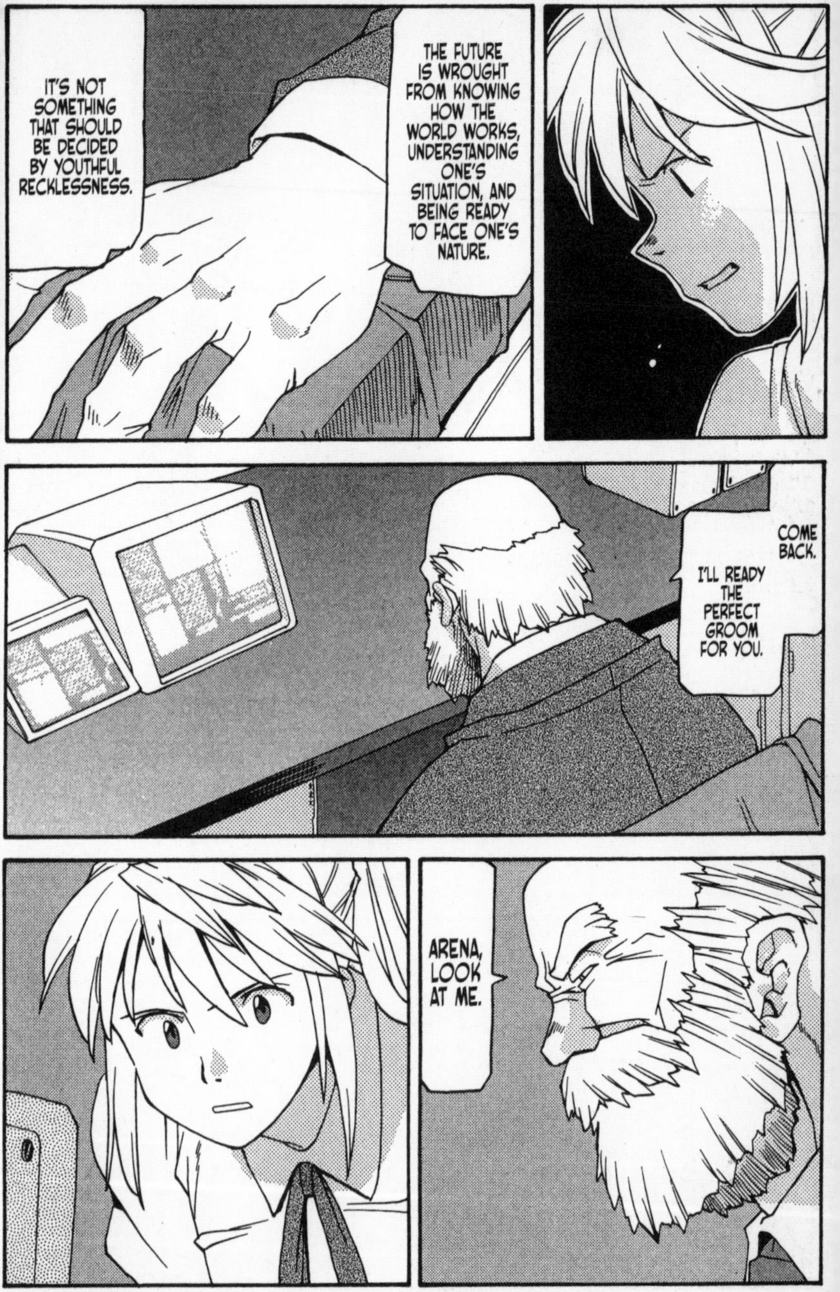
THE FUTURE IS WROUGHT FROM KNOWING HOW THE WORLD WORKS, UNDERSTANDING ONE'S SITUATION, AND BEING READY TO FACE ONE'S NATURE.
IT'S NOT SOMETHING THAT SHOULD BE DECIDED BY YOUTHFUL RECKLESSNESS.
COME BACK.
I'LL READY THE PERFECT GROOM FOR YOU.
ARENA, LOOK AT ME.

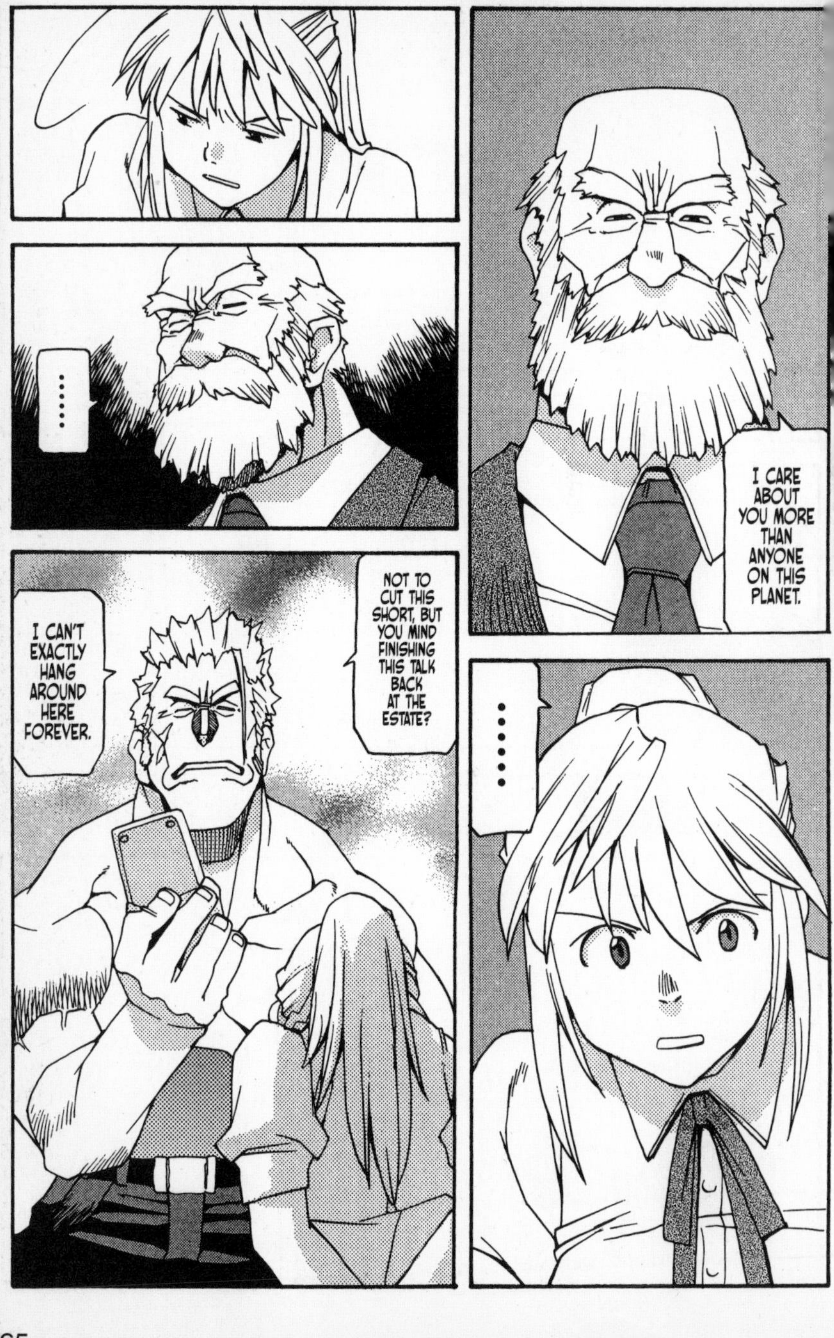
I CARE ABOUT YOU MORE THAN ANYONE ON THIS PLANET.
......
......
NOT TO CUT THIS SHORT, BUT YOU MIND FINISHING THIS TALK BACK AT THE ESTATE?
I CAN'T EXACTLY HANG AROUND HERE FOREVER.

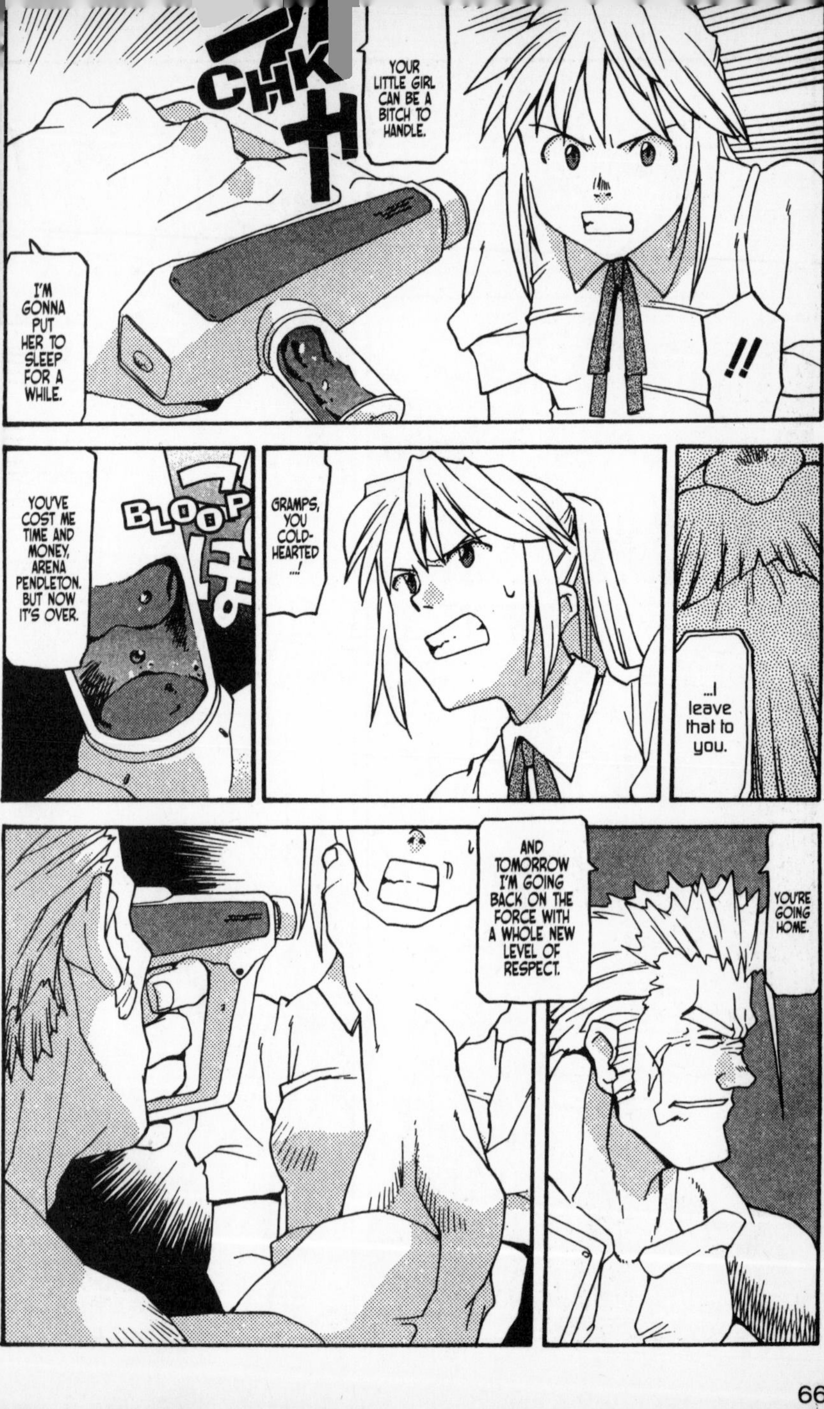
CHK
YOUR LITTLE GIRL CAN BE A BITCH TO HANDLE.
I'M GONNA PUT HER TO SLEEP FOR A WHILE.
!!
...I leave that to you.
GRAMPS, YOU COLD-HEARTED ...!
BLOOP
YOU'VE COST ME TIME AND MONEY, ARENA PENDLETON. BUT NOW IT'S OVER.
YOU'RE GOING HOME.
AND TOMORROW I'M GOING BACK ON THE FORCE WITH A WHOLE NEW LEVEL OF RESPECT.

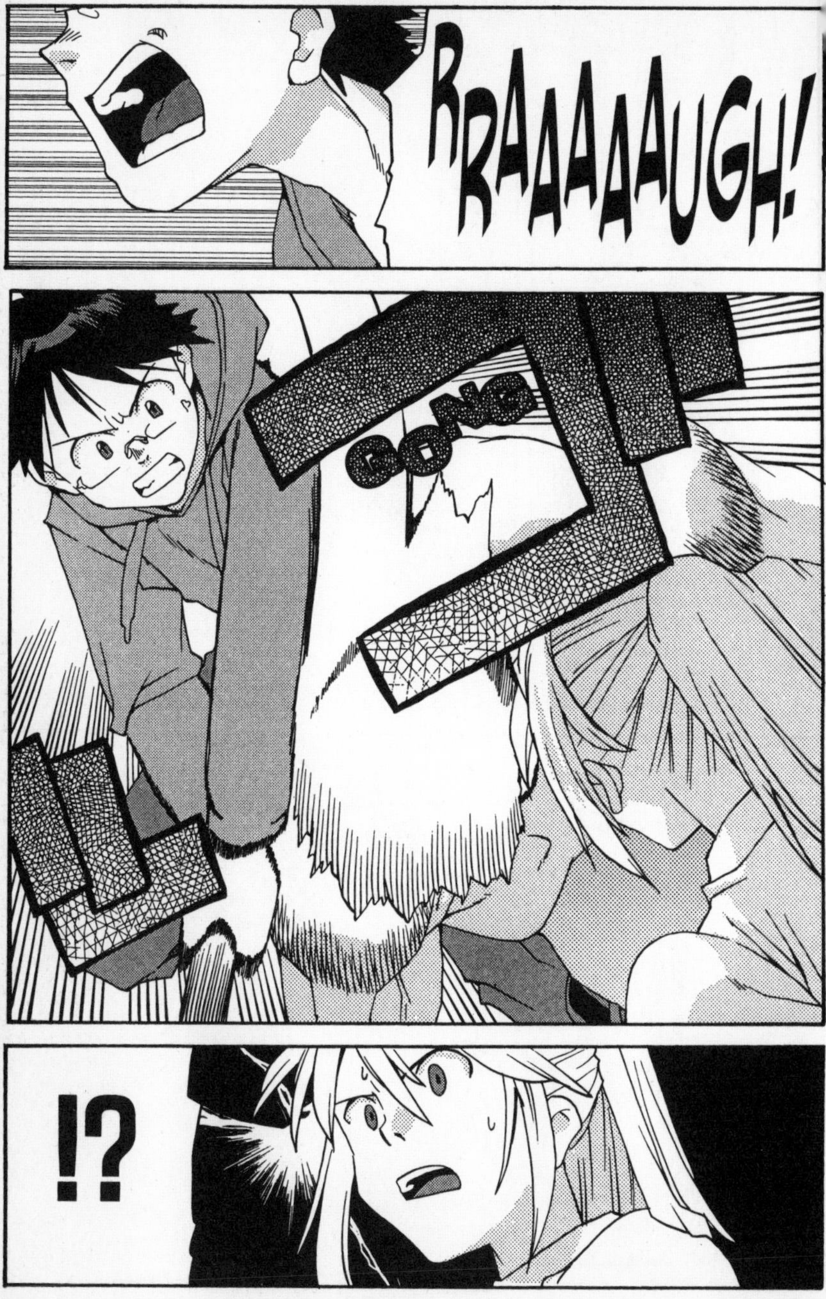
RRAAAAAUGH!
GONG
!?

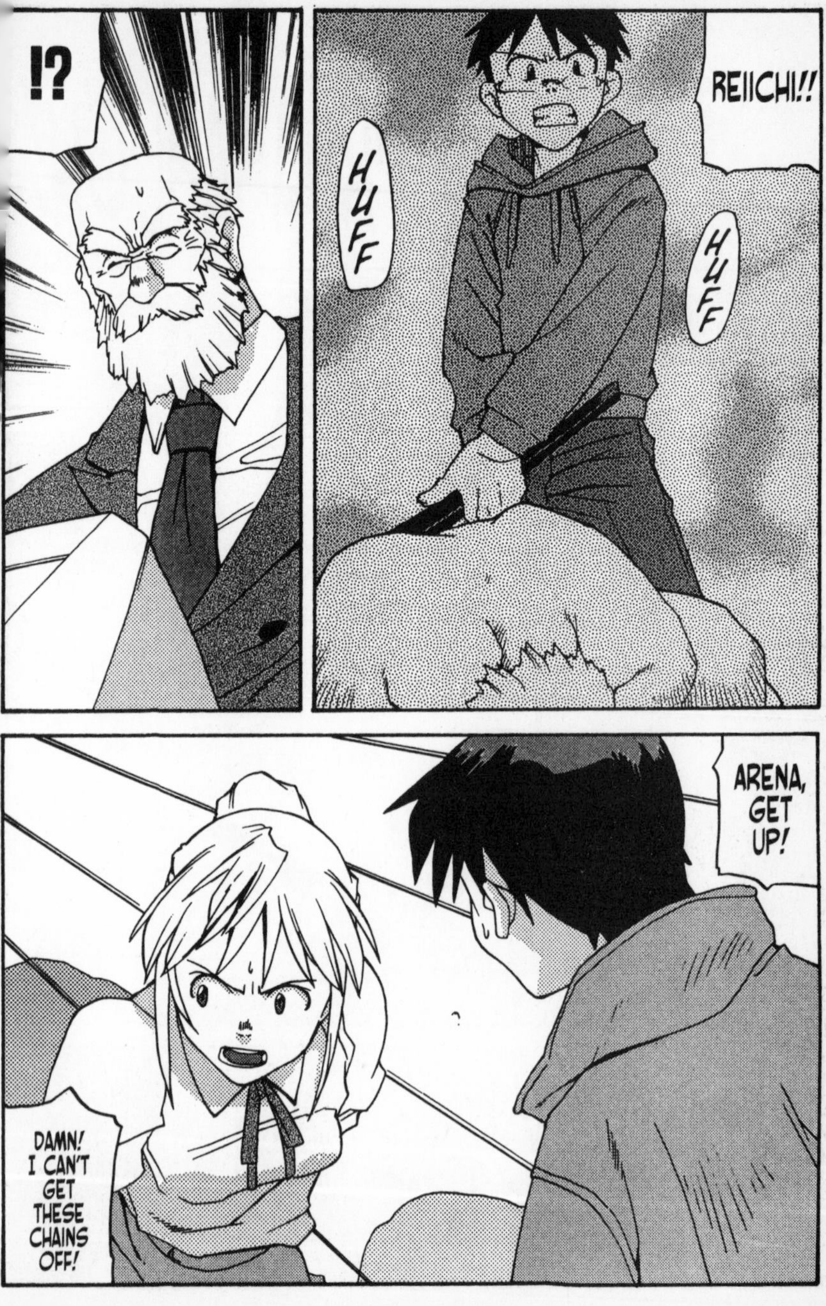
REIICHI!!
HUFF
HUFF
!?
ARENA, GET UP!
DAMN! I CAN'T GET THESE CHAINS OFF!

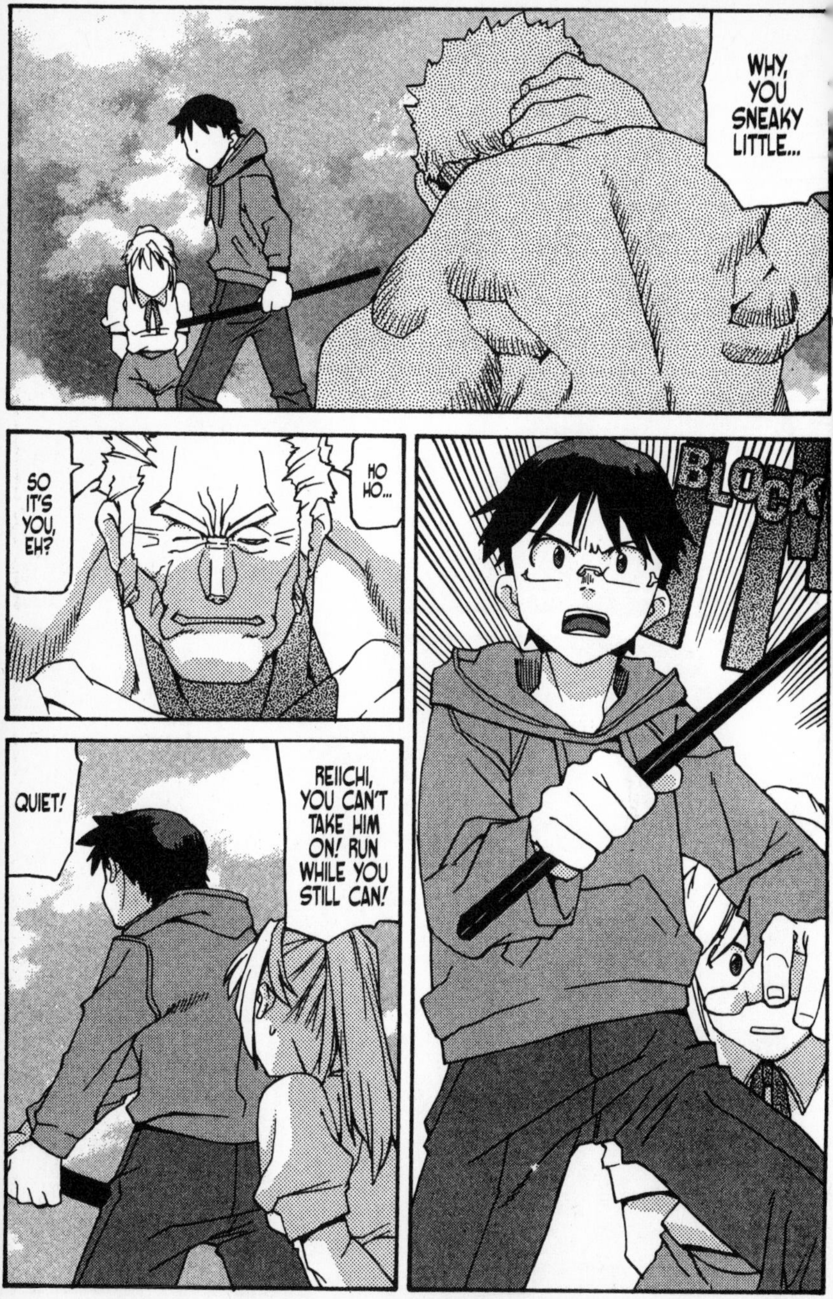
WHY, YOU SNEAKY LITTLE...
BLOCK
HO HO...
SO IT'S YOU, EH?
REIICHI, YOU CAN'T TAKE HIM ON! RUN WHILE YOU STILL CAN!
QUIET!

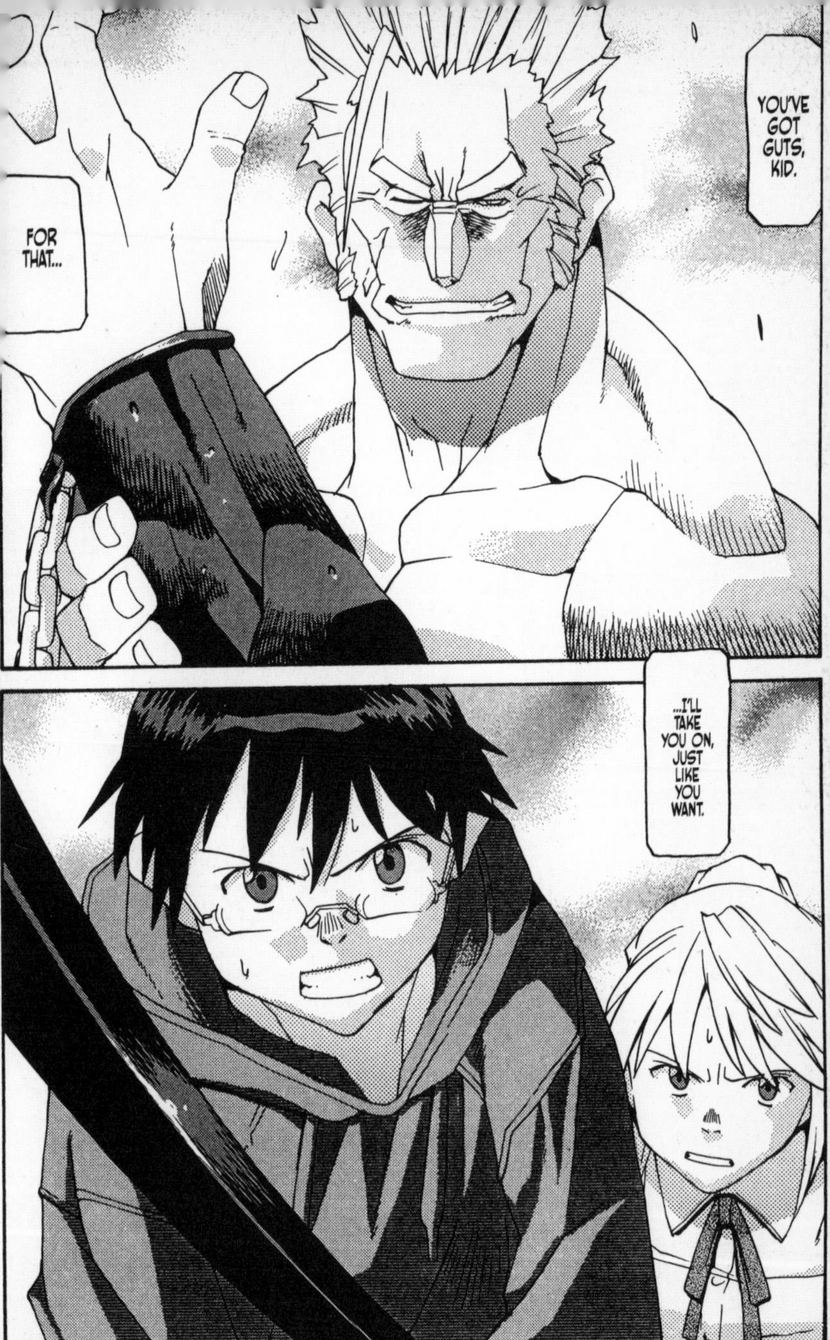
YOU'VE GOT GUTS, KID.
FOR THAT...
...I'LL TAKE YOU ON, JUST LIKE YOU WANT.

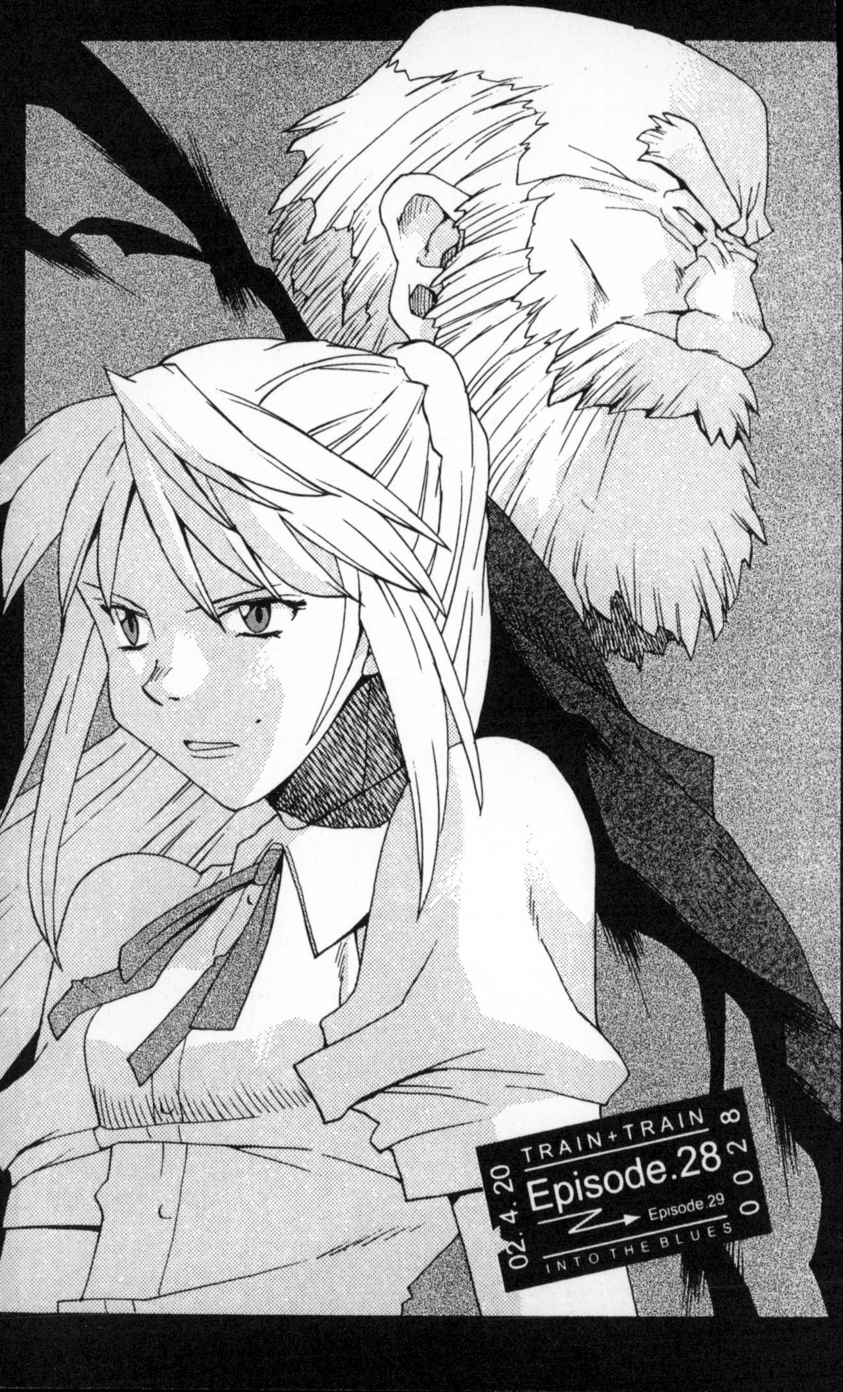
02. 4. 20
TRAIN+TRAIN
Episode.28
Episode.29
INTO THE BLUES
0028

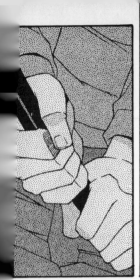

THAT
KATANA
....!

HEY,
KID.

S
TA
N
CE

72

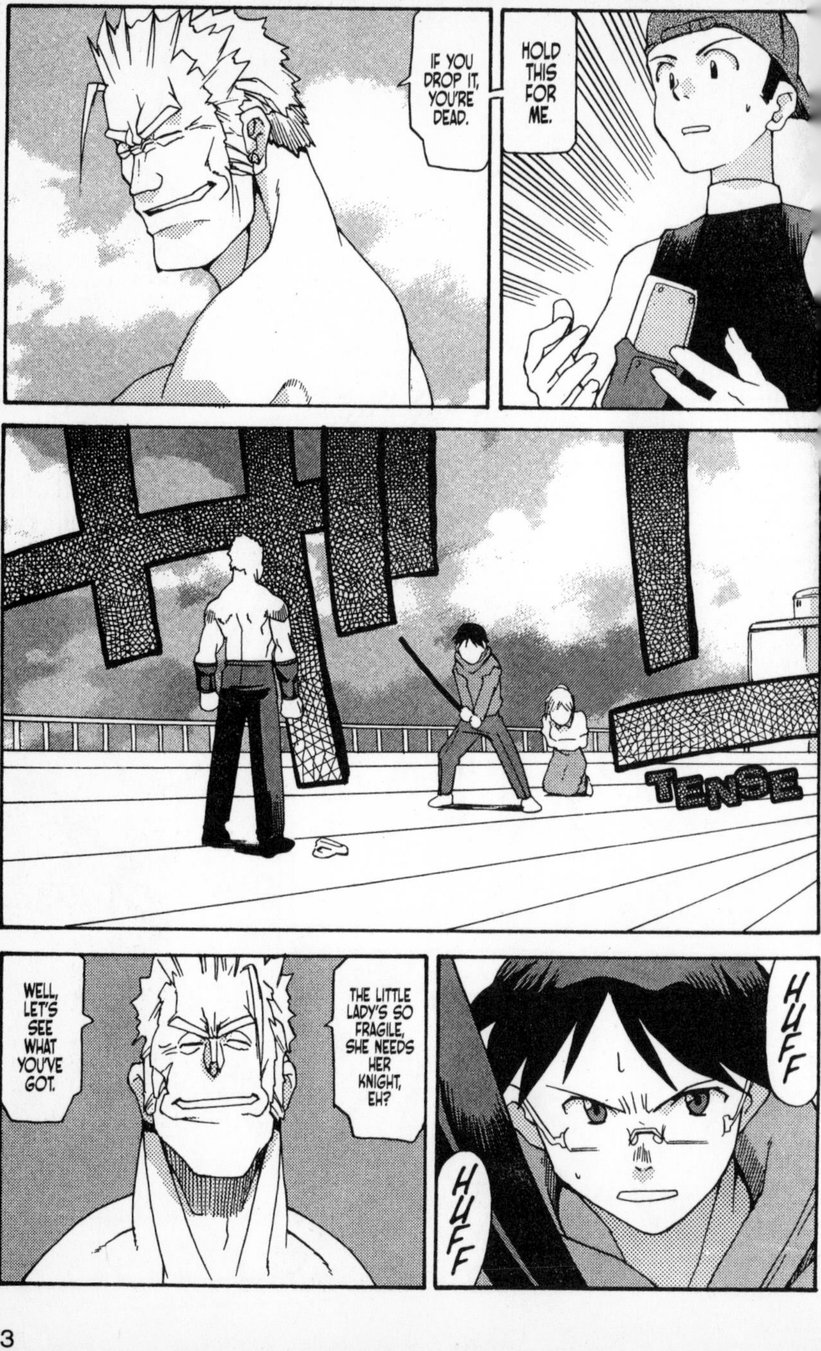
HOLD THIS FOR ME.
IF YOU DROP IT, YOU'RE DEAD.
TENSE
HUFF
HUFF
THE LITTLE LADY'S SO FRAGILE, SHE NEEDS HER KNIGHT, EH?
WELL, LET'S SEE WHAT YOU'VE GOT.

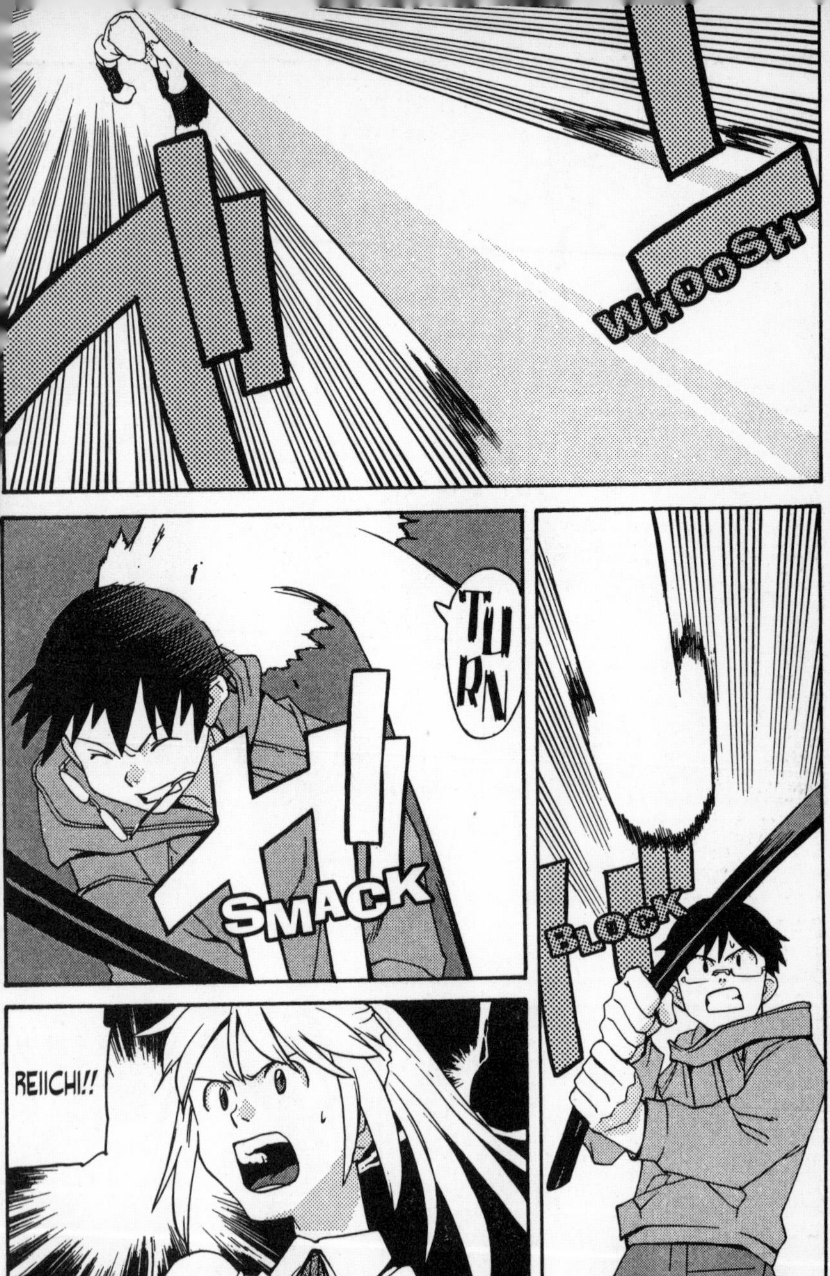
WHOOSH
BLOCK
TURN
SMACK
REIICHI!!

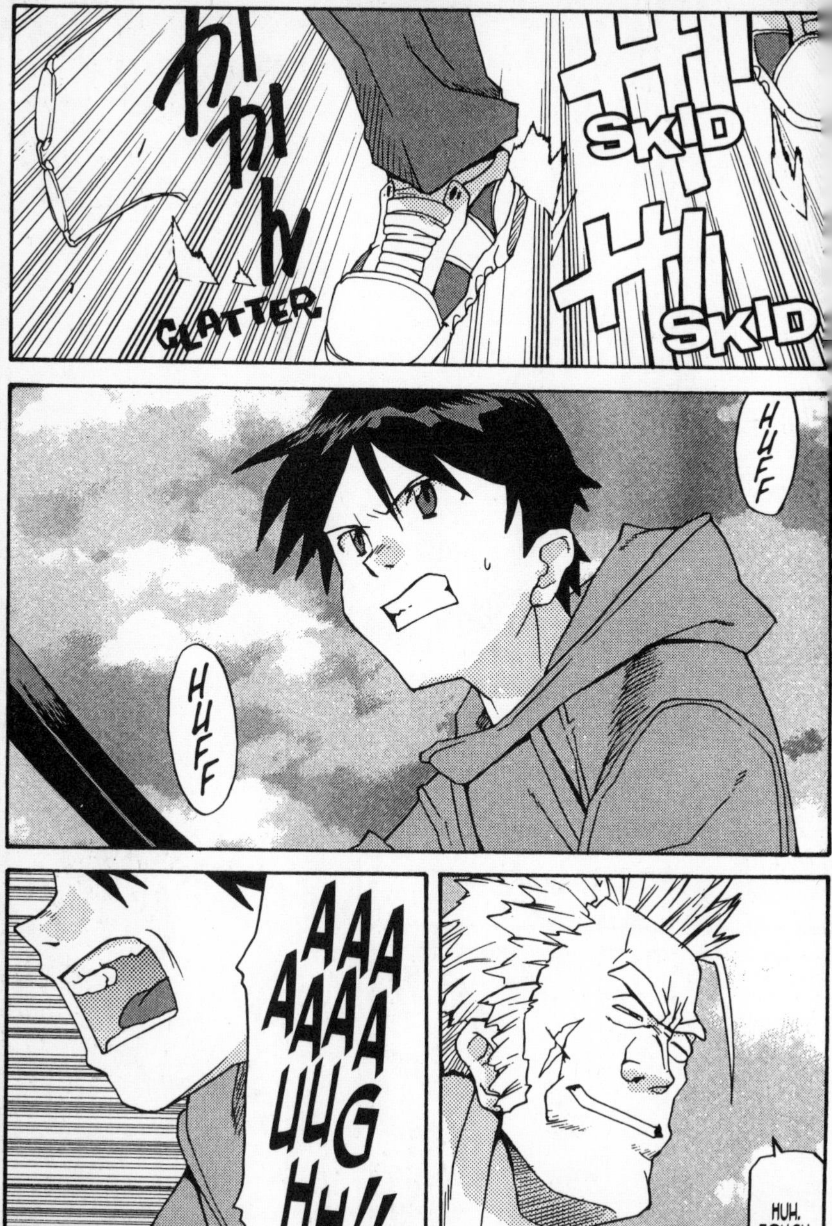
SKID
SKID
CLATTER
HUFF
HUFF
HUH. TOUGH.
AAAAAAAUUGHH!!

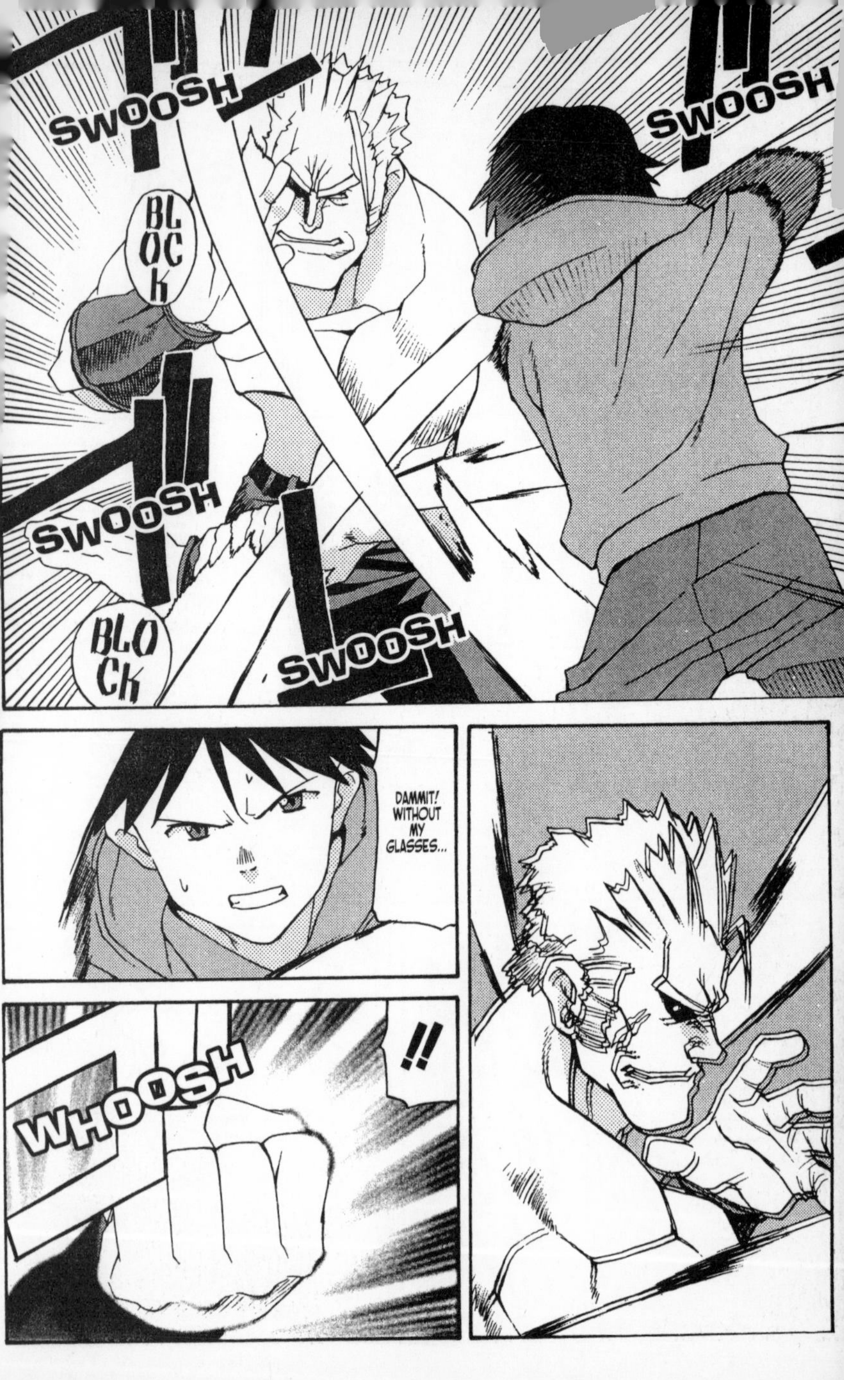
SWOOSH
SWOOSH
BLOCK
SWOOSH
BLOCK
SWOOSH
DAMMIT! WITHOUT MY GLASSES...
!!
WHOOSH

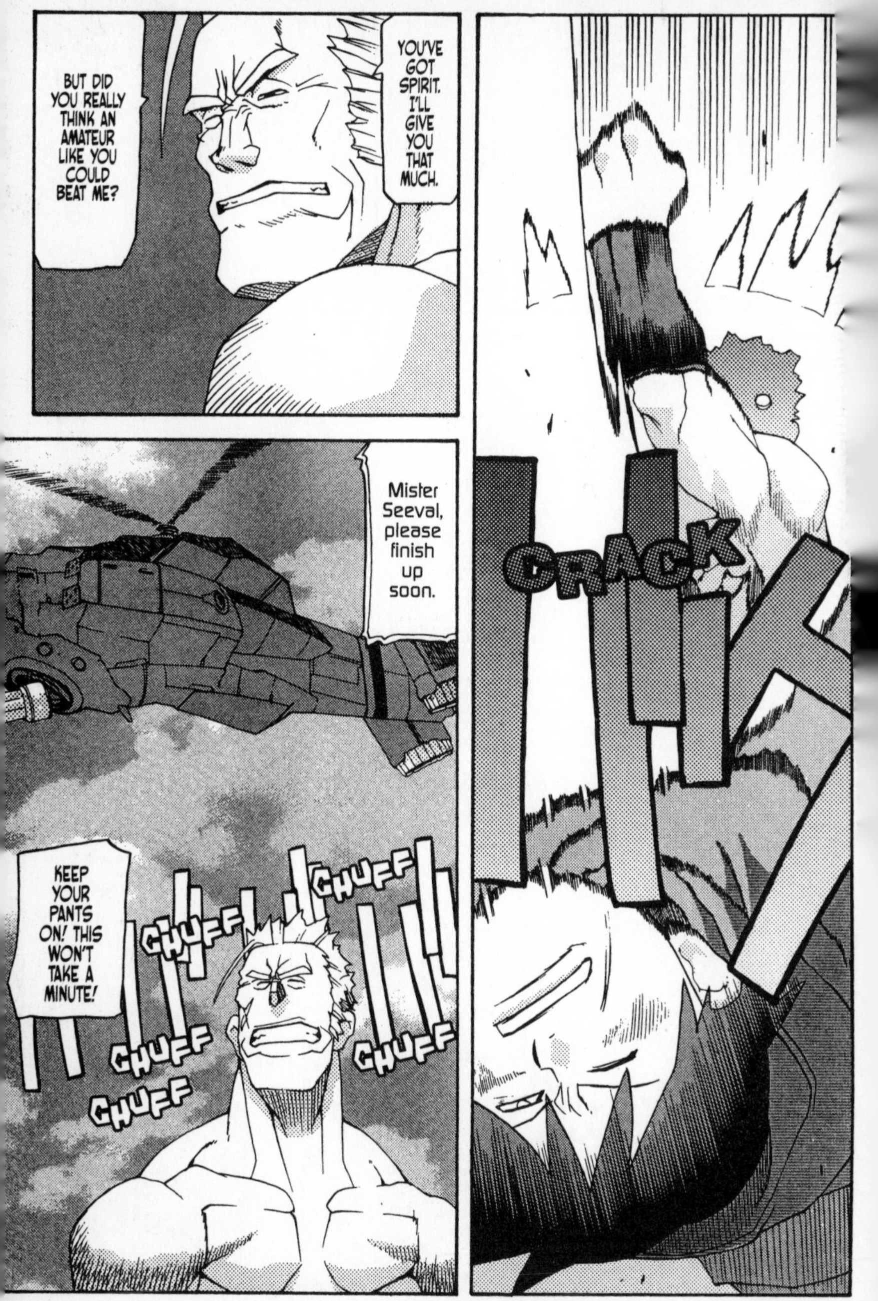
CRACK
YOU'VE GOT SPIRIT. I'LL GIVE YOU THAT MUCH.
BUT DID YOU REALLY THINK AN AMATEUR LIKE YOU COULD BEAT ME?
Mister Seeval, please finish up soon.
KEEP YOUR PANTS ON! THIS WON'T TAKE A MINUTE!
CHUFF
CHUFF
CHUFF
CHUFF
CHUFF

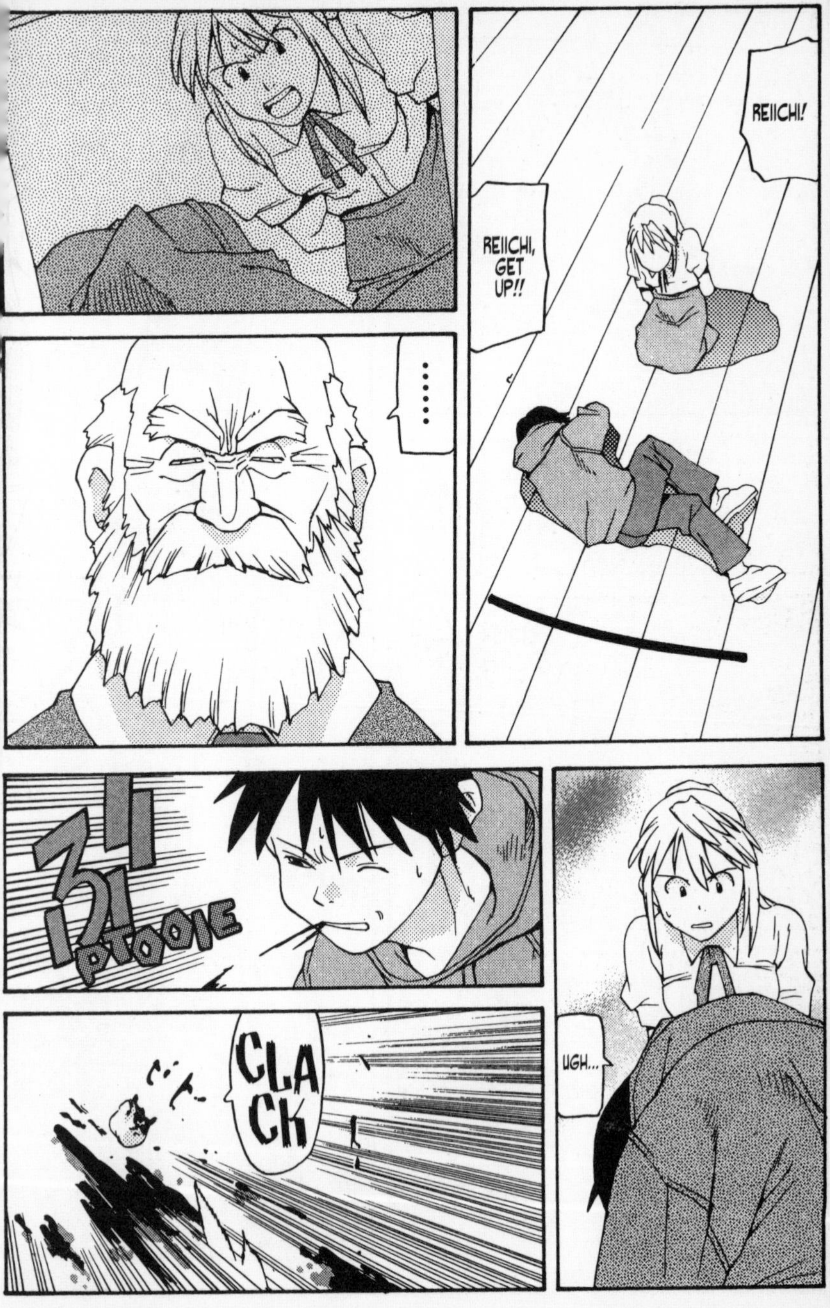
REIICHI!
REIICHI, GET UP!!
......
UGH...
PTOOIE
CLACK

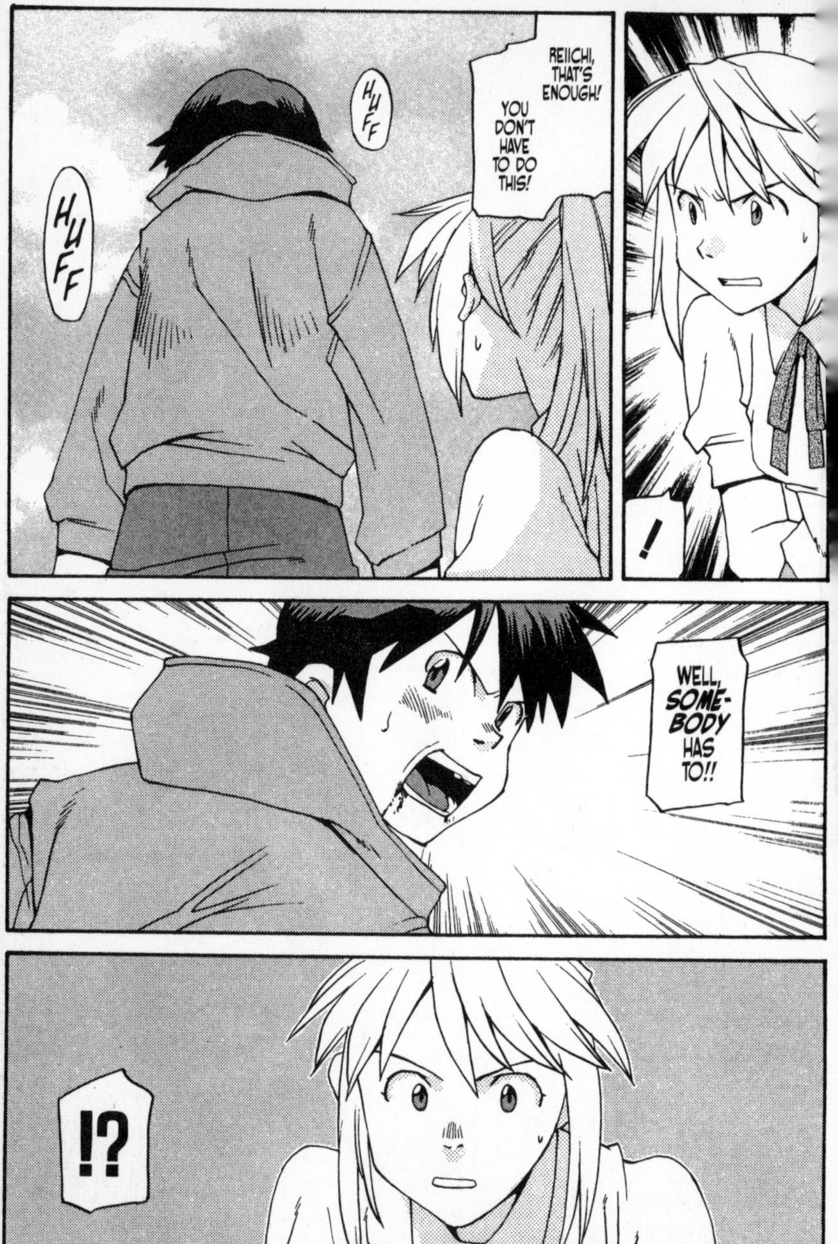
!
REIICHI, THAT'S ENOUGH!
YOU DON'T HAVE TO DO THIS!
HUFF
HUFF
WELL, SOMEBODY HAS TO!!
!?

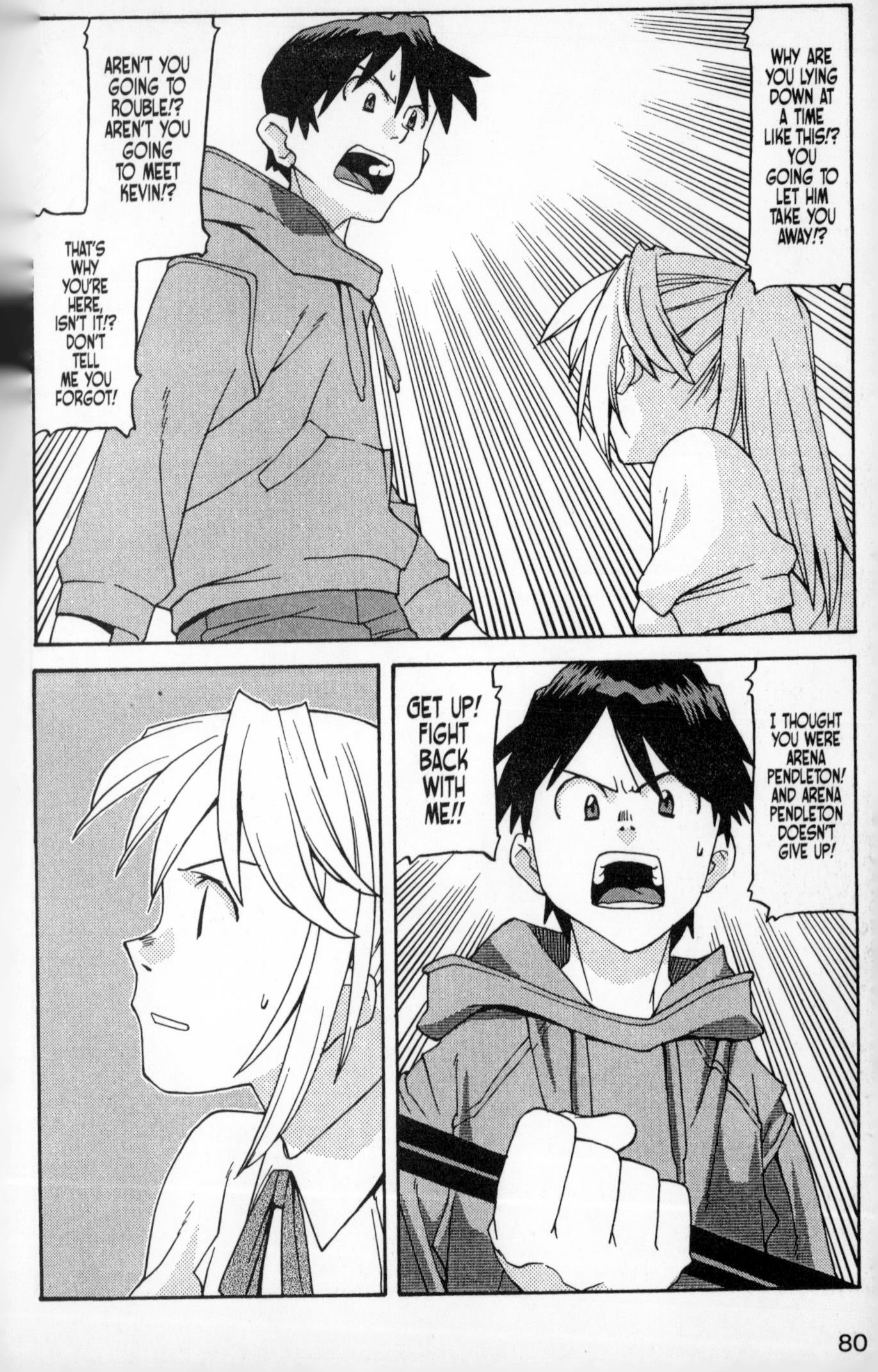
WHY ARE YOU LYING DOWN AT A TIME LIKE THIS!? YOU GOING TO LET HIM TAKE YOU AWAY!?
AREN'T YOU GOING TO ROUBLE!? AREN'T YOU GOING TO MEET KEVIN!?
THAT'S WHY YOU'RE HERE, ISN'T IT!? DON'T TELL ME YOU FORGOT!
I THOUGHT YOU WERE ARENA PENDLETON! AND ARENA PENDLETON DOESN'T GIVE UP!
GET UP! FIGHT BACK WITH ME!!

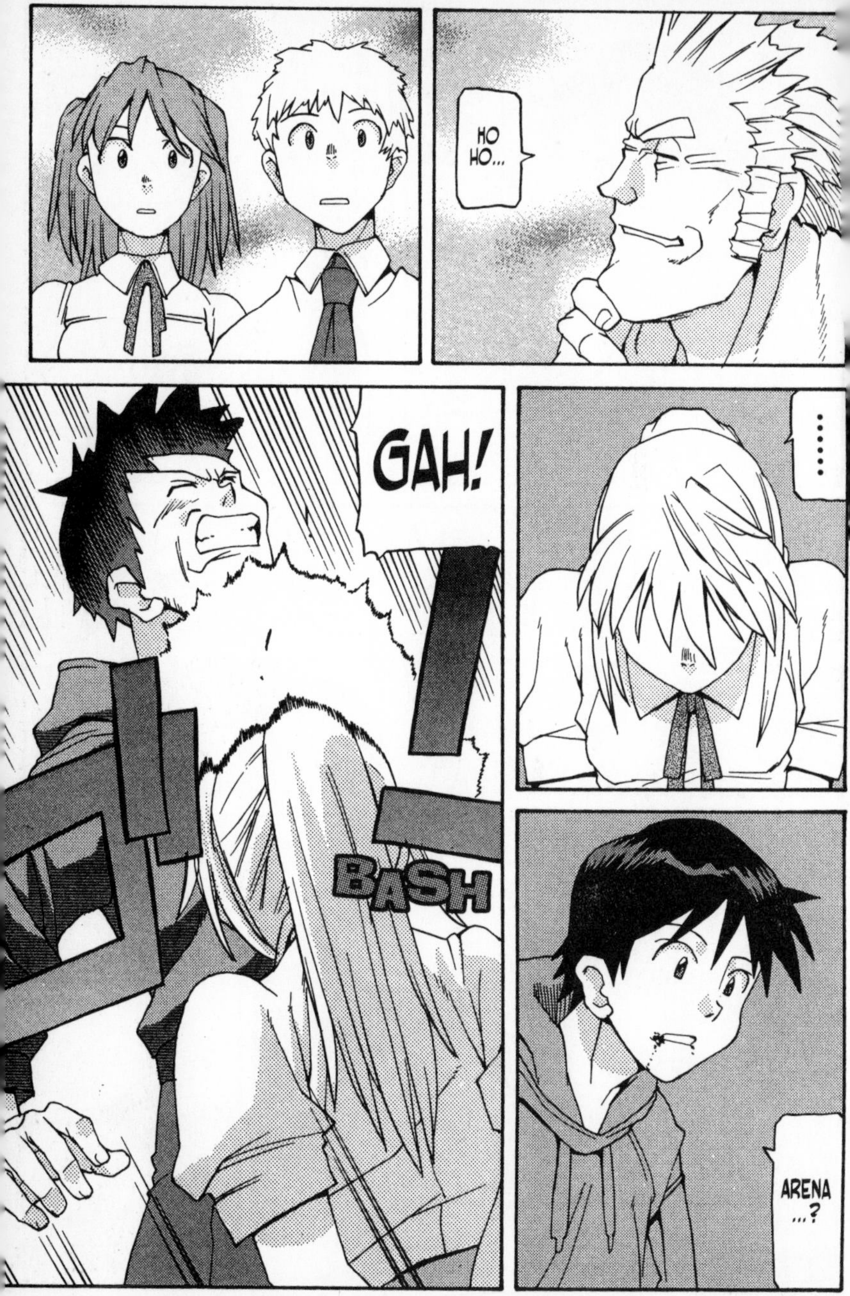
HO HO...
......
ARENA ...?
GAH!
BASH

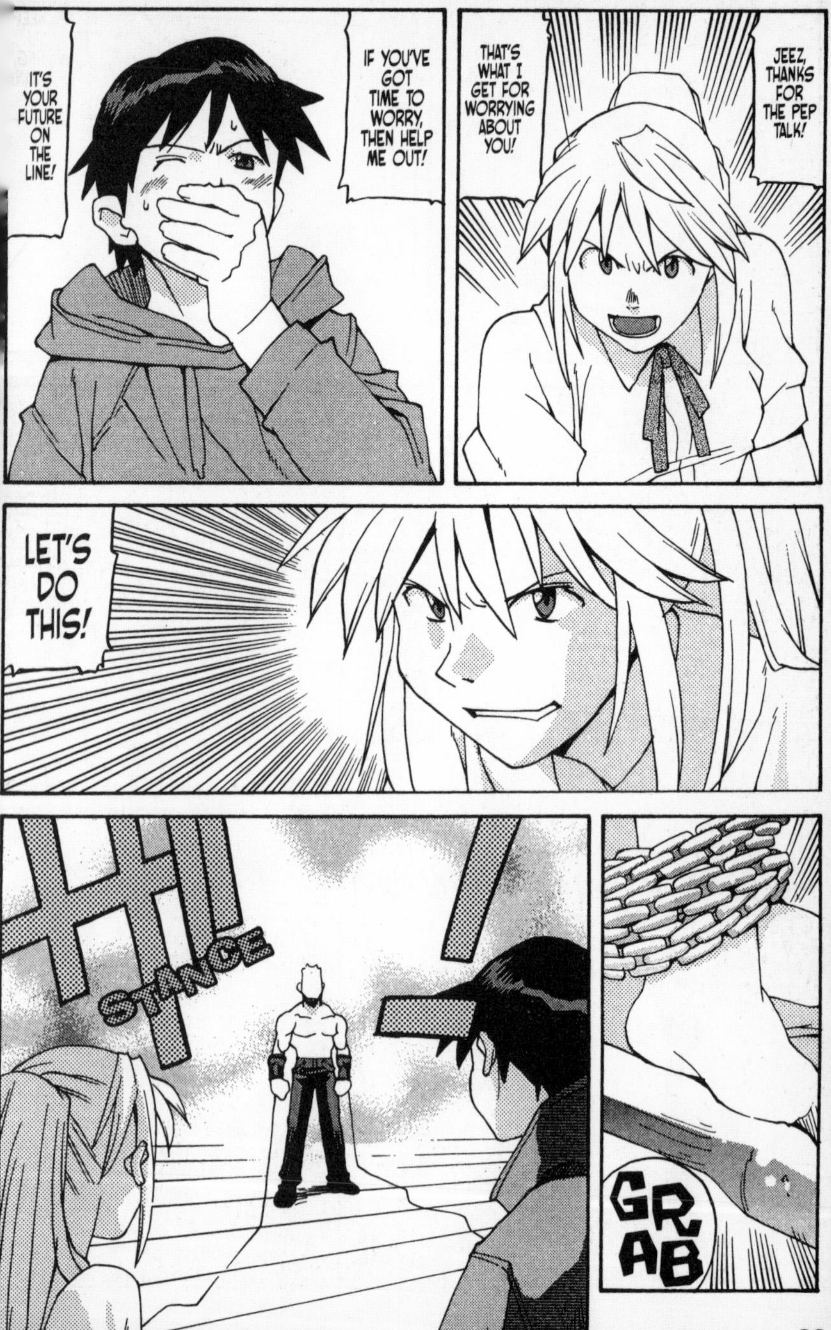
JEEZ, THANKS FOR THE PEP TALK!
THAT'S WHAT I GET FOR WORRYING ABOUT YOU!
IF YOU'VE GOT TIME TO WORRY, THEN HELP ME OUT!
IT'S YOUR FUTURE ON THE LINE!
LET'S DO THIS!
GRAB
STANCE

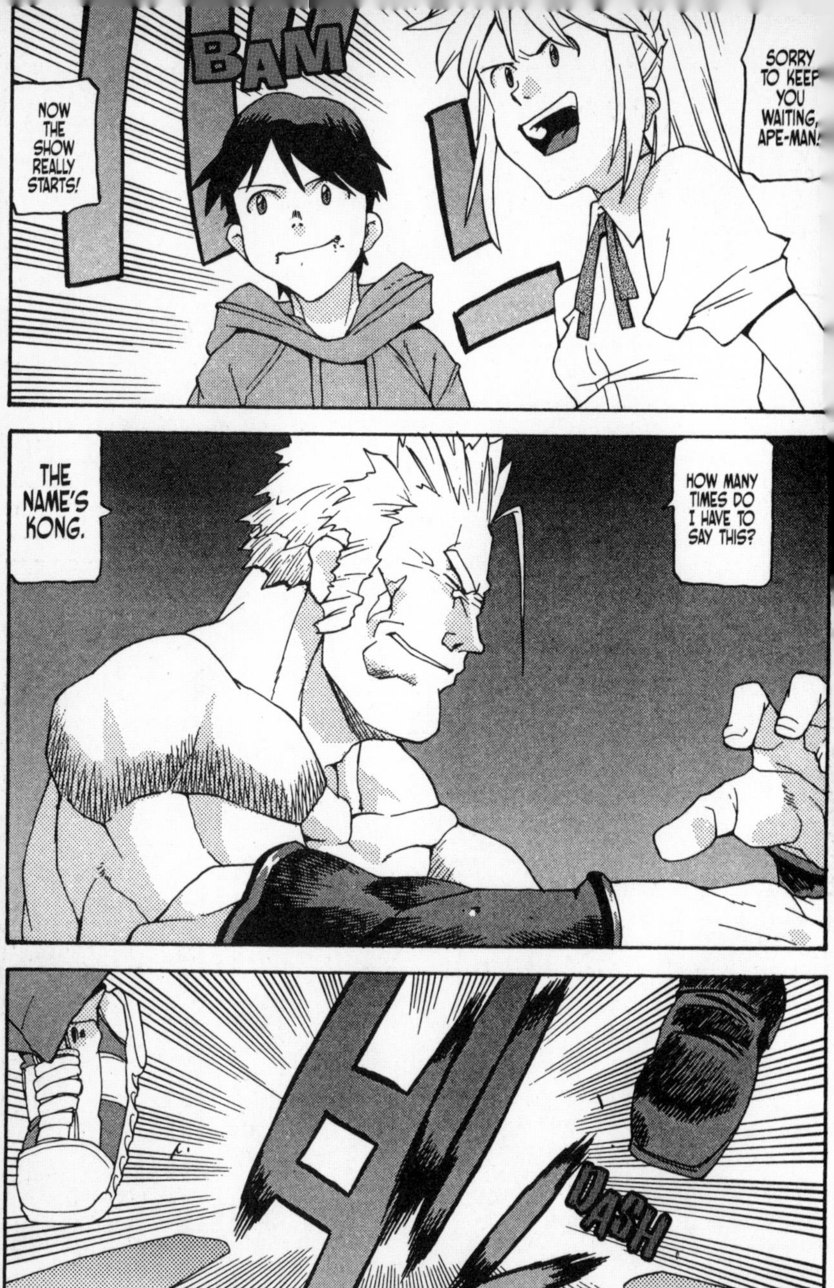
SORRY TO KEEP YOU WAITING, APE-MAN!
BAM
NOW THE SHOW REALLY STARTS!
HOW MANY TIMES DO I HAVE TO SAY THIS?
THE NAME'S KONG.
DASH

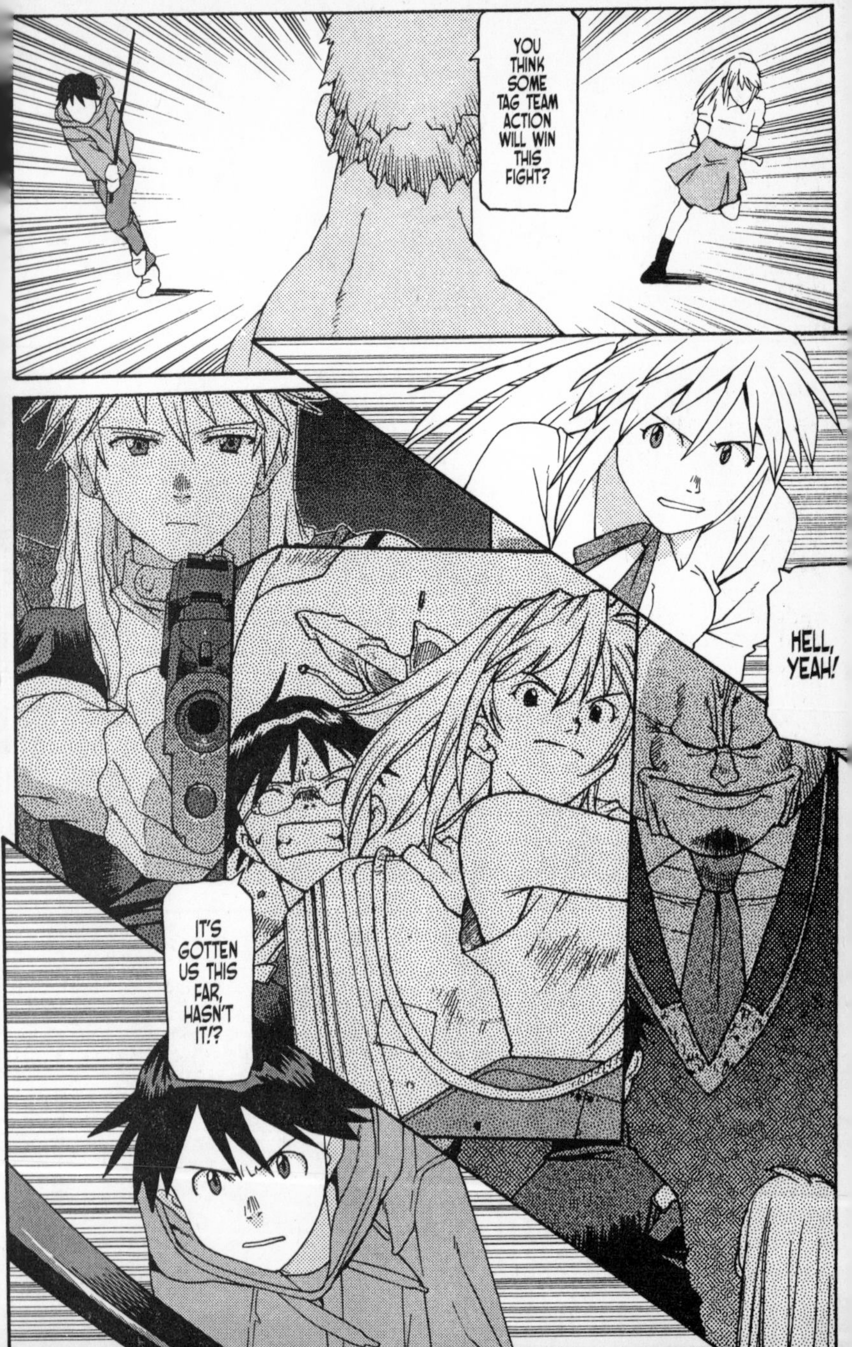
YOU THINK SOME TAG TEAM ACTION WILL WIN THIS FIGHT?
HELL, YEAH!
IT'S GOTTEN US THIS FAR, HASN'T IT!?

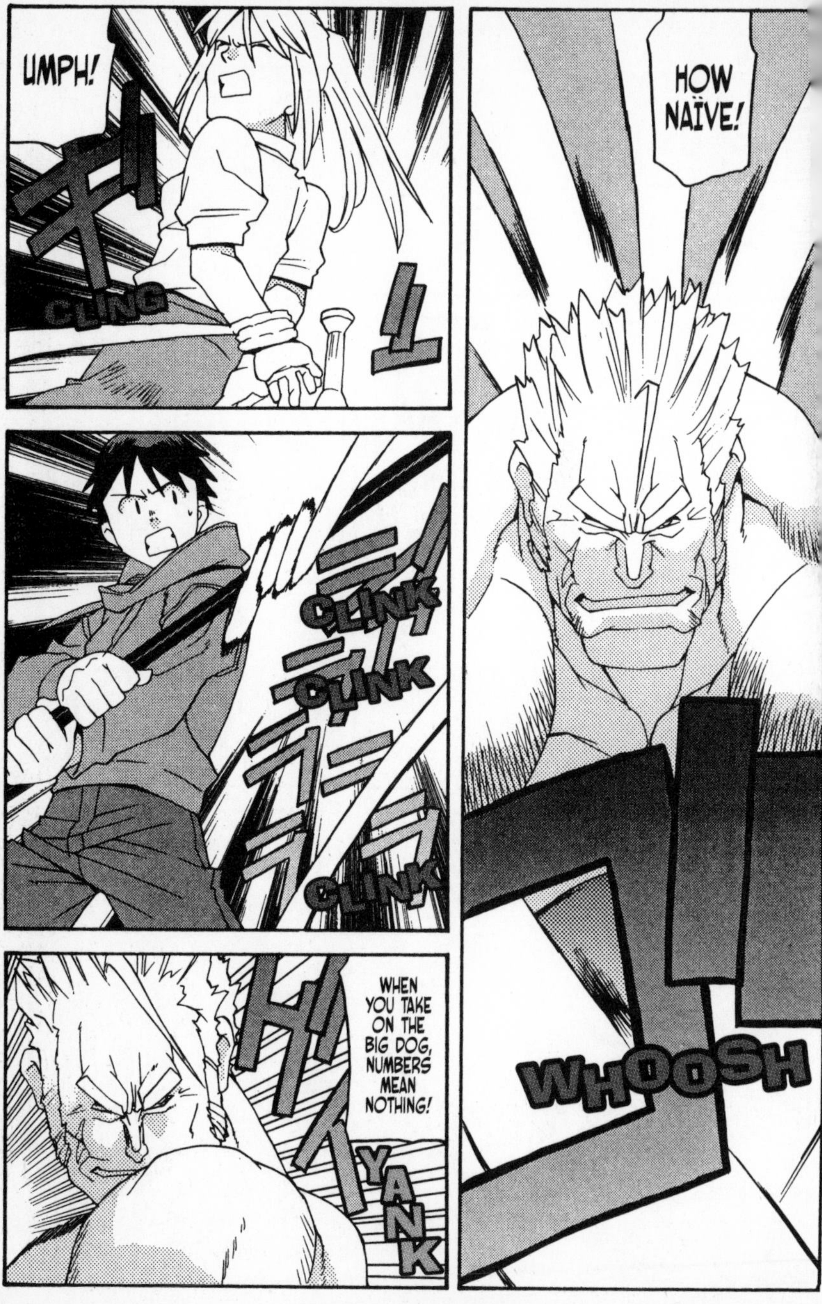
HOW NAÏVE!
WHOOSH
UMPH!
CLING
CLINK
CLINK
CLINK
WHEN YOU TAKE ON THE BIG DOG, NUMBERS MEAN NOTHING!
YANK

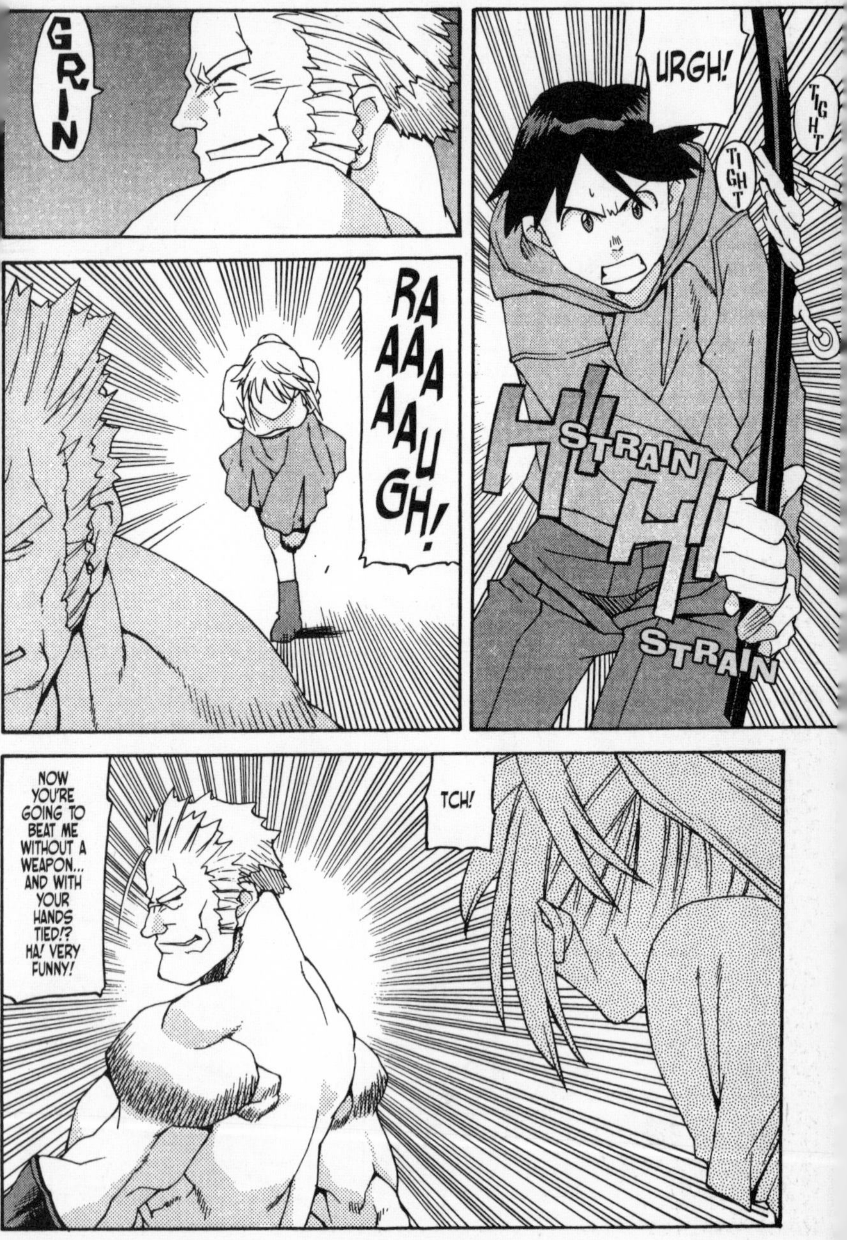
URGH!
TIGHT
TIGHT
STRAIN
STRAIN
GRIN
RAAAAAAUGH!
TCH!
NOW YOU'RE GOING TO BEAT ME WITHOUT A WEAPON... AND WITH YOUR HANDS TIED!? HA! VERY FUNNY!

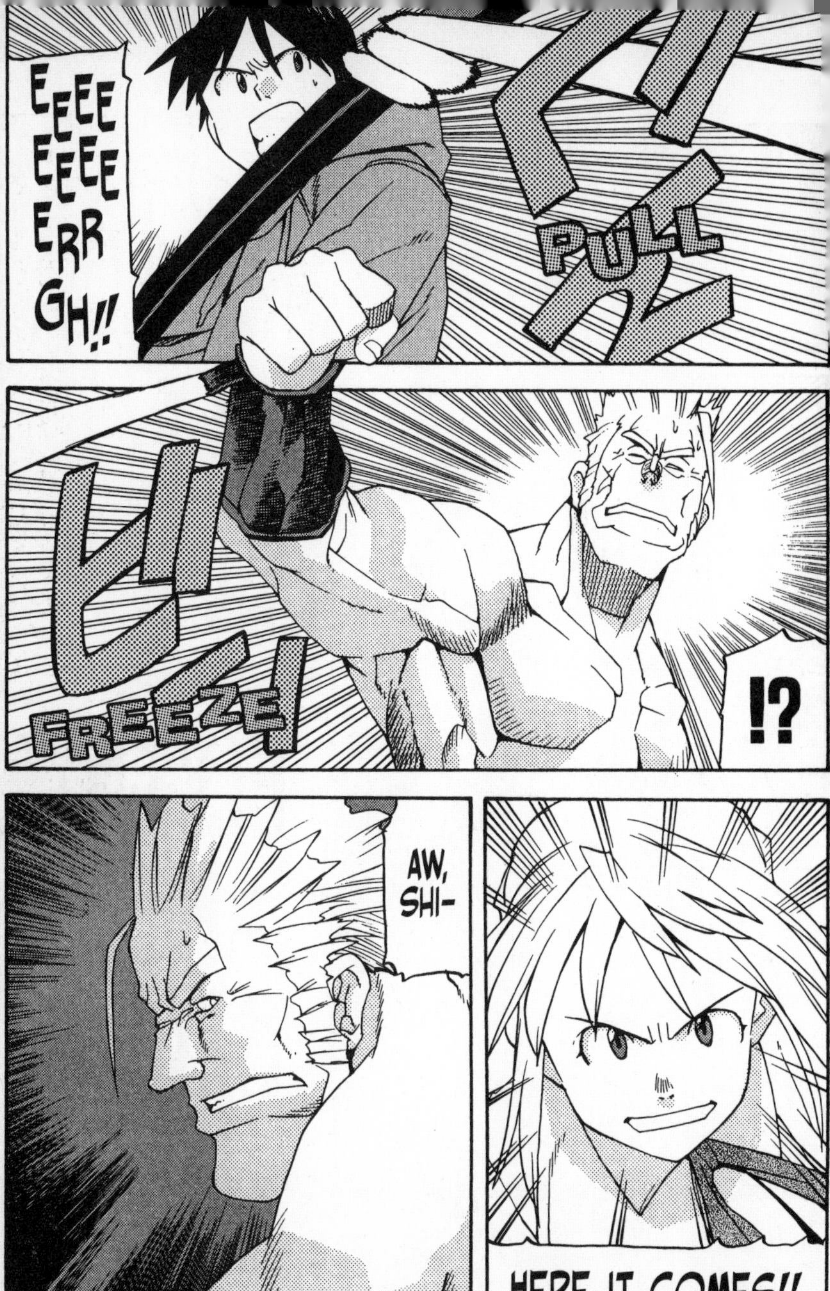
PULL
EEEEEEEEERRGH!!
!?
FREEZE!
HERE IT COMES!!
AW, SHI-

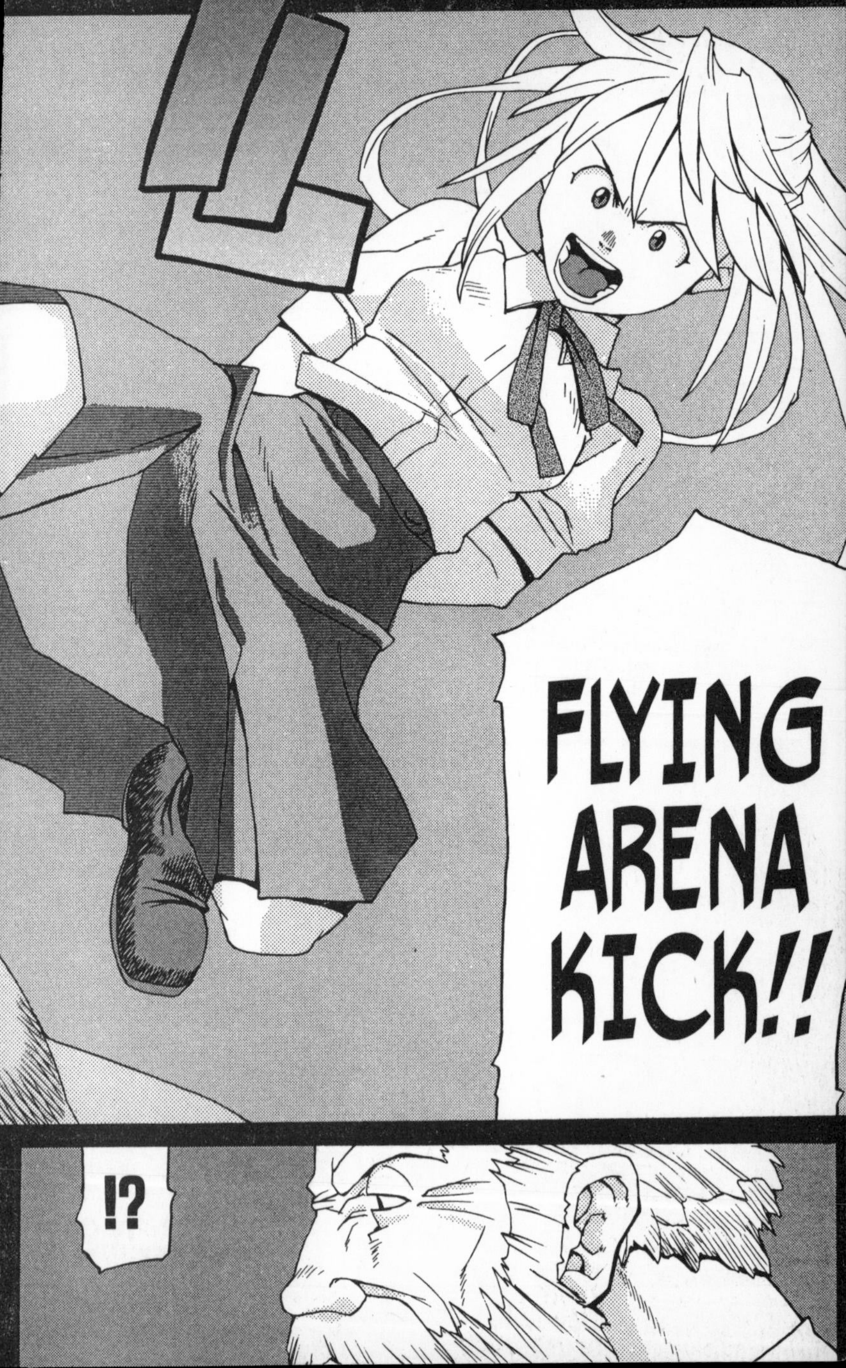
FLYING ARENA KICK!!
!?

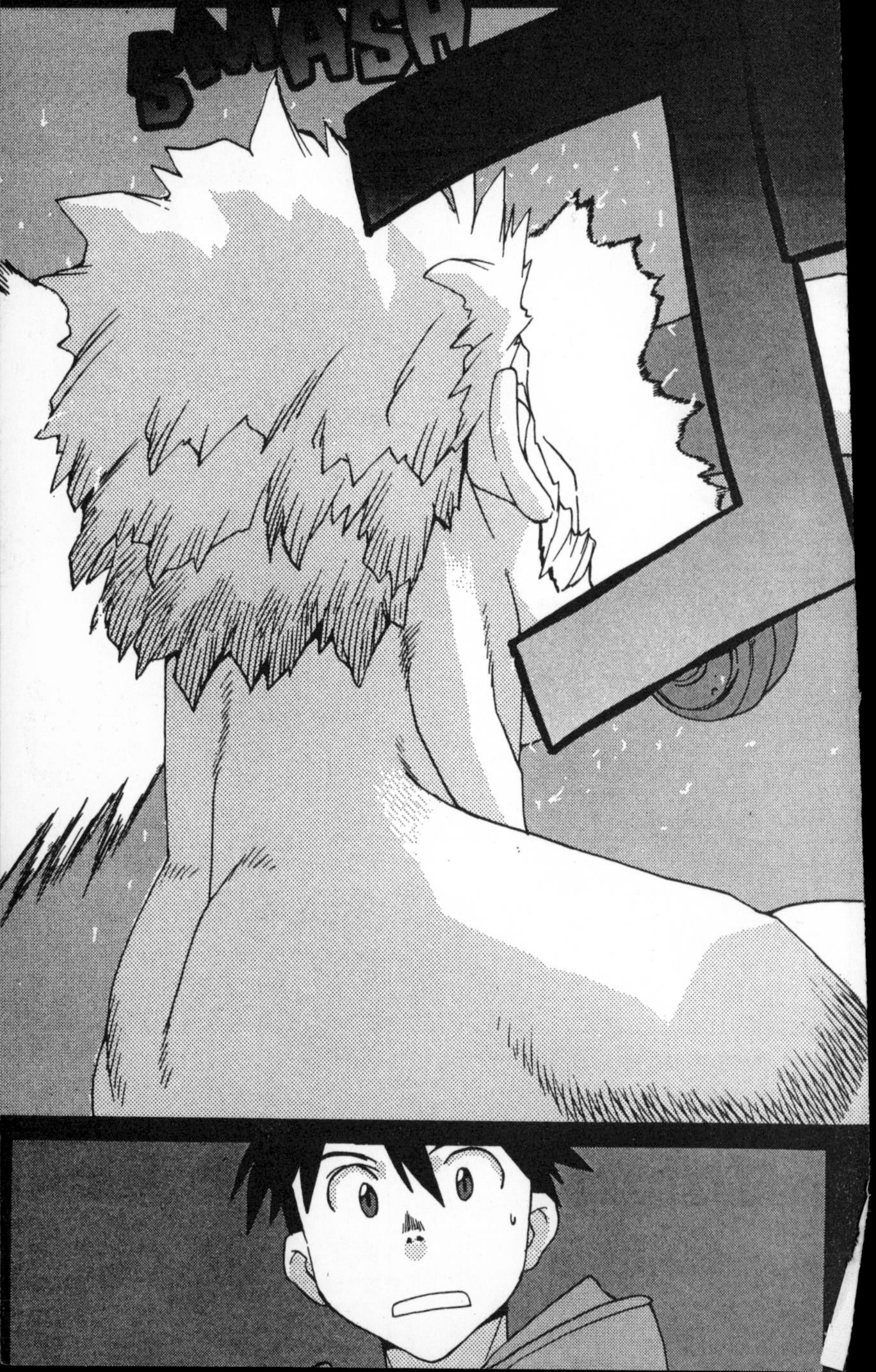
SMASH

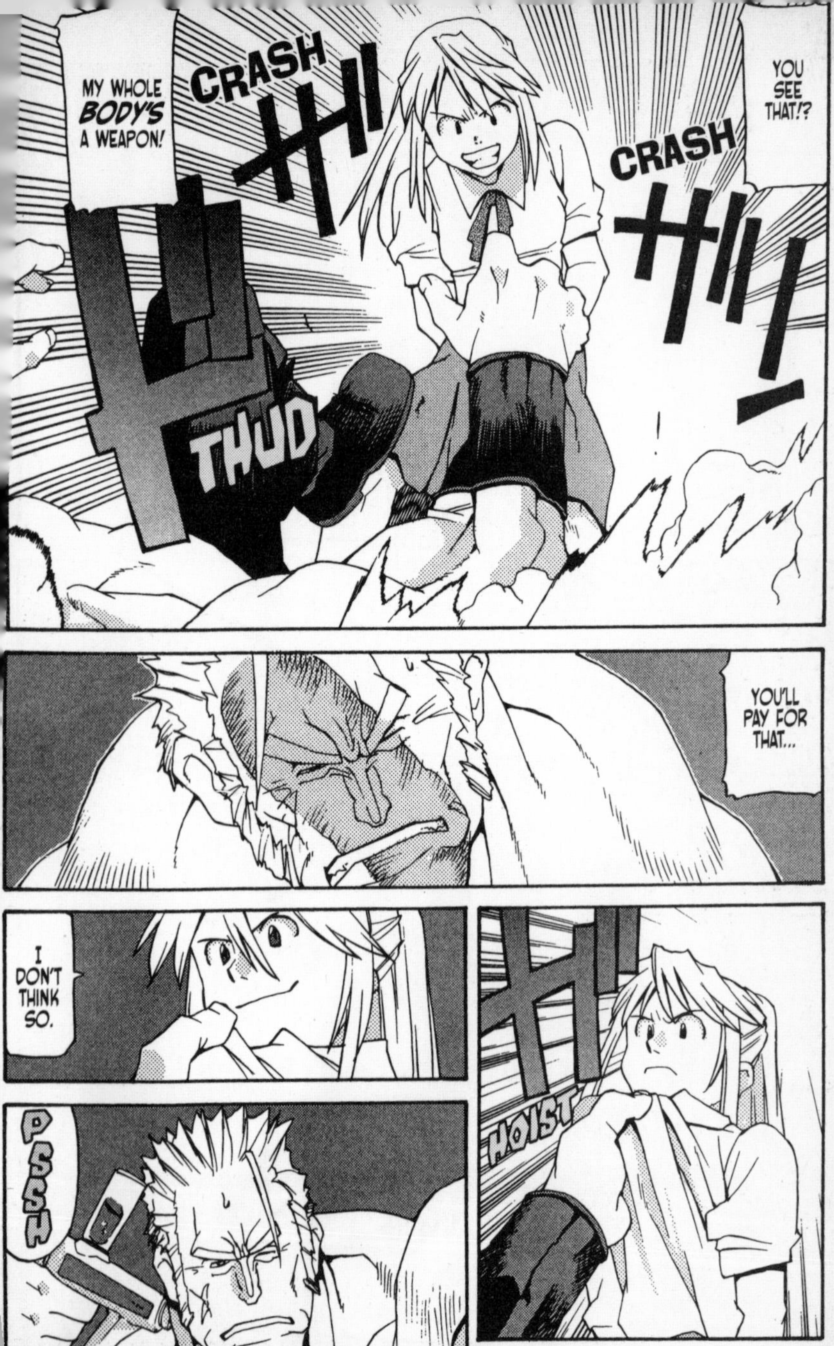
YOU SEE THAT!?
CRASH
CRASH
MY WHOLE BODY'S A WEAPON!
THUD
YOU'LL PAY FOR THAT...
HOIST
I DON'T THINK SO.
PSSH

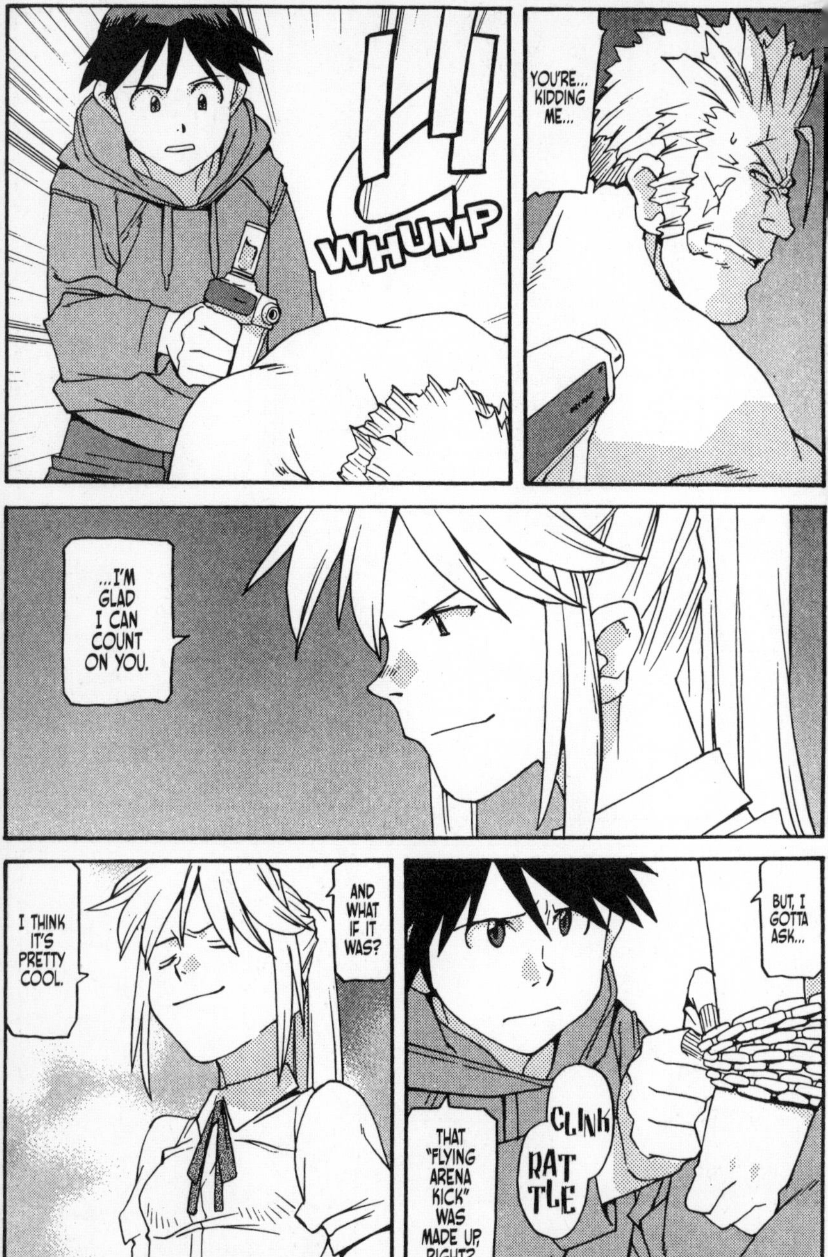
YOU'RE... KIDDING ME...
WHUMP
...I'M GLAD I CAN COUNT ON YOU.
BUT, I GOTTA ASK...
CLINK
RATTLE
THAT "FLYING ARENA KICK" WAS MADE UP, RIGHT?
AND WHAT IF IT WAS?
I THINK IT'S PRETTY COOL.

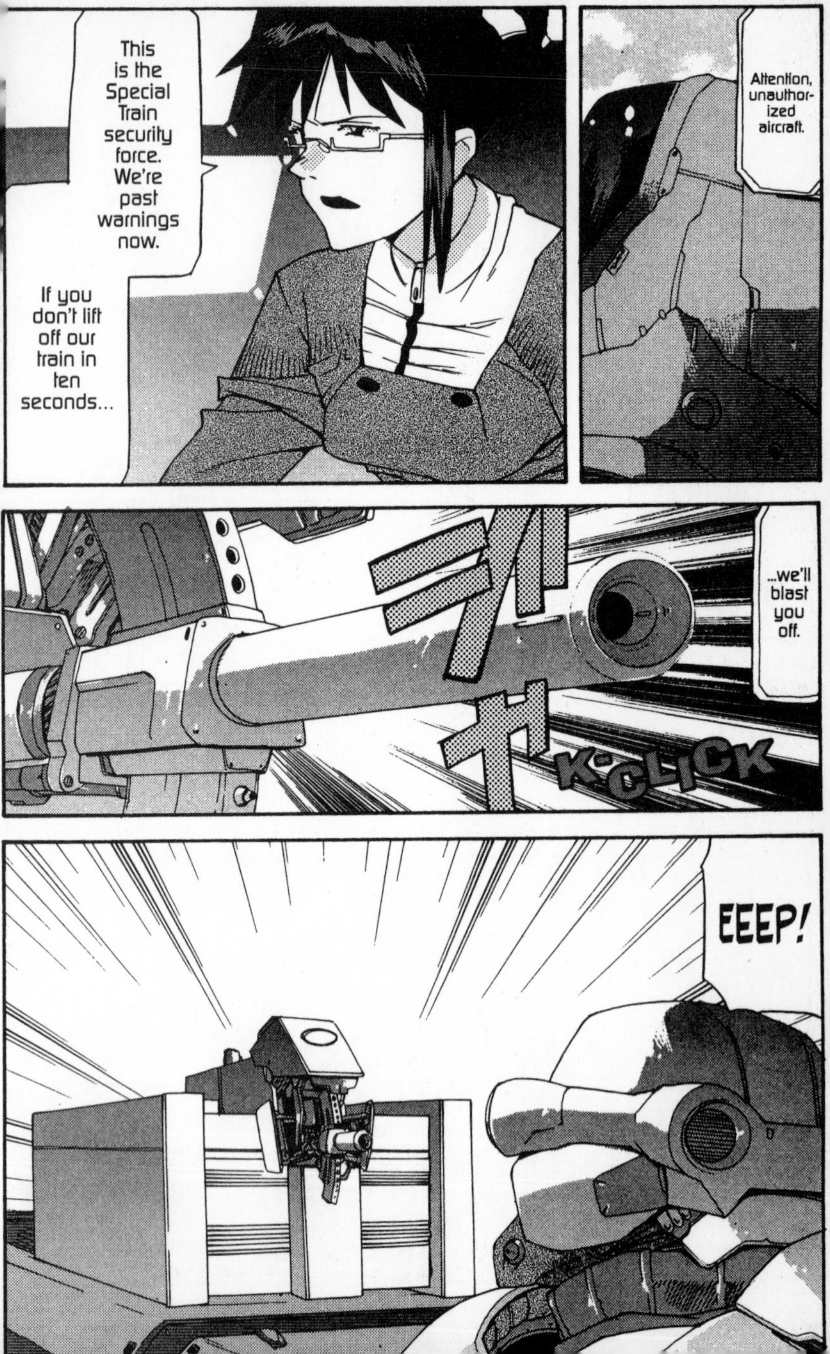
Attention, unauthorized aircraft.
This is the Special Train security force. We're past warnings now.
If you don't lift off our train in ten seconds...
...we'll blast you off.
K-CLICK
EEEP!

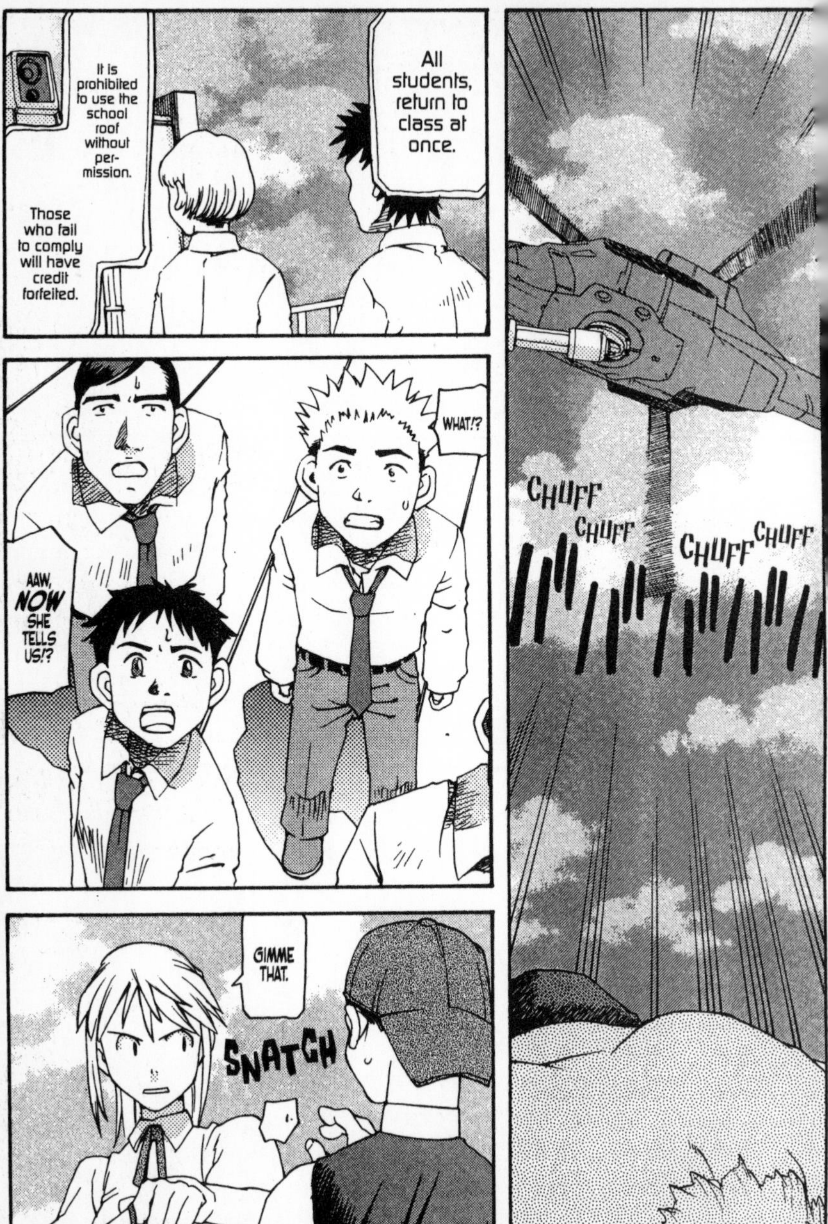
CHUFF
CHUFF
CHUFF
CHUFF
All students, return to class at once.
It is prohibited to use the school roof without per-mission.
Those who fail to comply will have credit forfeited.
WHAT!?
AAW, NOW SHE TELLS US!?
GIMME THAT.
SNATCH

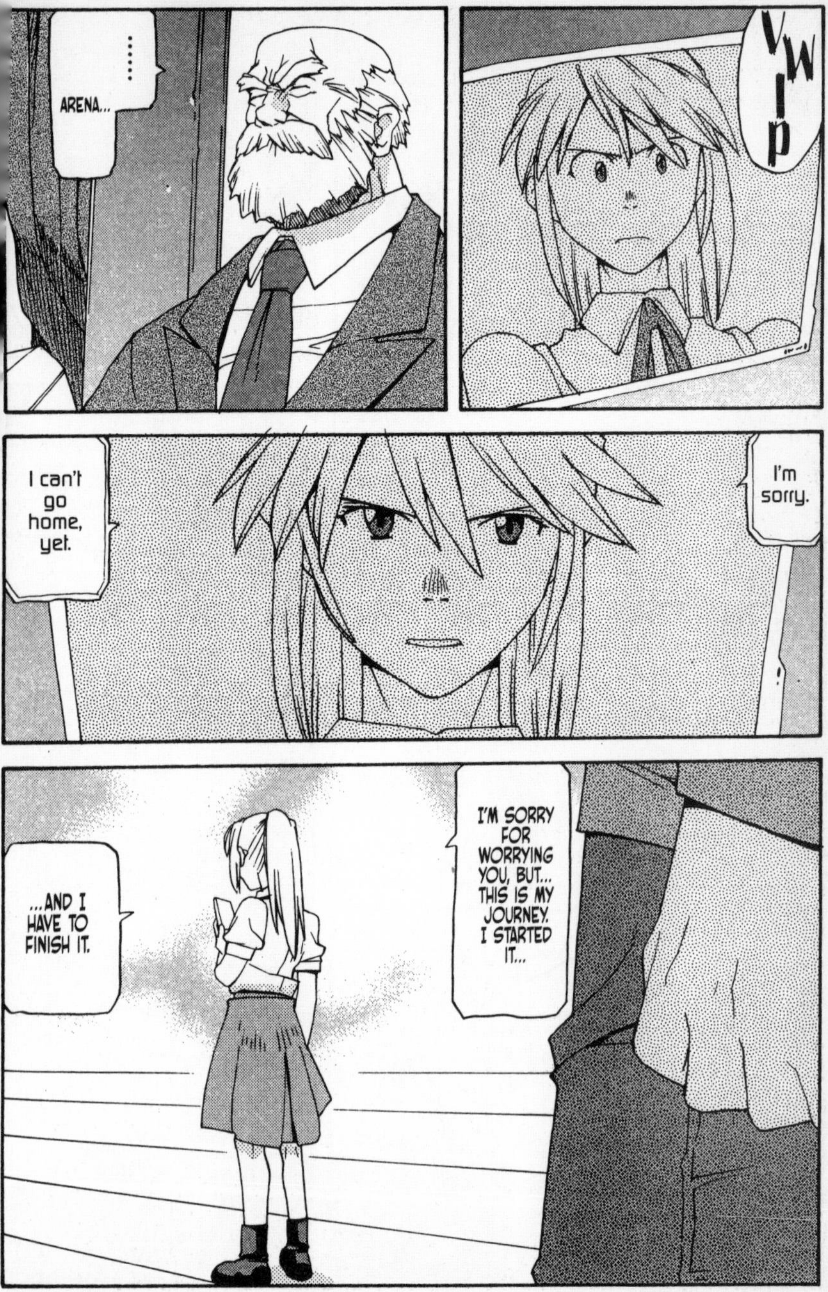
VWIP
......
ARENA...
I'm sorry.
I can't go home, yet.
I'M SORRY FOR WORRYING YOU, BUT... THIS IS MY JOURNEY. I STARTED IT...
...AND I HAVE TO FINISH IT.

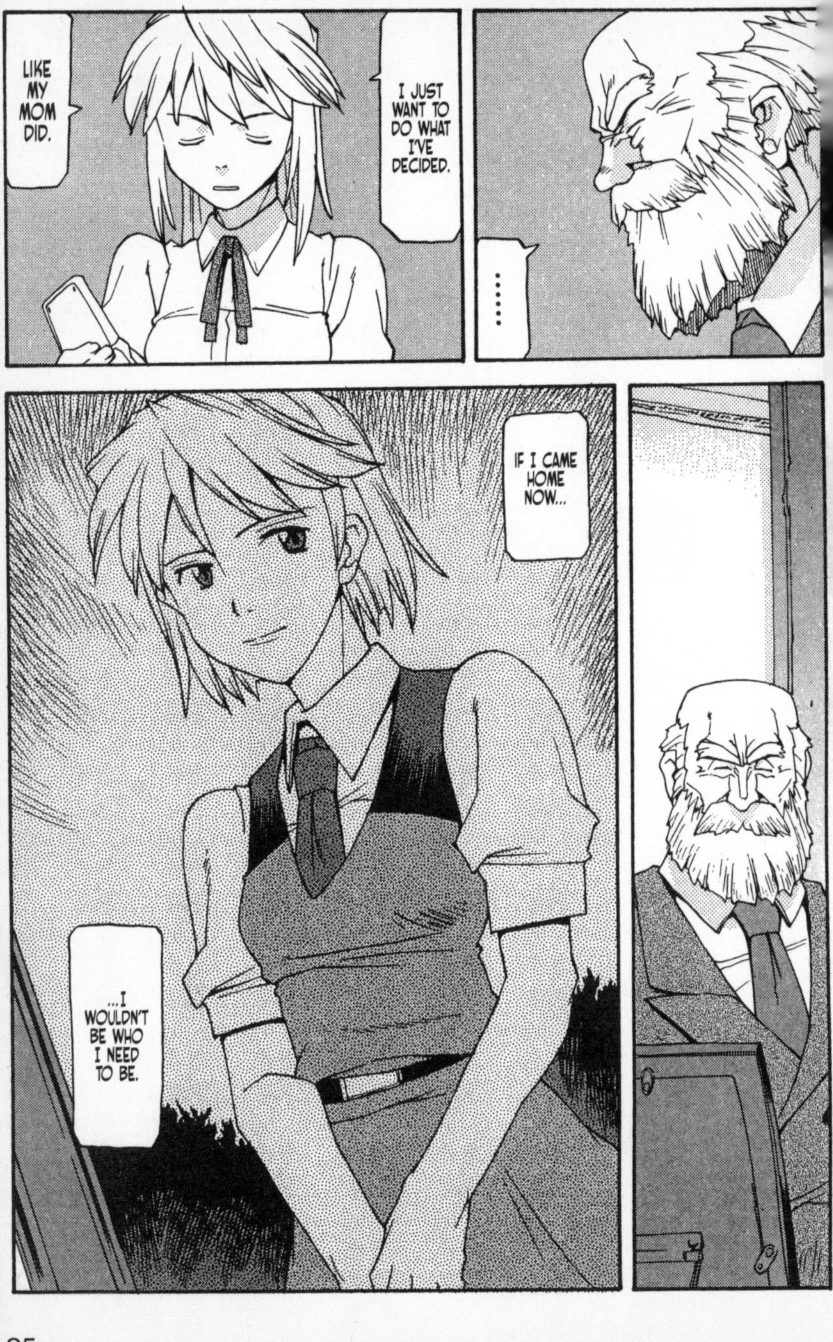
......
I JUST WANT TO DO WHAT I'VE DECIDED.
LIKE MY MOM DID.
IF I CAME HOME NOW...
...I WOULDN'T BE WHO I NEED TO BE.

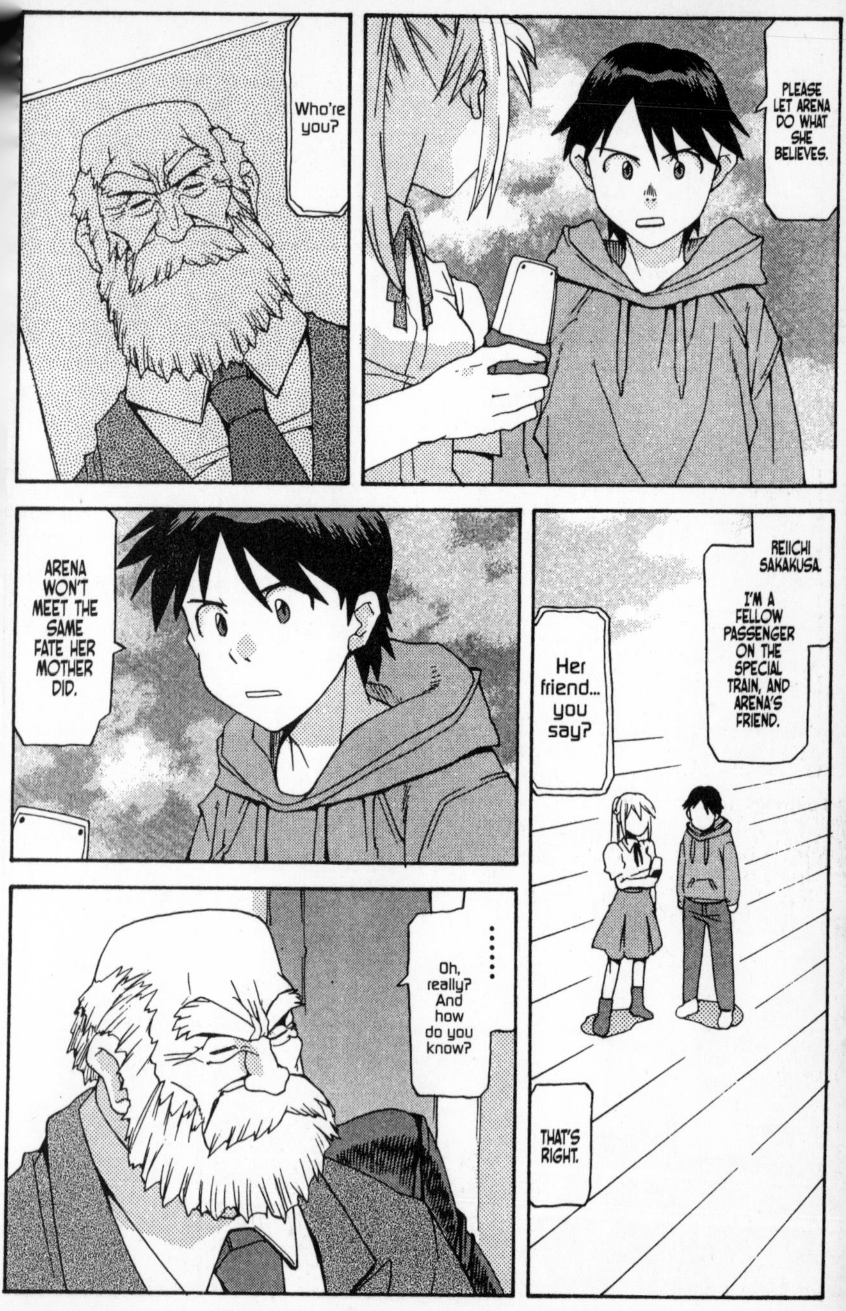
PLEASE LET ARENA DO WHAT SHE BELIEVES.
Who're you?
REIICHI SAKAKUSA.
I'M A FELLOW PASSENGER ON THE SPECIAL TRAIN, AND ARENA'S FRIEND.
Her friend... you say?
THAT'S RIGHT.
ARENA WON'T MEET THE SAME FATE HER MOTHER DID.
......
Oh, really? And how do you know?

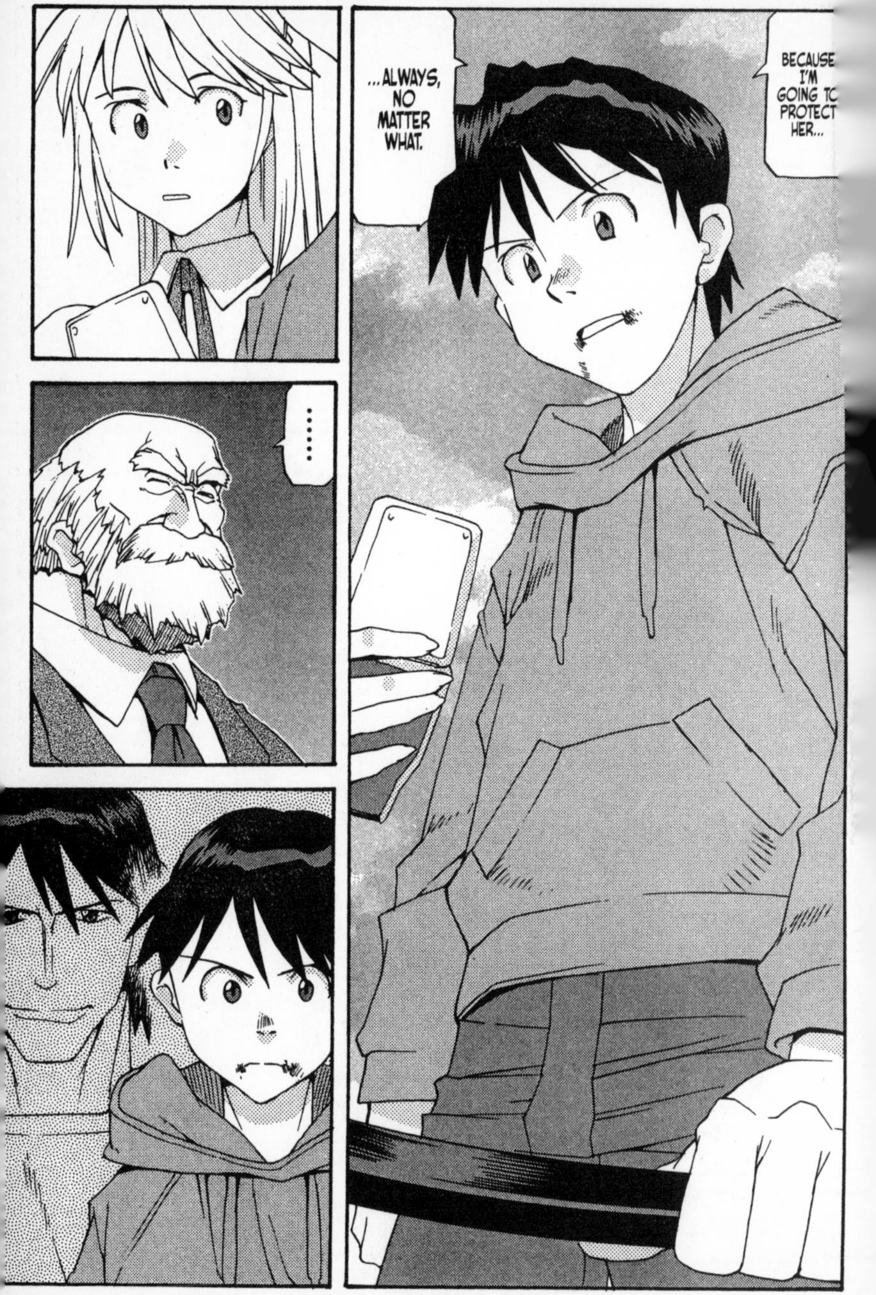
BECAUSE I'M GOING TO PROTECT HER...
...ALWAYS, NO MATTER WHAT.
......

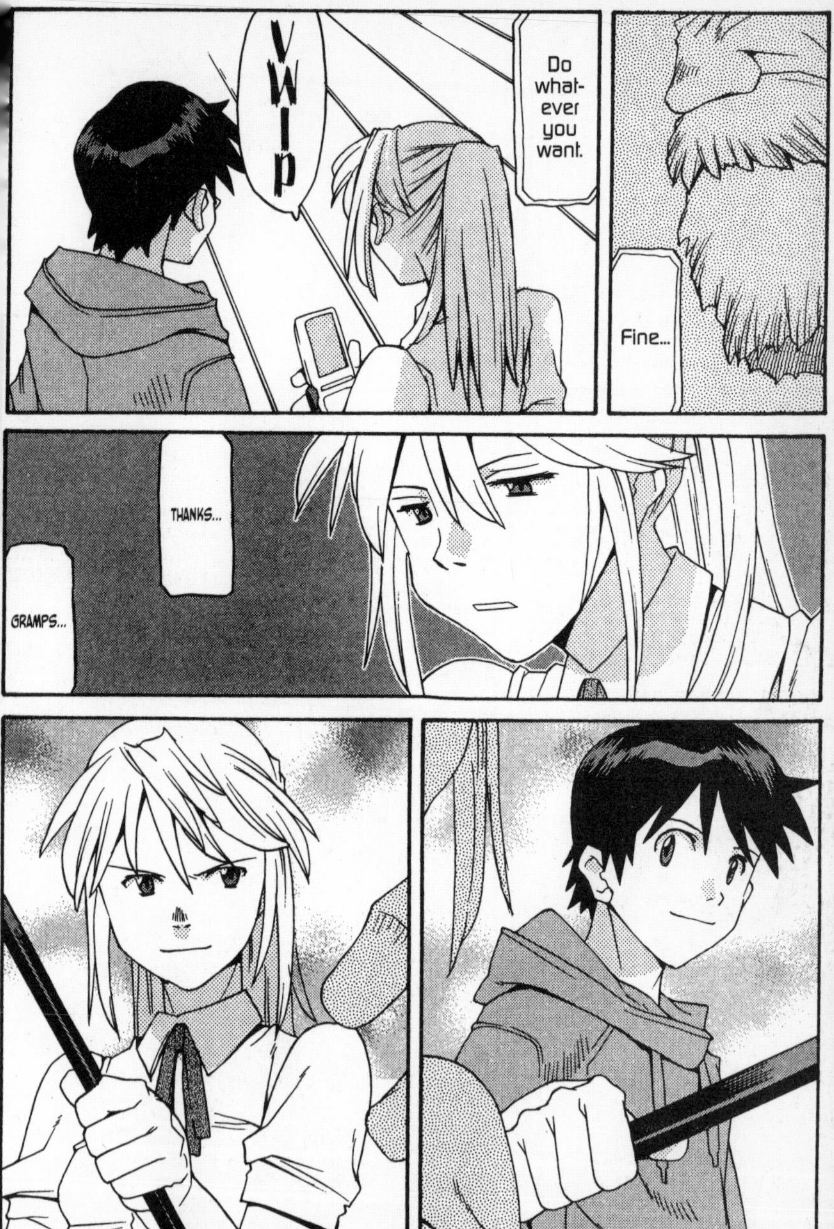

Fine...
Do what-ever you want.
VWIP
THANKS...
GRAMPS...

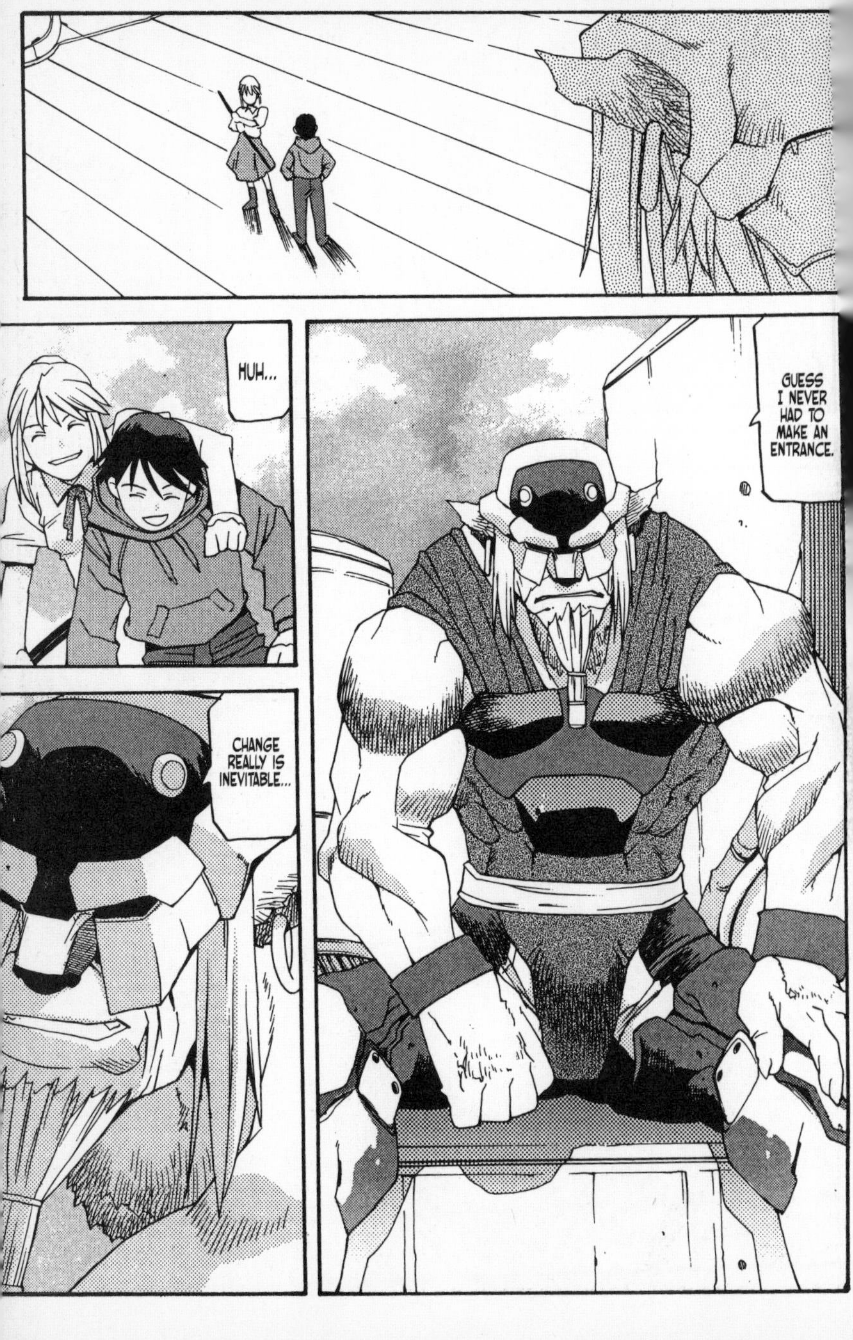
GUESS I NEVER HAD TO MAKE AN ENTRANCE.
HUH...
CHANGE REALLY IS INEVITABLE...

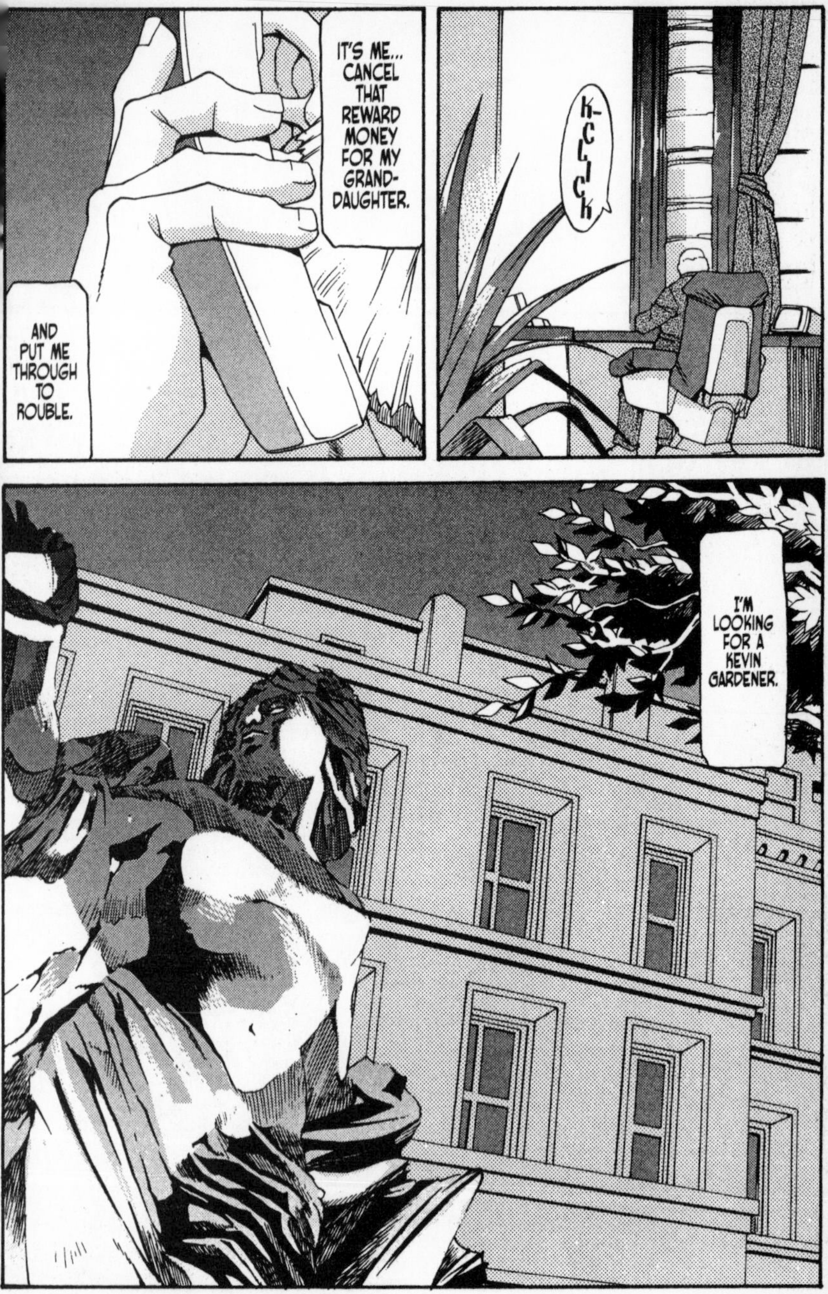
K-CLICK
IT'S ME... CANCEL THAT REWARD MONEY FOR MY GRAND-DAUGHTER.
AND PUT ME THROUGH TO ROUBLE.
I'M LOOKING FOR A KEVIN GARDENER.

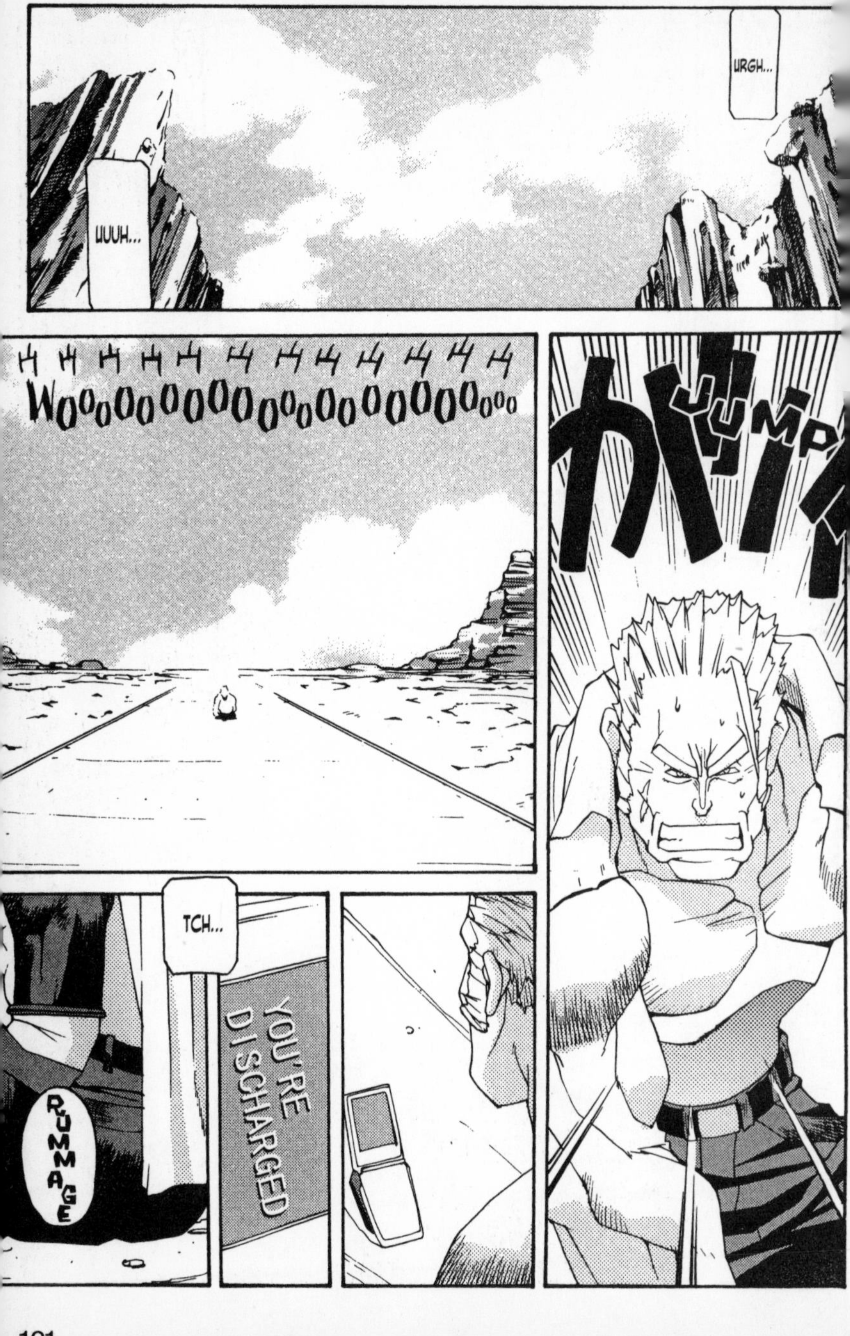
URGH...
UUUH...
JUMP
WOOOOOOOOOOOOOOOOOOOO
TCH...
YOU'RE DISCHARGED
RUMMAGE

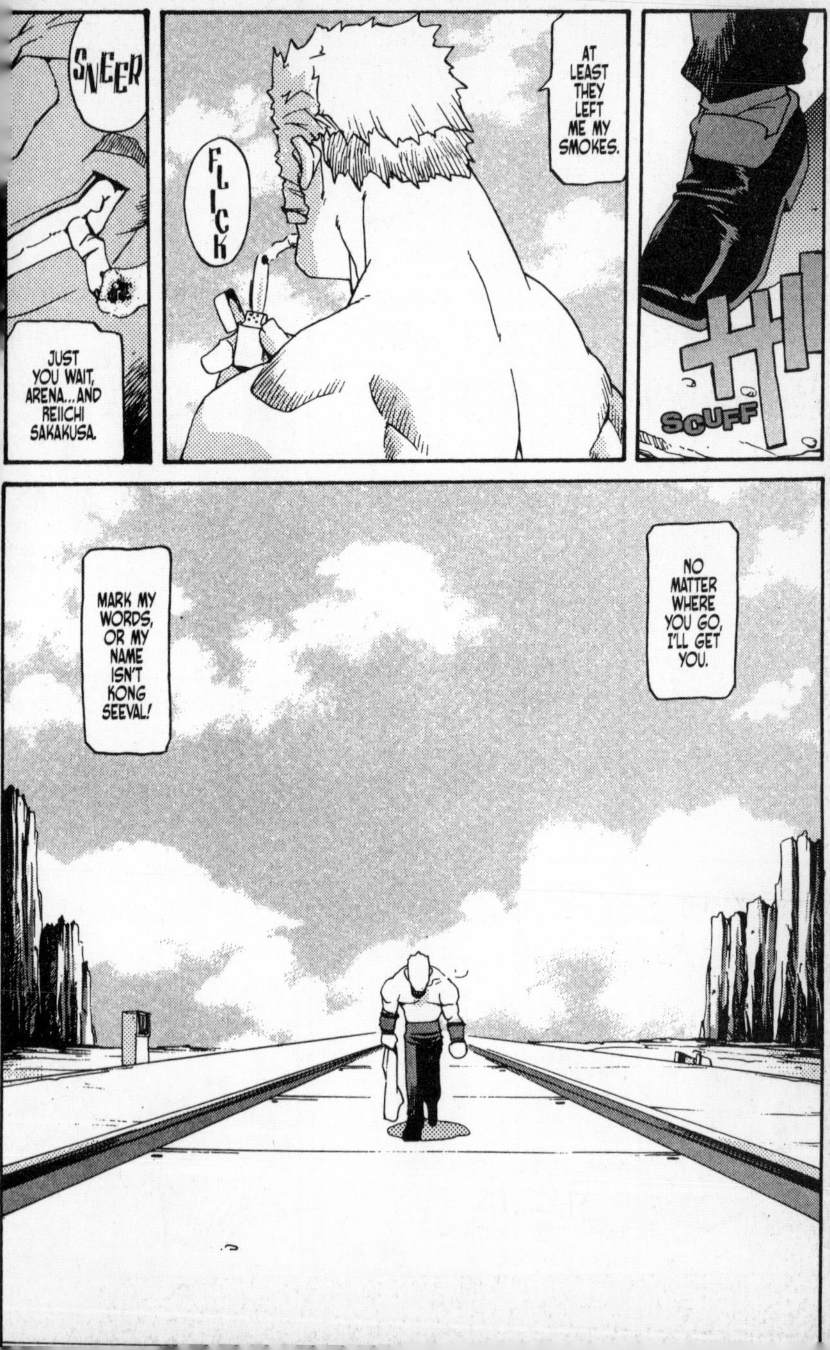
SCUFF
AT LEAST THEY LEFT ME MY SMOKES.
FLICK
SNEER
JUST YOU WAIT, ARENA...AND REIICHI SAKAKUSA.
NO MATTER WHERE YOU GO, I'LL GET YOU.
MARK MY WORDS, OR MY NAME ISN'T KONG SEEVAL!

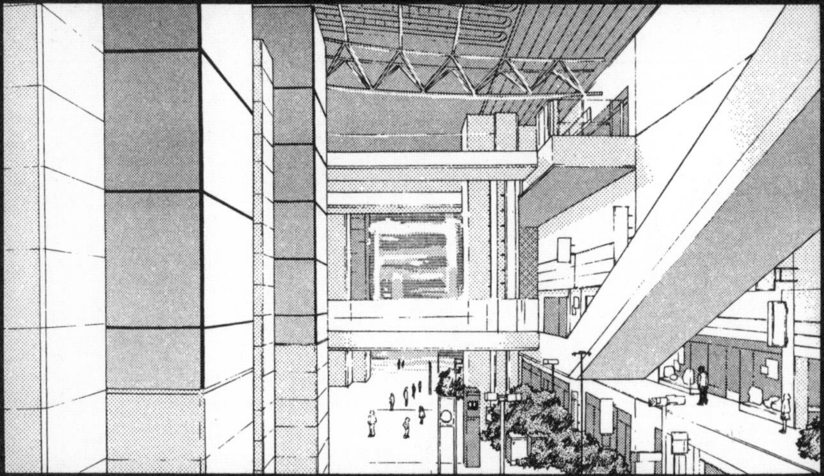

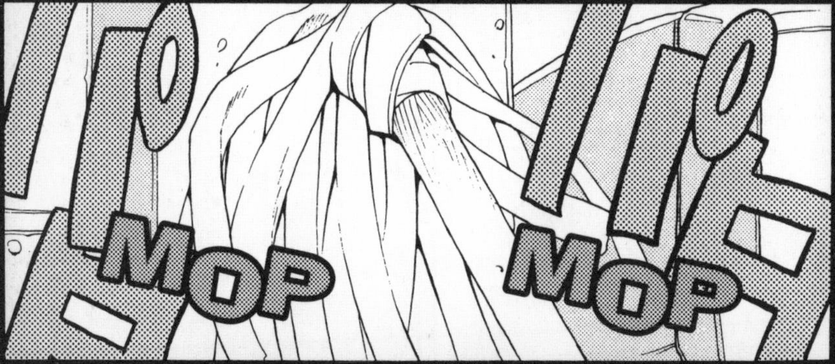
MOP
MOP

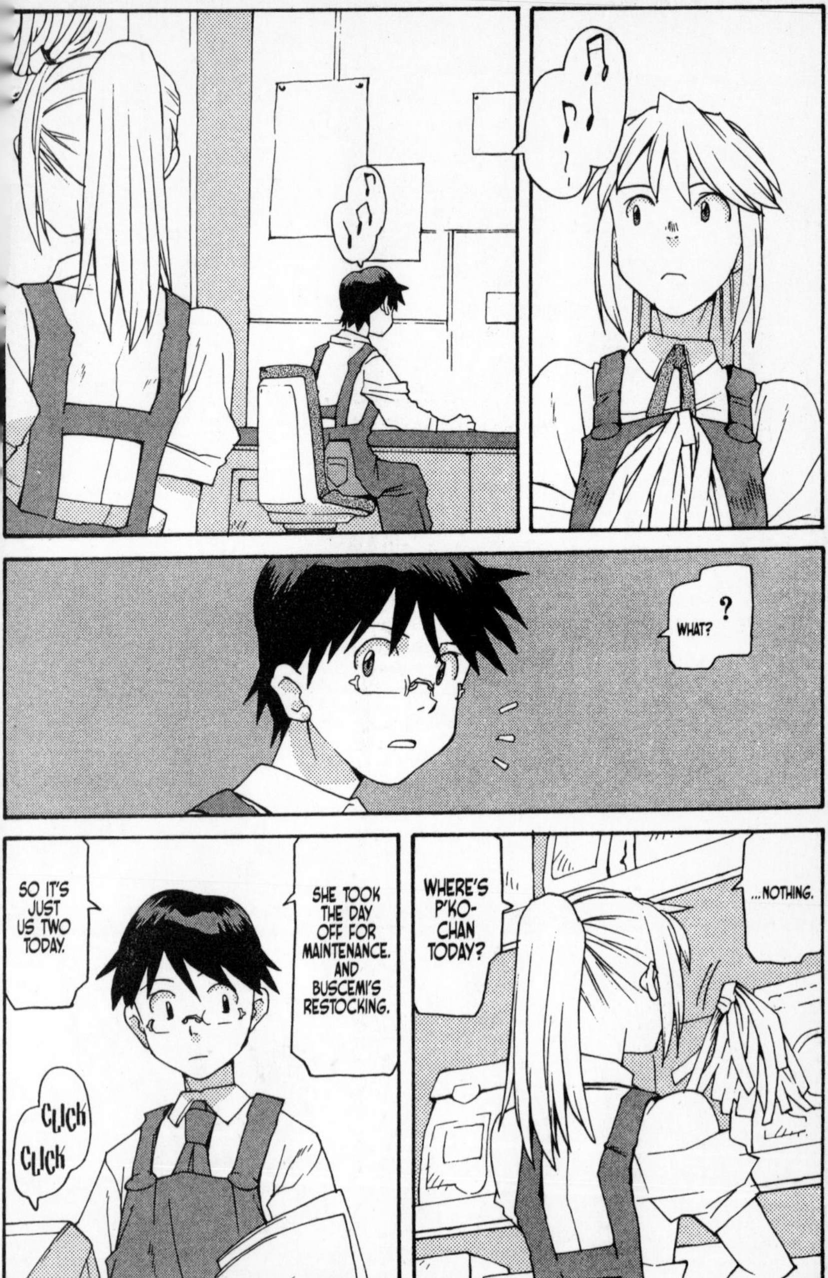
WHAT? ?
...NOTHING.
WHERE'S P'KO-CHAN TODAY?
SHE TOOK THE DAY OFF FOR MAINTENANCE. AND BUSCEMI'S RESTOCKING.
SO IT'S JUST US TWO TODAY.
CLICK CLICK

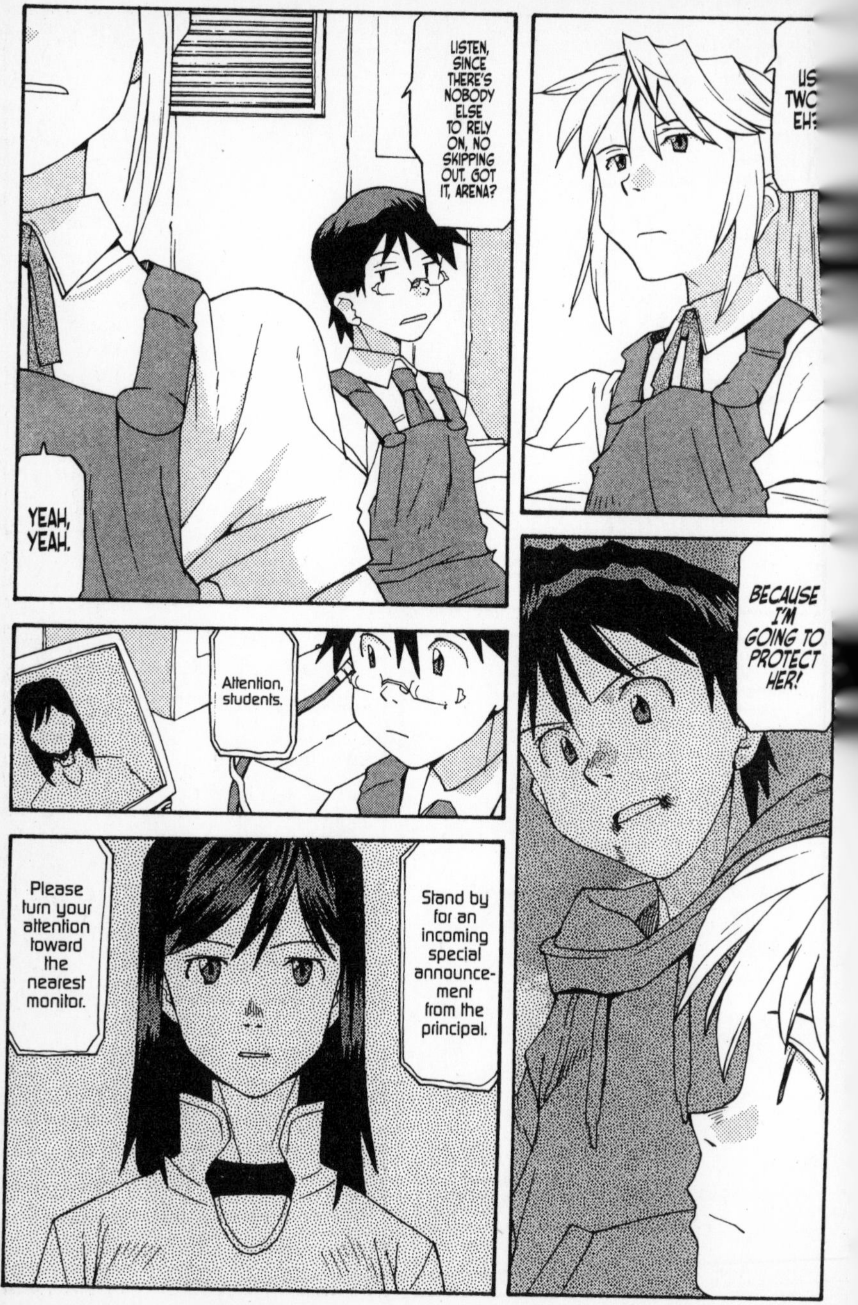
LISTEN, SINCE THERE'S NOBODY ELSE TO RELY ON, NO SKIPPING OUT. GOT IT, ARENA?
YEAH, YEAH.
BECAUSE I'M GOING TO PROTECT HER!
Attention, students.
Stand by for an incoming special announcement from the principal.
Please turn your attention toward the nearest monitor.

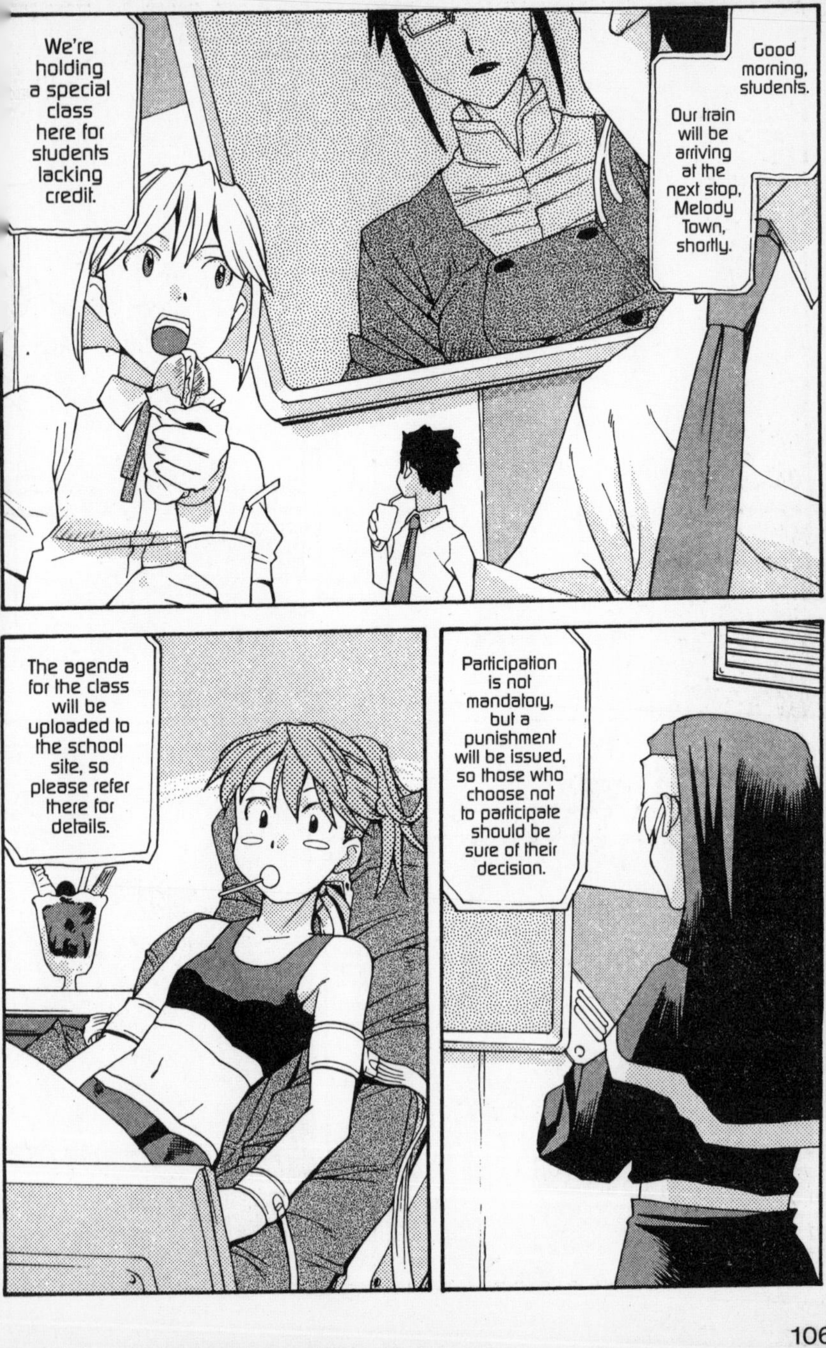
Good morning, students.
Our train will be arriving at the next stop, Melody Town, shortly.
We're holding a special class here for students lacking credit.
Participation is not mandatory, but a punishment will be issued, so those who choose not to participate should be sure of their decision.
The agenda for the class will be uploaded to the school site, so please refer there for details.

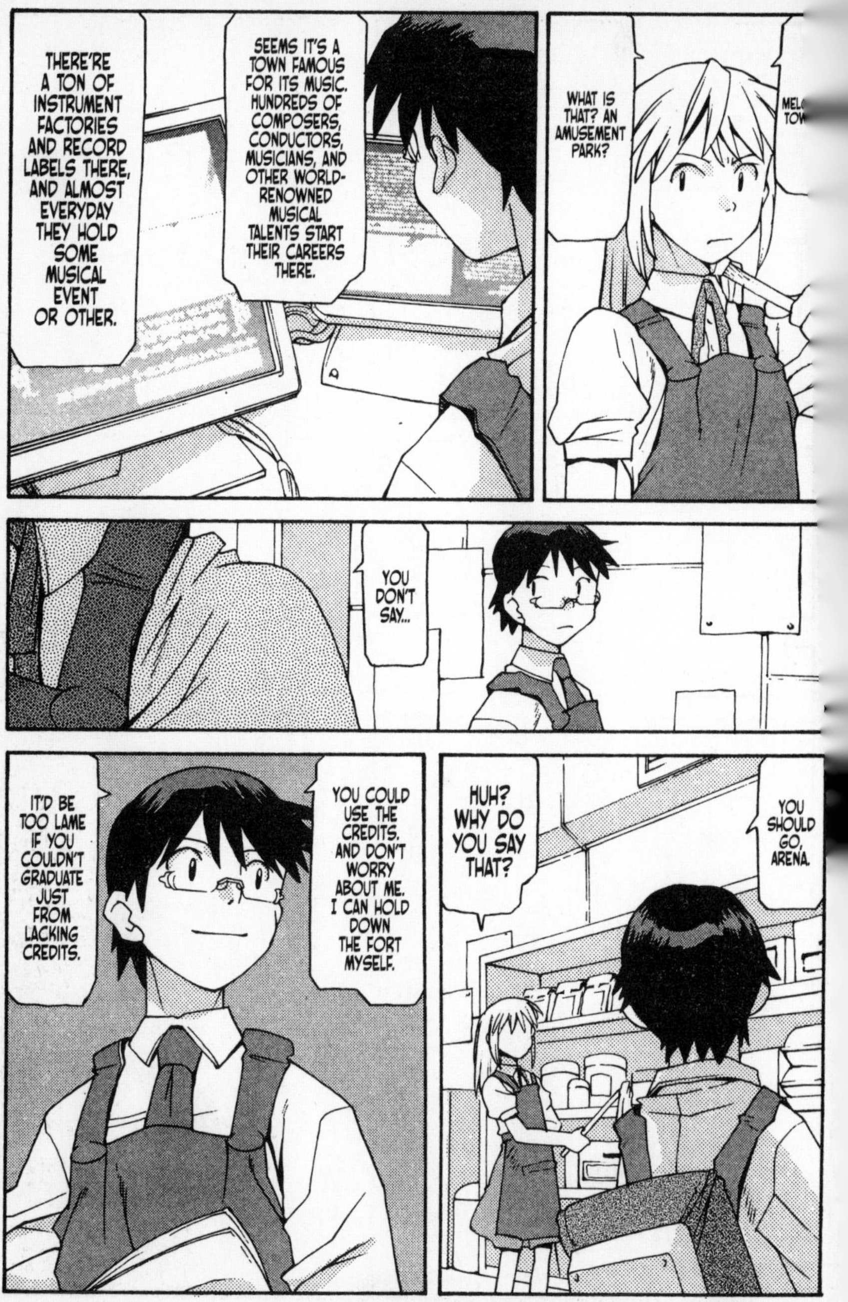
WHAT IS THAT? AN AMUSEMENT PARK?
SEEMS IT'S A TOWN FAMOUS FOR ITS MUSIC. HUNDREDS OF COMPOSERS, CONDUCTORS, MUSICIANS, AND OTHER WORLD-RENOWNED MUSICAL TALENTS START THEIR CAREERS THERE.
THERE'RE A TON OF INSTRUMENT FACTORIES AND RECORD LABELS THERE, AND ALMOST EVERYDAY THEY HOLD SOME MUSICAL EVENT OR OTHER.
YOU DON'T SAY...
YOU SHOULD GO, ARENA.
HUH? WHY DO YOU SAY THAT?
YOU COULD USE THE CREDITS. AND DON'T WORRY ABOUT ME. I CAN HOLD DOWN THE FORT MYSELF.
IT'D BE TOO LAME IF YOU COULDN'T GRADUATE JUST FROM LACKING CREDITS.

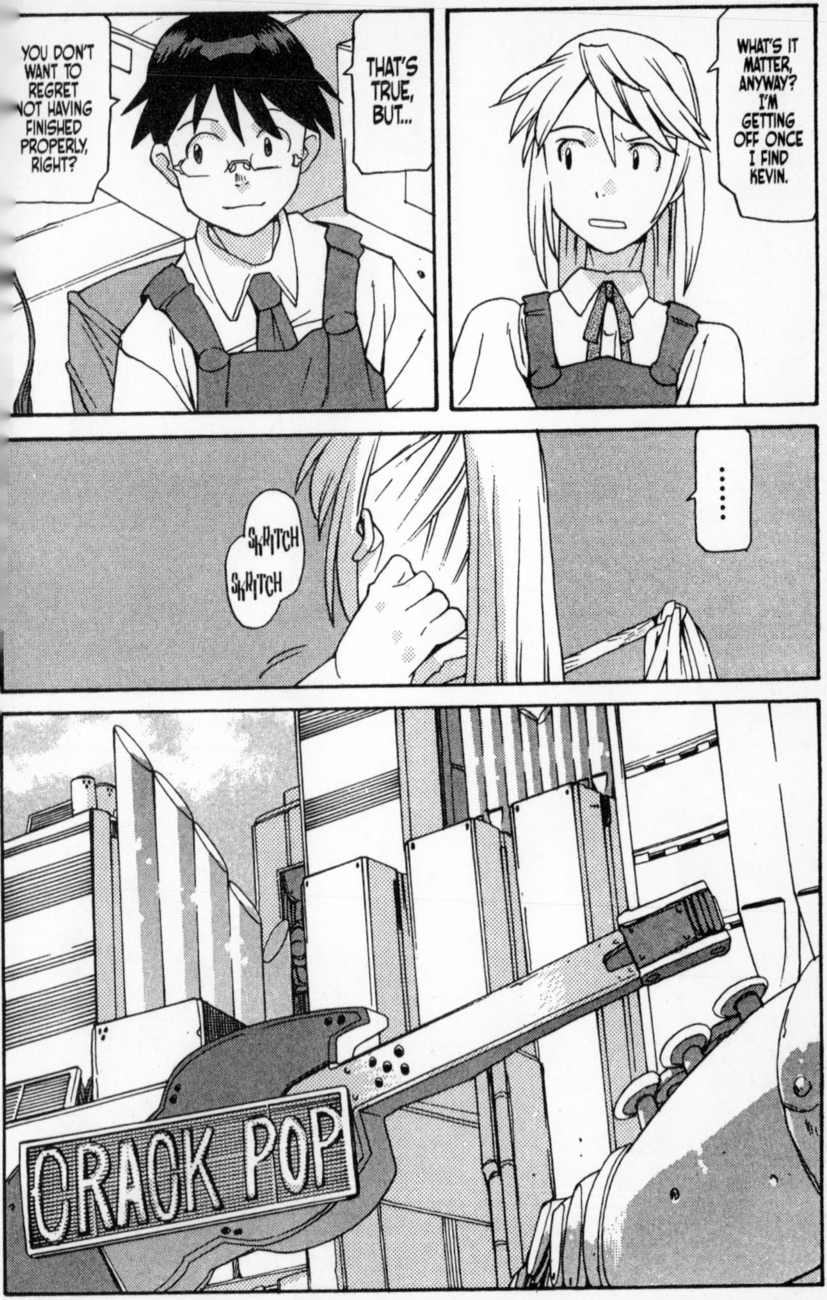
WHAT'S IT MATTER, ANYWAY? I'M GETTING OFF ONCE I FIND KEVIN.
THAT'S TRUE, BUT...
YOU DON'T WANT TO REGRET NOT HAVING FINISHED PROPERLY, RIGHT?
......
SKRITCH
SKRITCH
CRACK POP

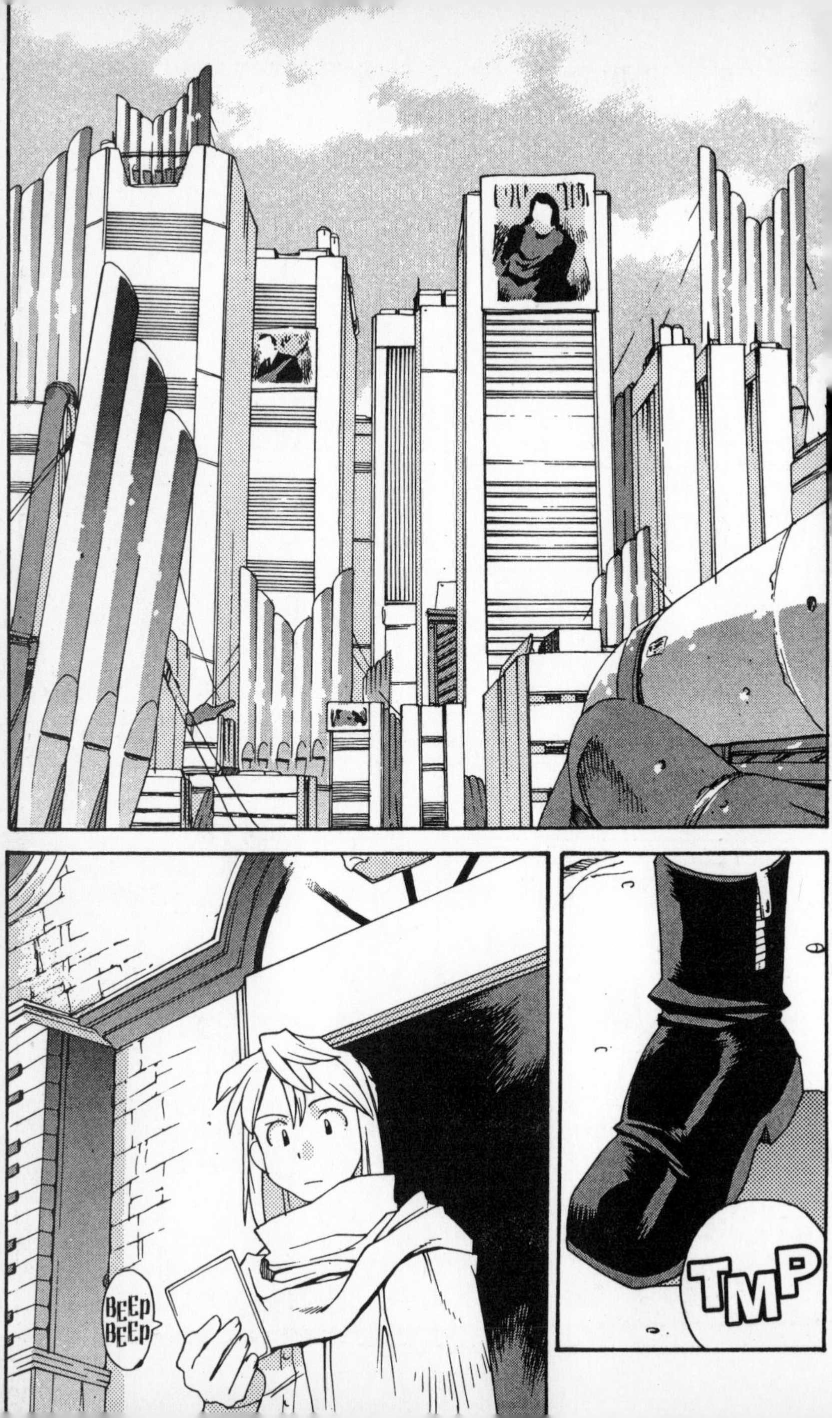
TMP
BEEP BEEP

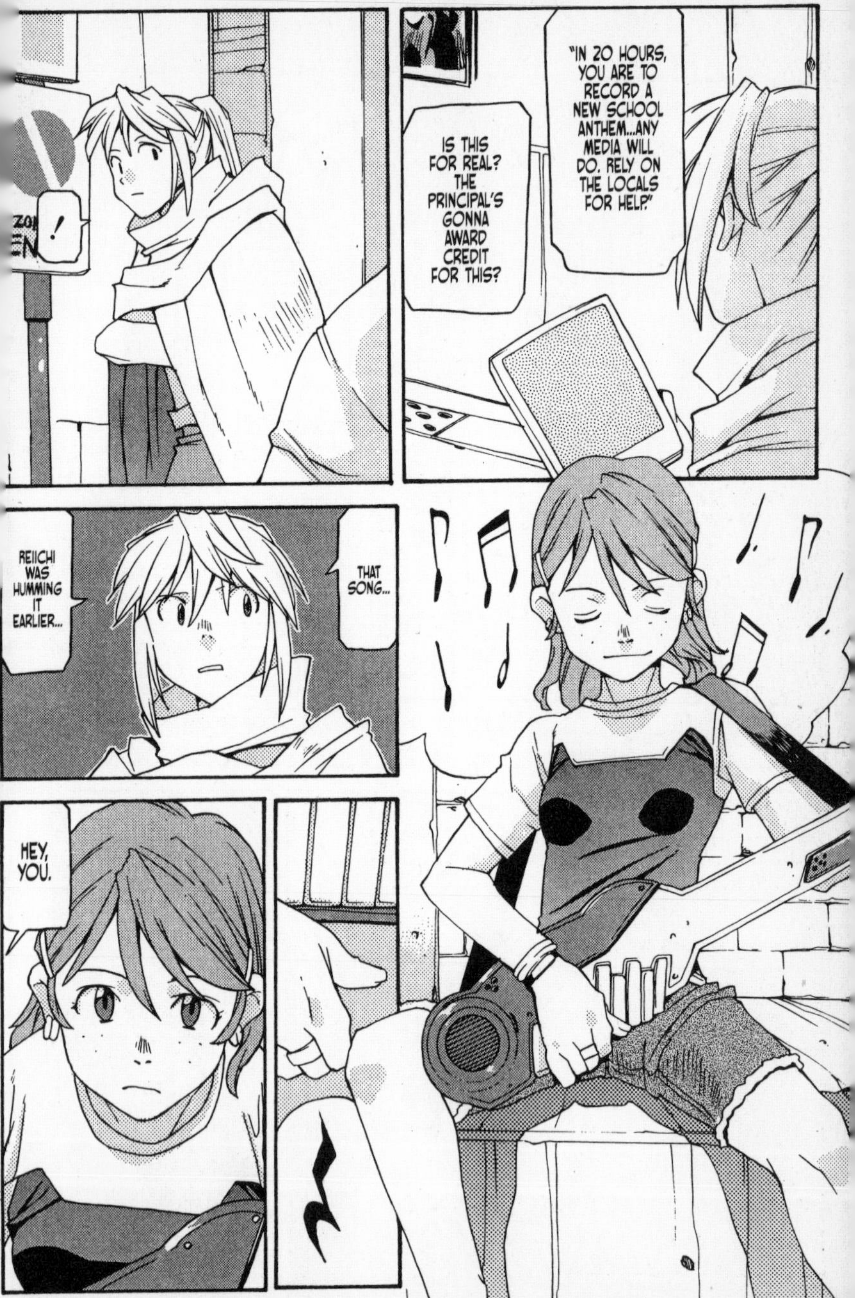
"IN 20 HOURS, YOU ARE TO RECORD A NEW SCHOOL ANTHEM...ANY MEDIA WILL DO. RELY ON THE LOCALS FOR HELP."
IS THIS FOR REAL? THE PRINCIPAL'S GONNA AWARD CREDIT FOR THIS?
!
THAT SONG...
REIICHI WAS HUMMING IT EARLIER...
HEY, YOU.